Special thanks to Mom and Dad, Kera, Myoyu Roshi, Misun, Kazuaki Tanahashi, Cecily Fuhr at Rochester Zen Center, and all the therapists and medical personnel who offered me their assistance. Forge.

"Heart of Perfect Wisdom (Prajñā Pāramitā Hridaya Sutra)" translation © copyright 2005 Rochester Zen Center. rzc.org. Used with permission.

"Tung-Shan's 'No Cold, No Heat'" contains an element of a translation by Kazuaki Tanahashi and Katherine Thanas. My thanks to Mr. Tanahashi for his assistance and guidance. brushmind.net.

"Mercy" originally appeared in *The Comics Journal Special Edition Volume Two: Cartoonists on Music*, June 2002, Fantagraphics Books.

For more information on John's work please visit king-cat.net.
drawnandquarterly.com

First edition: September 2014
Printed in Malaysia
10 9 8 7 6 5 4 3 2 1

Library and Archives Canada Cataloguing in Publication
Porcellino, John, author, illustrator.
    The Hospital Suite / John Porcellino.
ISBN 978-1-77046-164-2 (pbk.)
    1. Graphic novels. I. Title.
PN6727.P67H67 2014   741.5'973   C2013-908474-6

Published in the USA by Drawn & Quarterly, a client publisher of
Farrar, Straus and Giroux
Orders: 888.330.8477

Published in Canada by Drawn & Quarterly, a client publisher of
Raincoast Books
Orders: 800.663.5714

Published in the UK by Drawn & Quarterly, a client publisher of
Publishers Group UK
Orders: info@pguk.co.uk

THE HOSPITAL SUITE

John Porcellino

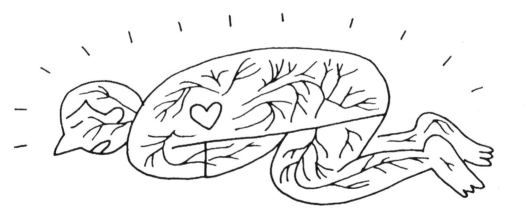

DRAWN and QUARTERLY

THE HOSPITAL SUITE

THE HOSPITAL SUITE

Part One

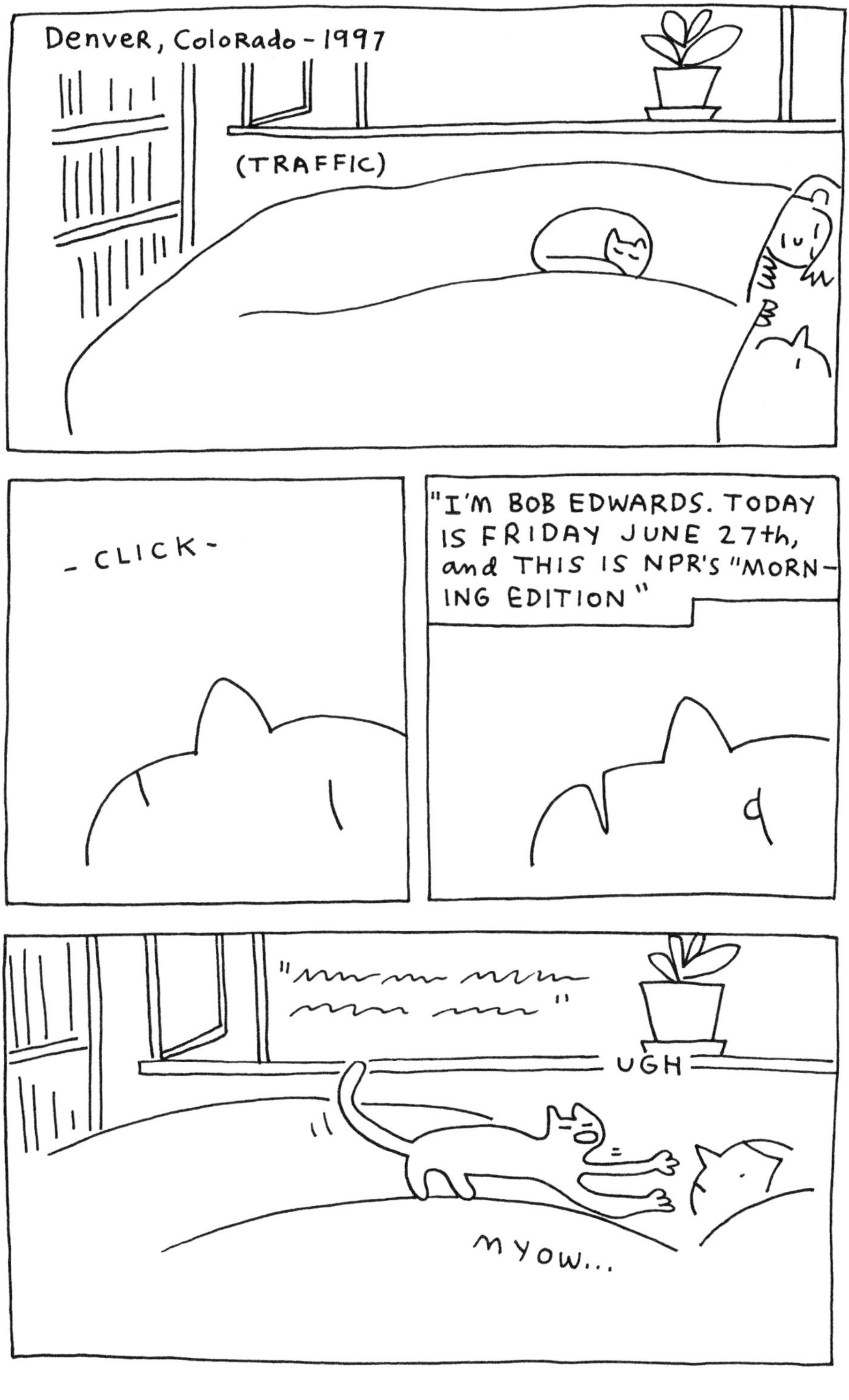
Denver, Colorado - 1997
(TRAFFIC)
- CLICK -
"I'M BOB EDWARDS. TODAY IS FRIDAY JUNE 27th, and THIS IS NPR'S "MORNING EDITION"
UGH
MYOW...

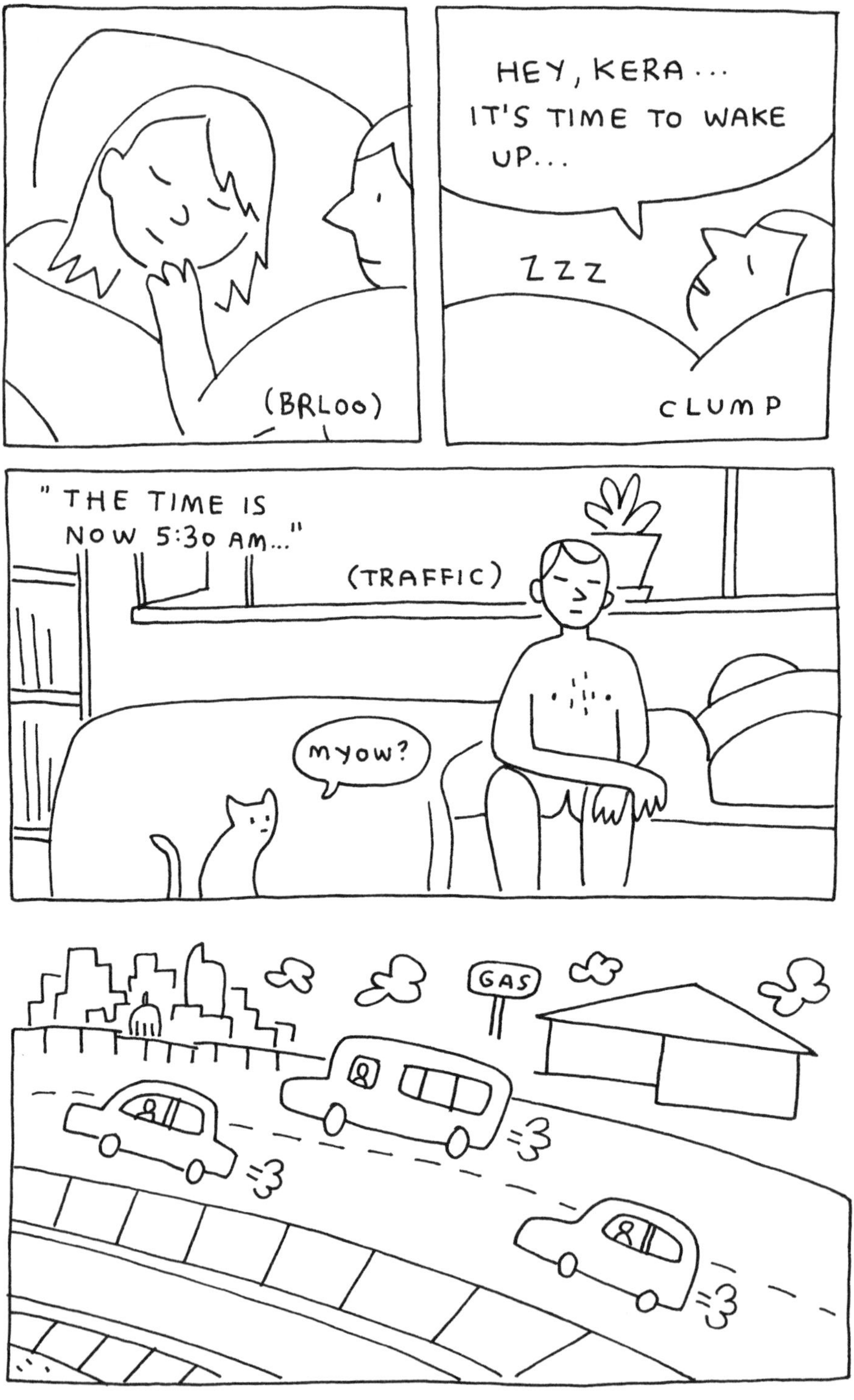
(BRLOO)
HEY, KERA... IT'S TIME TO WAKE UP...
ZZZ
CLUMP
"THE TIME IS NOW 5:30 AM..."
(TRAFFIC)
MYOW?
GAS

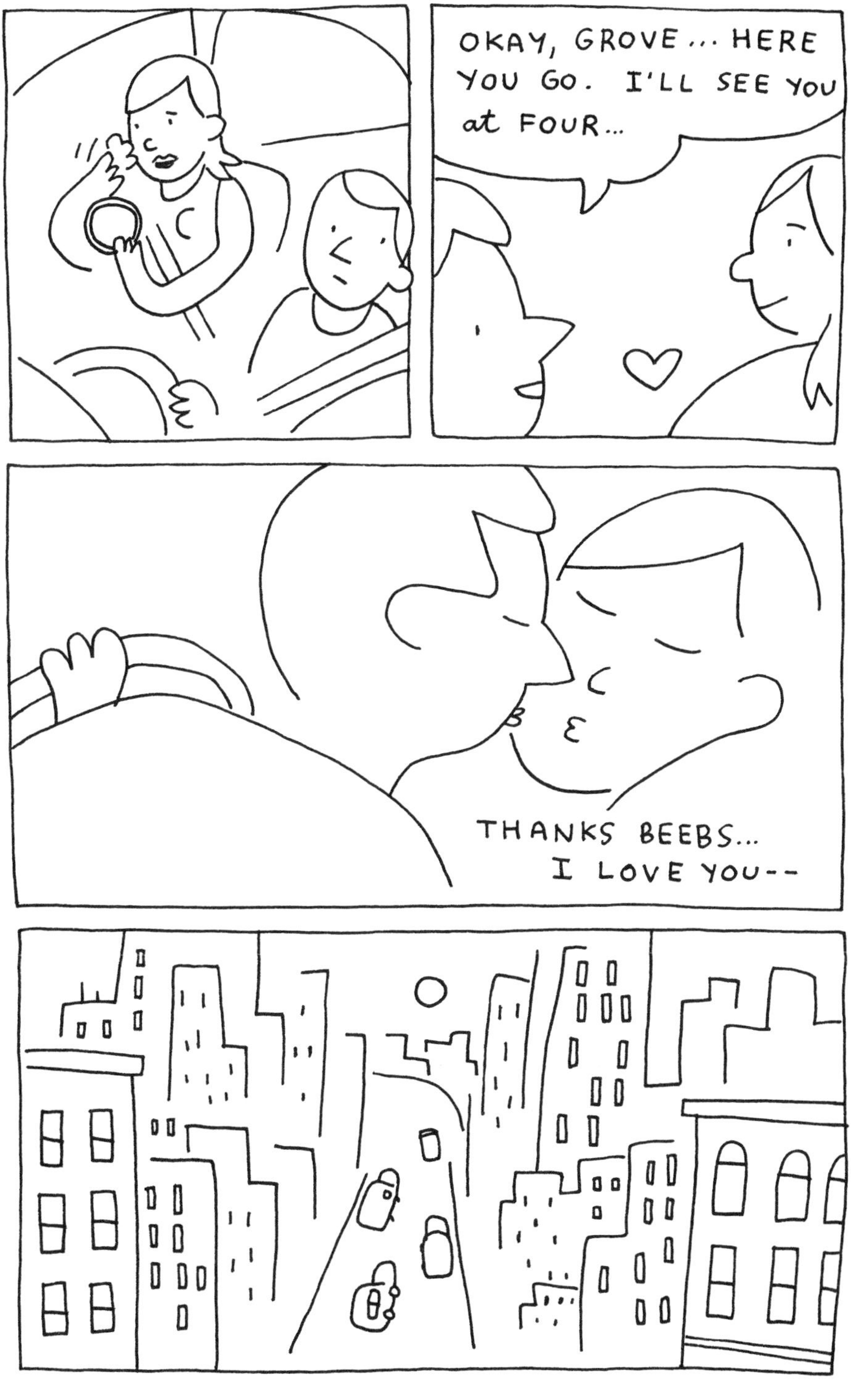
OKAY, GROVE... HERE YOU GO. I'LL SEE YOU at FOUR...
THANKS BEEBS... I LOVE YOU--

CITY PARK

THIS DIET FOR MY EARS IS KILLIN' ME... IT'S TOO HARD...

OKAY — I NEED TO BACK UP A LITTLE...

In January of 1995, I'd developed a hearing disorder called Hyperacusis — where everyday, average sounds could be extremely painful... Things like closing the car door, dropping a fork on a plate, or even turning on a light switch could result in pain and pressure in my ears that lasted anywhere from a day to a month...

After seeing doctor after doctor with no relief, I finally turned to alternative healers. I began seeing an acupuncturist, who helped me a lot, and then a naturopath, who'd recommended a diet free from wheat, yeast, and dairy products...

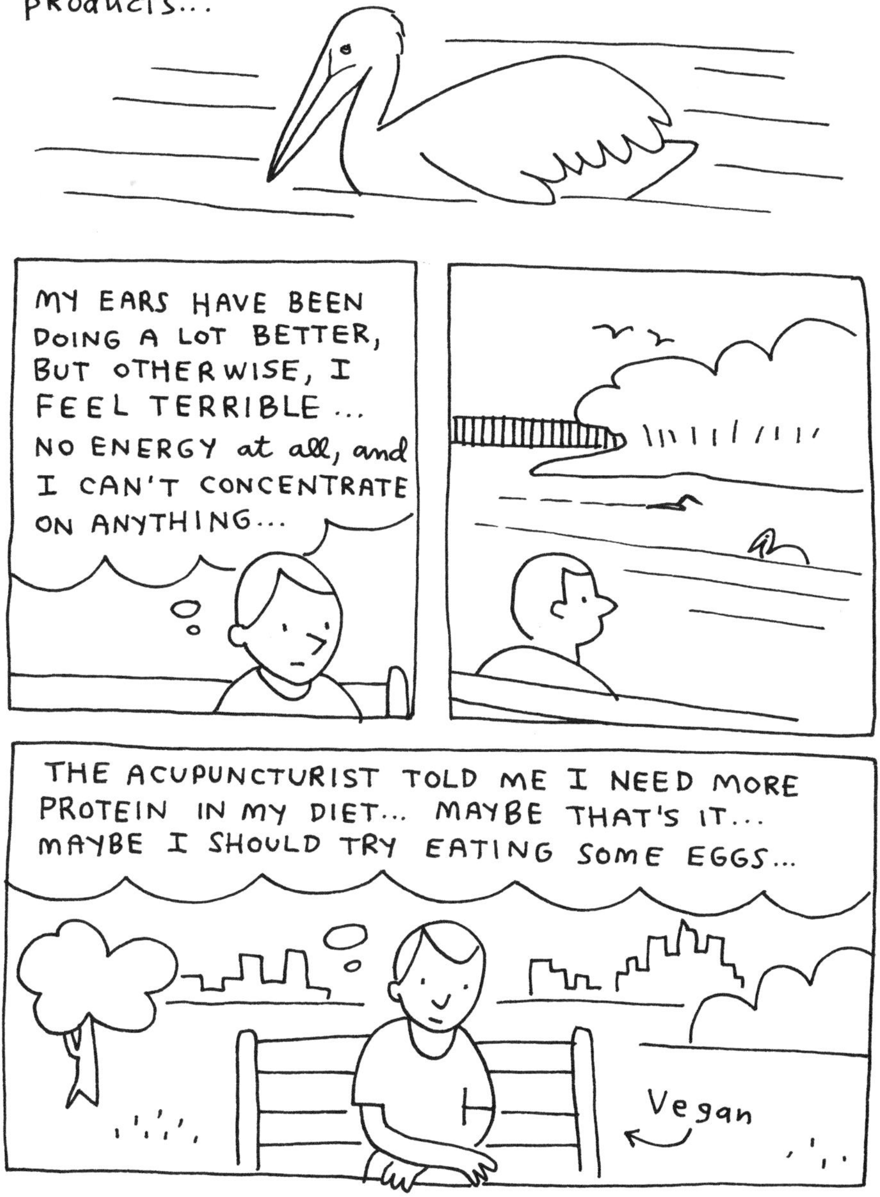

MY EARS HAVE BEEN DOING A LOT BETTER, BUT OTHERWISE, I FEEL TERRIBLE... NO ENERGY at all, and I CAN'T CONCENTRATE ON ANYTHING...
THE ACUPUNCTURIST TOLD ME I NEED MORE PROTEIN IN MY DIET... MAYBE THAT'S IT... MAYBE I SHOULD TRY EATING SOME EGGS...
Vegan

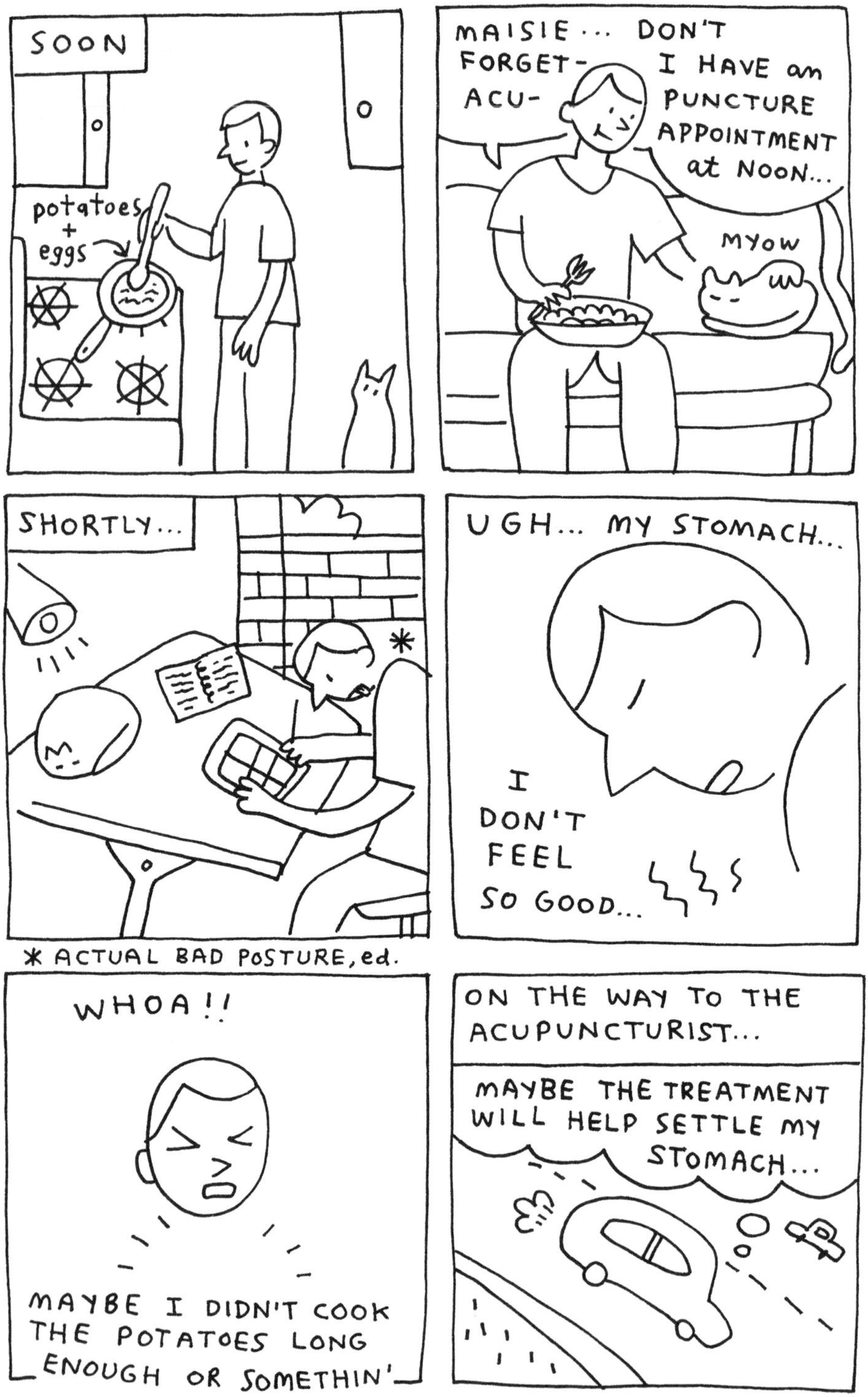
SOON
potatoes + eggs
MAISIE... DON'T FORGET- I HAVE an ACU- PUNCTURE APPOINTMENT at NOON...
MYOW
SHORTLY...
*
UGH... MY STOMACH...
I DON'T FEEL SO GOOD...
* ACTUAL BAD POSTURE, ed.
WHOA!!
MAYBE I DIDN'T COOK THE POTATOES LONG ENOUGH OR SOMETHIN'
ON THE WAY TO THE ACUPUNCTURIST...
MAYBE THE TREATMENT WILL HELP SETTLE MY STOMACH...

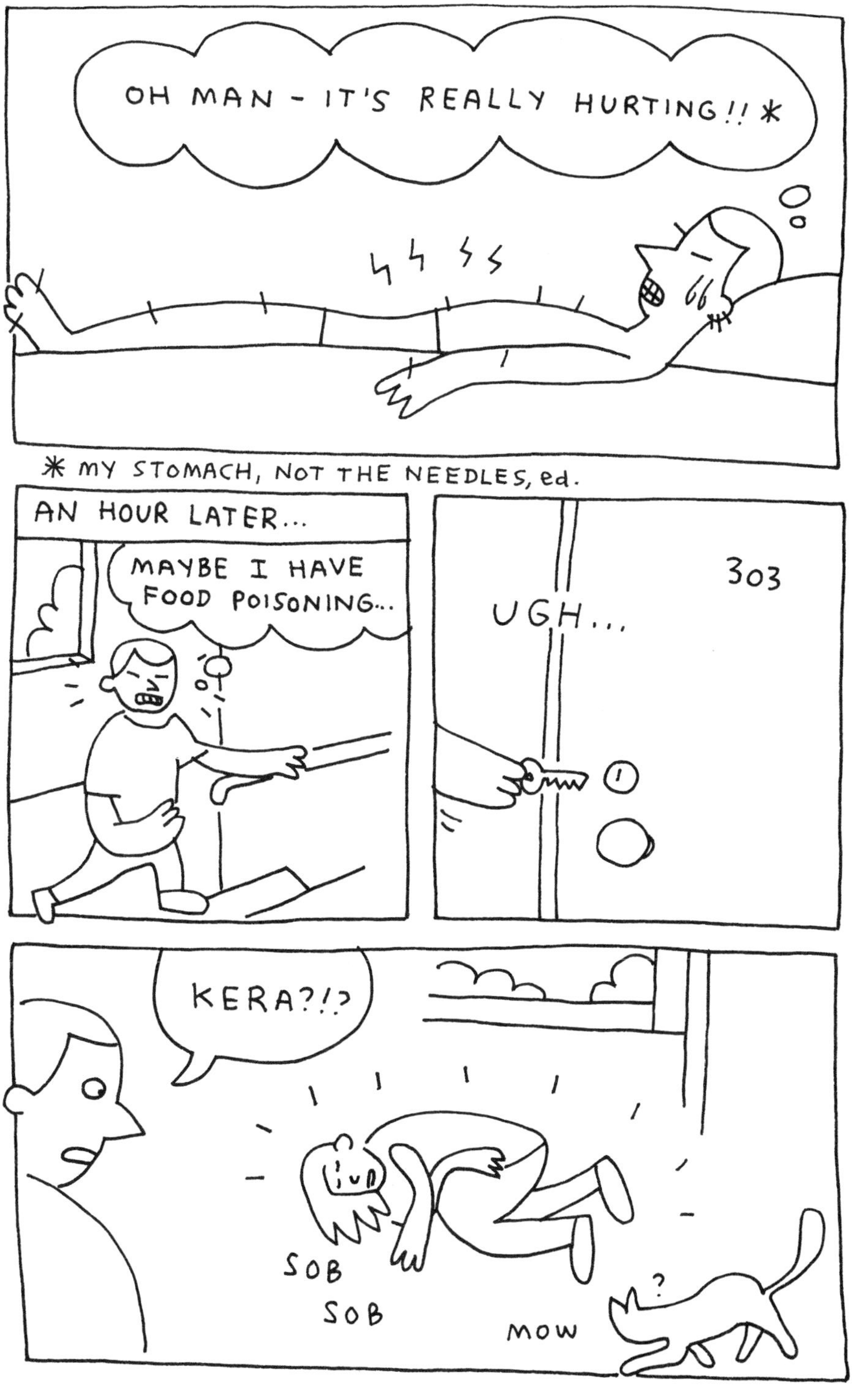
OH MAN - IT'S REALLY HURTING!! *
* MY STOMACH, NOT THE NEEDLES, ed.
AN HOUR LATER...
MAYBE I HAVE FOOD POISONING...
303
UGH...
KERA?!?
SOB
SOB
MOW
?

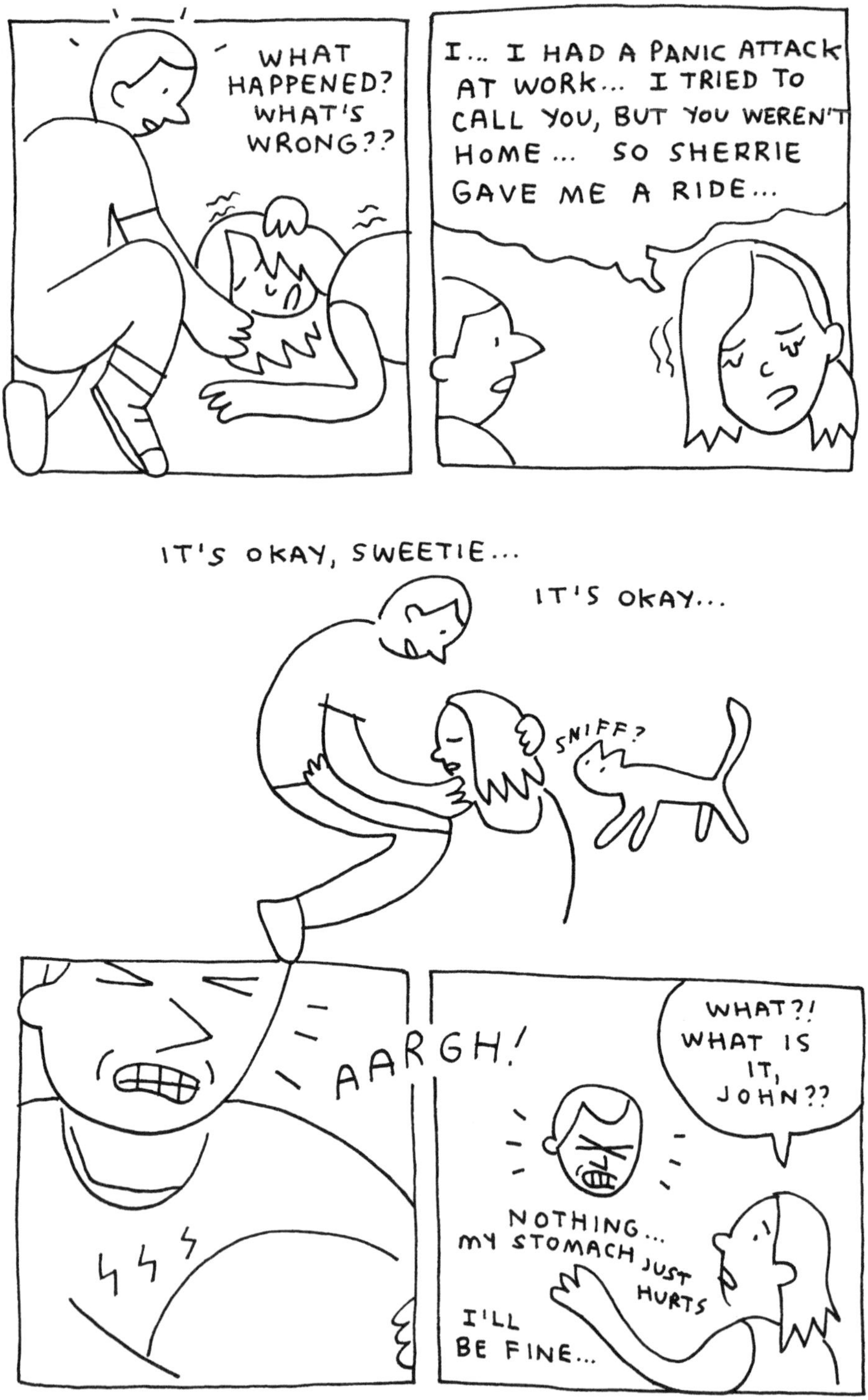
WHAT HAPPENED? WHAT'S WRONG??
I... I HAD A PANIC ATTACK AT WORK... I TRIED TO CALL YOU, BUT YOU WEREN'T HOME... SO SHERRIE GAVE ME A RIDE...
IT'S OKAY, SWEETIE...
IT'S OKAY...
SNIFF?
AARGH!
WHAT?! WHAT IS IT, JOHN??
NOTHING... MY STOMACH JUST HURTS
I'LL BE FINE...

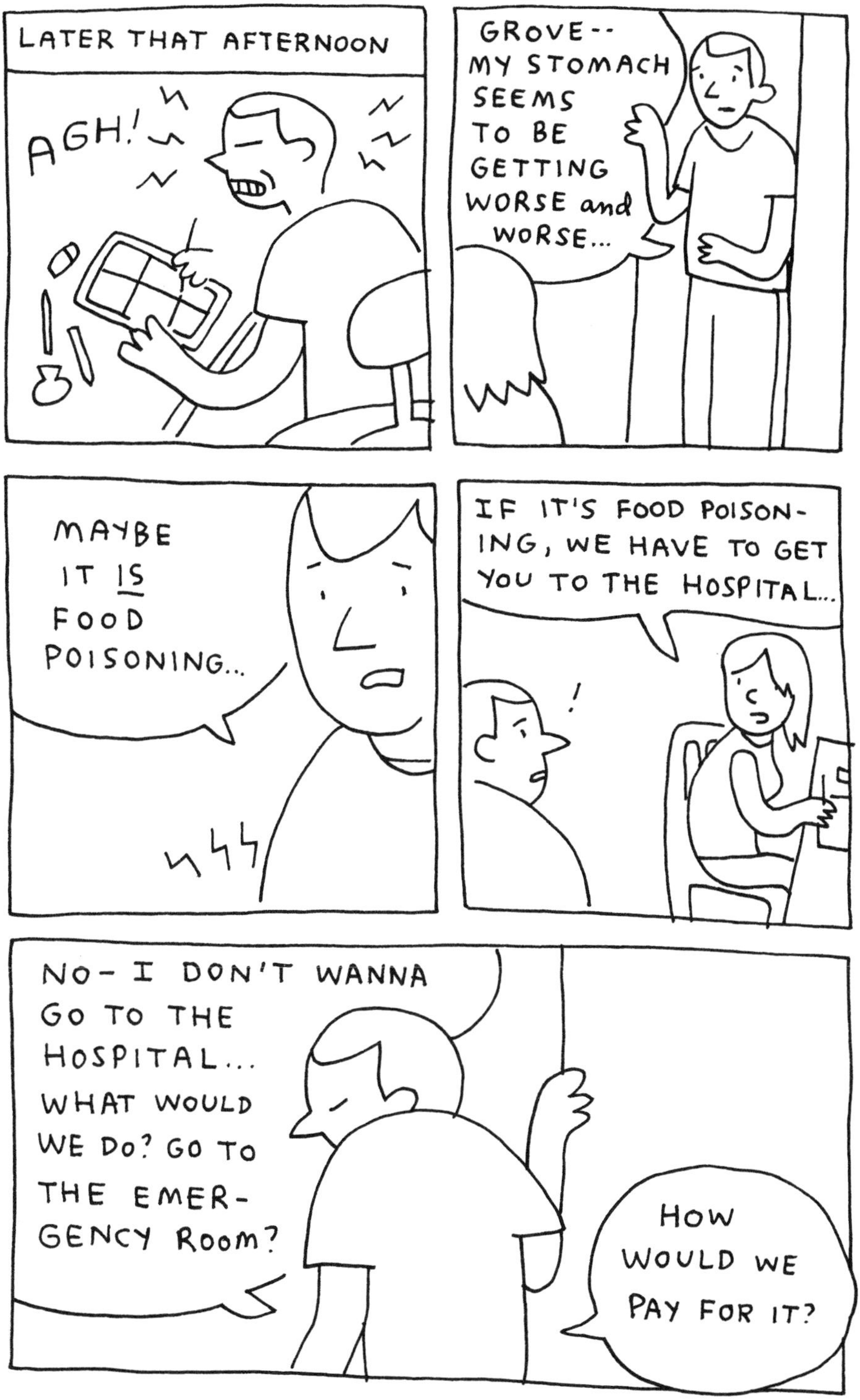
LATER THAT AFTERNOON
AGH!
GROVE-- MY STOMACH SEEMS TO BE GETTING WORSE and WORSE...
MAYBE IT IS FOOD POISONING...
IF IT'S FOOD POISON-ING, WE HAVE TO GET YOU TO THE HOSPITAL...
!
NO- I DON'T WANNA GO TO THE HOSPITAL... WHAT WOULD WE DO? GO TO THE EMER-GENCY ROOM?
HOW WOULD WE PAY FOR IT?

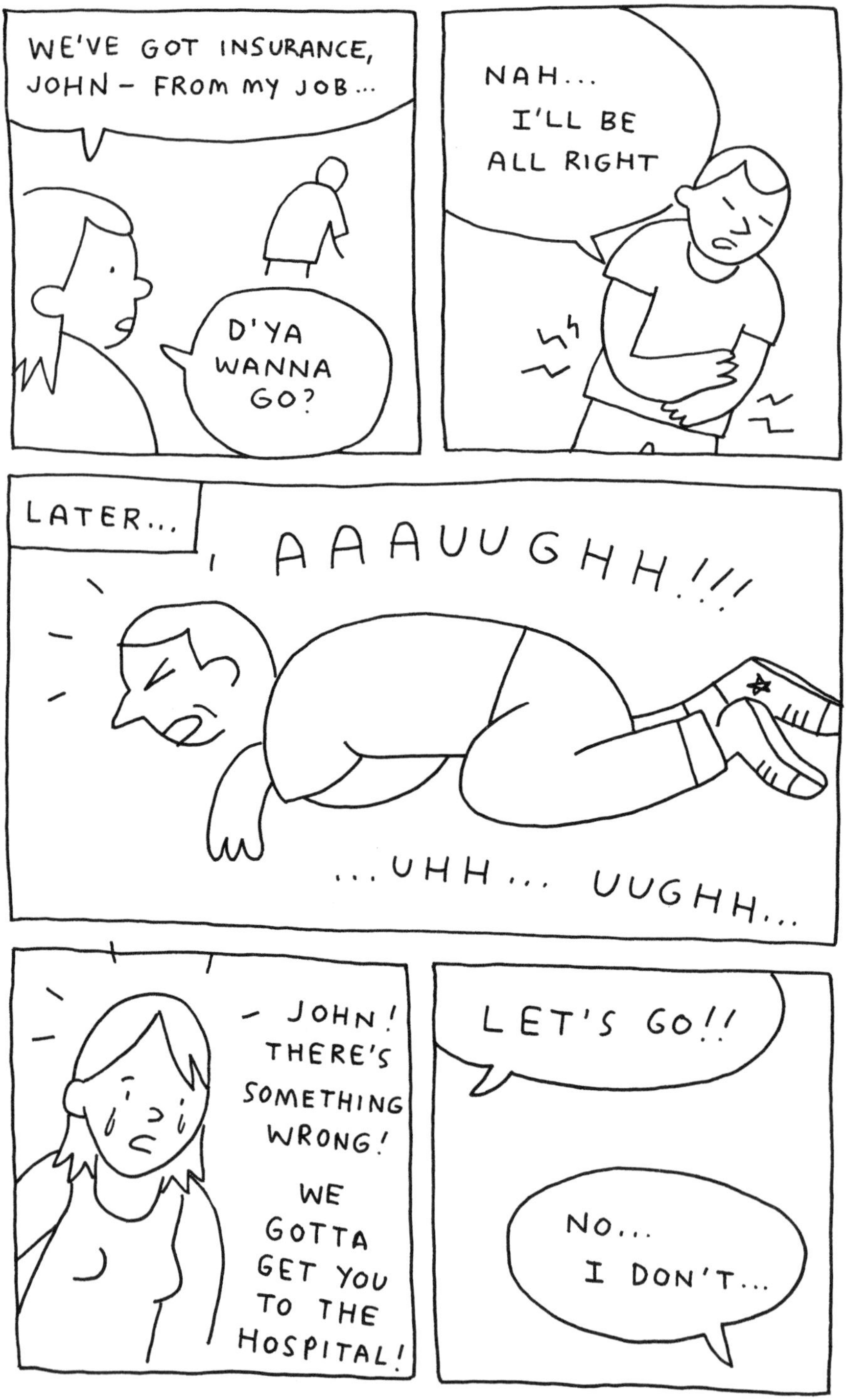
WE'VE GOT INSURANCE, JOHN - FROM MY JOB...
D'YA WANNA GO?
NAH... I'LL BE ALL RIGHT
LATER...
AAAUUGHH!!!!
...UHH... UUGHH...
JOHN! THERE'S SOMETHING WRONG!
WE GOTTA GET YOU TO THE HOSPITAL!
LET'S GO!!
NO... I DON'T...

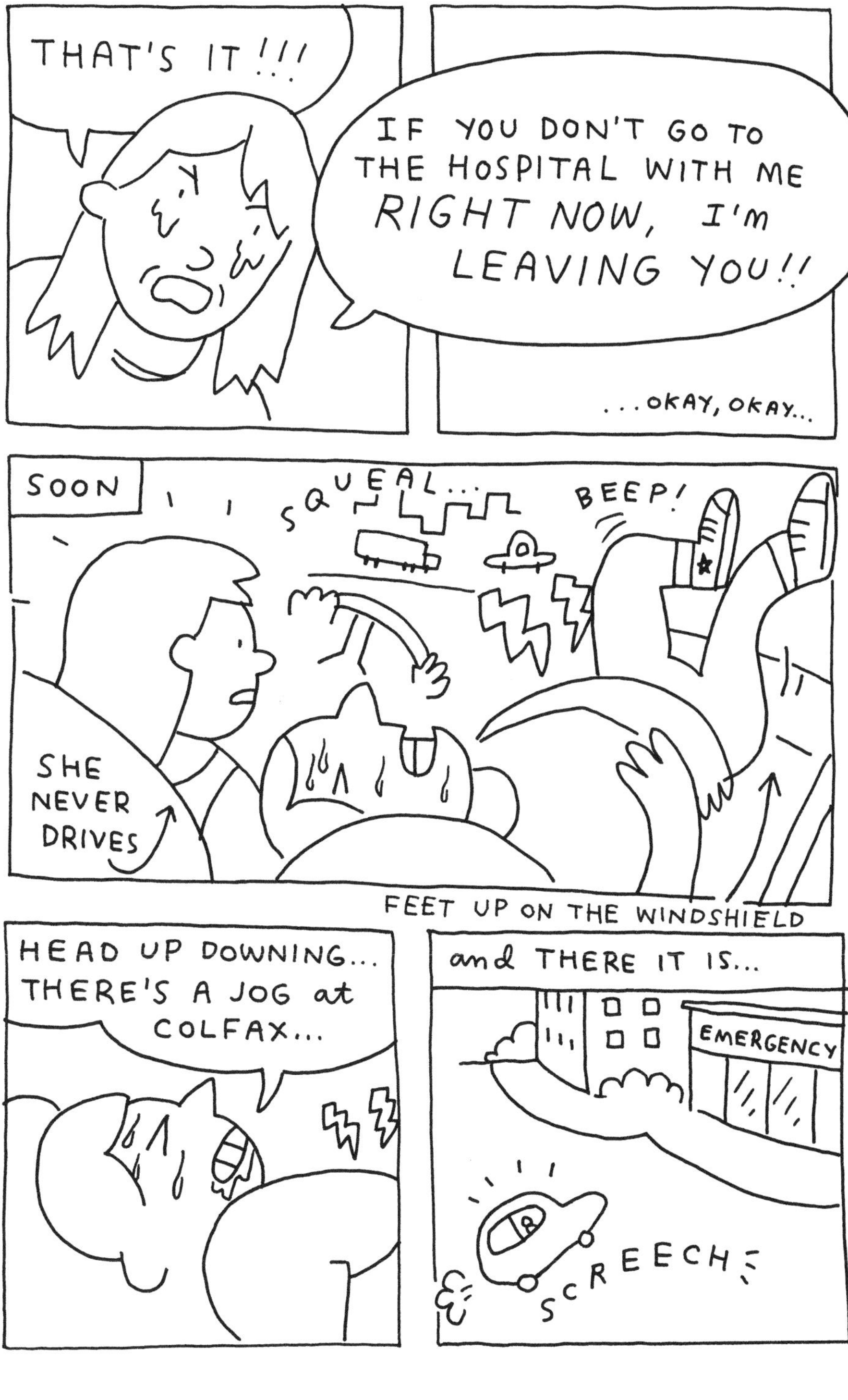
THAT'S IT!!!
IF YOU DON'T GO TO THE HOSPITAL WITH ME RIGHT NOW, I'M LEAVING YOU!!
...OKAY, OKAY...
SOON
SQUEAL...
BEEP!
SHE NEVER DRIVES
FEET UP ON THE WINDSHIELD
HEAD UP DOWNING... THERE'S A JOG at COLFAX...
and THERE IT IS...
EMERGENCY
SCREECH

NAME? JOHN PORCELLINO - AGE? 28 WHERE DOES IT HURT, JOHN? MY STOM ACH? WHERE EXACTLY DOES IT HURT? I DON'T KNOW EVERYWHERE - HAVE YOU EVER HAD APPENDICITIS? WHEN I WAS A KID THEY TOOK IT OUT- WHAT HAVE YO TEN TODAY? EGGS and POTATOES CURRENTLY ON ANY MEDICATI HE TOOK A DOSE OF NIZORAL THIS RNING - NIZORAL? IT'S AN ANTIFUNGAL MEDICATION -- HIS DOCTOR TOLD HIM HE HAS A FULL BODY YEAST INFECTION - HAVE YOU EVER BEEN TESTED FOR A YEAST INFECTION? NO- ARE THERE ANY PRE-EXISTING COND ITIONS? CHRONIC PROSTATITIS - AND HIS EARS ARE VERY SENSITIVE TO SOUND - HE'S HARD OF HEARING? NO THE OPPOSITE HIS EARS ARE VERY SENSITIVE, IT'S VERY PAINFUL - HOW LONG HAVE YOU BEEN HAVING THE STOMACH PAIN? SINCE ABOUT NINE A.M. - HOW WOULD YOU DESCRIBE THE PAIN? WHAT? IS IT DULL? SHARP?

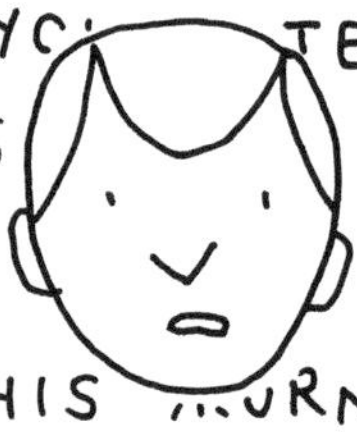

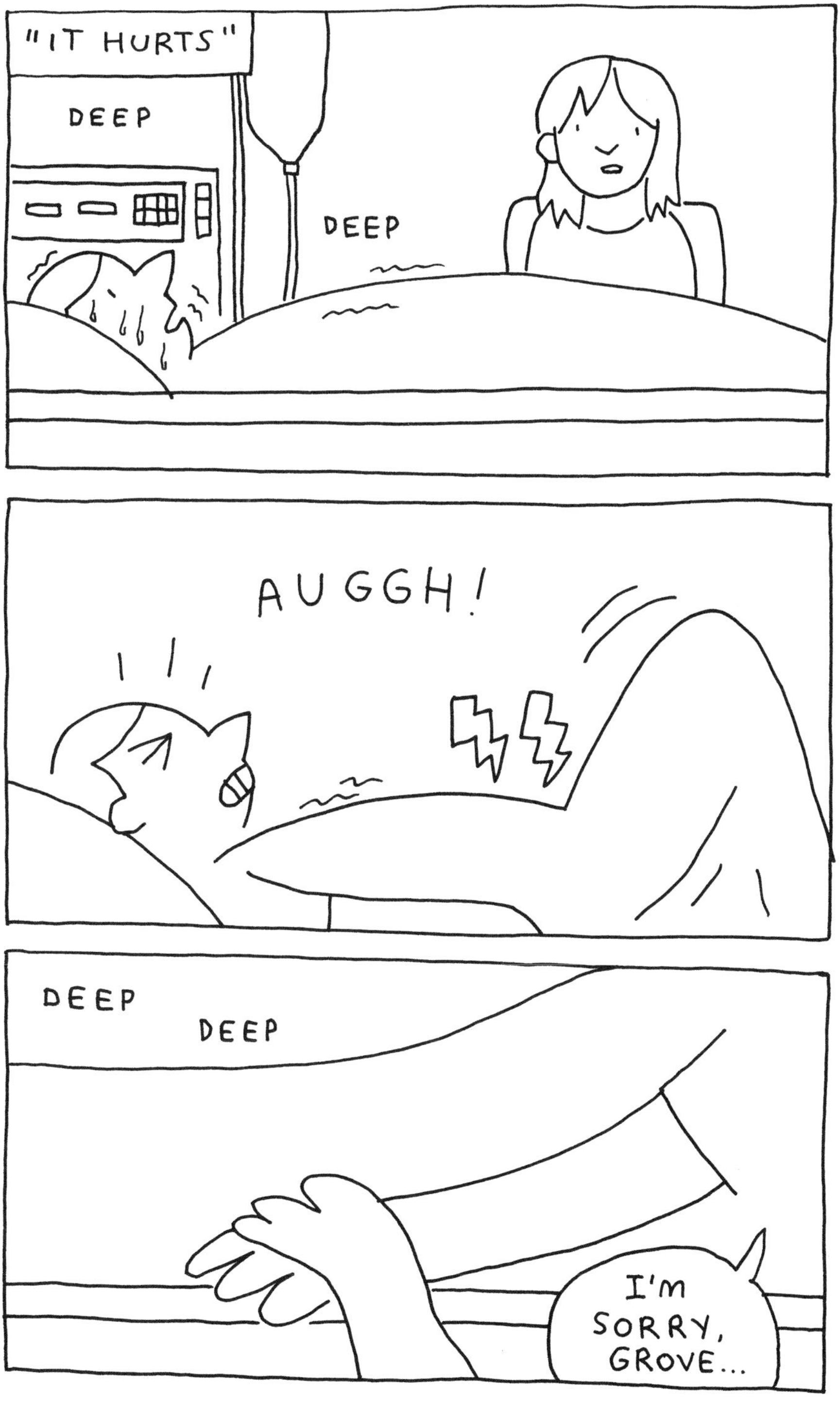
"IT HURTS"
DEEP
DEEP
AUGGH!
DEEP
DEEP
I'M SORRY, GROVE...

DOCTORS and NURSES WERE COMING IN and OUT, ASKING QUESTIONS and WRITING ON CLIP-BOARDS...

HAVE YOU EVER HAD YOUR APPENDIX OUT?

"POTATOES and EGGS"

WHAT KIND OF PAIN IS IT? IS IT A BURNING PAIN?

I DON'T KNOW -- IT JUST HURTS...

DOES IT COME and GO, OR DOES IT STAY THE SAME?

IT JUST HURTS- all the TIME...

THEY WERE TAKING MY BLOOD, HOOKING ME UP TO MACHINES...

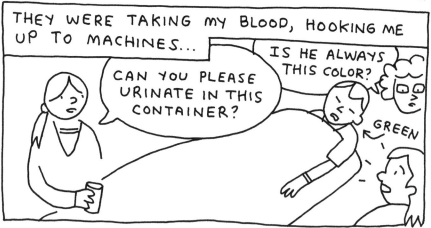

CAN YOU PLEASE URINATE IN THIS CONTAINER?

IS HE ALWAYS THIS COLOR?

GREEN

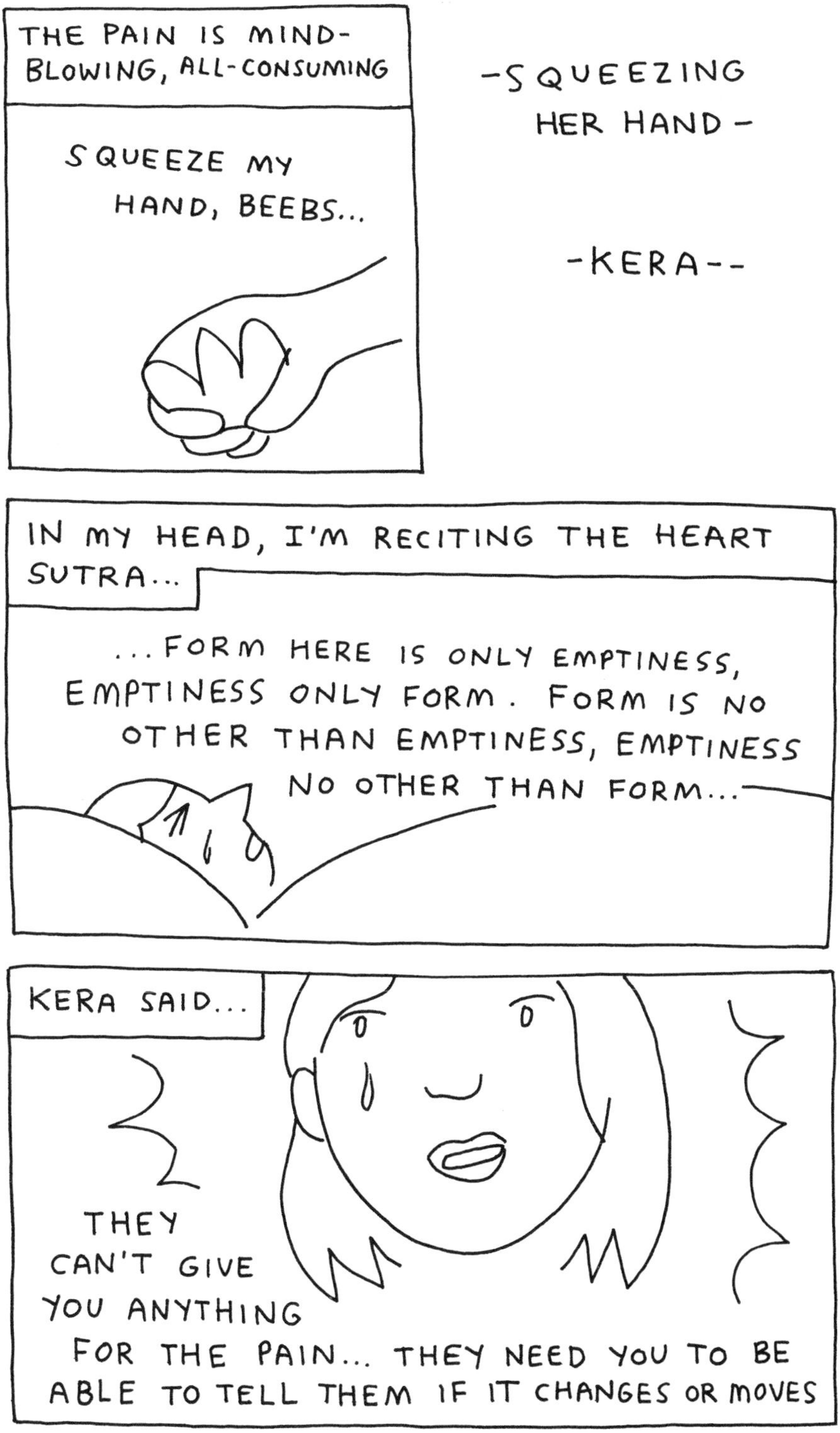
THE PAIN IS MIND-BLOWING, ALL-CONSUMING
SQUEEZE MY HAND, BEEBS...
-SQUEEZING HER HAND-
-KERA--
IN MY HEAD, I'M RECITING THE HEART SUTRA...
...FORM HERE IS ONLY EMPTINESS, EMPTINESS ONLY FORM. FORM IS NO OTHER THAN EMPTINESS, EMPTINESS NO OTHER THAN FORM...
KERA SAID...
THEY CAN'T GIVE YOU ANYTHING FOR THE PAIN... THEY NEED YOU TO BE ABLE TO TELL THEM IF IT CHANGES OR MOVES

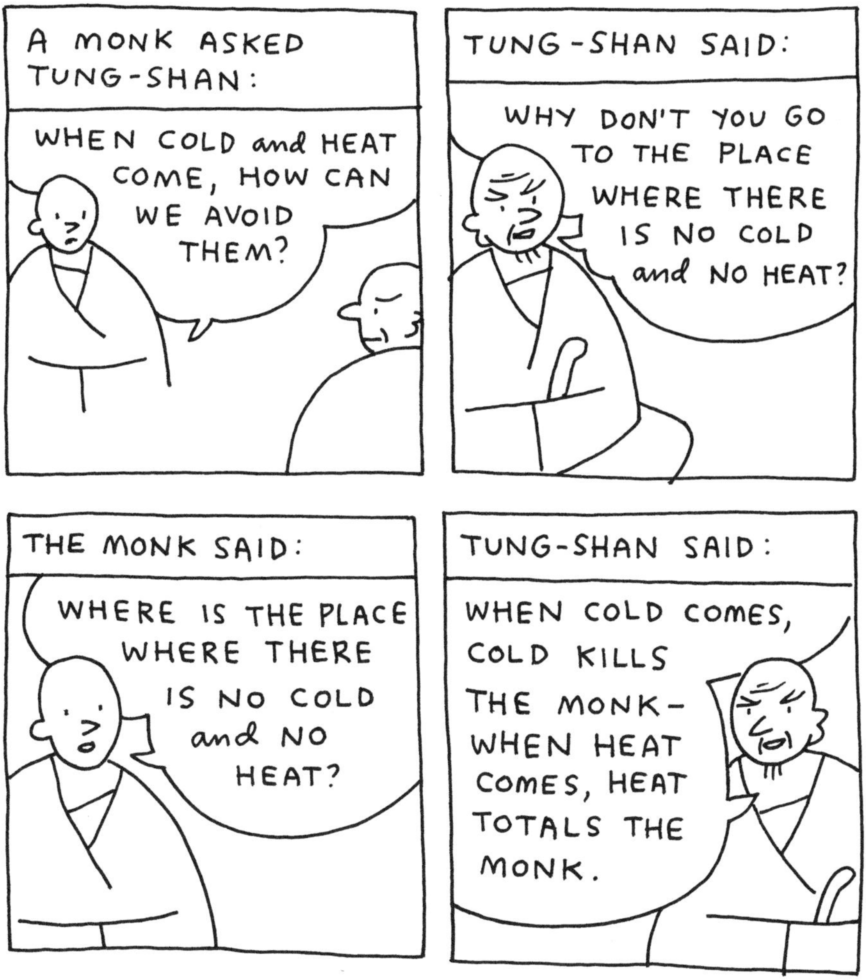
A MONK ASKED TUNG-SHAN:
WHEN COLD and HEAT COME, HOW CAN WE AVOID THEM?
TUNG-SHAN SAID:
WHY DON'T YOU GO TO THE PLACE WHERE THERE IS NO COLD and NO HEAT?
THE MONK SAID:
WHERE IS THE PLACE WHERE THERE IS NO COLD and NO HEAT?
TUNG-SHAN SAID:
WHEN COLD COMES, COLD KILLS THE MONK- WHEN HEAT COMES, HEAT TOTALS THE MONK.

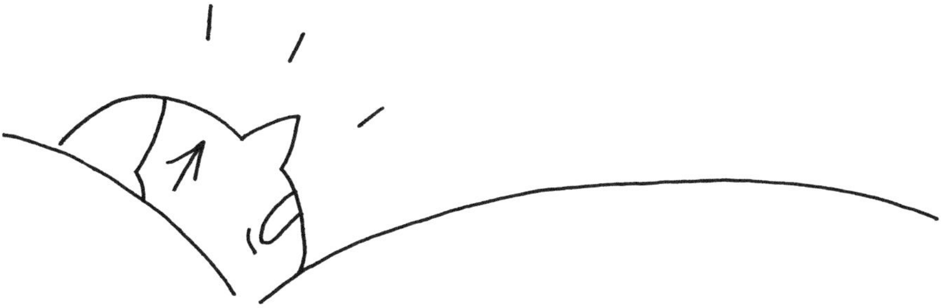

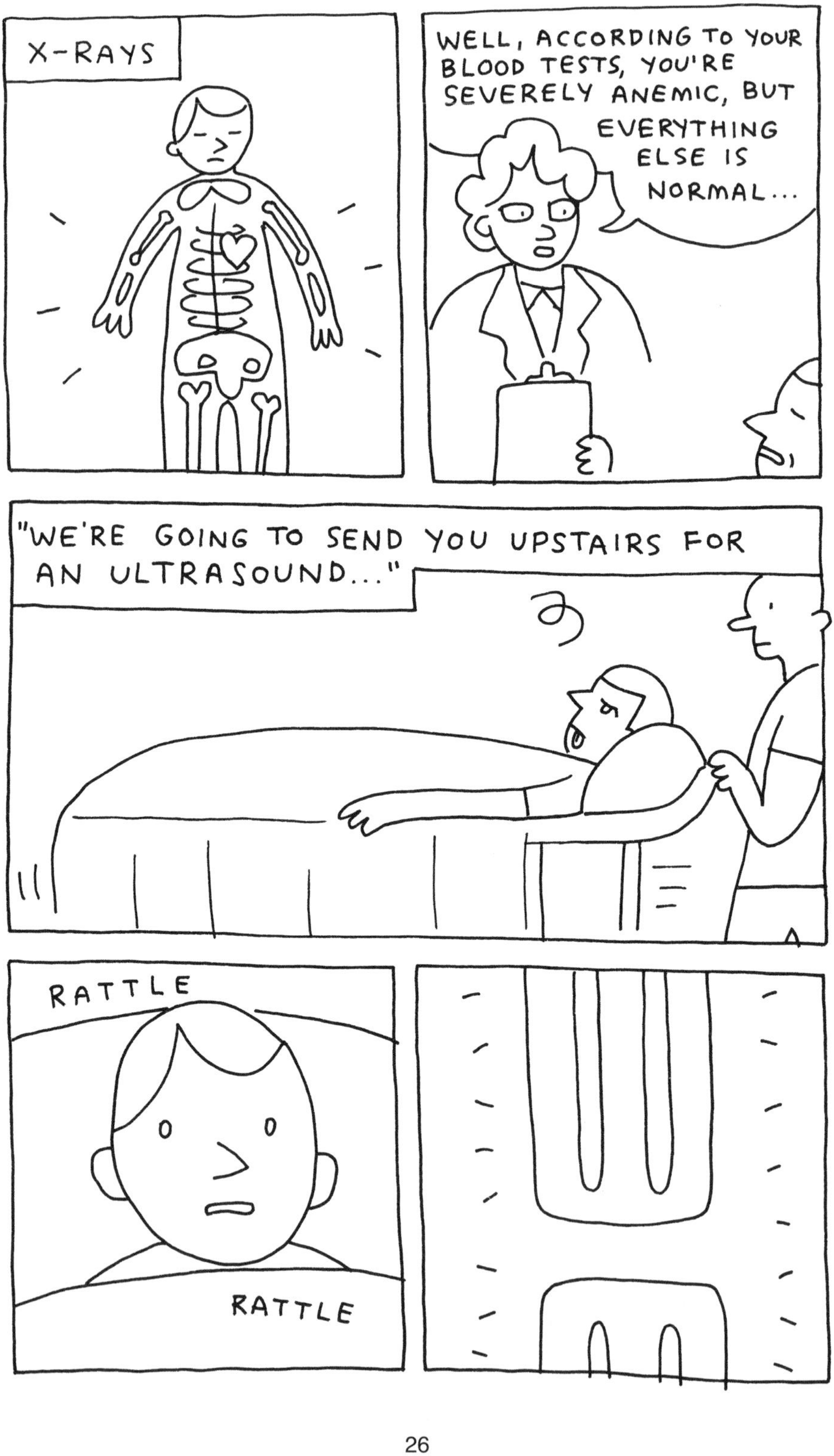
X-RAYS
WELL, ACCORDING TO YOUR BLOOD TESTS, YOU'RE SEVERELY ANEMIC, BUT EVERYTHING ELSE IS NORMAL...
"WE'RE GOING TO SEND YOU UPSTAIRS FOR AN ULTRASOUND..."
RATTLE
RATTLE

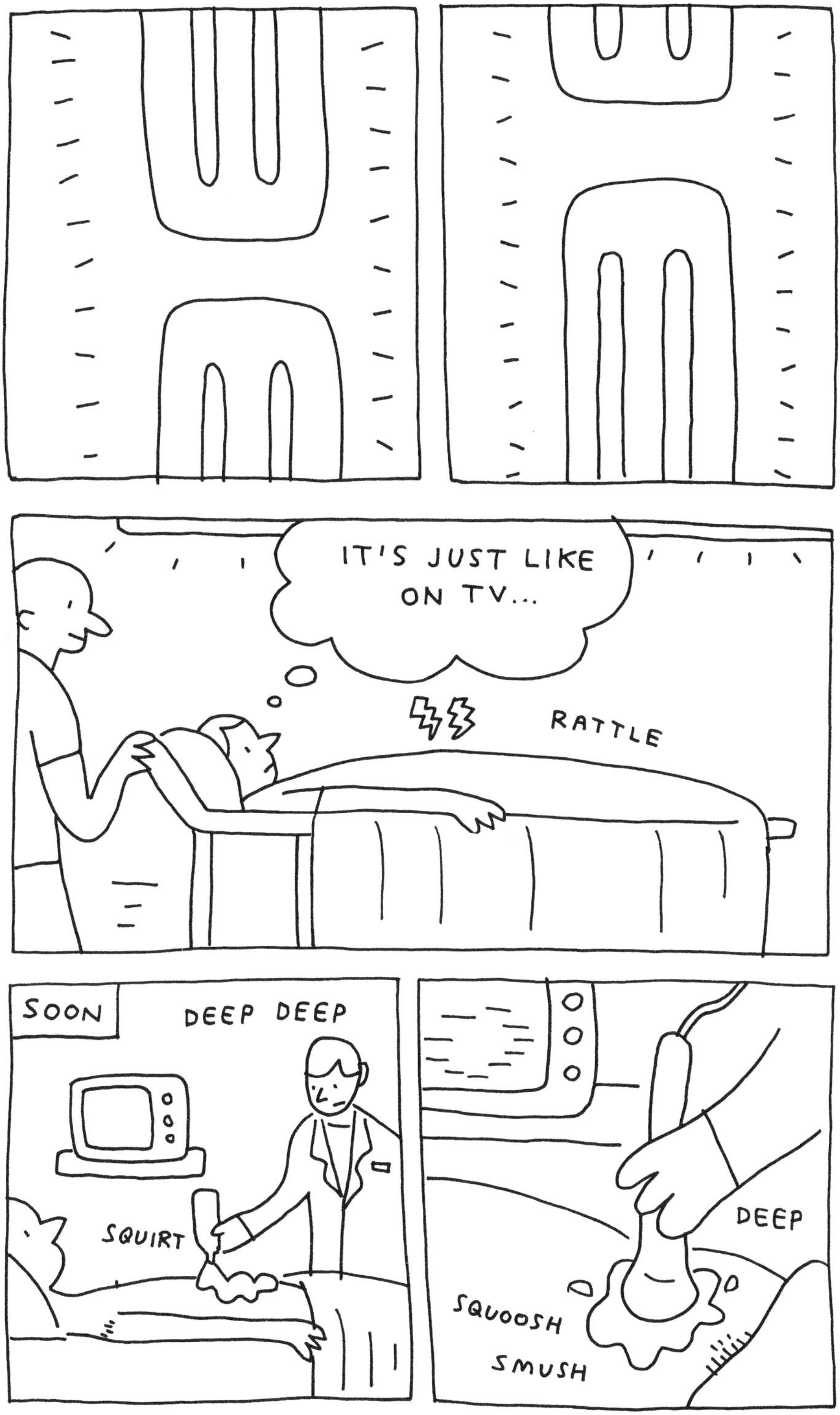
IT'S JUST LIKE ON TV...
RATTLE
SOON
DEEP DEEP
SQUIRT
DEEP
SQUOOSH
SMUSH

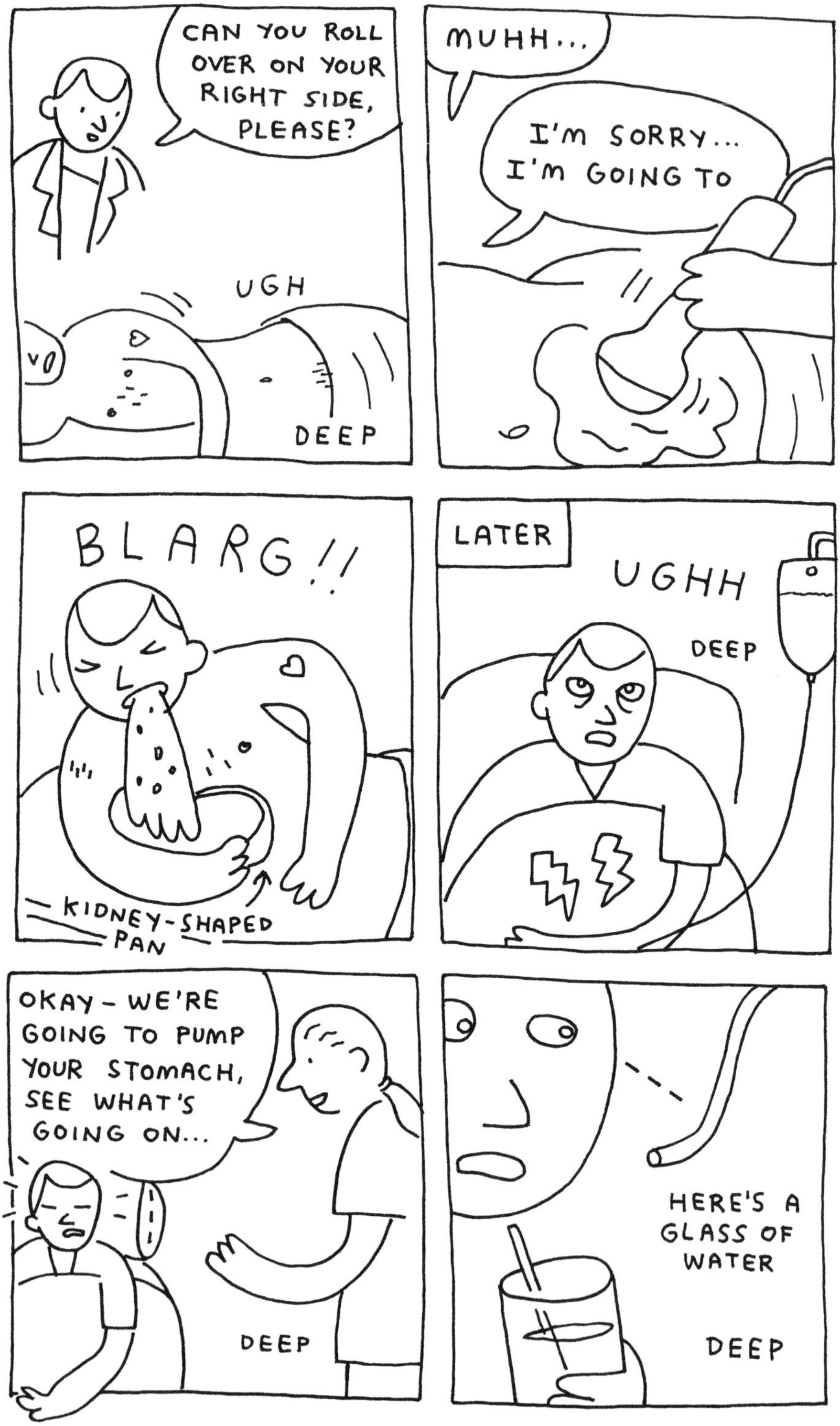
CAN YOU ROLL OVER ON YOUR RIGHT SIDE, PLEASE?
UGH
DEEP
MUHH...
I'M SORRY... I'M GOING TO
BLARG!!
KIDNEY-SHAPED PAN
LATER
UGHH
DEEP
OKAY - WE'RE GOING TO PUMP YOUR STOMACH, SEE WHAT'S GOING ON...
DEEP
HERE'S A GLASS OF WATER
DEEP

THE TUBE'S GONNA GO THROUGH YOUR NOSE and INTO YOUR STOMACH... WHEN I TELL YOU TO DRINK, DRINK... and KEEP SWALLOWING TILL I TELL YOU TO STOP...

ALL RIGHT... DRINK!

DEEP

GULP GULP

DRINK... KEEP DRINKING... KEEP DRINKING... OKAY.

I HAVE A TUBE IN MY NOSE...

DEEP

SNORK

SLORK

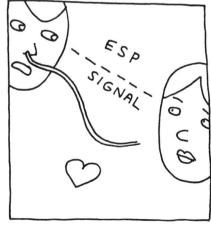

IT'S ALL BLACK

!!

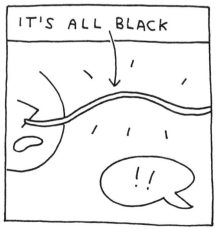

ESP SIGNAL

29

HE TOOK CHARCOAL PILLS THIS AFTERNOON, CUZ HE THOUGHT HE MIGHT HAVE FOOD POISONING... THAT'S WHY IT'S BLACK...

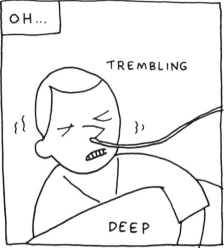

OH...

TREMBLING

DEEP

WAITING and WAITING

DEEP IV

GROVE

BEEBS

I THOUGHT TO MYSELF, "I MIGHT BE DYING..."

NO IGNORANCE OR END OF IT...

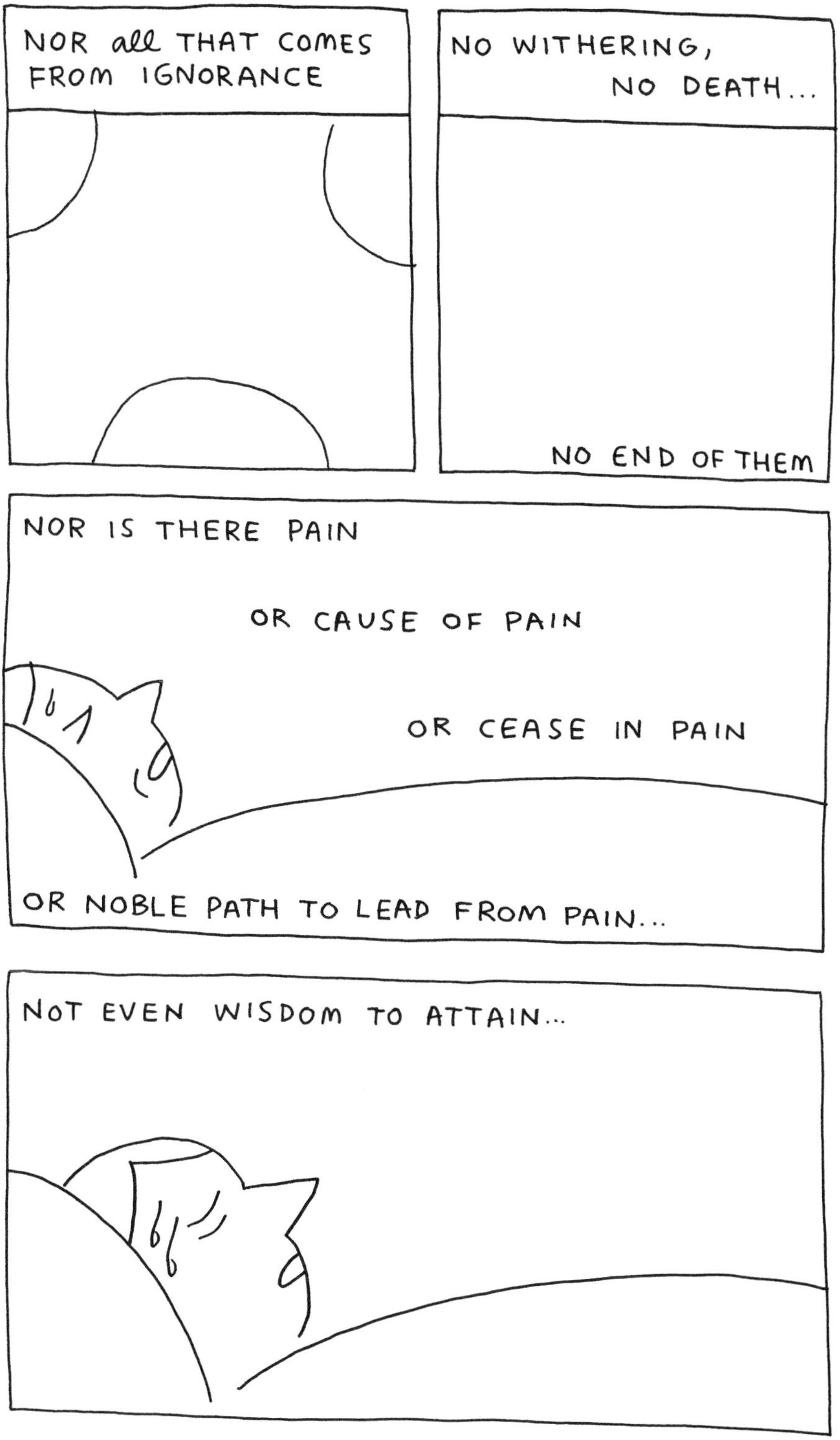
NOR all THAT COMES FROM IGNORANCE
NO WITHERING, NO DEATH...
NO END OF THEM
NOR IS THERE PAIN
OR CAUSE OF PAIN
OR CEASE IN PAIN
OR NOBLE PATH TO LEAD FROM PAIN...
NOT EVEN WISDOM TO ATTAIN...

ATTAINMENT, TOO,
IS EMPTINESS

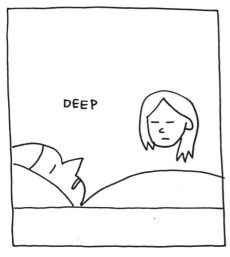

DEEP

PATIENT SLEEPING

COMPLAINS OF ABDOMINAL PAIN WHEN AWOKEN

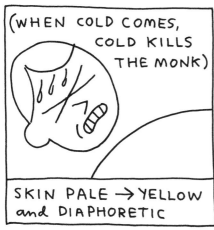

(WHEN COLD COMES, COLD KILLS THE MONK)

SKIN PALE → YELLOW and DIAPHORETIC

(WHEN HEAT COMES, HEAT TOTALS THE MONK)

WIFE at BEDSIDE

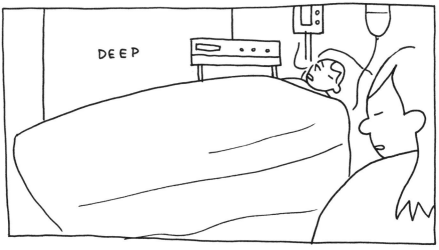

DEEP

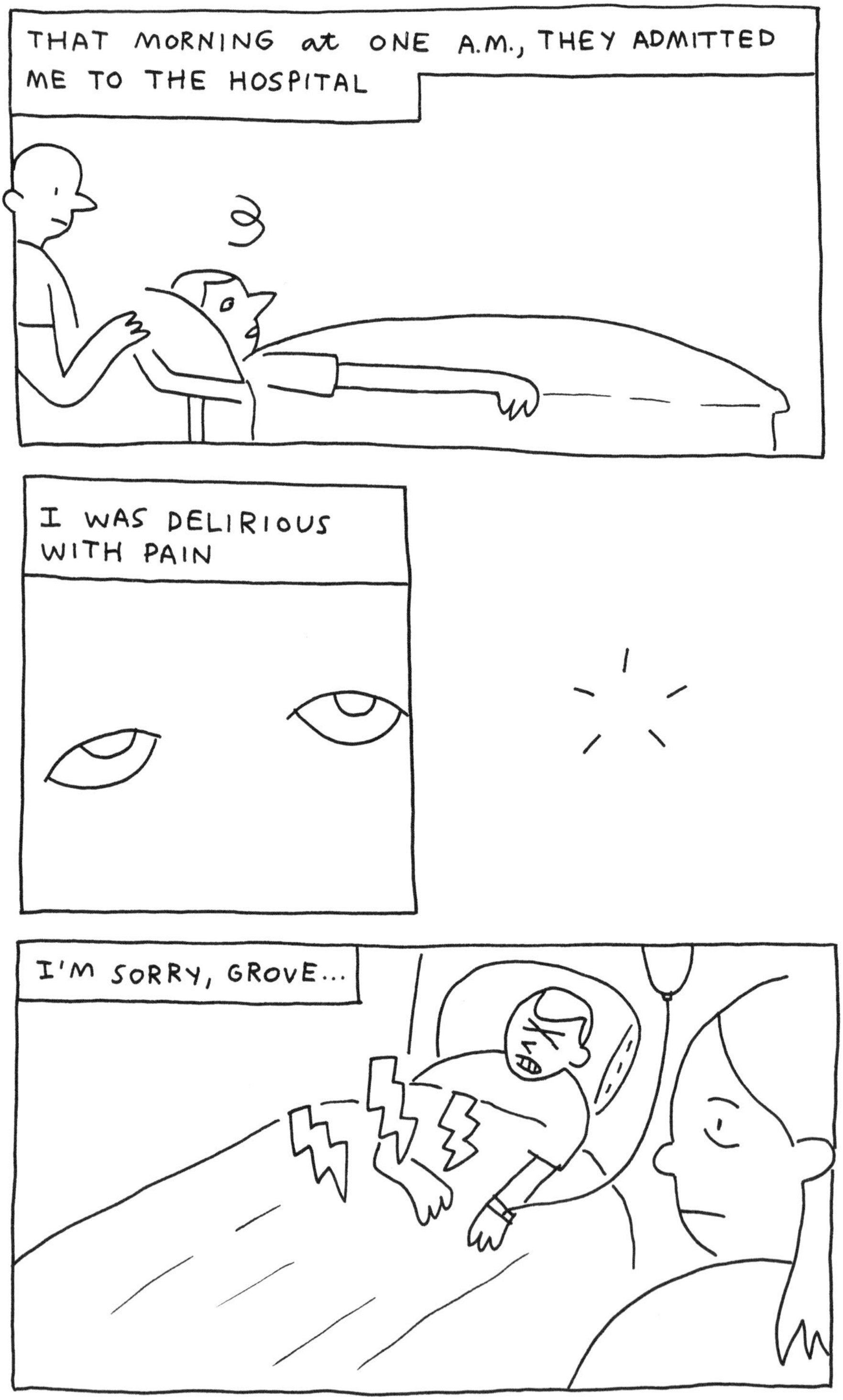
THAT MORNING at ONE A.M., THEY ADMITTED ME TO THE HOSPITAL
I WAS DELIRIOUS WITH PAIN
I'M SORRY, GROVE...

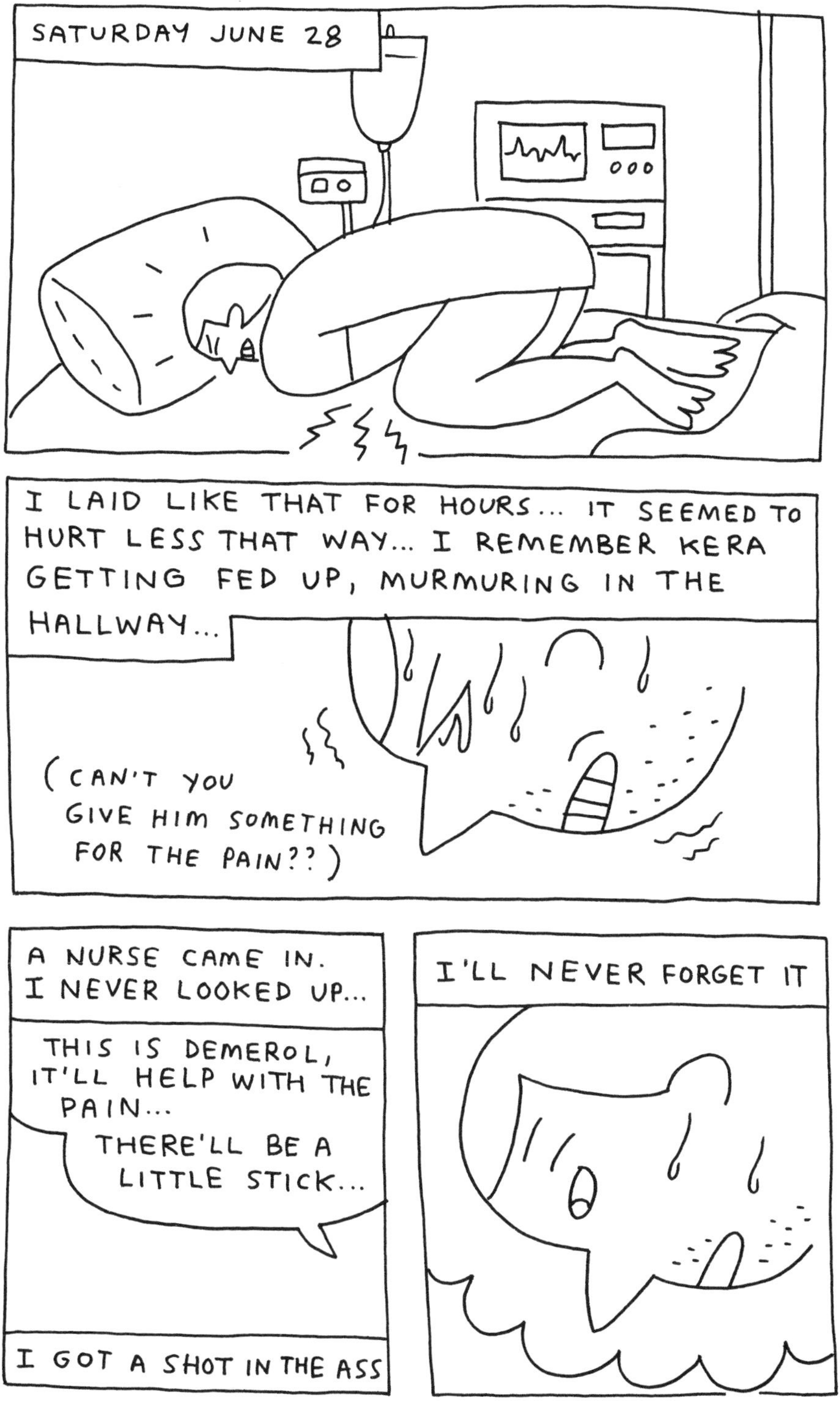
SATURDAY JUNE 28
I LAID LIKE THAT FOR HOURS... IT SEEMED TO HURT LESS THAT WAY... I REMEMBER KERA GETTING FED UP, MURMURING IN THE HALLWAY...
(CAN'T YOU GIVE HIM SOMETHING FOR THE PAIN??)
A NURSE CAME IN. I NEVER LOOKED UP...
THIS IS DEMEROL, IT'LL HELP WITH THE PAIN... THERE'LL BE A LITTLE STICK...
I GOT A SHOT IN THE ASS
I'LL NEVER FORGET IT

THE DRUG COURSED THROUGH EVERY VEIN IN MY BODY

and EVERYWHERE IT WENT

BLISS

I SLEPT FOR A DAY

DEEP   DEEP   DEEP   DEEP

SNNGKK

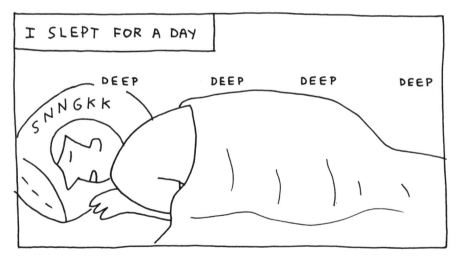

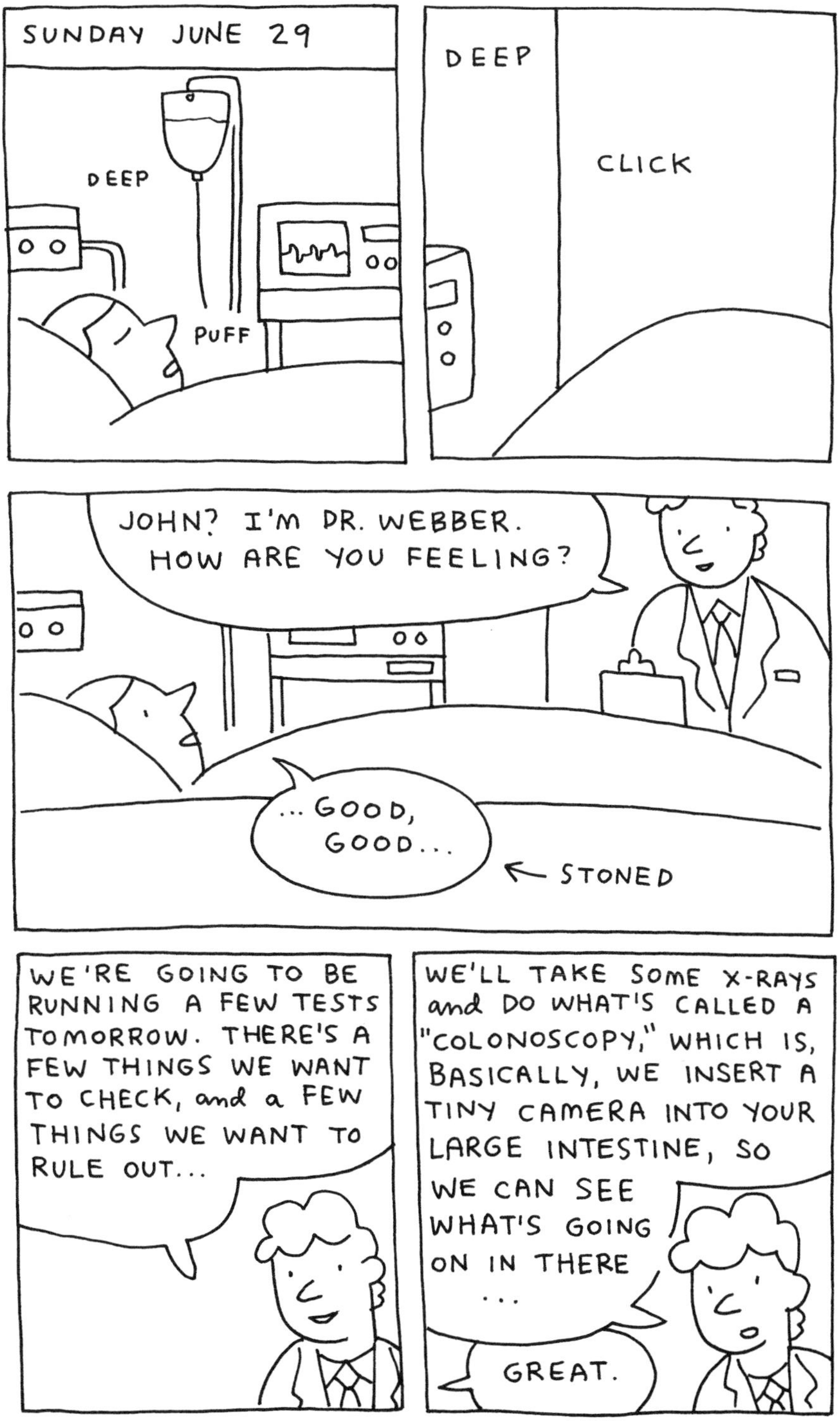
SUNDAY JUNE 29
DEEP
PUFF
DEEP
CLICK
JOHN? I'M DR. WEBBER. HOW ARE YOU FEELING?
...GOOD, GOOD...
STONED
WE'RE GOING TO BE RUNNING A FEW TESTS TOMORROW. THERE'S A FEW THINGS WE WANT TO CHECK, and a FEW THINGS WE WANT TO RULE OUT...
WE'LL TAKE SOME X-RAYS and DO WHAT'S CALLED A "COLONOSCOPY," WHICH IS, BASICALLY, WE INSERT A TINY CAMERA INTO YOUR LARGE INTESTINE, SO WE CAN SEE WHAT'S GOING ON IN THERE
...
GREAT.

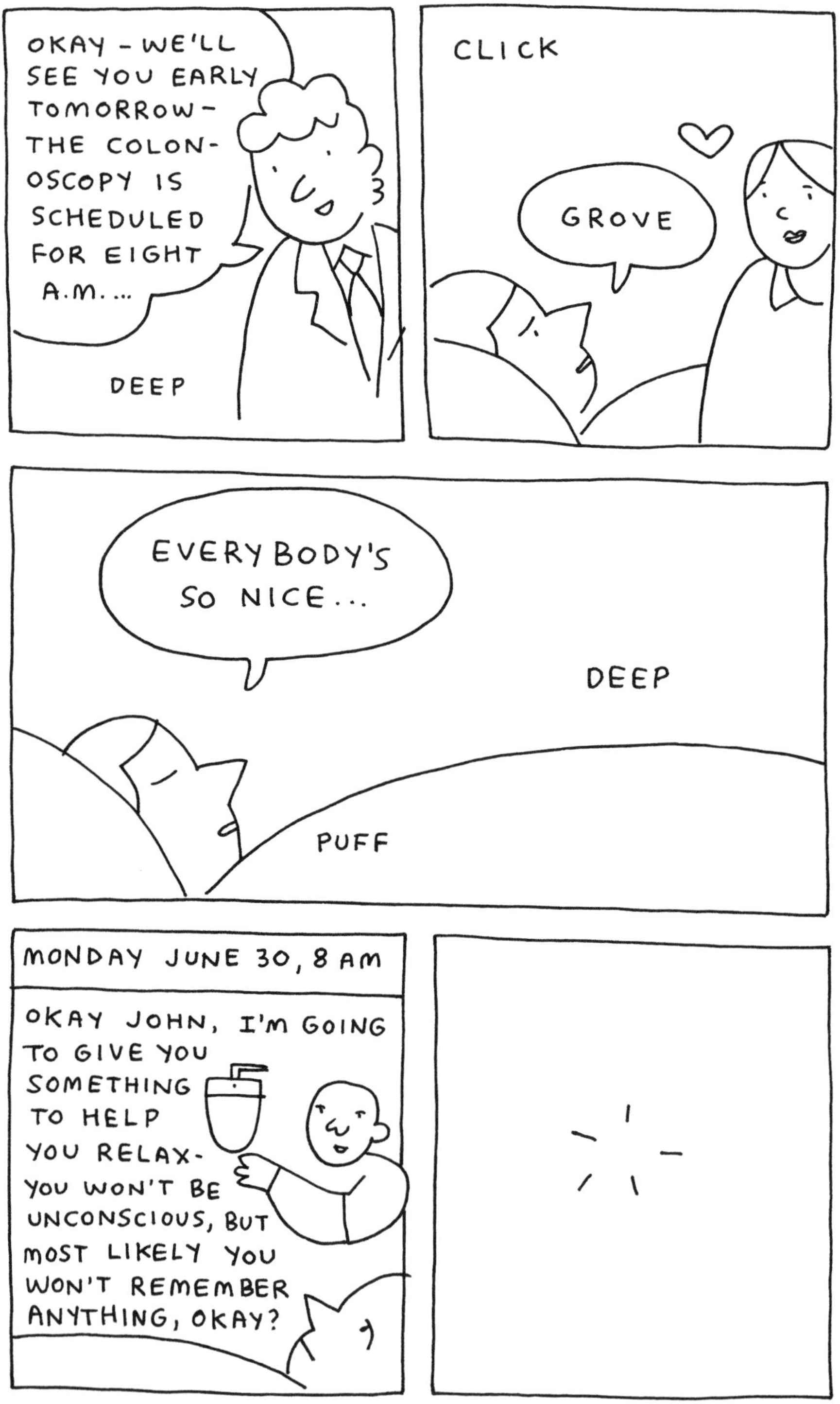
OKAY - WE'LL SEE YOU EARLY TOMORROW - THE COLON-OSCOPY IS SCHEDULED FOR EIGHT A.M. ...
DEEP
CLICK
GROVE
EVERYBODY'S SO NICE...
DEEP
PUFF
MONDAY JUNE 30, 8 AM
OKAY JOHN, I'M GOING TO GIVE YOU SOMETHING TO HELP YOU RELAX- YOU WON'T BE UNCONSCIOUS, BUT MOST LIKELY YOU WON'T REMEMBER ANYTHING, OKAY?

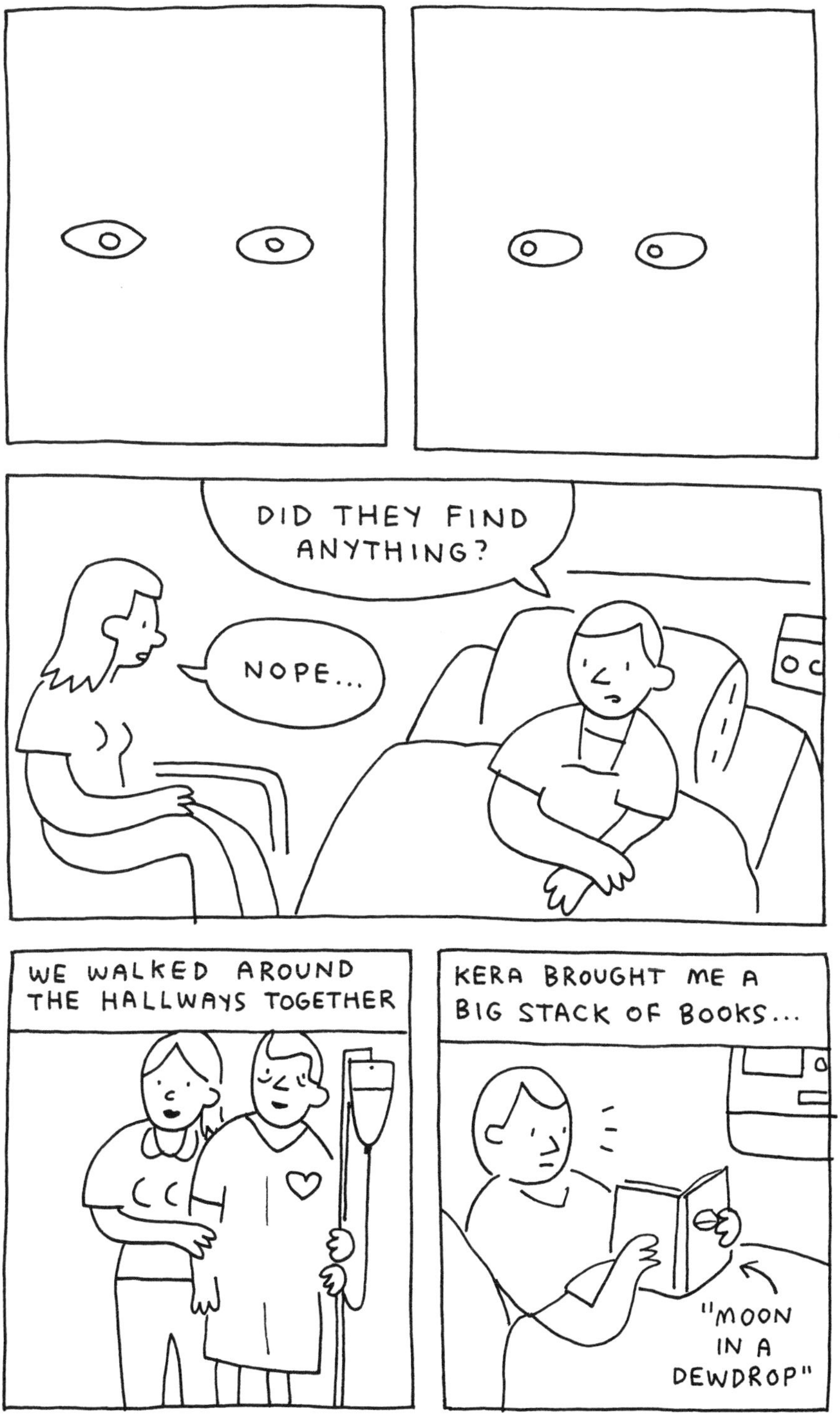
DID THEY FIND ANYTHING?
NOPE...
WE WALKED AROUND THE HALLWAYS TOGETHER
KERA BROUGHT ME A BIG STACK OF BOOKS...
"MOON IN A DEWDROP"

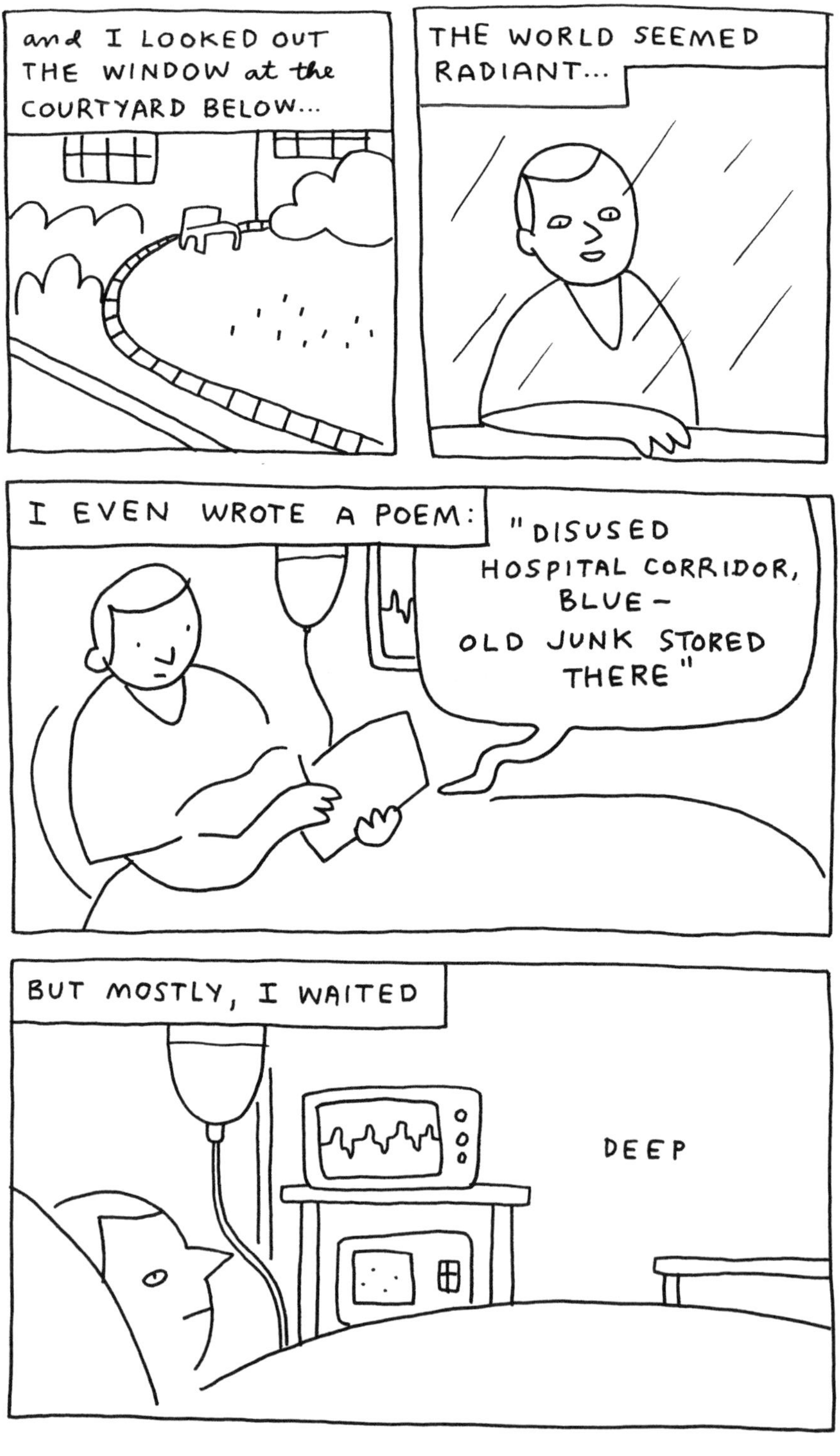
and I LOOKED OUT THE WINDOW at the COURTYARD BELOW...
THE WORLD SEEMED RADIANT...
I EVEN WROTE A POEM:
"DISUSED HOSPITAL CORRIDOR, BLUE – OLD JUNK STORED THERE"
BUT MOSTLY, I WAITED
DEEP

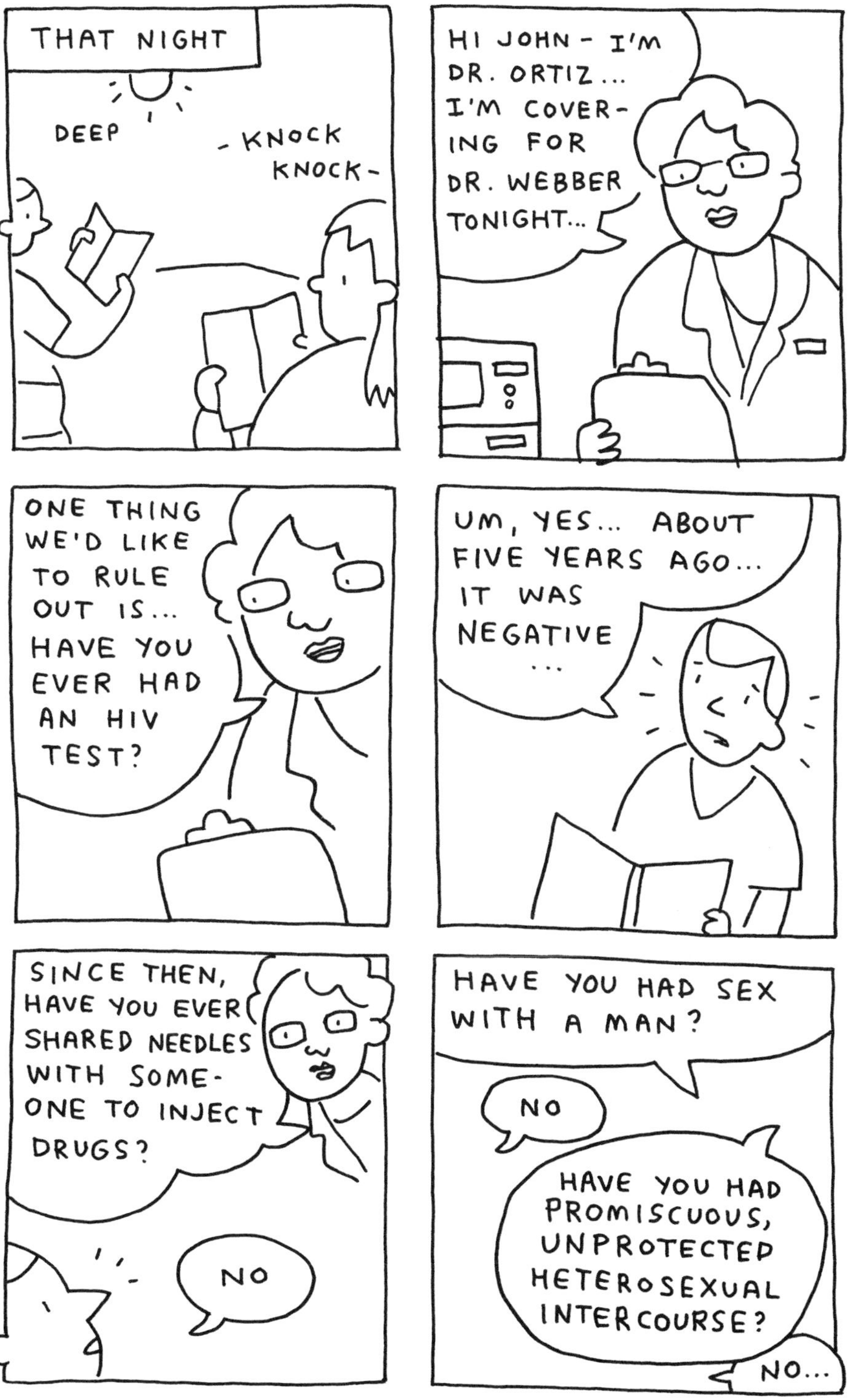
THAT NIGHT
DEEP
- KNOCK KNOCK -
HI JOHN - I'M DR. ORTIZ... I'M COVERING FOR DR. WEBBER TONIGHT...
ONE THING WE'D LIKE TO RULE OUT IS... HAVE YOU EVER HAD AN HIV TEST?
UM, YES... ABOUT FIVE YEARS AGO... IT WAS NEGATIVE ...
SINCE THEN, HAVE YOU EVER SHARED NEEDLES WITH SOMEONE TO INJECT DRUGS?
NO
HAVE YOU HAD SEX WITH A MAN?
NO
HAVE YOU HAD PROMISCUOUS, UNPROTECTED HETEROSEXUAL INTERCOURSE?
NO...

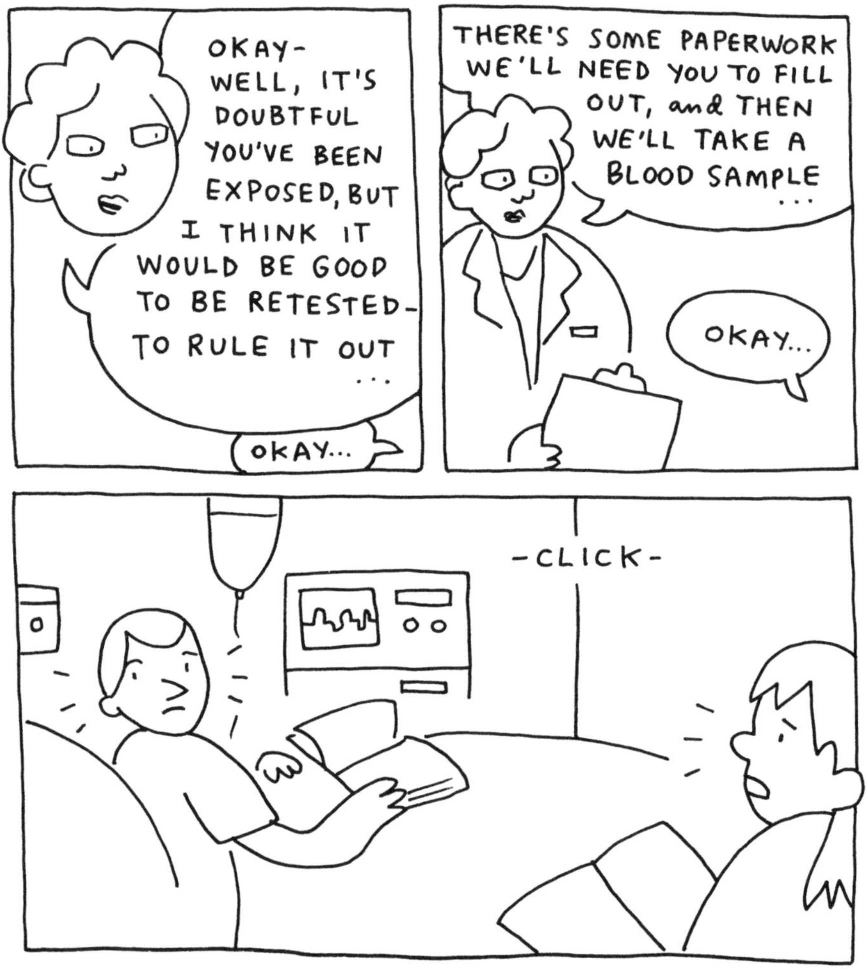
OKAY- WELL, IT'S DOUBTFUL YOU'VE BEEN EXPOSED, BUT I THINK IT WOULD BE GOOD TO BE RETESTED- TO RULE IT OUT ...
OKAY...
THERE'S SOME PAPERWORK WE'LL NEED YOU TO FILL OUT, and THEN WE'LL TAKE A BLOOD SAMPLE ...
OKAY...
-CLICK-

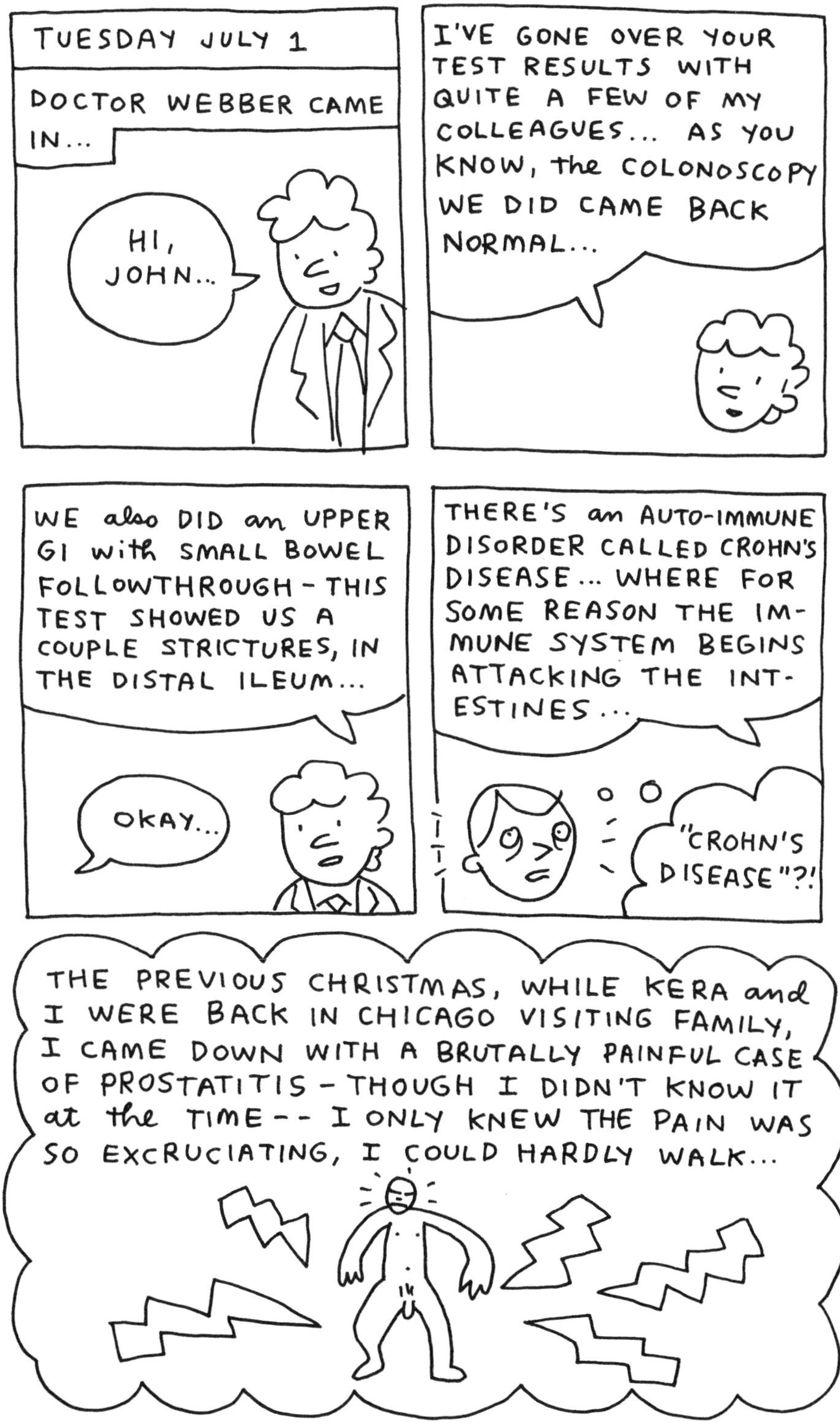
TUESDAY JULY 1
DOCTOR WEBBER CAME IN...
HI, JOHN...
I'VE GONE OVER YOUR TEST RESULTS WITH QUITE A FEW OF MY COLLEAGUES... AS YOU KNOW, the COLONOSCOPY WE DID CAME BACK NORMAL...
WE also DID an UPPER GI with SMALL BOWEL FOLLOWTHROUGH - THIS TEST SHOWED US A COUPLE STRICTURES, IN THE DISTAL ILEUM...
OKAY...
THERE'S an AUTO-IMMUNE DISORDER CALLED CROHN'S DISEASE... WHERE FOR SOME REASON THE IMMUNE SYSTEM BEGINS ATTACKING THE INTESTINES...
"CROHN'S DISEASE"?!
THE PREVIOUS CHRISTMAS, WHILE KERA and I WERE BACK IN CHICAGO VISITING FAMILY, I CAME DOWN WITH A BRUTALLY PAINFUL CASE OF PROSTATITIS - THOUGH I DIDN'T KNOW IT at the TIME -- I ONLY KNEW THE PAIN WAS SO EXCRUCIATING, I COULD HARDLY WALK...

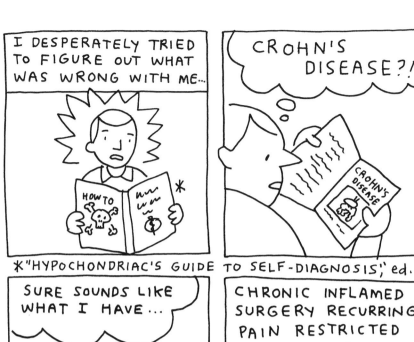

I DESPERATELY TRIED TO FIGURE OUT WHAT WAS WRONG WITH ME...

CROHN'S DISEASE?!

*"HYPOCHONDRIAC'S GUIDE TO SELF-DIAGNOSIS," ed.

SURE SOUNDS LIKE WHAT I HAVE...

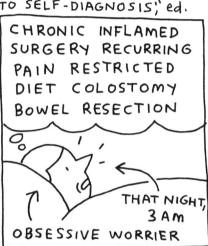

CHRONIC INFLAMED SURGERY RECURRING PAIN RESTRICTED DIET COLOSTOMY BOWEL RESECTION

THAT NIGHT, 3 AM
OBSESSIVE WORRIER

EVENTUALLY THE PAIN WENT AWAY ON ITS OWN, BUT I ALWAYS REMEMBERED MY FEAR OF CROHN'S...

NOW, PEOPLE WITH CROHN'S NEED TO TAKE MEDICATION, and WATCH WHAT THEY EAT, BUT IN GENERAL THEY GO ON TO LIVE RELATIVELY NORMAL LIVES...

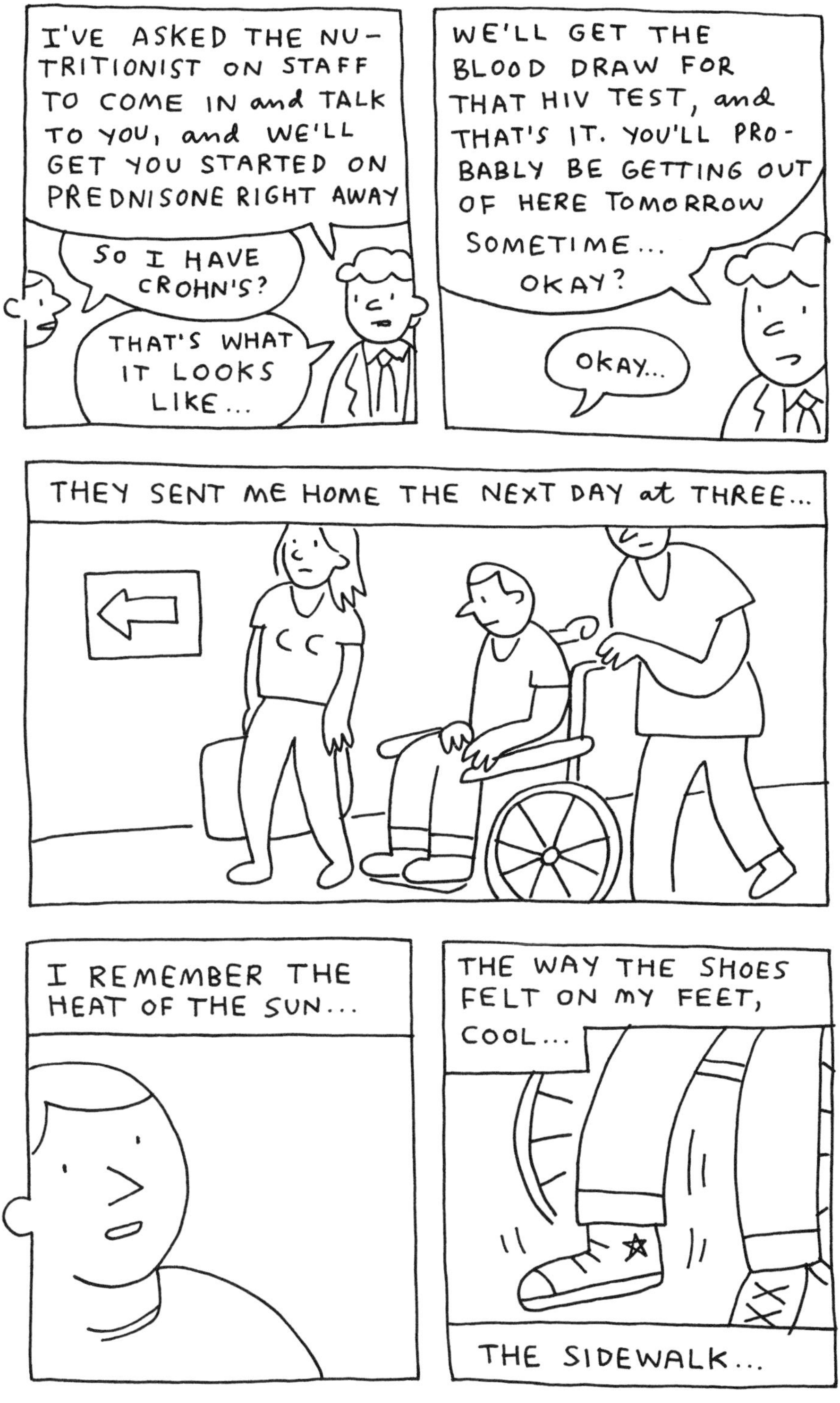
I'VE ASKED THE NUTRITIONIST ON STAFF TO COME IN and TALK TO YOU, and WE'LL GET YOU STARTED ON PREDNISONE RIGHT AWAY
SO I HAVE CROHN'S?
THAT'S WHAT IT LOOKS LIKE...
WE'LL GET THE BLOOD DRAW FOR THAT HIV TEST, and THAT'S IT. YOU'LL PROBABLY BE GETTING OUT OF HERE TOMORROW SOMETIME... OKAY?
OKAY...
THEY SENT ME HOME THE NEXT DAY at THREE...
I REMEMBER THE HEAT OF THE SUN...
THE WAY THE SHOES FELT ON MY FEET, COOL...
THE SIDEWALK...

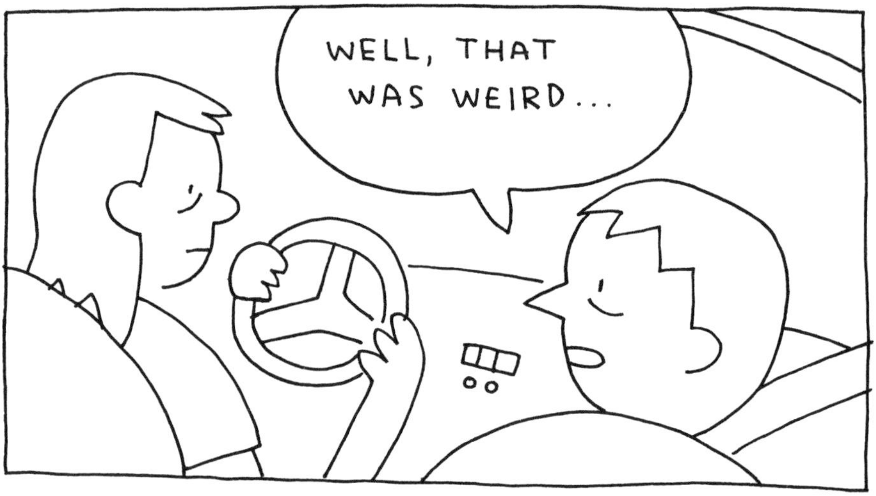
WELL, THAT WAS WEIRD...

Part Two

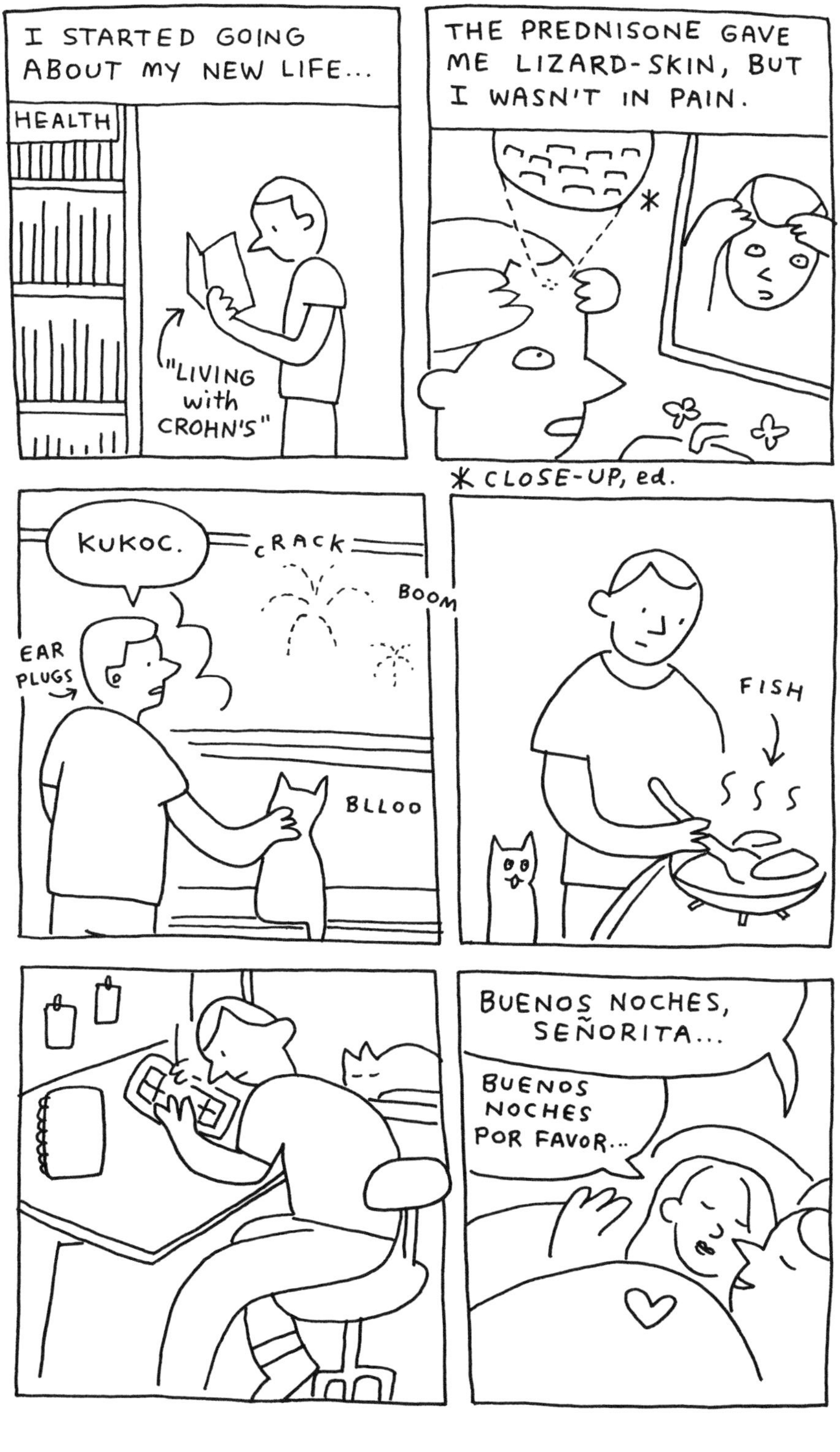

I STARTED GOING ABOUT MY NEW LIFE...
HEALTH
"LIVING with CROHN'S"
THE PREDNISONE GAVE ME LIZARD-SKIN, BUT I WASN'T IN PAIN.
* CLOSE-UP, ed.
KUKOC.
CRACK
BOOM
EAR PLUGS
BLLOO
FISH
BUENOS NOCHES, SEÑORITA...
BUENOS NOCHES POR FAVOR...

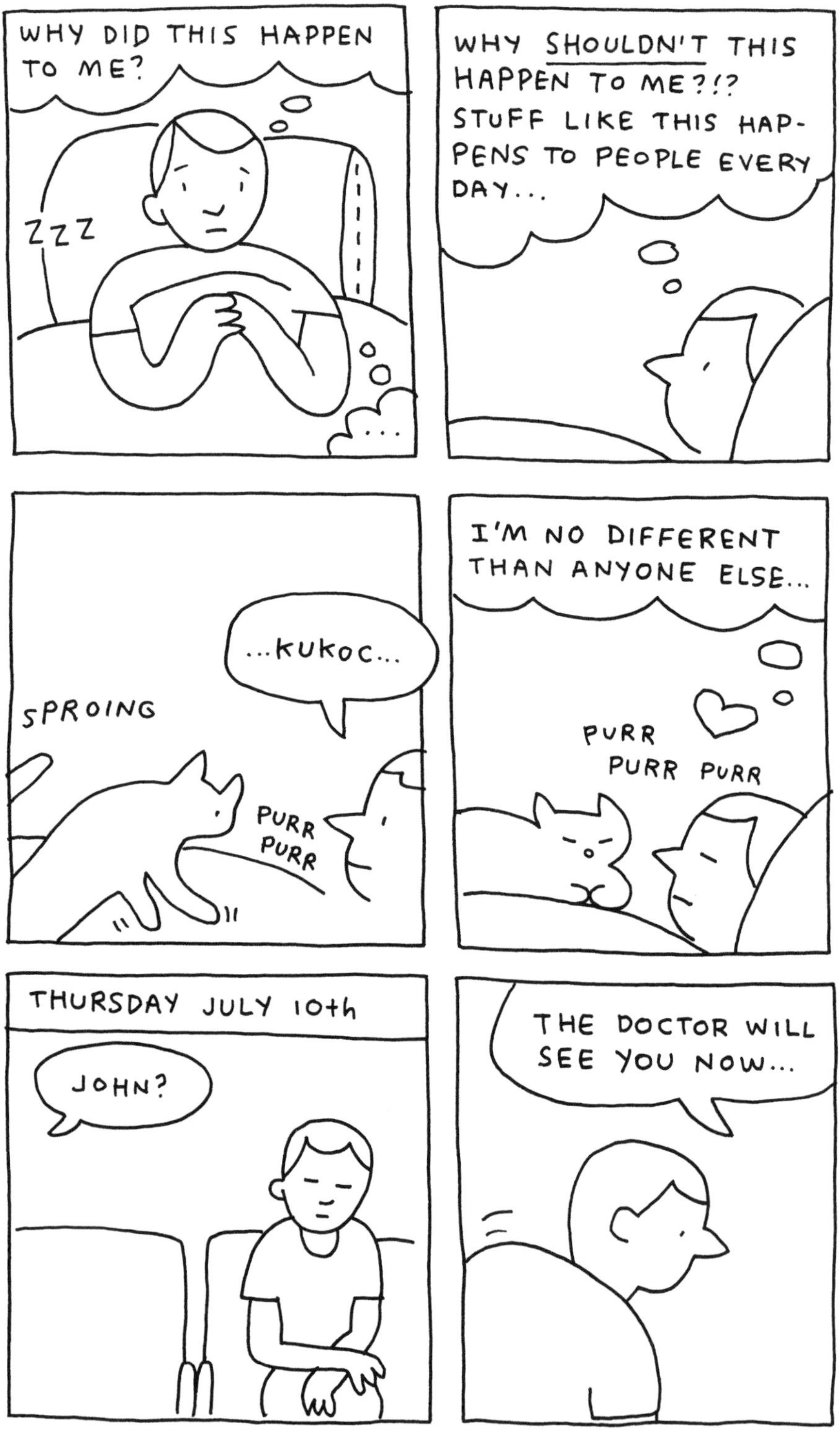
WHY DID THIS HAPPEN TO ME?
ZZZ
...
WHY SHOULDN'T THIS HAPPEN TO ME?!? STUFF LIKE THIS HAPPENS TO PEOPLE EVERY DAY...
...KUKOC...
SPROING
PURR PURR
I'M NO DIFFERENT THAN ANYONE ELSE...
PURR
PURR PURR
THURSDAY JULY 10th
JOHN?
THE DOCTOR WILL SEE YOU NOW...

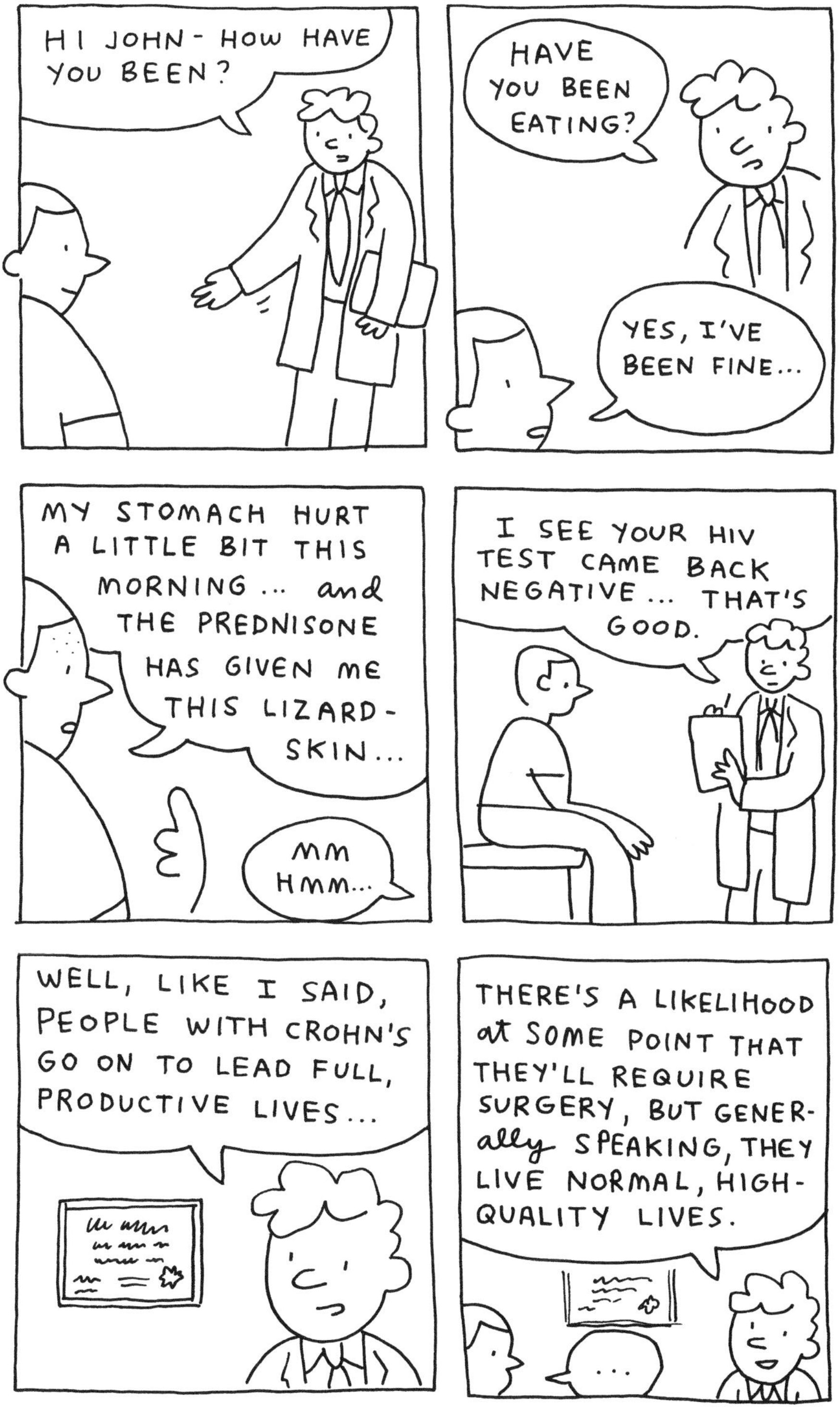
HI JOHN - HOW HAVE YOU BEEN?
HAVE YOU BEEN EATING?
YES, I'VE BEEN FINE...
MY STOMACH HURT A LITTLE BIT THIS MORNING... and THE PREDNISONE HAS GIVEN ME THIS LIZARD-SKIN...
MM HMM...
I SEE YOUR HIV TEST CAME BACK NEGATIVE... THAT'S GOOD.
WELL, LIKE I SAID, PEOPLE WITH CROHN'S GO ON TO LEAD FULL, PRODUCTIVE LIVES...
THERE'S A LIKELIHOOD at SOME POINT THAT THEY'LL REQUIRE SURGERY, BUT GENERally SPEAKING, THEY LIVE NORMAL, HIGH-QUALITY LIVES.
...

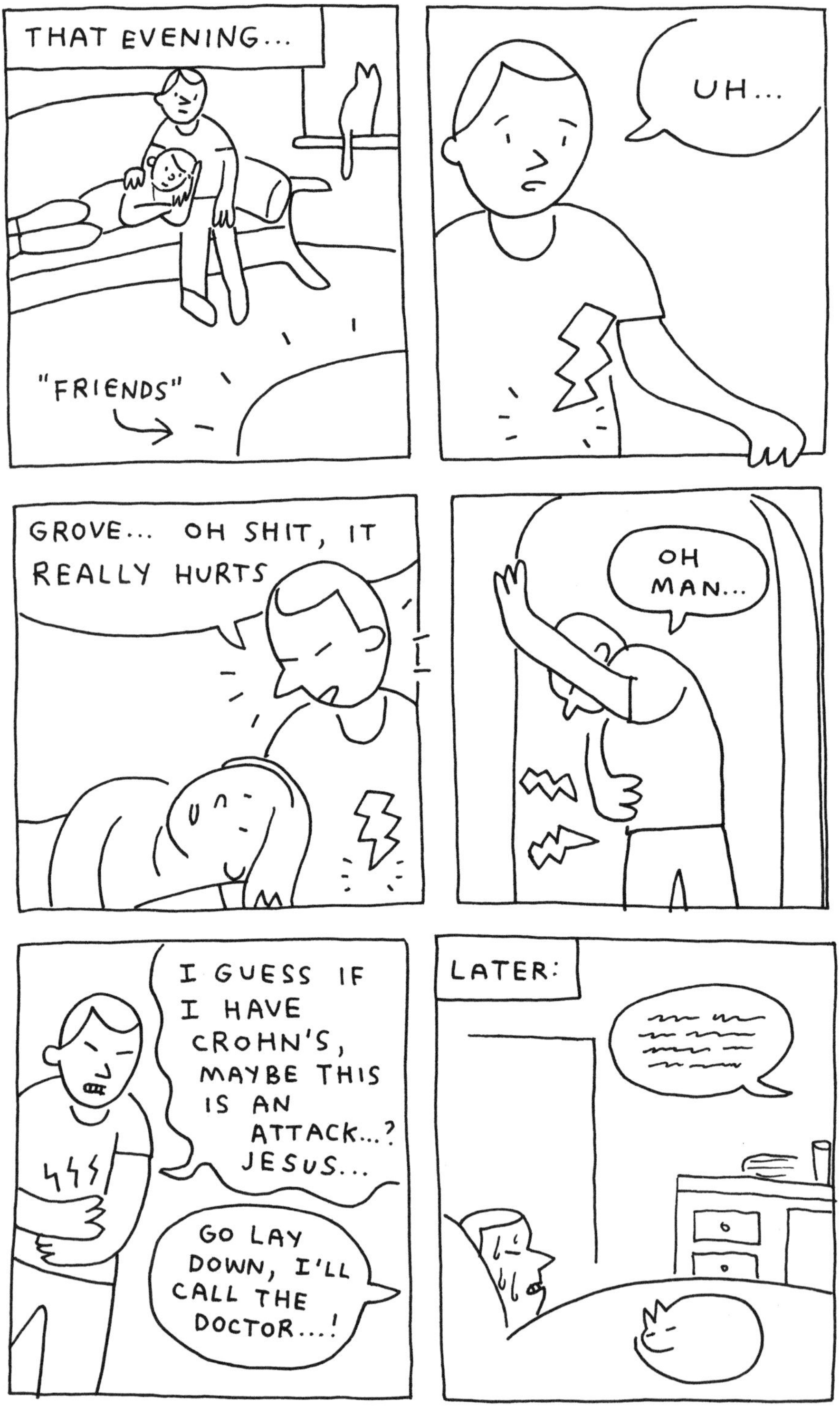
THAT EVENING...
"FRIENDS"
UH...
GROVE... OH SHIT, IT REALLY HURTS
OH MAN...
I GUESS IF I HAVE CROHN'S, MAYBE THIS IS AN ATTACK...? JESUS...
GO LAY DOWN, I'LL CALL THE DOCTOR...!
LATER:

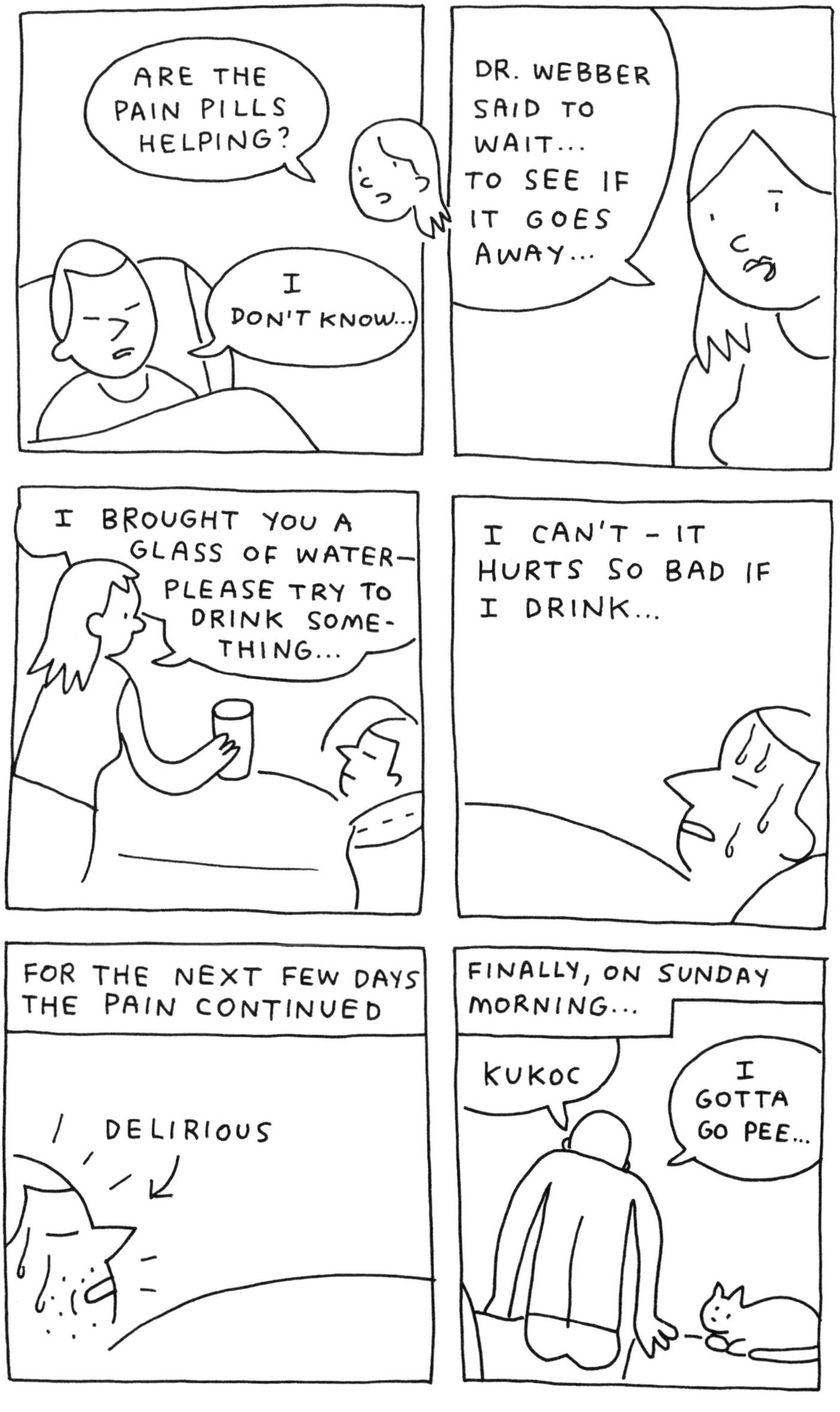
ARE THE PAIN PILLS HELPING?
I DON'T KNOW...
DR. WEBBER SAID TO WAIT... TO SEE IF IT GOES AWAY...
I BROUGHT YOU A GLASS OF WATER— PLEASE TRY TO DRINK SOME-THING...
I CAN'T - IT HURTS SO BAD IF I DRINK...
FOR THE NEXT FEW DAYS THE PAIN CONTINUED
DELIRIOUS
FINALLY, ON SUNDAY MORNING...
KUKOC
I GOTTA GO PEE...

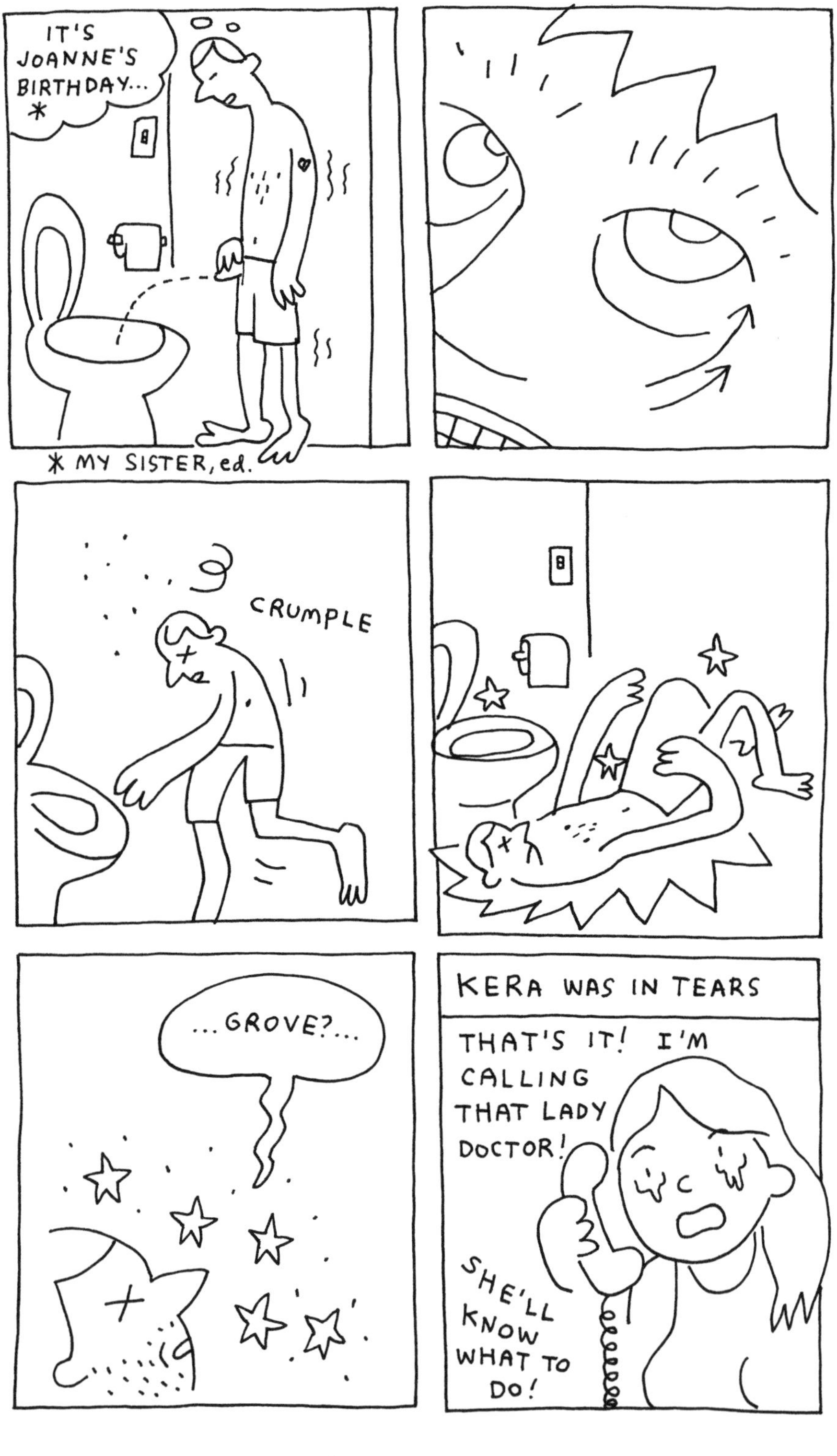
IT'S JOANNE'S BIRTHDAY... *
* MY SISTER, ed.
CRUMPLE
...GROVE?...
KERA WAS IN TEARS
THAT'S IT! I'M CALLING THAT LADY DOCTOR!
SHE'LL KNOW WHAT TO DO!

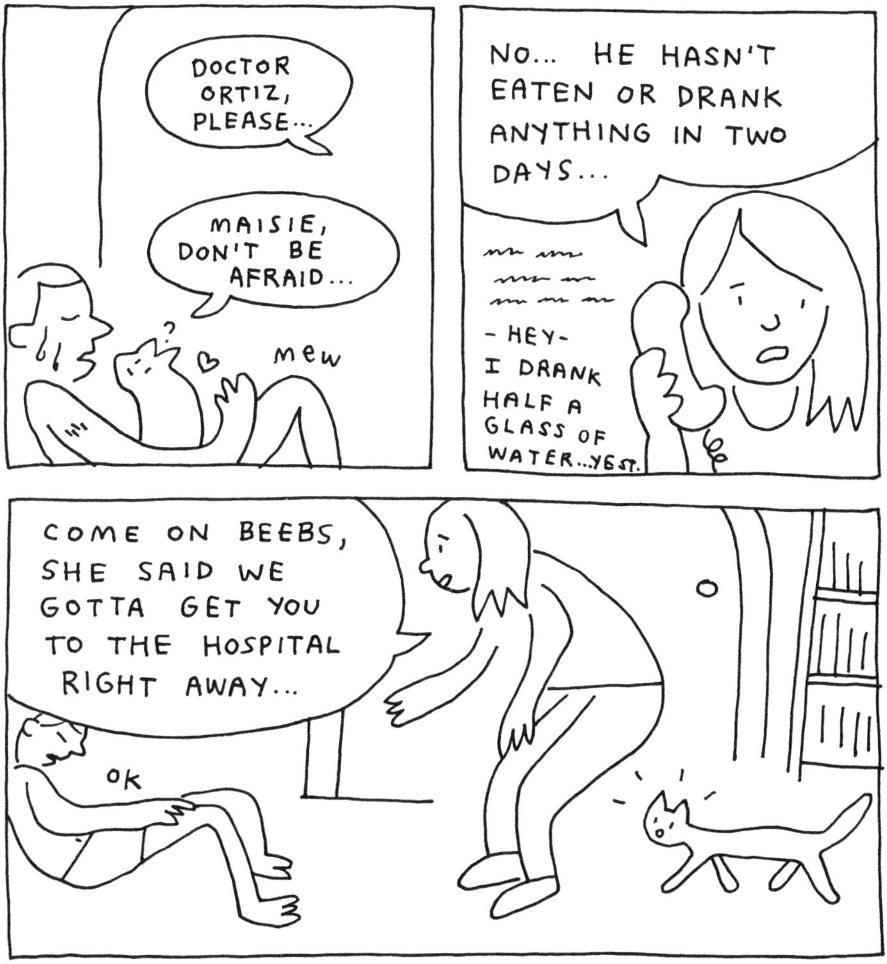
DOCTOR ORTIZ, PLEASE...
MAISIE, DON'T BE AFRAID...
MEW
NO... HE HASN'T EATEN OR DRANK ANYTHING IN TWO DAYS...
- HEY-
I DRANK HALF A GLASS OF WATER...YEST.
COME ON BEEBS, SHE SAID WE GOTTA GET YOU TO THE HOSPITAL RIGHT AWAY...
OK

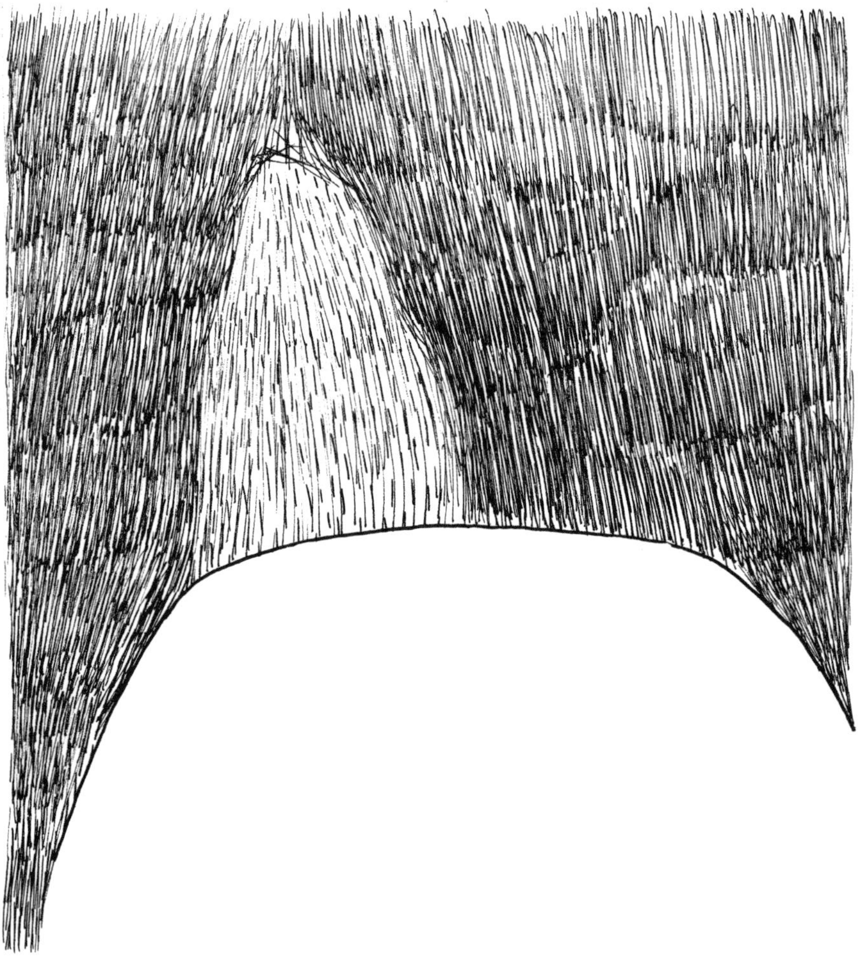

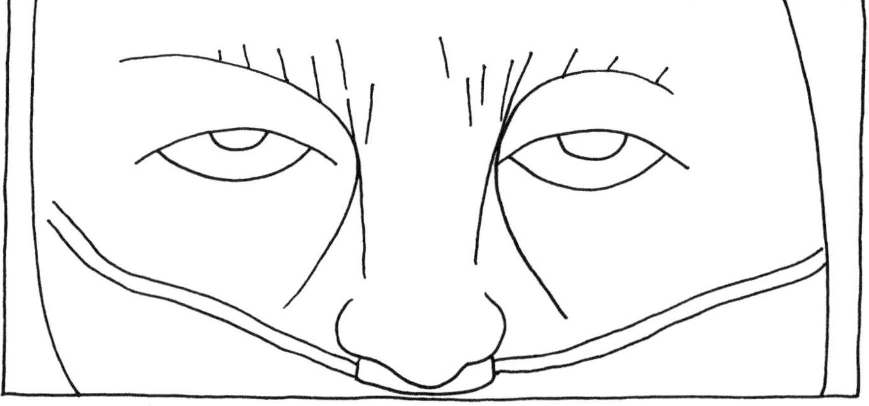

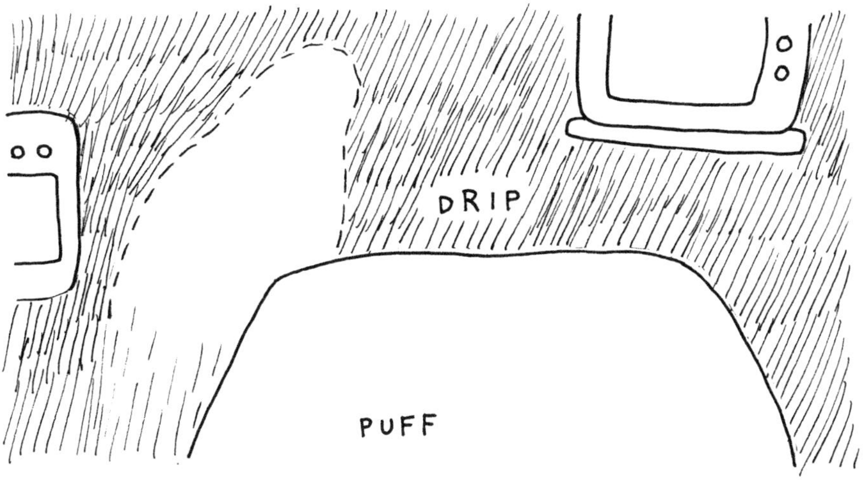
DRIP
PUFF

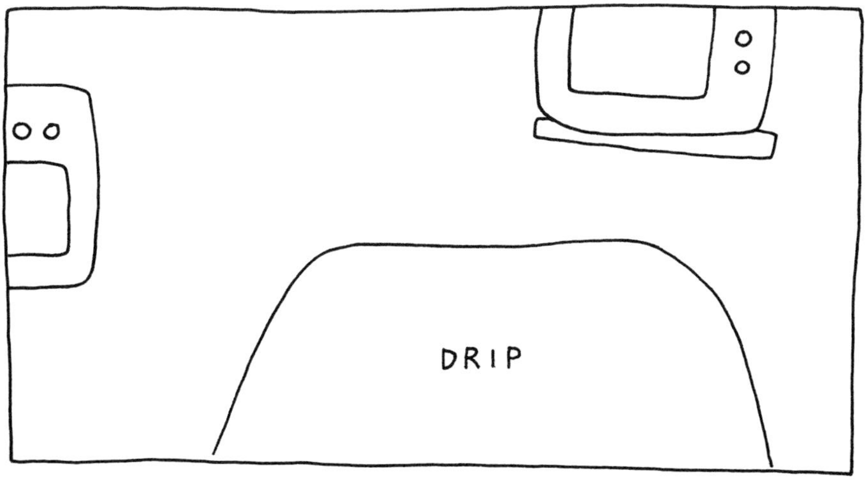
DRIP

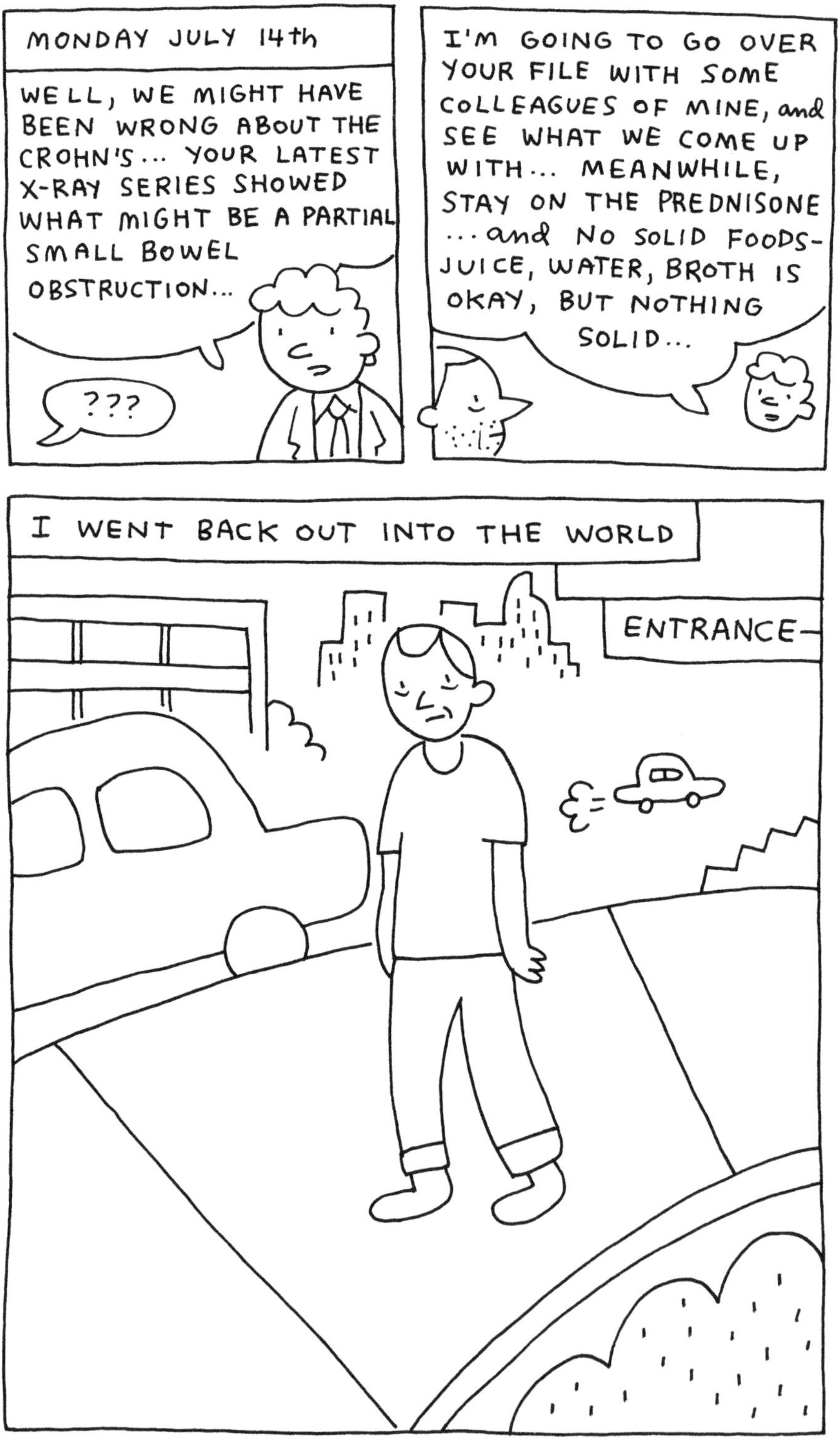
MONDAY JULY 14th
WELL, WE MIGHT HAVE BEEN WRONG ABOUT THE CROHN'S... YOUR LATEST X-RAY SERIES SHOWED WHAT MIGHT BE A PARTIAL SMALL BOWEL OBSTRUCTION...
???
I'M GOING TO GO OVER YOUR FILE WITH SOME COLLEAGUES OF MINE, and SEE WHAT WE COME UP WITH... MEANWHILE, STAY ON THE PREDNISONE ...and NO SOLID FOODS- JUICE, WATER, BROTH IS OKAY, BUT NOTHING SOLID...
I WENT BACK OUT INTO THE WORLD
ENTRANCE

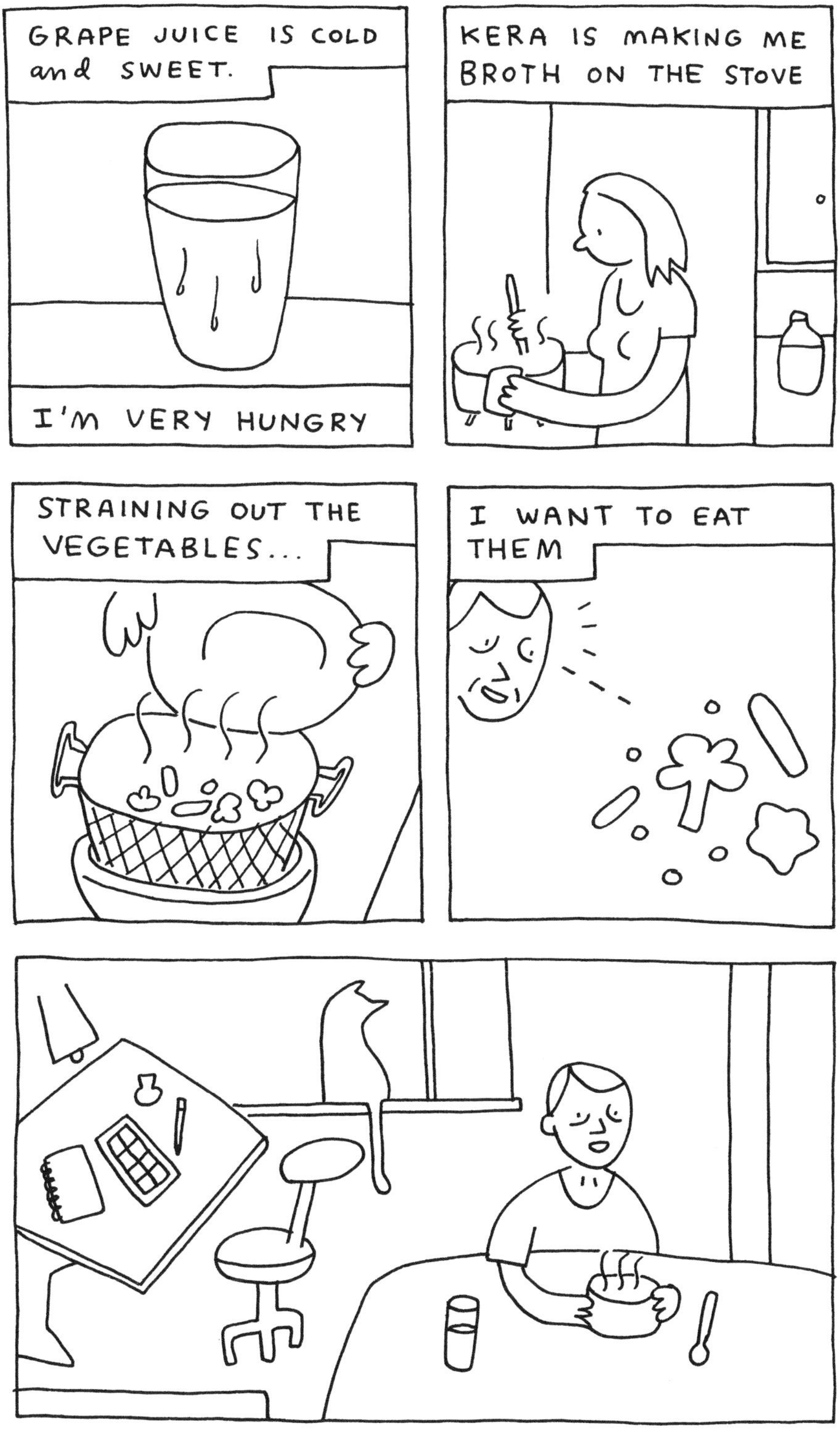
GRAPE JUICE IS COLD and SWEET.
I'M VERY HUNGRY
KERA IS MAKING ME BROTH ON THE STOVE
STRAINING OUT THE VEGETABLES...
I WANT TO EAT THEM

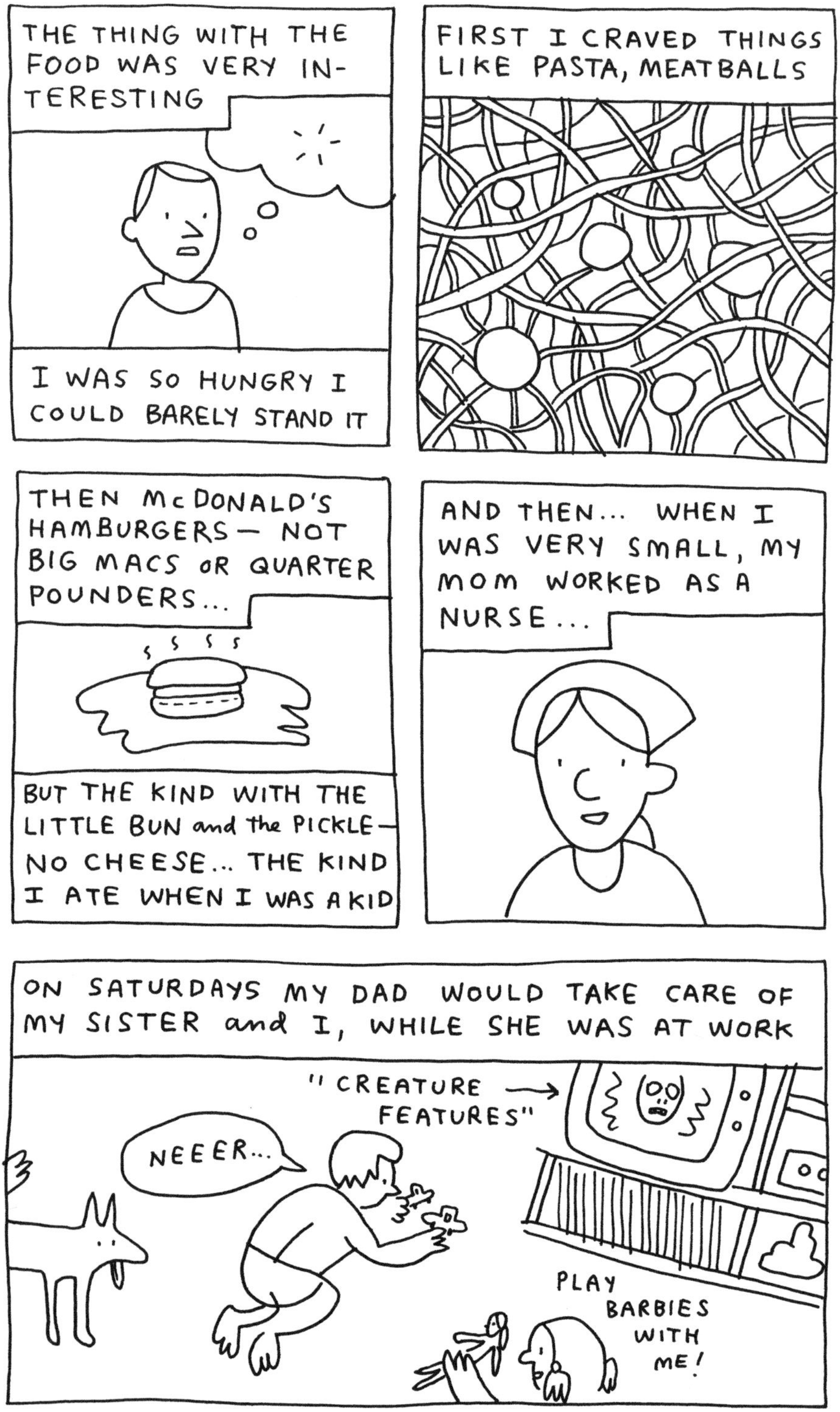
THE THING WITH THE FOOD WAS VERY INTERESTING
I WAS SO HUNGRY I COULD BARELY STAND IT
FIRST I CRAVED THINGS LIKE PASTA, MEATBALLS
THEN McDONALD'S HAMBURGERS — NOT BIG MACS OR QUARTER POUNDERS...
BUT THE KIND WITH THE LITTLE BUN and the PICKLE — NO CHEESE... THE KIND I ATE WHEN I WAS A KID
AND THEN... WHEN I WAS VERY SMALL, MY MOM WORKED AS A NURSE...
ON SATURDAYS MY DAD WOULD TAKE CARE OF MY SISTER and I, WHILE SHE WAS AT WORK
"CREATURE FEATURES"
NEEER...
PLAY BARBIES WITH ME!

FOR LUNCH HE'D MAKE US THE SAME THING EVERY TIME...

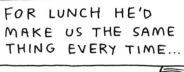

WHITE BREAD
BOLOGNA

SWISS CHEESE

THEN, WITH YELLOW MUSTARD, HE'D DRAW A SMILEY FACE, OR WRITE OUR NAMES...

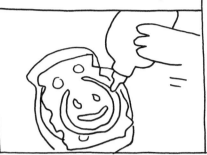

BREAD ON TOP and WE'D EAT THEM WITH FRITOS WHILE WATCH- ING MONSTER MOVIES

"BEAST WITH A MILLION EYES"

AFTER THE McDONALD'S CRAVING, I CRAVED THOSE SANDWICHES

. . .

AND AFTER THAT WAS DONE, I DIDN'T CARE ABOUT FOOD ANYMORE

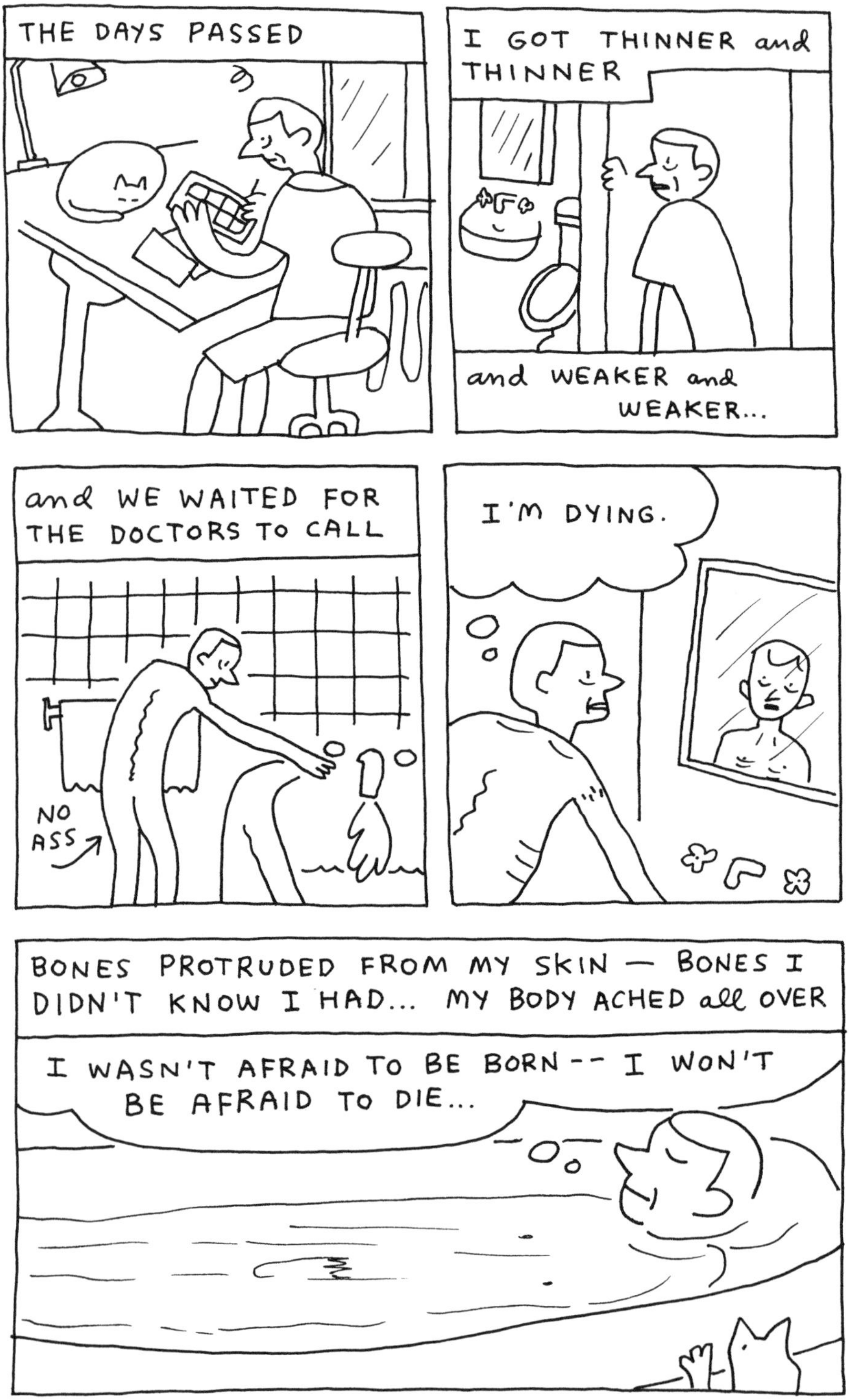
THE DAYS PASSED
I GOT THINNER and THINNER
and WEAKER and WEAKER...
and WE WAITED FOR THE DOCTORS TO CALL
NO ASS
I'M DYING.
BONES PROTRUDED FROM MY SKIN — BONES I DIDN'T KNOW I HAD... MY BODY ACHED all OVER
I WASN'T AFRAID TO BE BORN -- I WON'T BE AFRAID TO DIE...

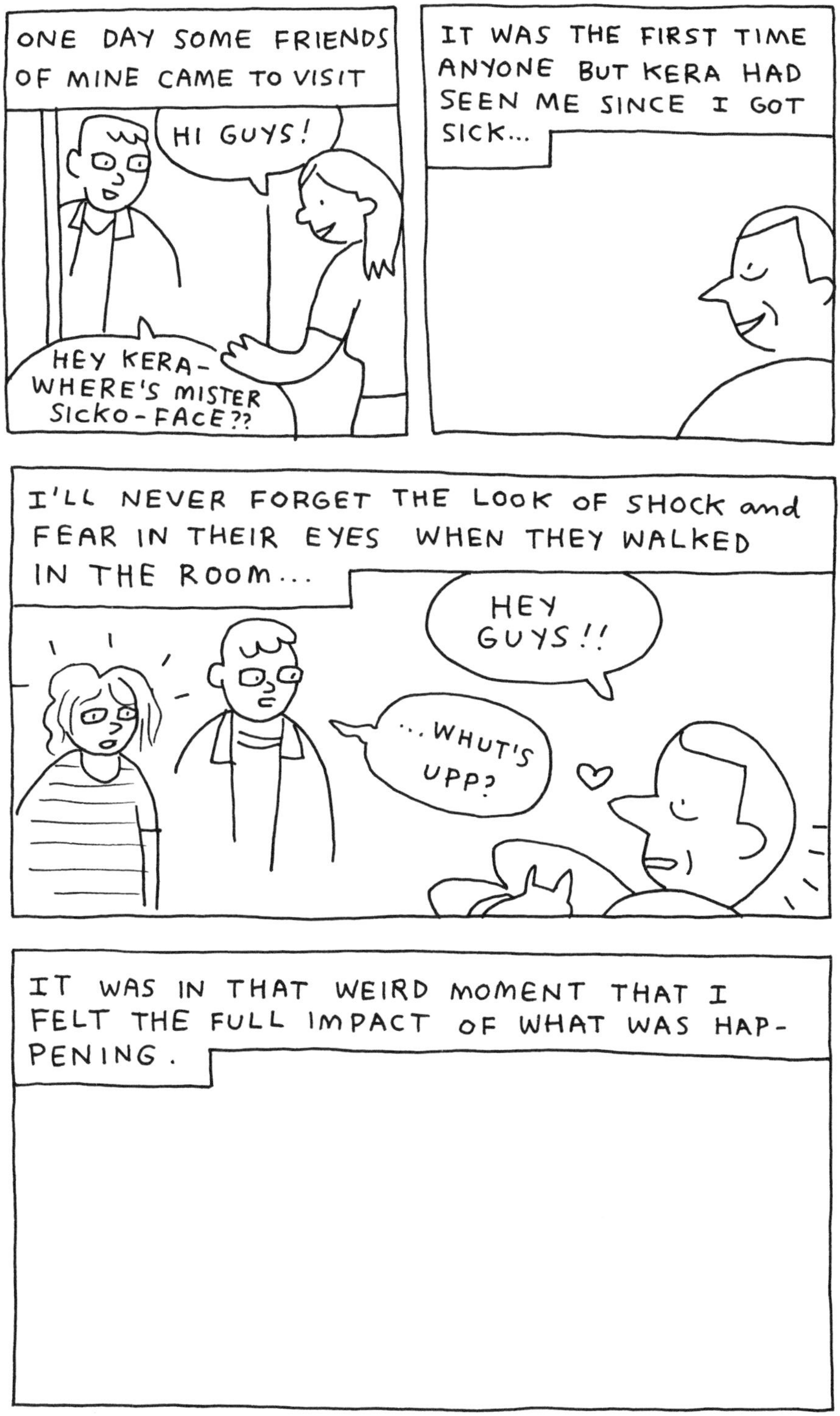
ONE DAY SOME FRIENDS OF MINE CAME TO VISIT
HI GUYS!
HEY KERA- WHERE'S MISTER SICKO-FACE??
IT WAS THE FIRST TIME ANYONE BUT KERA HAD SEEN ME SINCE I GOT SICK...
I'LL NEVER FORGET THE LOOK OF SHOCK and FEAR IN THEIR EYES WHEN THEY WALKED IN THE ROOM...
HEY GUYS!!
...WHUT'S UPP?
IT WAS IN THAT WEIRD MOMENT THAT I FELT THE FULL IMPACT OF WHAT WAS HAP-PENING.

FINALLY, THE DOCTOR CALLED...

WE'D LIKE YOU TO COME IN FOR A CAT SCAN... THAT WILL GIVE US A BETTER PICTURE OF WHAT'S GOING ON...

*

* SPEAKERPHONE USED DUE TO BAD EARS, ed.

FRIDAY JULY 18th

THE CAT SCAN IS SCHEDULED FOR NOON, BUT I'M READY at EIGHT— All I WANT TO KNOW IS WHAT'S WRONG WITH ME

I DON'T CARE WHAT IT IS, I JUST WANT TO KNOW

WHMMM

MRRR

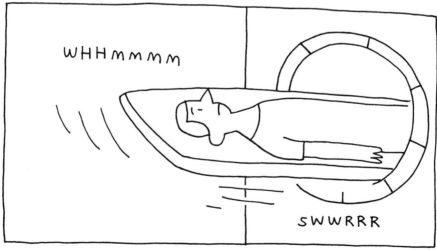

WHHMMMM

SWWRRR

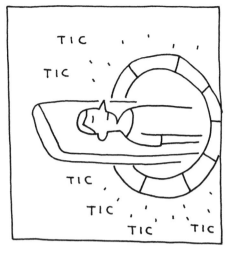

TIC TIC TIC TIC TIC

WHIRRR

OKAY— ONCE MORE, BUT THIS TIME I'M GOING TO INJECT YOU WITH A KIND OF DYE FIRST

"IT'LL HELP THE DOCTORS GET A BETTER LOOK at WHAT'S GOING ON..."

WAIT — DYE?!? ISN'T THAT WHAT KILLED PAULY??✱ HE HAD AN ALLERGIC REACTION OR SOMETHING??

✱Dad's Cousin's Husband, ed.

WHAT IF I HAVE an ALLERGIC REACTION TO IT and I DIE??!

ALL RIGHT... WHEN IT GOES IN IT'S GOING TO MAKE YOU FEEL LIKE YOU HAVE TO PEE...

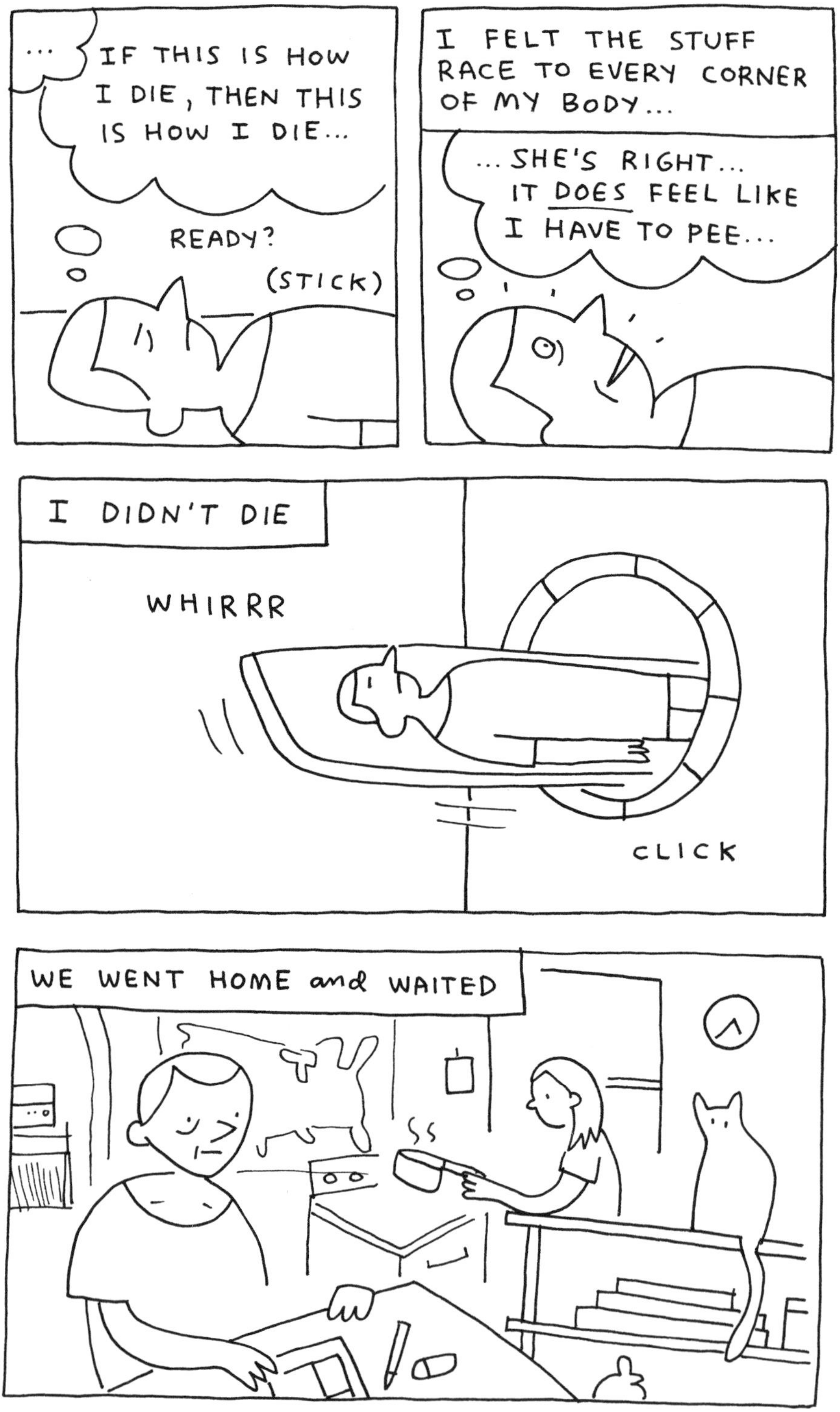
... IF THIS IS HOW I DIE, THEN THIS IS HOW I DIE...
READY?
(STICK)
I FELT THE STUFF RACE TO EVERY CORNER OF MY BODY...
... SHE'S RIGHT... IT DOES FEEL LIKE I HAVE TO PEE...
I DIDN'T DIE
WHIRRR
CLICK
WE WENT HOME and WAITED

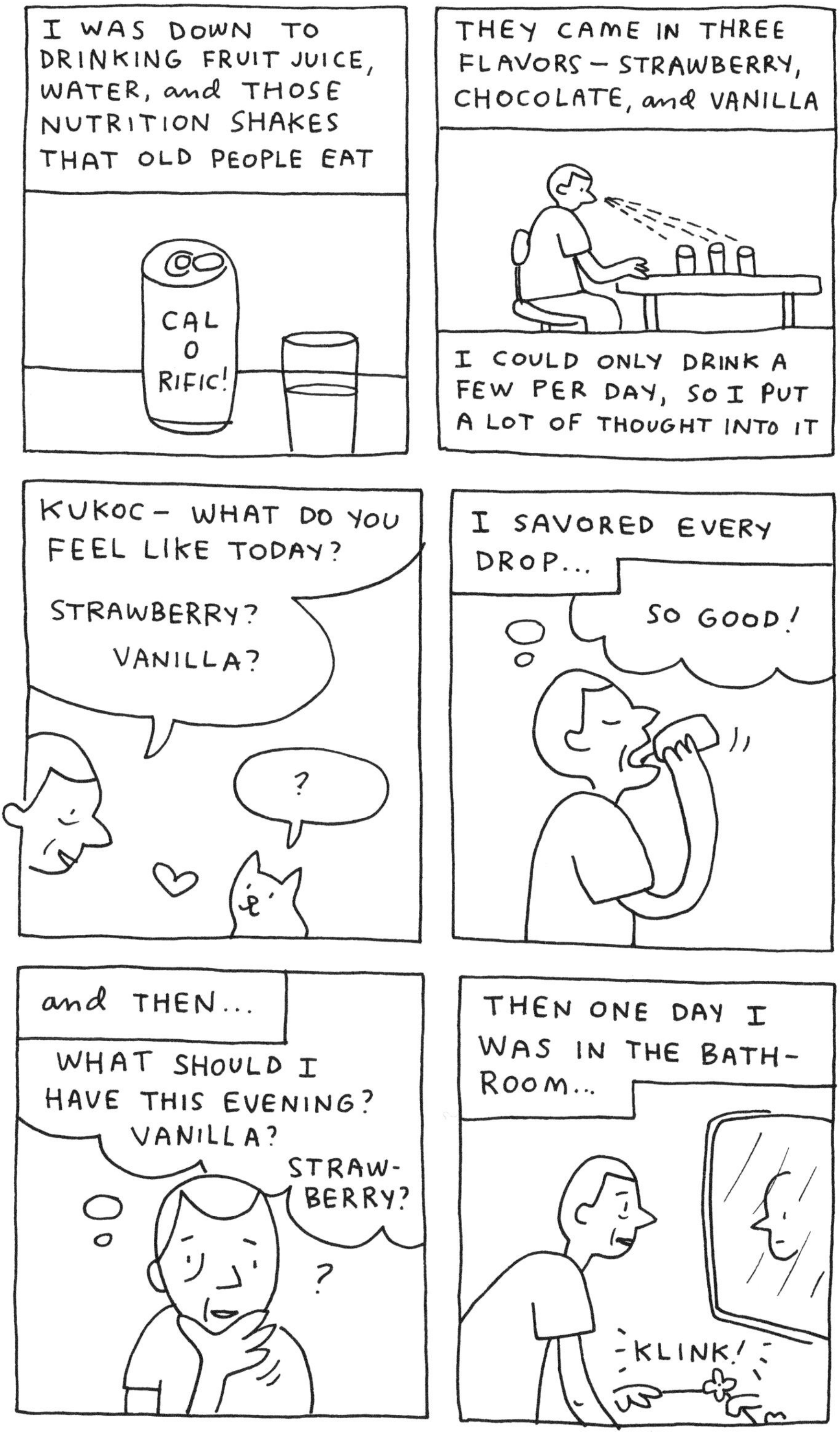
I WAS DOWN TO DRINKING FRUIT JUICE, WATER, and THOSE NUTRITION SHAKES THAT OLD PEOPLE EAT
CAL O RIFIC!
THEY CAME IN THREE FLAVORS – STRAWBERRY, CHOCOLATE, and VANILLA
I COULD ONLY DRINK A FEW PER DAY, SO I PUT A LOT OF THOUGHT INTO IT
KUKOC – WHAT DO YOU FEEL LIKE TODAY?
STRAWBERRY?
VANILLA?
?
I SAVORED EVERY DROP...
SO GOOD!
and THEN...
WHAT SHOULD I HAVE THIS EVENING?
VANILLA?
STRAW-BERRY?
?
THEN ONE DAY I WAS IN THE BATH-ROOM...
KLINK!

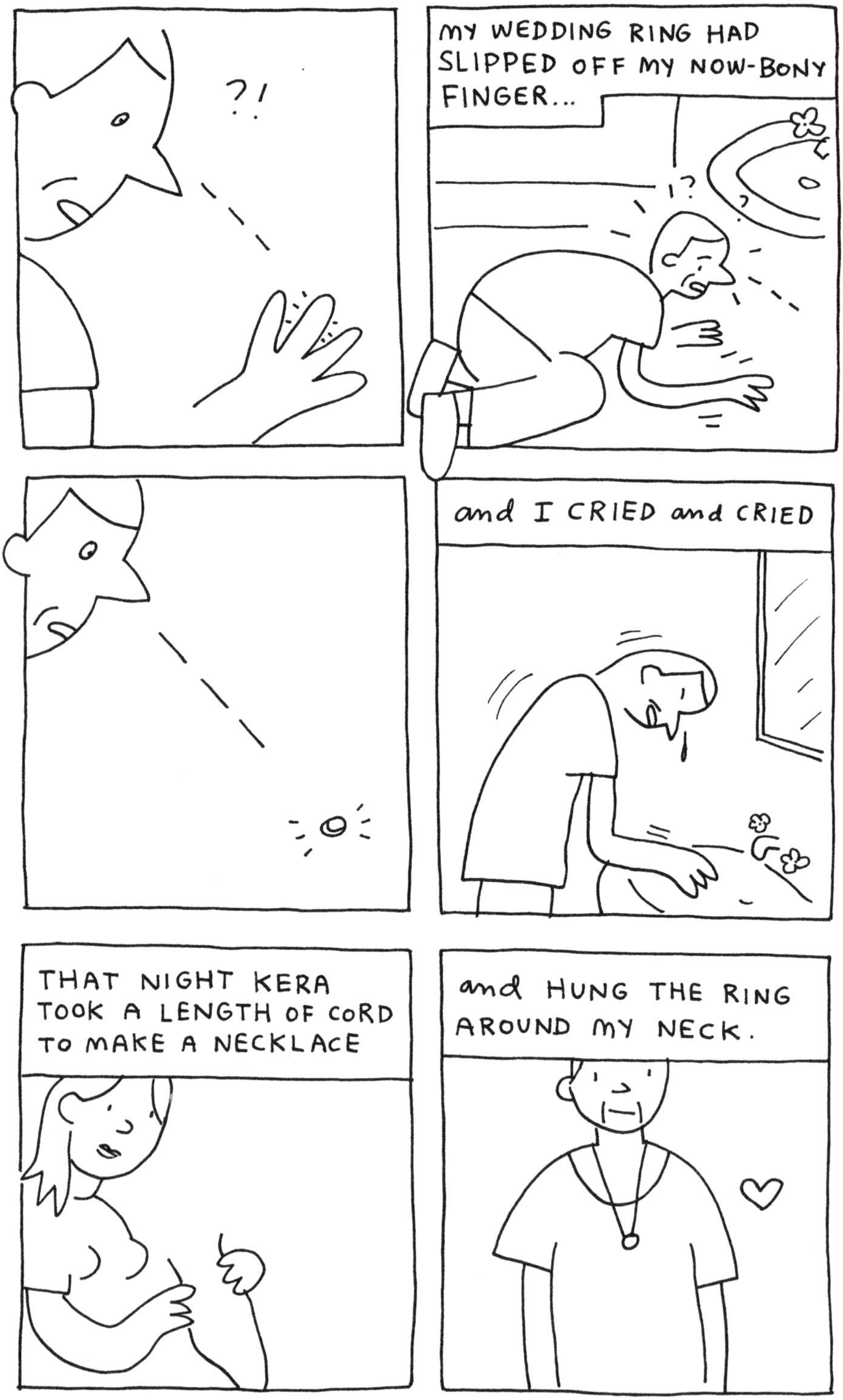
?!
MY WEDDING RING HAD SLIPPED OFF MY NOW-BONY FINGER...
!?
?
and I CRIED and CRIED
THAT NIGHT KERA TOOK A LENGTH OF CORD TO MAKE A NECKLACE
and HUNG THE RING AROUND MY NECK.

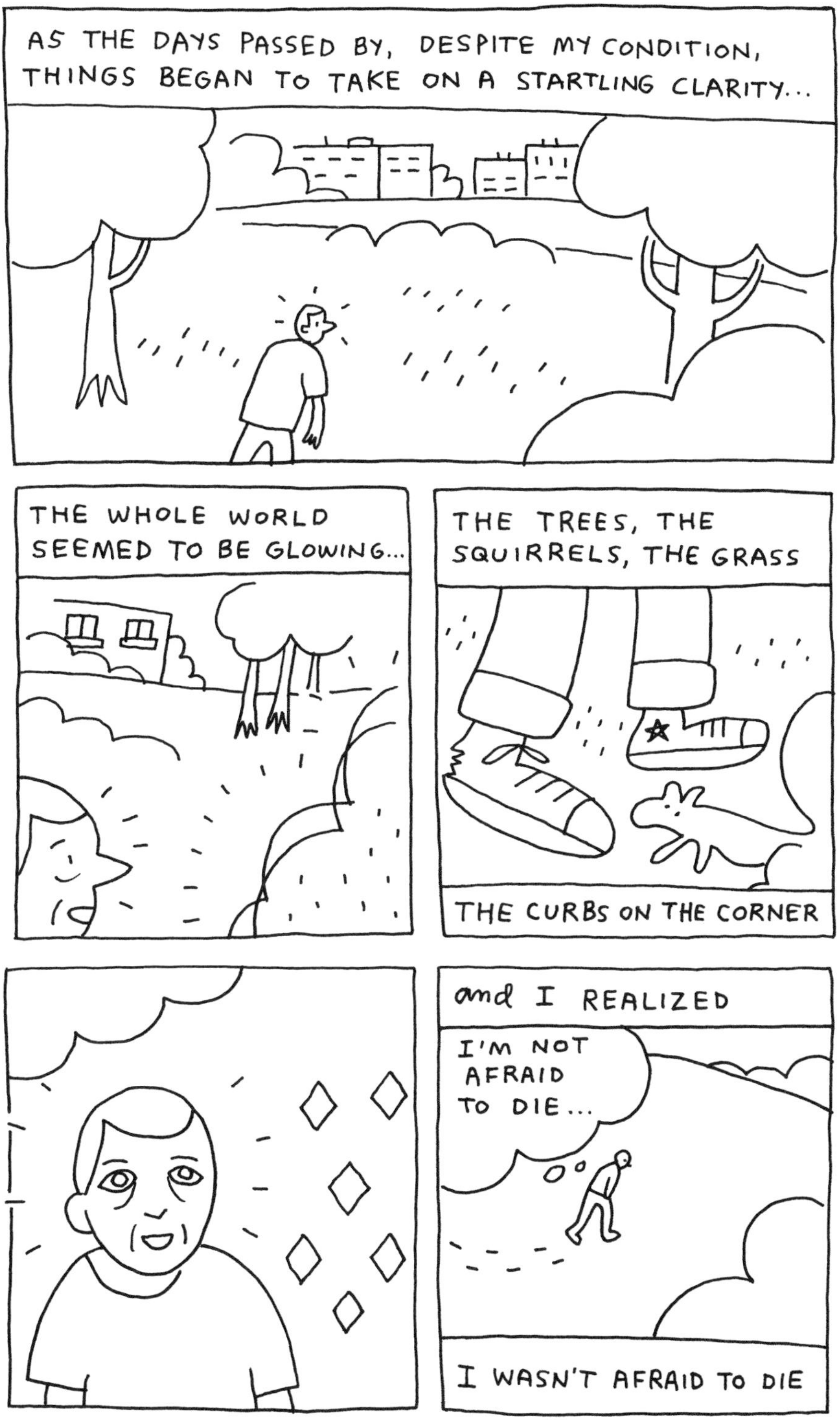
AS THE DAYS PASSED BY, DESPITE MY CONDITION, THINGS BEGAN TO TAKE ON A STARTLING CLARITY...
THE WHOLE WORLD SEEMED TO BE GLOWING...
THE TREES, THE SQUIRRELS, THE GRASS
THE CURBS ON THE CORNER
and I REALIZED
I'M NOT AFRAID TO DIE...
I WASN'T AFRAID TO DIE

Part Three

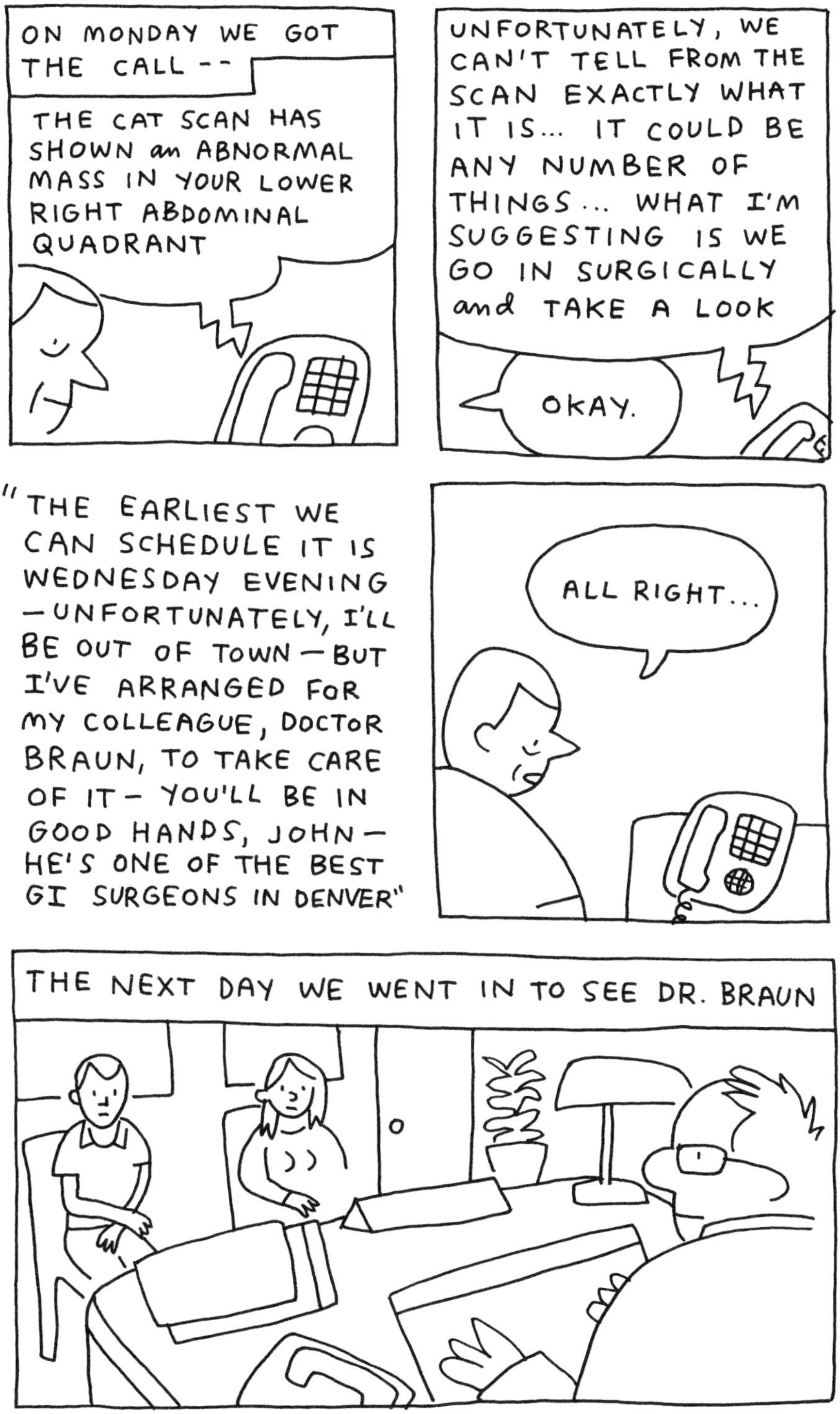
ON MONDAY WE GOT THE CALL --
THE CAT SCAN HAS SHOWN an ABNORMAL MASS IN YOUR LOWER RIGHT ABDOMINAL QUADRANT
UNFORTUNATELY, WE CAN'T TELL FROM THE SCAN EXACTLY WHAT IT IS... IT COULD BE ANY NUMBER OF THINGS... WHAT I'M SUGGESTING IS WE GO IN SURGICALLY and TAKE A LOOK
OKAY.
"THE EARLIEST WE CAN SCHEDULE IT IS WEDNESDAY EVENING —UNFORTUNATELY, I'LL BE OUT OF TOWN—BUT I'VE ARRANGED FOR MY COLLEAGUE, DOCTOR BRAUN, TO TAKE CARE OF IT— YOU'LL BE IN GOOD HANDS, JOHN— HE'S ONE OF THE BEST GI SURGEONS IN DENVER"
ALL RIGHT...
THE NEXT DAY WE WENT IN TO SEE DR. BRAUN

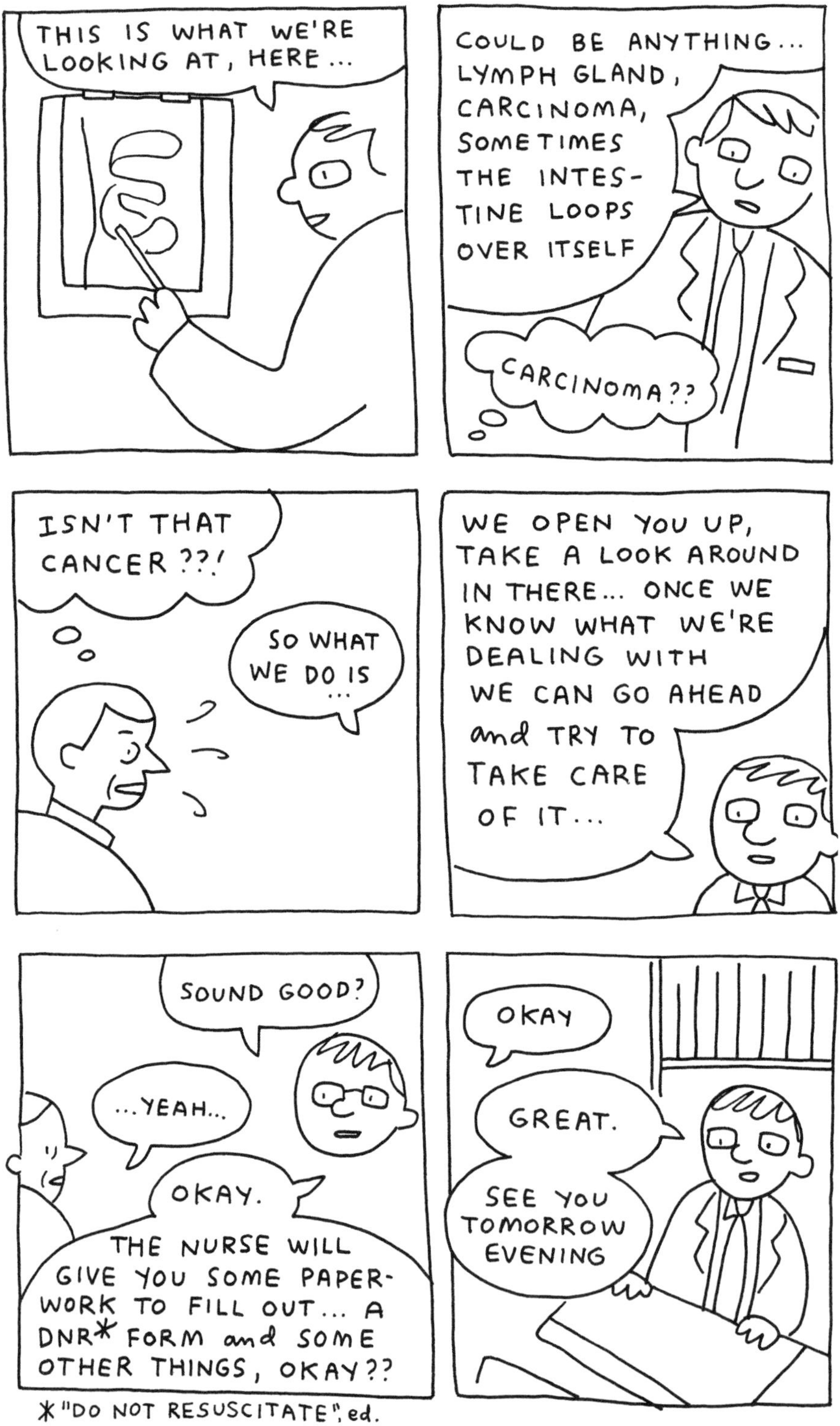
THIS IS WHAT WE'RE LOOKING AT, HERE...
COULD BE ANYTHING... LYMPH GLAND, CARCINOMA, SOMETIMES THE INTES-TINE LOOPS OVER ITSELF
CARCINOMA??
ISN'T THAT CANCER??!
SO WHAT WE DO IS ...
WE OPEN YOU UP, TAKE A LOOK AROUND IN THERE... ONCE WE KNOW WHAT WE'RE DEALING WITH WE CAN GO AHEAD and TRY TO TAKE CARE OF IT...
SOUND GOOD?
...YEAH...
OKAY.
THE NURSE WILL GIVE YOU SOME PAPER-WORK TO FILL OUT... A DNR* FORM and SOME OTHER THINGS, OKAY??
OKAY
GREAT.
SEE YOU TOMORROW EVENING

* "DO NOT RESUSCITATE", ed.

AT HOME...

KUKOC

I WONDER IF I SHOULD BOTHER SENDING OUT THE NEW CATALOGS? *

(* I RUN A MAIL-ORDER SERVICE FOR INDEPENDENT COMICS)

I GUESS I JUST NEED TO ACT AS IF I'M GOING TO SURVIVE

I MAILED THE CATALOGS

US MAIL

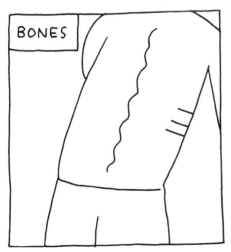

BONES

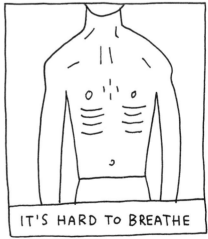

IT'S HARD TO BREATHE

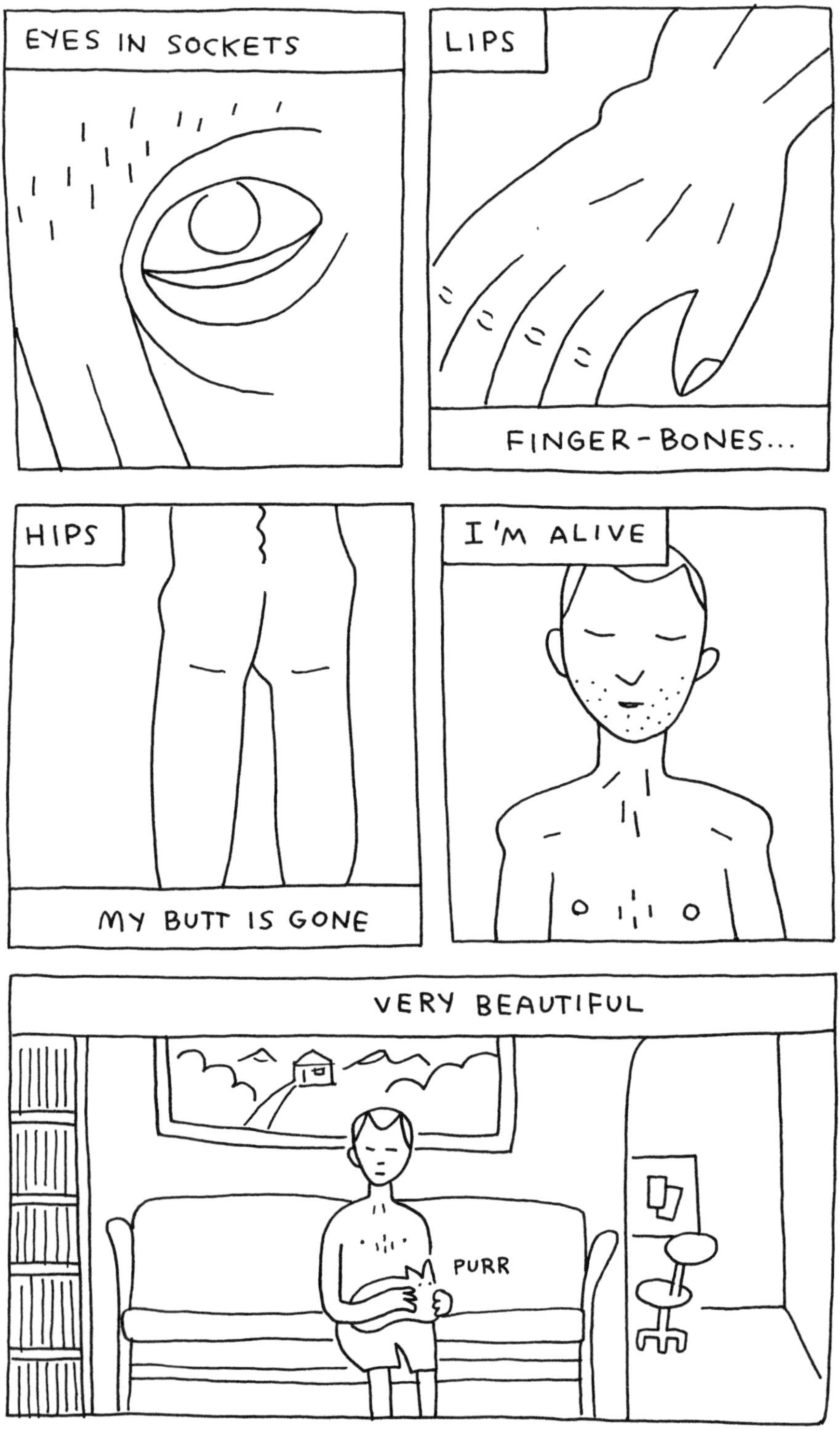
EYES IN SOCKETS
LIPS
FINGER-BONES...
HIPS
MY BUTT IS GONE
I'M ALIVE
VERY BEAUTIFUL
PURR

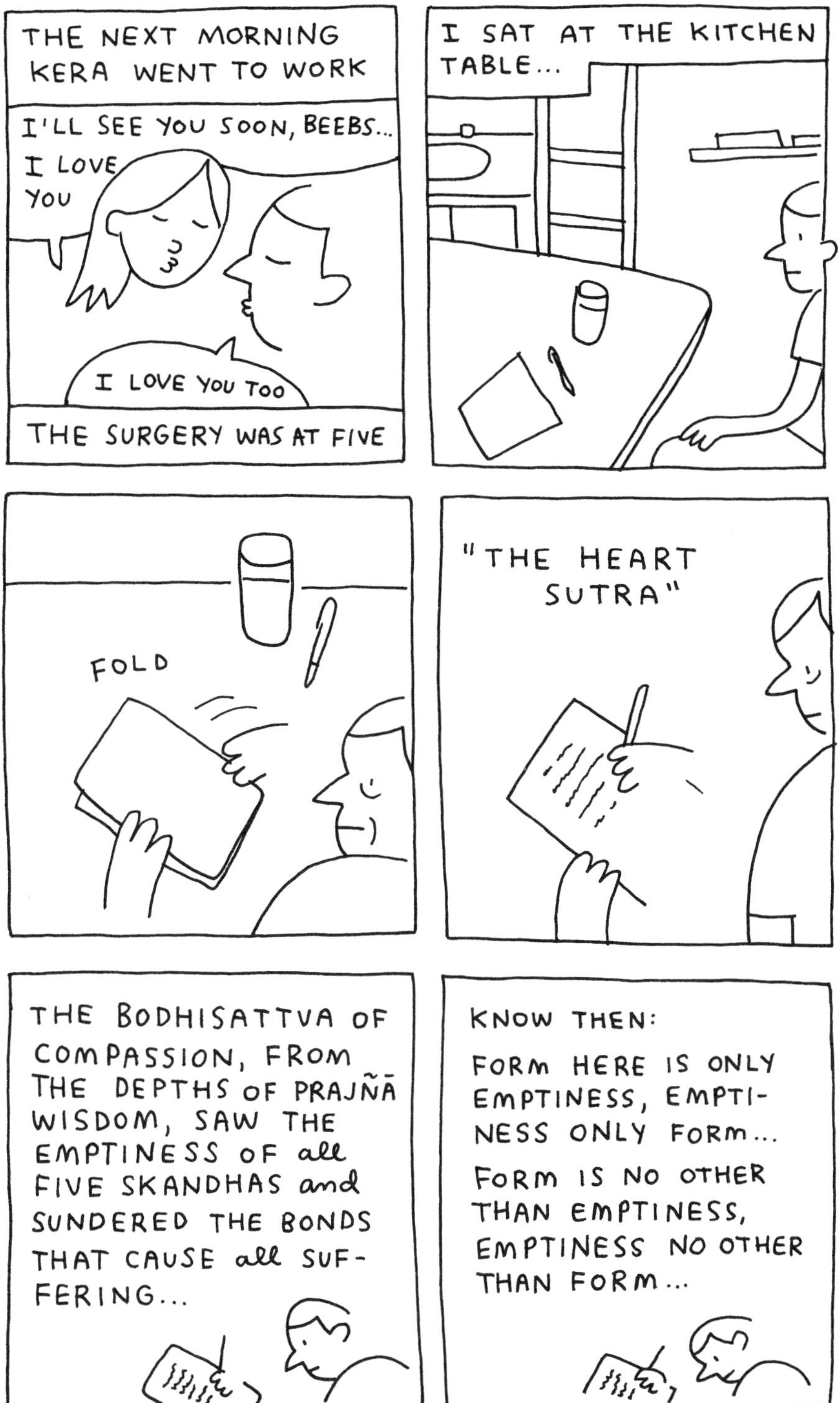
THE NEXT MORNING KERA WENT TO WORK
I'LL SEE YOU SOON, BEEBS... I LOVE YOU
I LOVE YOU TOO
THE SURGERY WAS AT FIVE
I SAT AT THE KITCHEN TABLE...
FOLD
"THE HEART SUTRA"
THE BODHISATTVA OF COMPASSION, FROM THE DEPTHS OF PRAJÑĀ WISDOM, SAW THE EMPTINESS OF all FIVE SKANDHAS and SUNDERED THE BONDS THAT CAUSE all SUF-FERING...
KNOW THEN:
FORM HERE IS ONLY EMPTINESS, EMPTI-NESS ONLY FORM...
FORM IS NO OTHER THAN EMPTINESS, EMPTINESS NO OTHER THAN FORM...

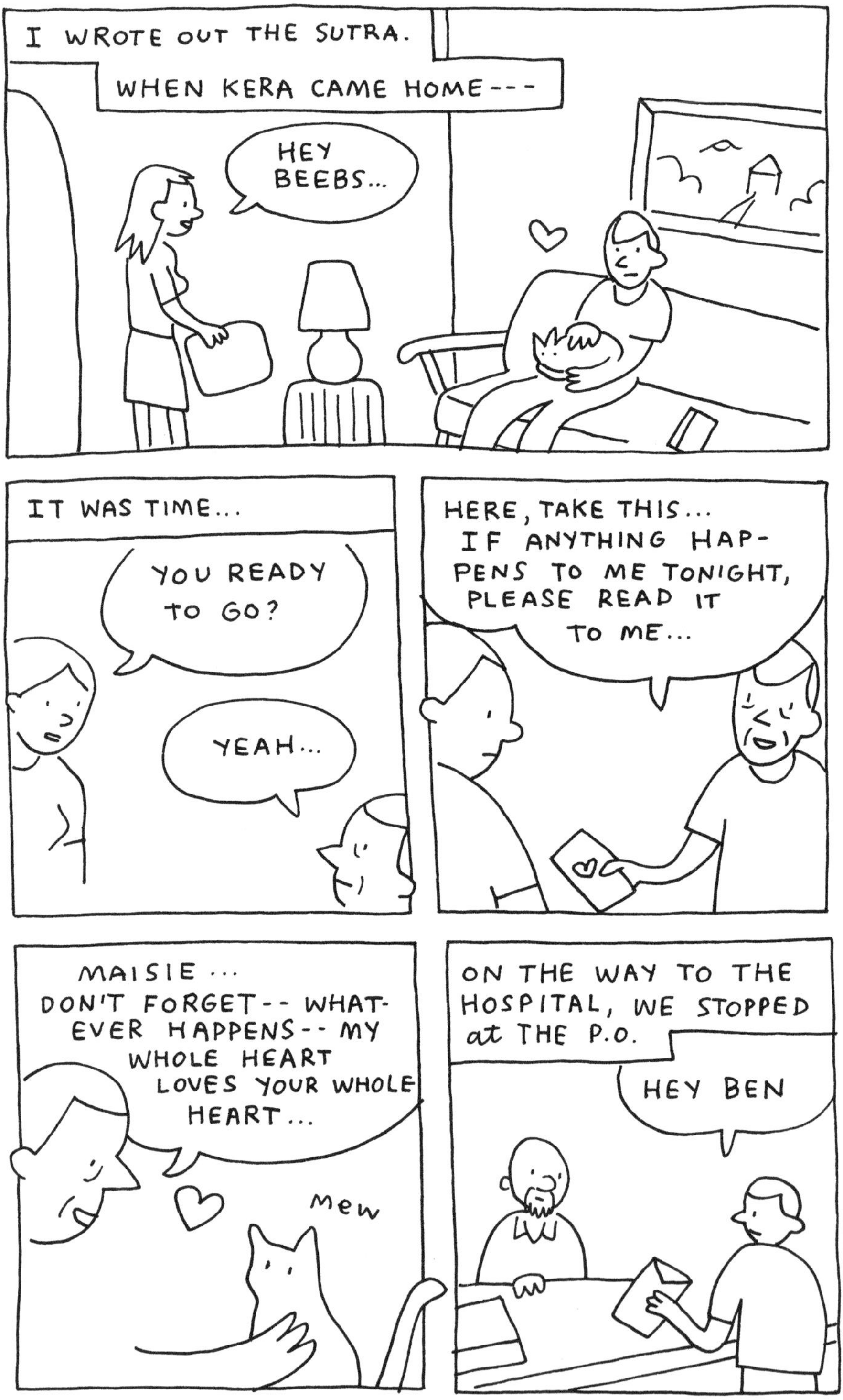
I WROTE OUT THE SUTRA.
WHEN KERA CAME HOME---
HEY BEEBS...
IT WAS TIME...
YOU READY TO GO?
YEAH...
HERE, TAKE THIS... IF ANYTHING HAPPENS TO ME TONIGHT, PLEASE READ IT TO ME...
MAISIE... DON'T FORGET-- WHATEVER HAPPENS-- MY WHOLE HEART LOVES YOUR WHOLE HEART...
mew
ON THE WAY TO THE HOSPITAL, WE STOPPED at THE P.O.
HEY BEN

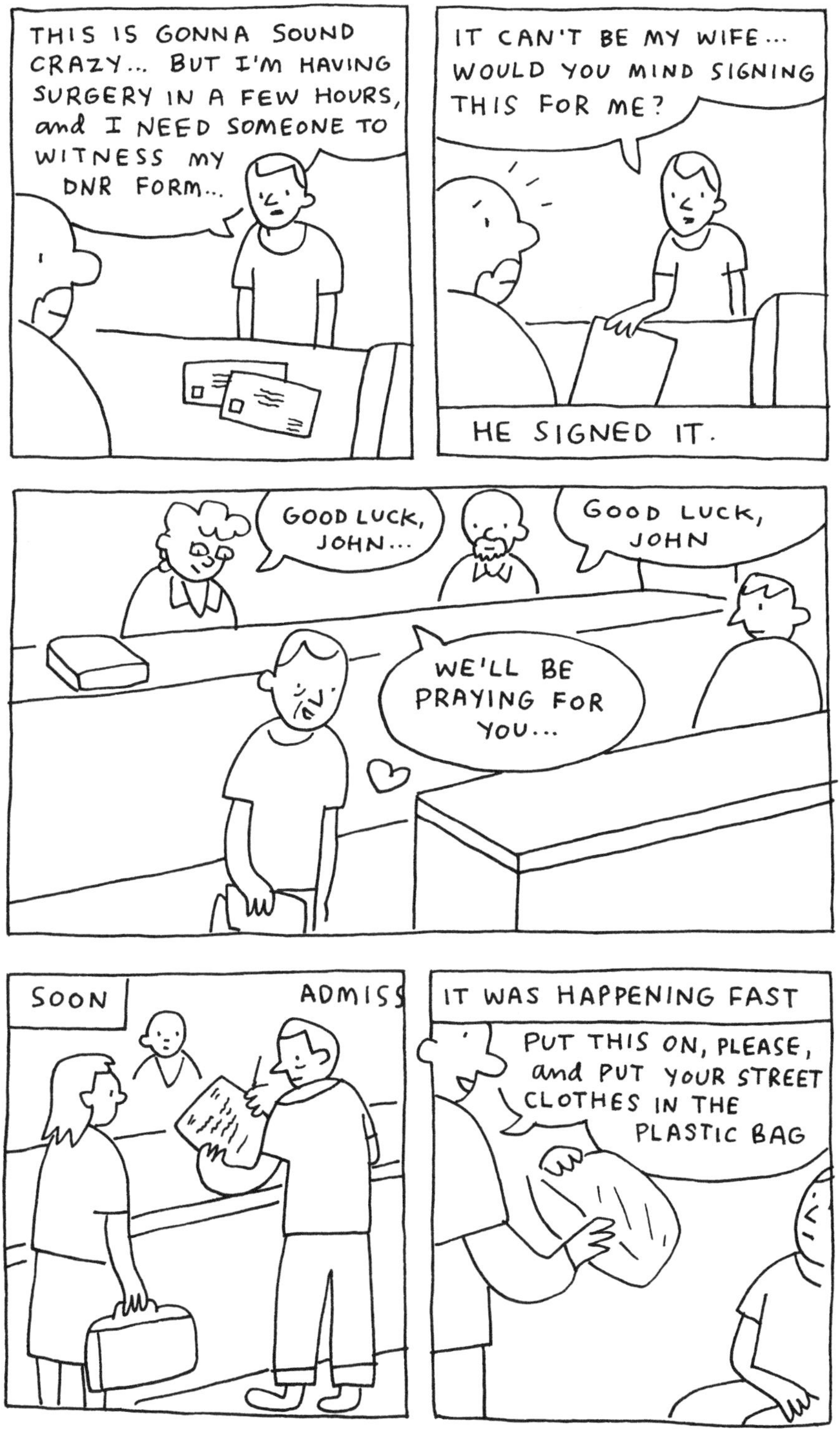
THIS IS GONNA SOUND CRAZY... BUT I'M HAVING SURGERY IN A FEW HOURS, and I NEED SOMEONE TO WITNESS MY DNR FORM...
IT CAN'T BE MY WIFE... WOULD YOU MIND SIGNING THIS FOR ME?
HE SIGNED IT.
GOOD LUCK, JOHN...
GOOD LUCK, JOHN
WE'LL BE PRAYING FOR YOU...
SOON
ADMISS
IT WAS HAPPENING FAST
PUT THIS ON, PLEASE, and PUT YOUR STREET CLOTHES IN THE PLASTIC BAG

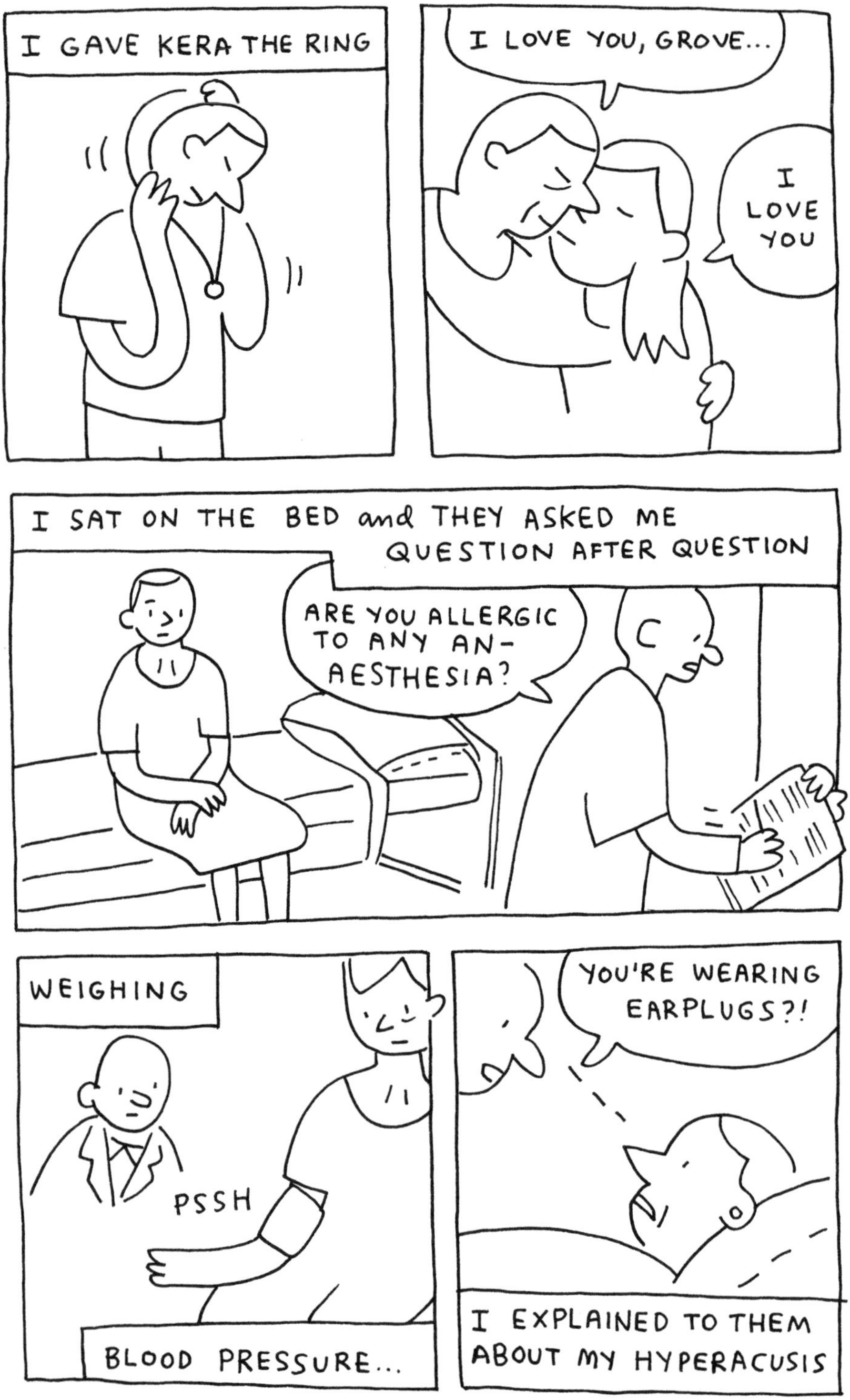
I GAVE KERA THE RING
I LOVE YOU, GROVE...
I LOVE YOU
I SAT ON THE BED and THEY ASKED ME QUESTION AFTER QUESTION
ARE YOU ALLERGIC TO ANY AN-AESTHESIA?
WEIGHING
PSSH
BLOOD PRESSURE...
YOU'RE WEARING EARPLUGS?!
I EXPLAINED TO THEM ABOUT MY HYPERACUSIS

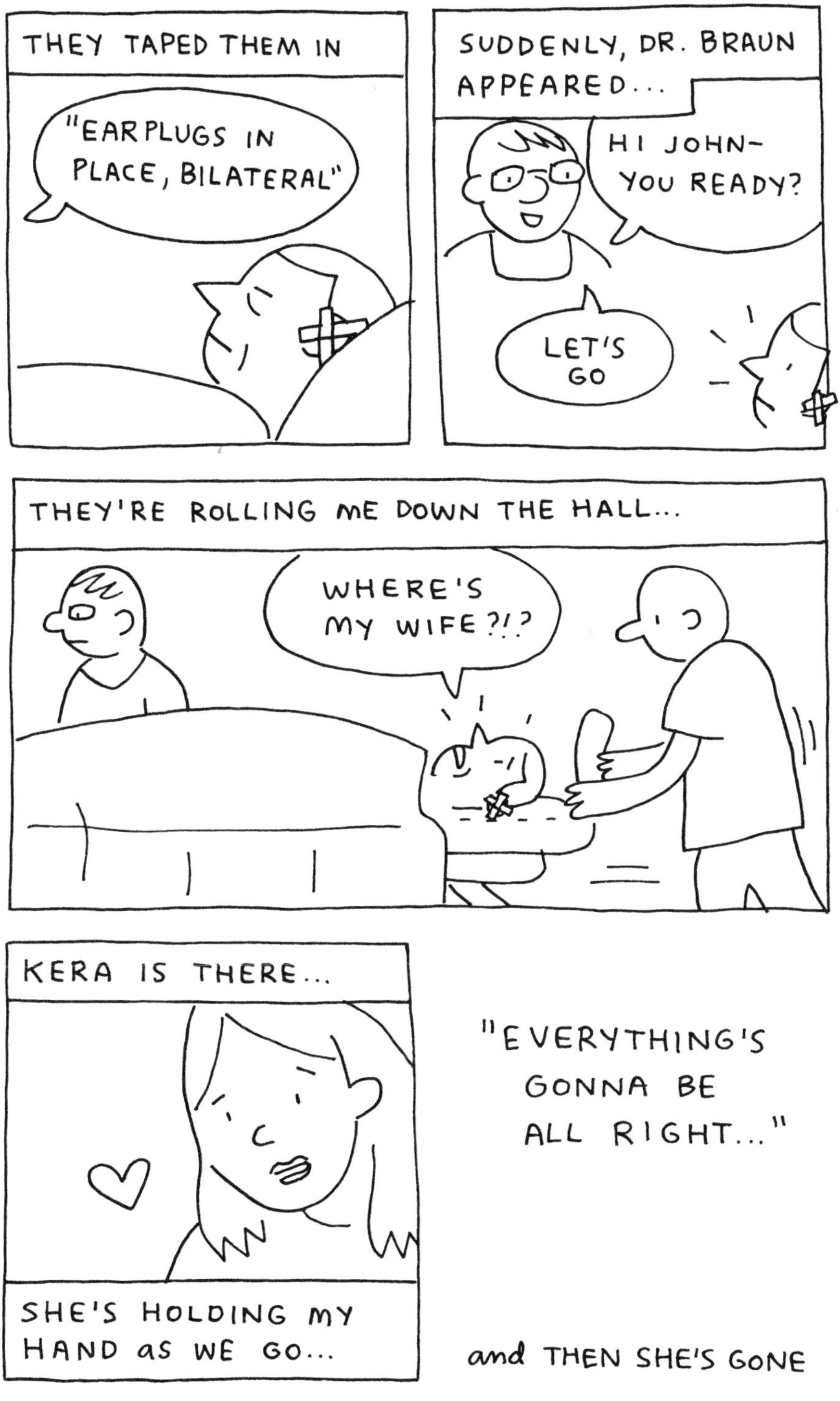
THEY TAPED THEM IN
"EARPLUGS IN PLACE, BILATERAL"
SUDDENLY, DR. BRAUN APPEARED...
HI JOHN- YOU READY?
LET'S GO
THEY'RE ROLLING ME DOWN THE HALL...
WHERE'S MY WIFE?!?
KERA IS THERE...
SHE'S HOLDING MY HAND as WE GO...
"EVERYTHING'S GONNA BE ALL RIGHT..."
and THEN SHE'S GONE

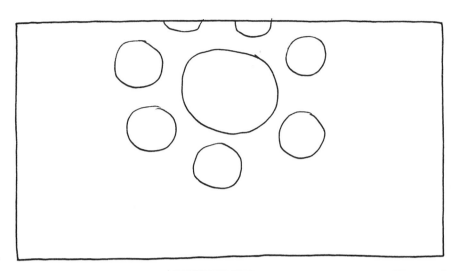

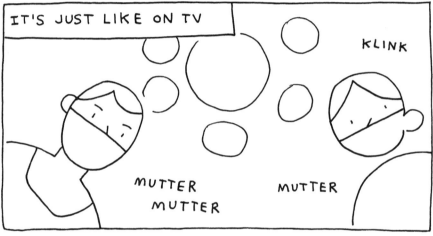

IT'S JUST LIKE ON TV

KLINK

MUTTER
MUTTER

MUTTER

DON'T WORRY- YOU'LL BE FINE...

DR. BRAUN IS THE BEST...

THEY'RE MAKING JOKES, LAUGHING... TRYING TO SET ME at EASE

HA

KLINK

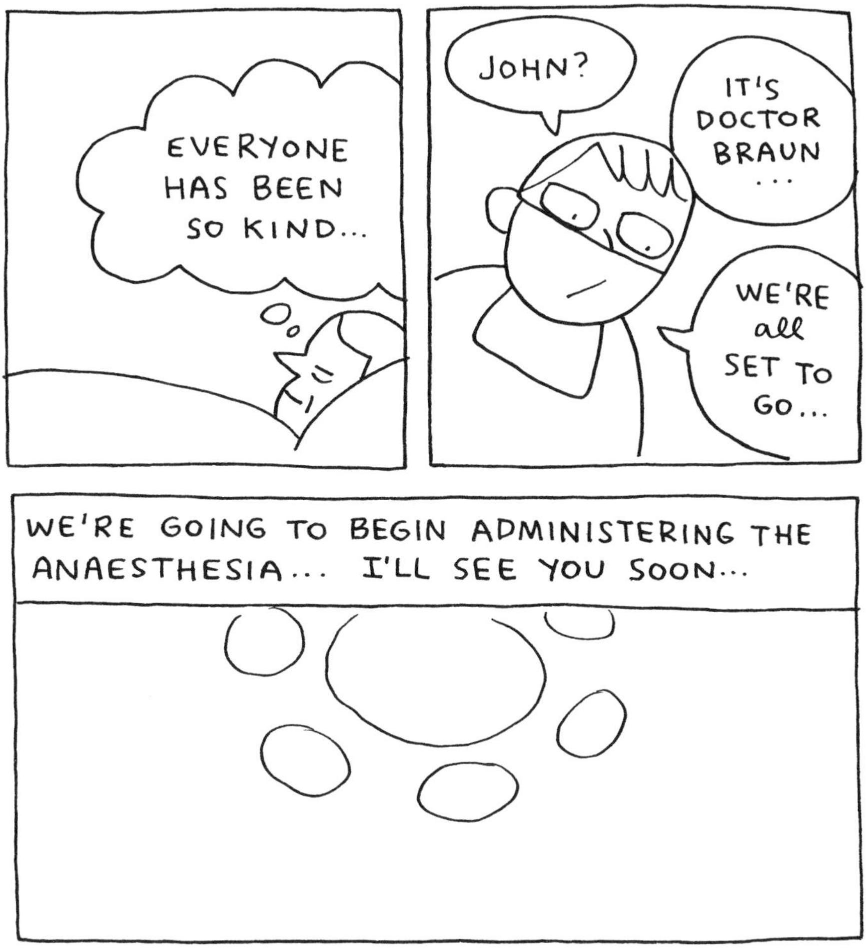
EVERYONE HAS BEEN SO KIND...
JOHN?
IT'S DOCTOR BRAUN ...
WE'RE all SET TO GO...
WE'RE GOING TO BEGIN ADMINISTERING THE ANAESTHESIA... I'LL SEE YOU SOON...

I WASN'T AFRAID TO BE BORN...

Part Four

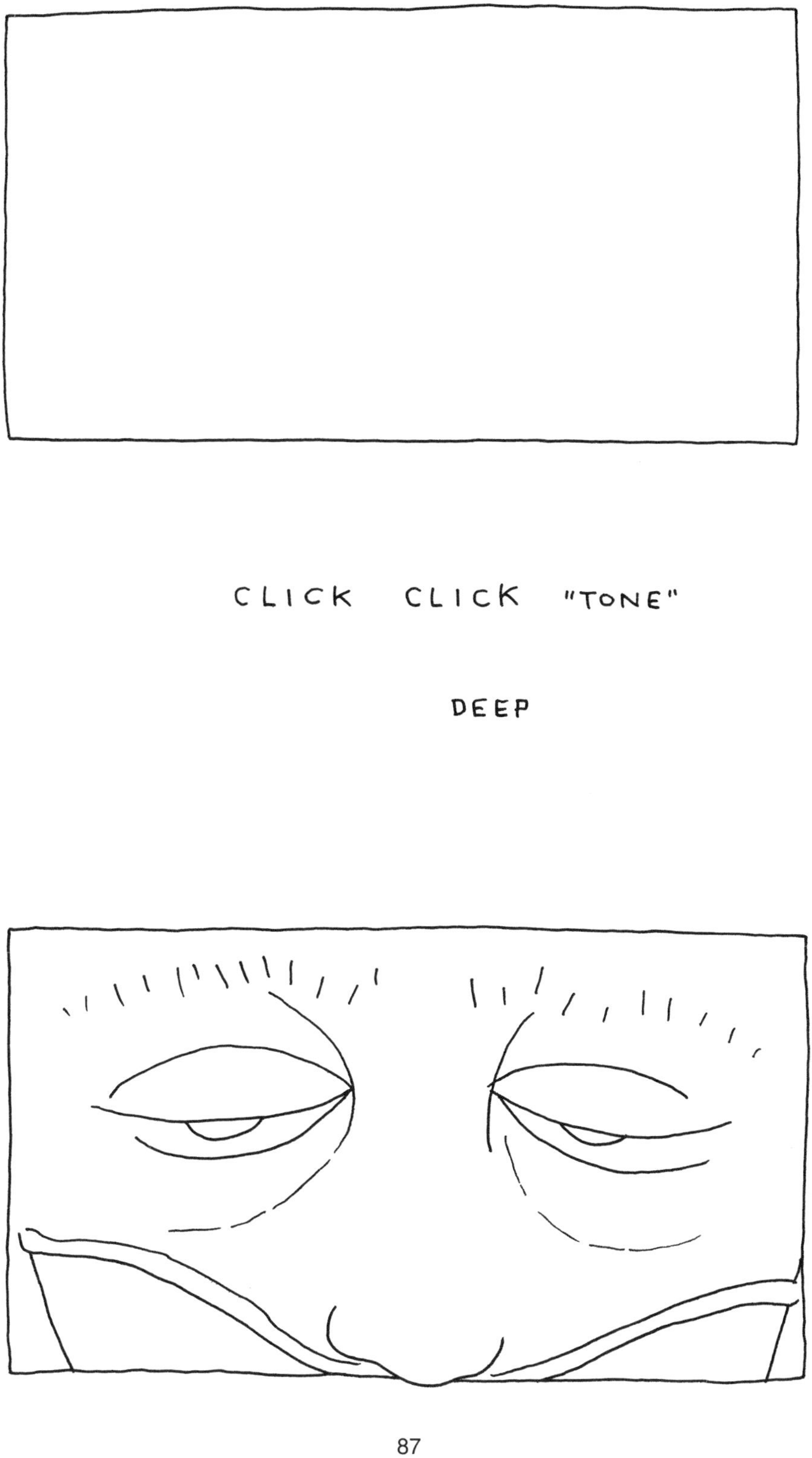
CLICK CLICK "TONE"
DEEP

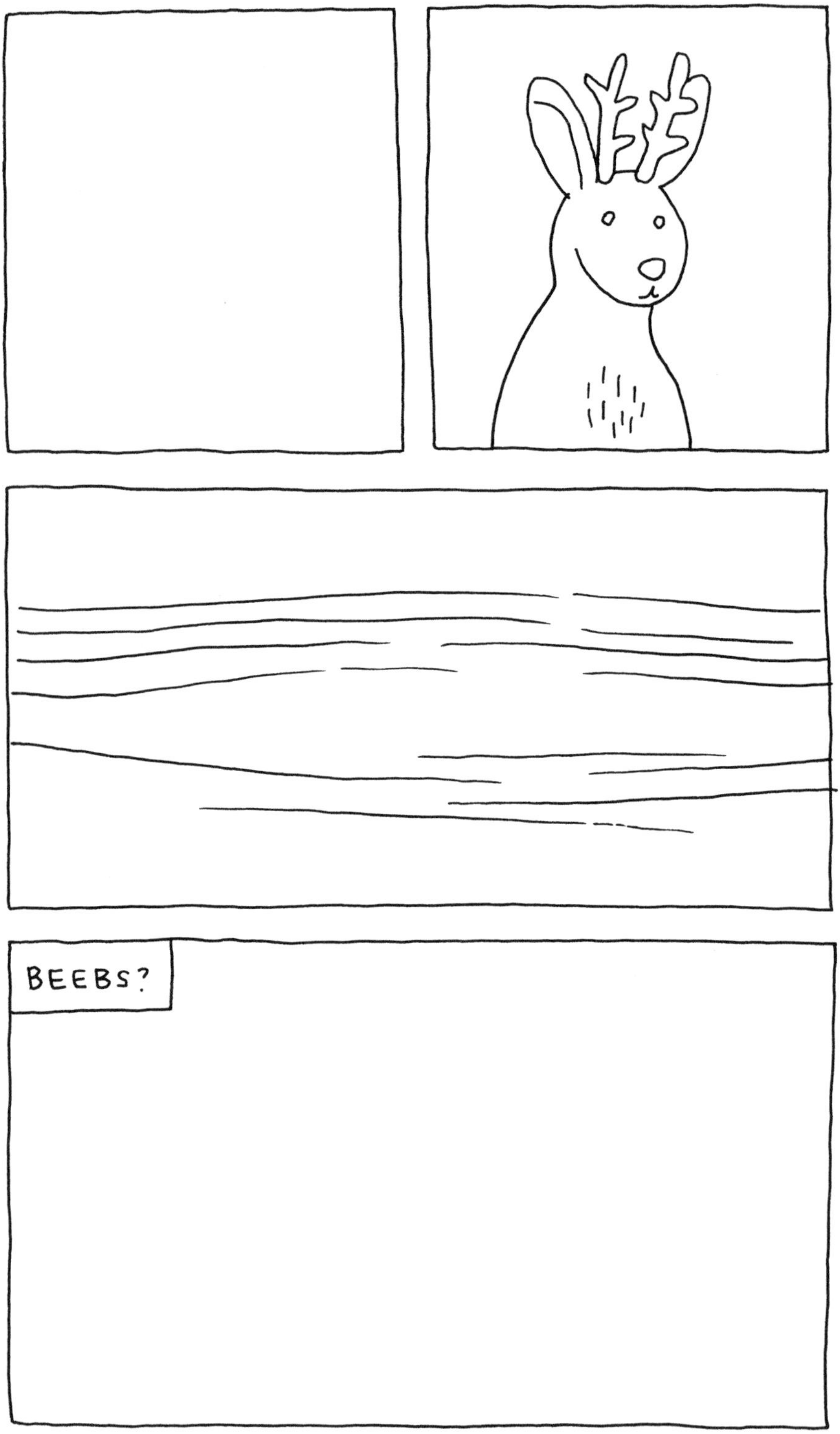
BEEBS?

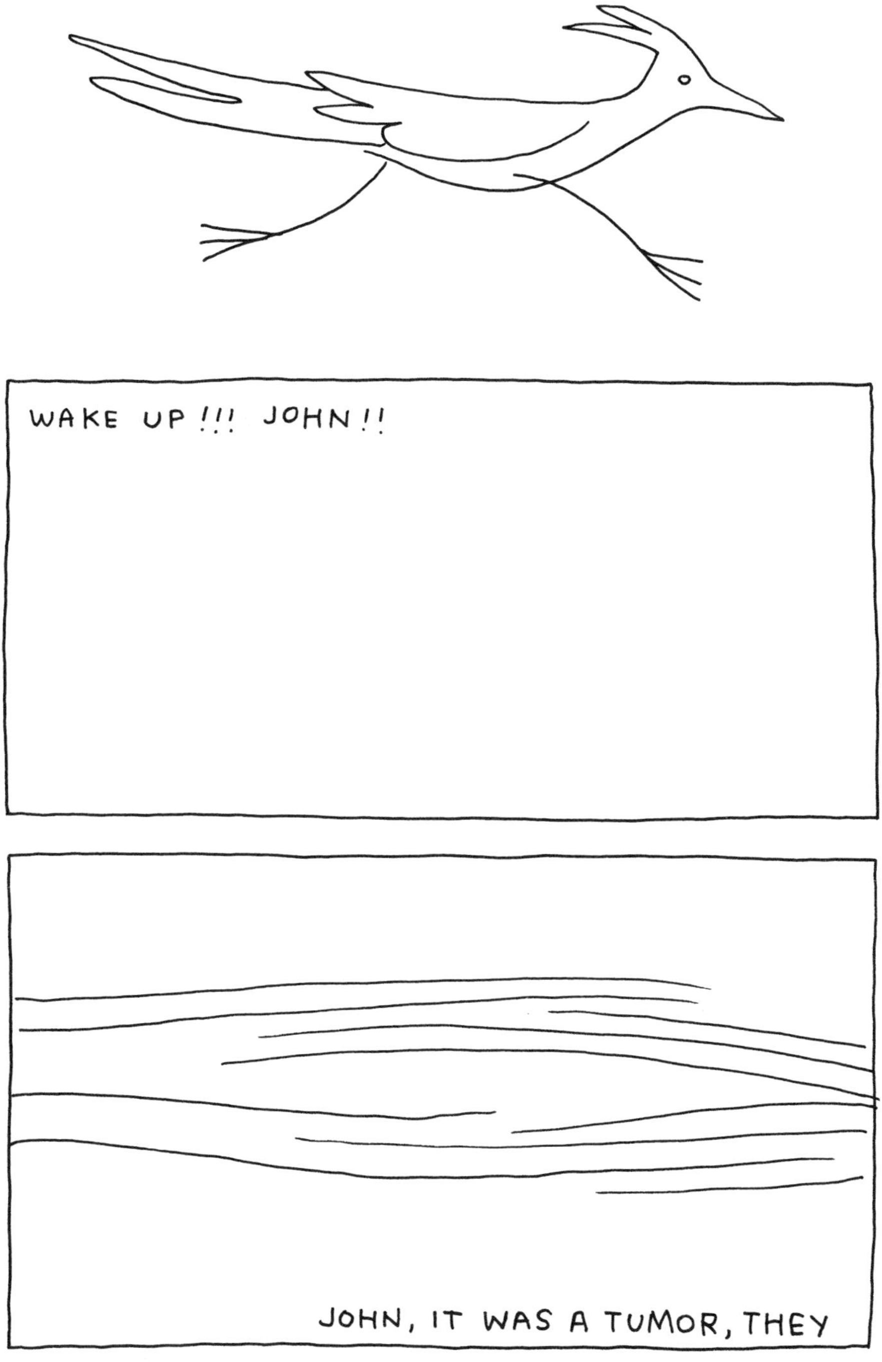
WAKE UP!!! JOHN!!
JOHN, IT WAS A TUMOR, THEY

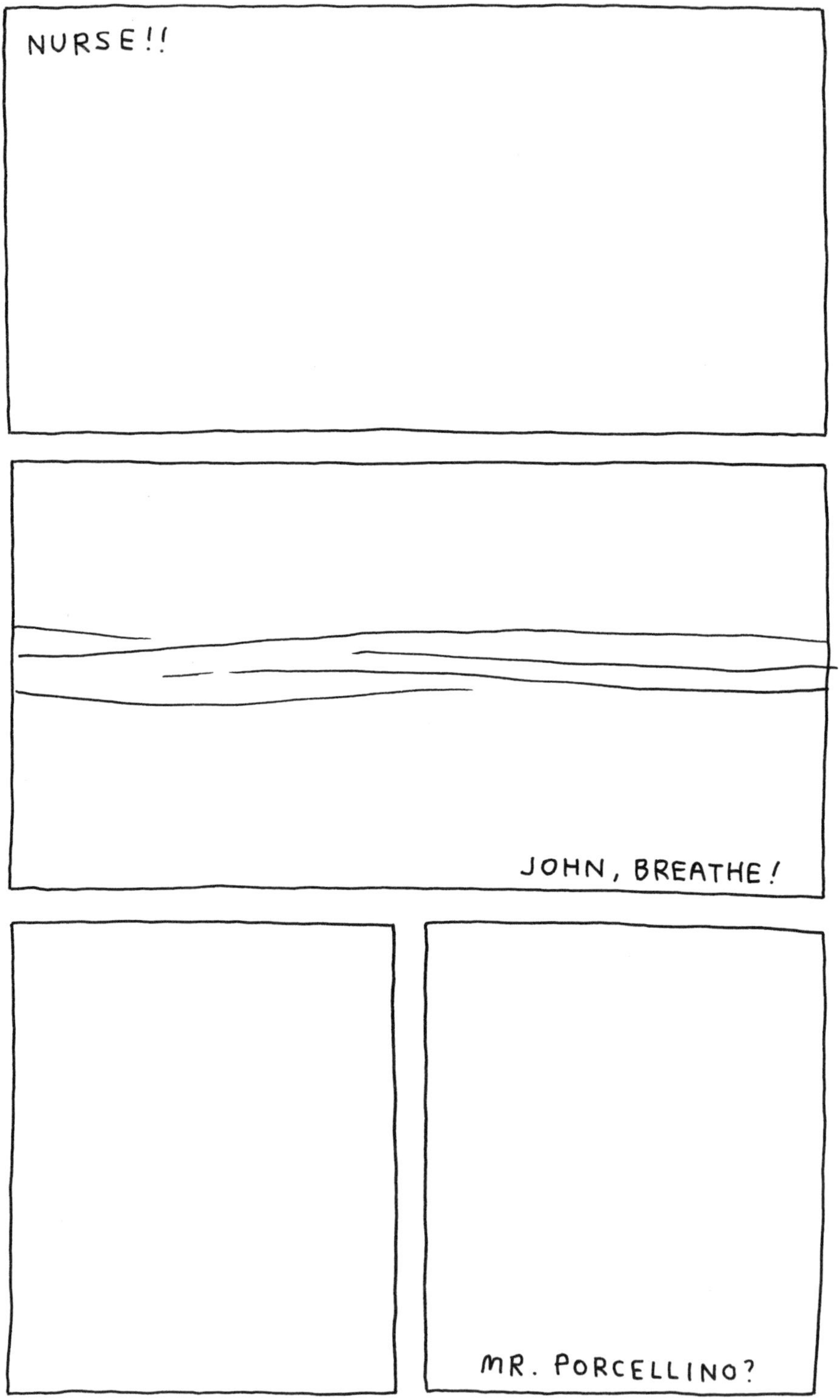
NURSE!!
JOHN, BREATHE!
MR. PORCELLINO?

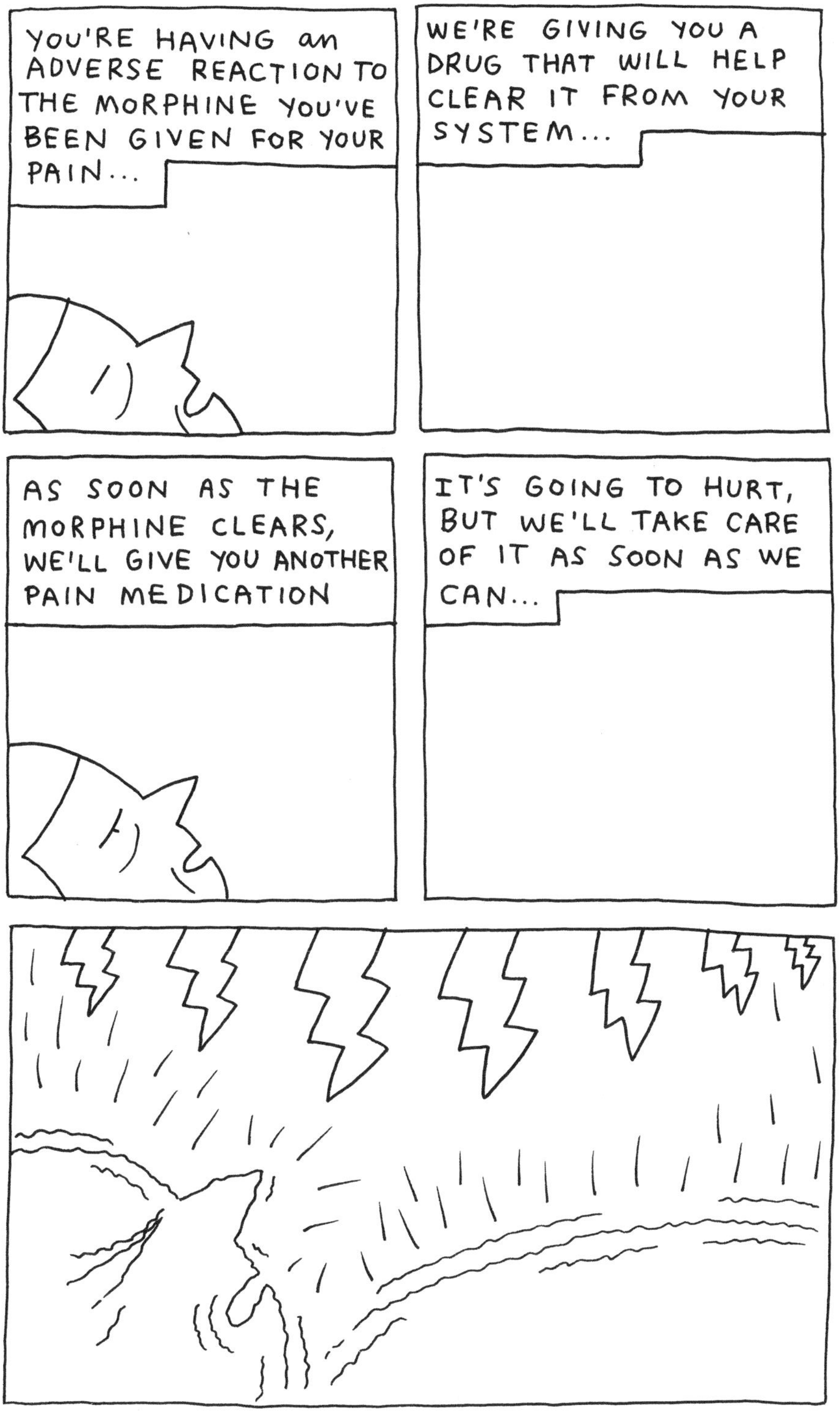
YOU'RE HAVING an ADVERSE REACTION TO THE MORPHINE YOU'VE BEEN GIVEN FOR YOUR PAIN...
WE'RE GIVING YOU A DRUG THAT WILL HELP CLEAR IT FROM YOUR SYSTEM...
AS SOON AS THE MORPHINE CLEARS, WE'LL GIVE YOU ANOTHER PAIN MEDICATION
IT'S GOING TO HURT, BUT WE'LL TAKE CARE OF IT AS SOON AS WE CAN...

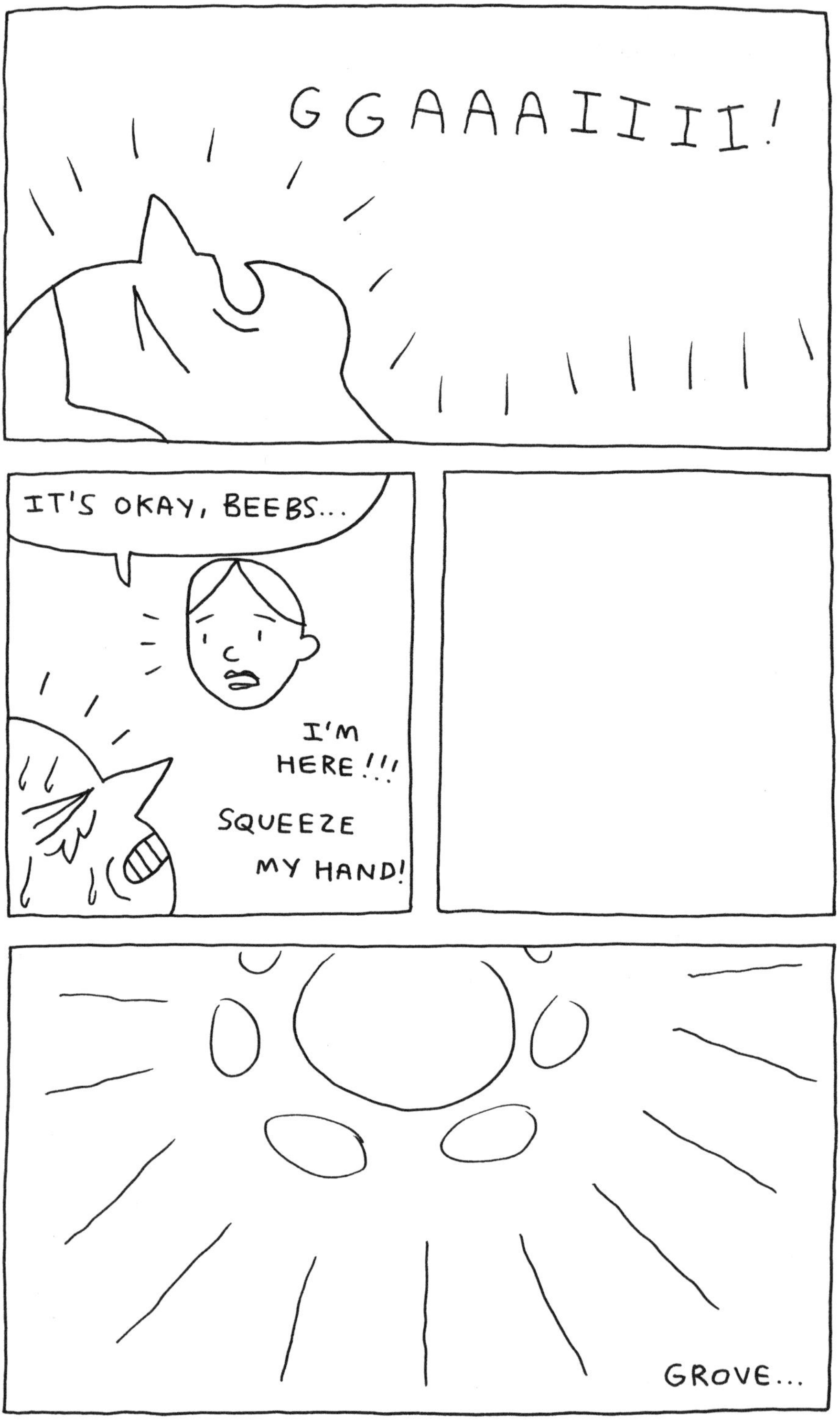
GGAAAIIII!
IT'S OKAY, BEEBS...
I'M HERE!!!
SQUEEZE MY HAND!
GROVE...

THEY GAVE YOU MOR-
PHINE and IT WAS
MAKING YOU SICK...
YOU KEPT FALLING
ASLEEP and
THEN YOU'D
STOP
BREATHING
and I'D
WAKE YOU
UP and THEN
YOU'D PASS OUT AGAIN

WHAT WAS IT?

IT WAS A TUMOR

THEY SAID THAT IT
WAS A GOOD THING,
CUZ THEY COULD
TAKE IT
all OUT...
and THEY
DON'T
THINK IT'S
CANCER...

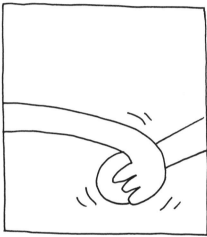

THEY TOOK PICTURES--
I SAW THEM...
I SAW YOUR GUTS!

WHAT DID
THEY LOOK
LIKE?

THEY LOOKED LIKE...
MUSTARD...

I SAW
JACKALOPES
and
ROADRUNNERS...

OH,
BEEBS...

DR. BRAUN CAME IN

HI JOHN -- WHAT HAP-
PENED WAS
YOU HAD A
TUMOR ATTACHED
TO THE WALL OF
YOUR SMALL
INTESTINE --

WHEN IT GOT BIG ENOUGH
IT BEGAN GETTING
PULLED INTO THE
LARGE INTESTINE,
BRINGING THE SMALL
INTESTINE along WITH
IT...

WE WERE ABLE TO
REMOVE THE ENTIRE
TUMOR, ALONG WITH
A BOUT EIGHT INCHES
OF INTESTINE, WHICH
ISN'T BAD...

OOO

OF all the POTENTIAL
OUTCOMES, THIS WAS
JUST ABOUT THE BEST-
WE GOT THE WHOLE
THING OUT... IT'S IN
THE LAB NOW, BUT IT
DOESN'T APPEAR TO
BE CANCEROUS...

WE'LL KEEP YOU HERE
IN INTENSIVE CARE FOR
A BIT, and THEN YOU'LL
HEAD UP TO A ROOM...
YOU'RE GOING TO BE
FINE...

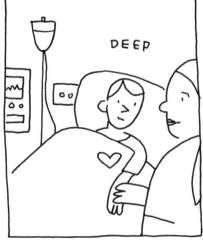

DEEP

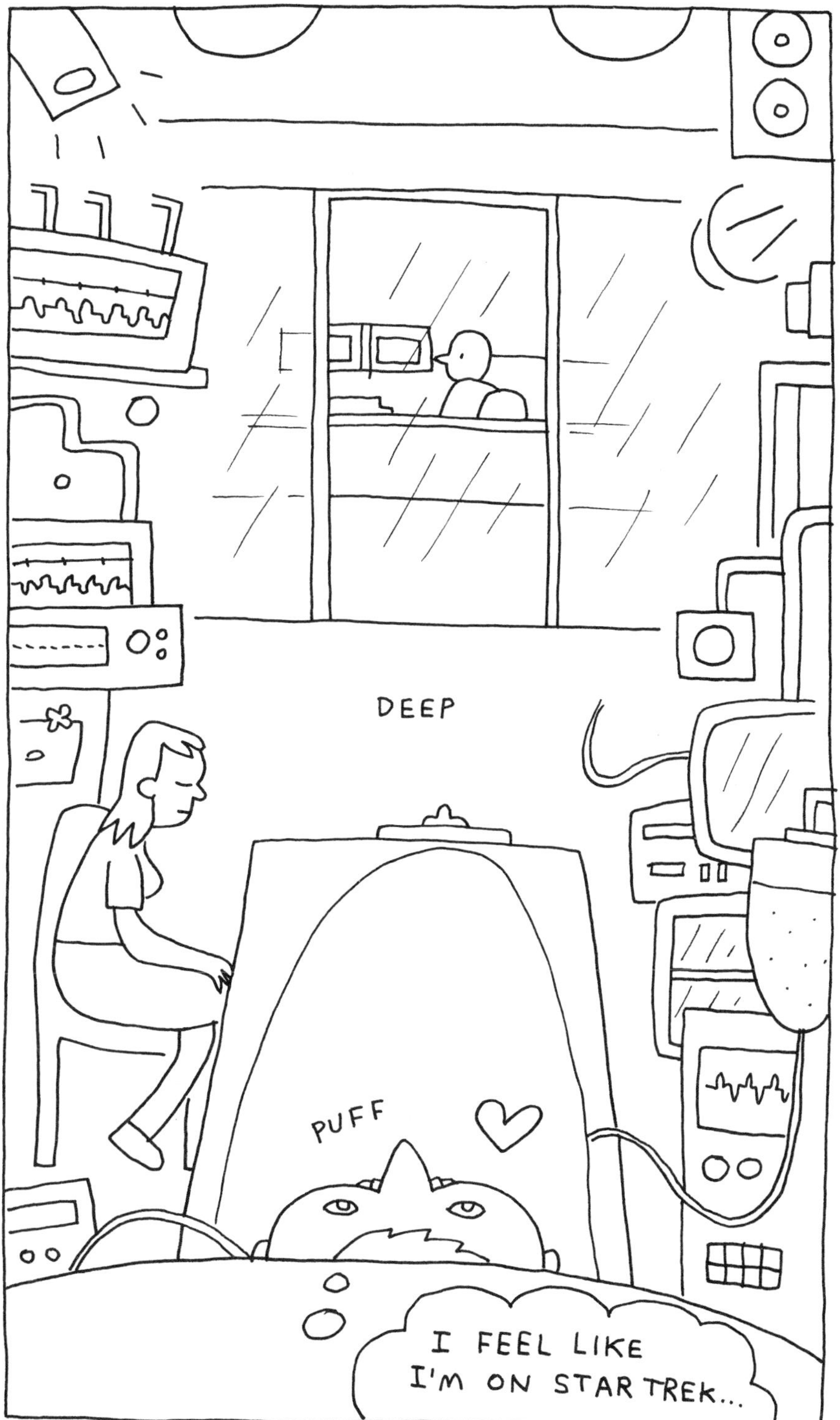
DEEP
PUFF
I FEEL LIKE I'M ON STAR TREK...

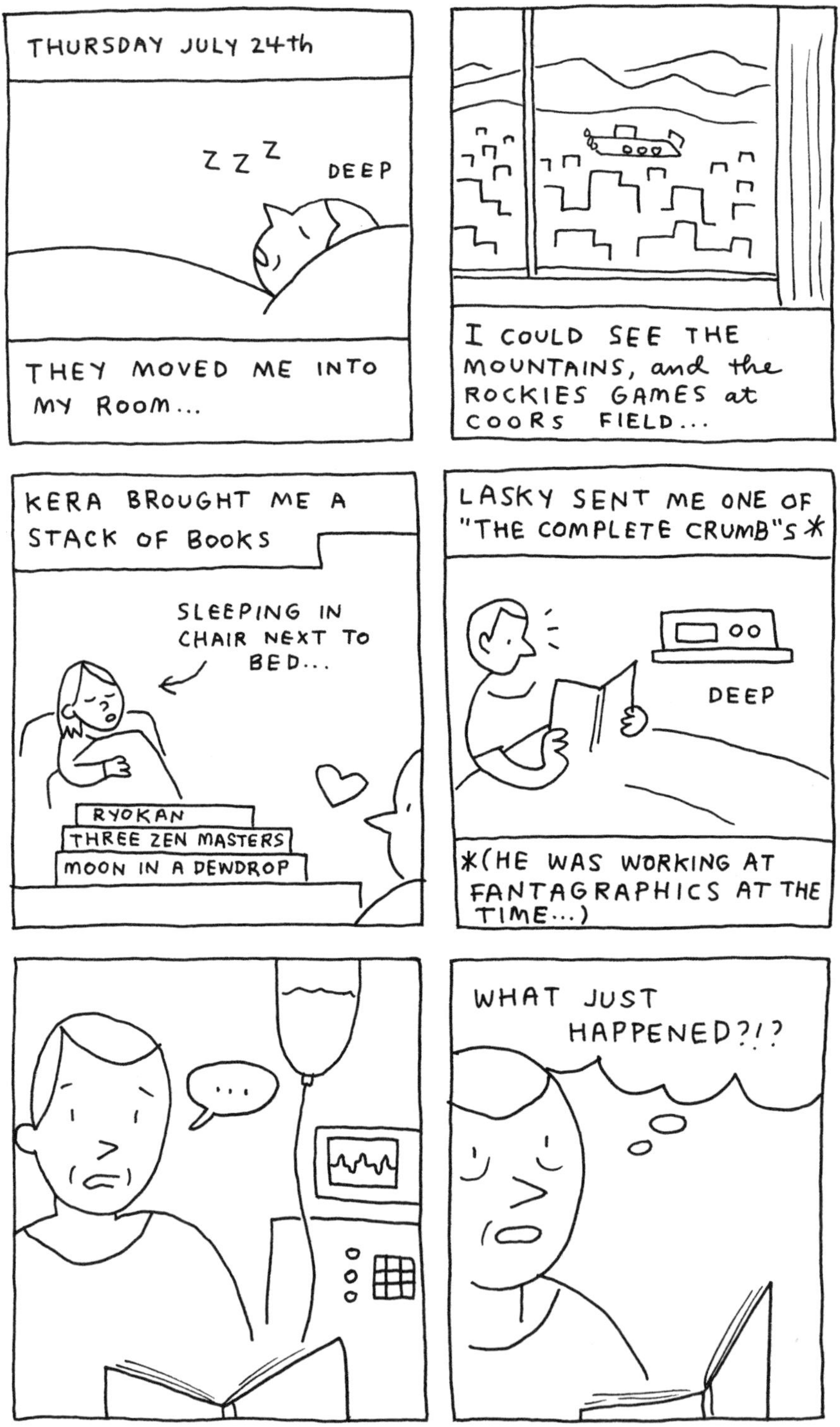
THURSDAY JULY 24th
Z Z Z
DEEP
THEY MOVED ME INTO MY ROOM...
I COULD SEE THE MOUNTAINS, and the ROCKIES GAMES at COORS FIELD...
KERA BROUGHT ME A STACK OF BOOKS
SLEEPING IN CHAIR NEXT TO BED...
RYOKAN
THREE ZEN MASTERS
MOON IN A DEWDROP
LASKY SENT ME ONE OF "THE COMPLETE CRUMB"S *
DEEP
*(HE WAS WORKING AT FANTAGRAPHICS AT THE TIME...)
...
WHAT JUST HAPPENED?!?

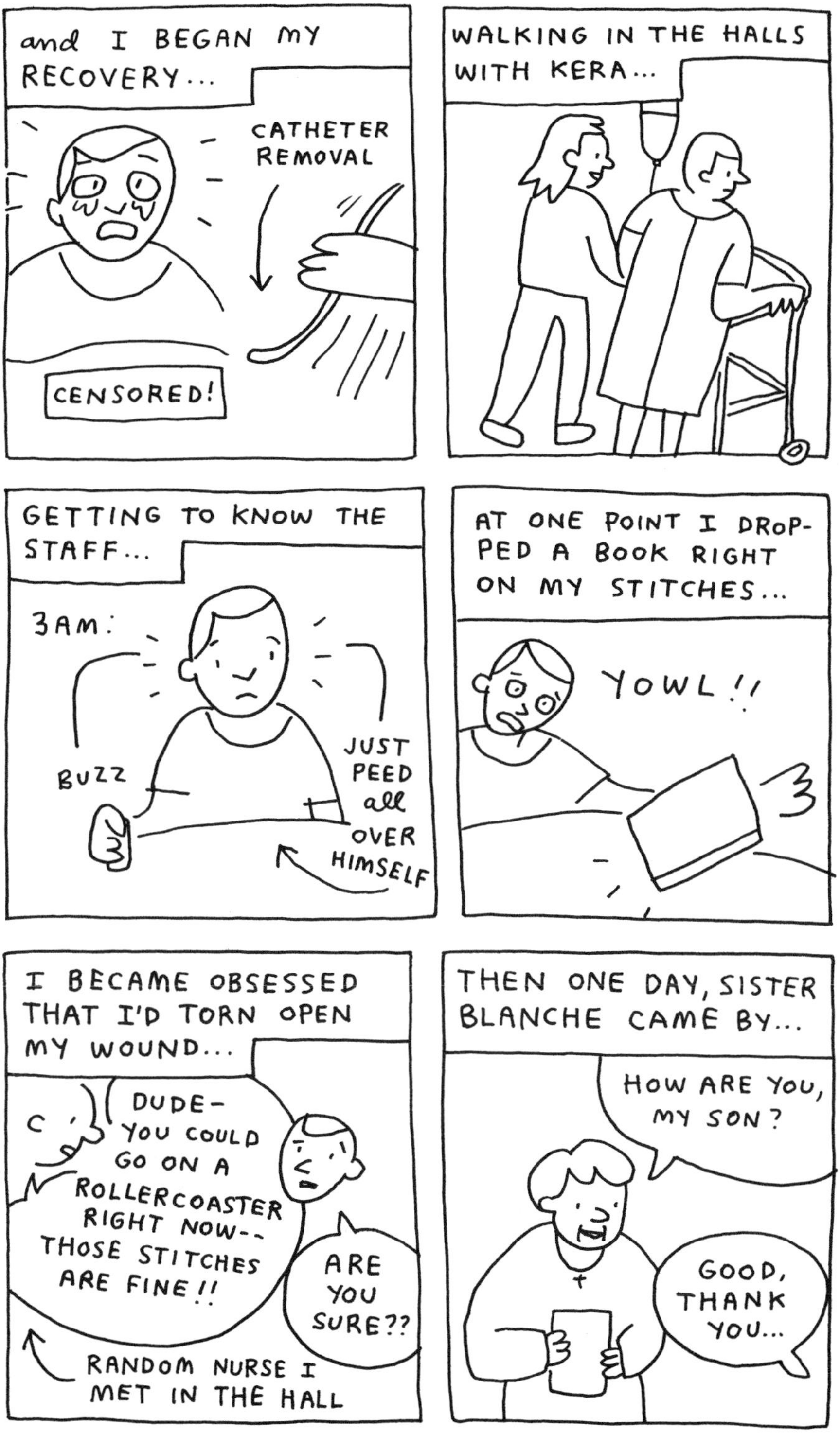

and I BEGAN MY RECOVERY...
CATHETER REMOVAL
CENSORED!
WALKING IN THE HALLS WITH KERA...
GETTING TO KNOW THE STAFF...
3AM:
BUZZ
JUST PEED all OVER HIMSELF
AT ONE POINT I DROPPED A BOOK RIGHT ON MY STITCHES...
YOWL!!
I BECAME OBSESSED THAT I'D TORN OPEN MY WOUND...
DUDE- YOU COULD GO ON A ROLLERCOASTER RIGHT NOW-- THOSE STITCHES ARE FINE!!
ARE YOU SURE??
RANDOM NURSE I MET IN THE HALL
THEN ONE DAY, SISTER BLANCHE CAME BY...
HOW ARE YOU, MY SON?
GOOD, THANK YOU...

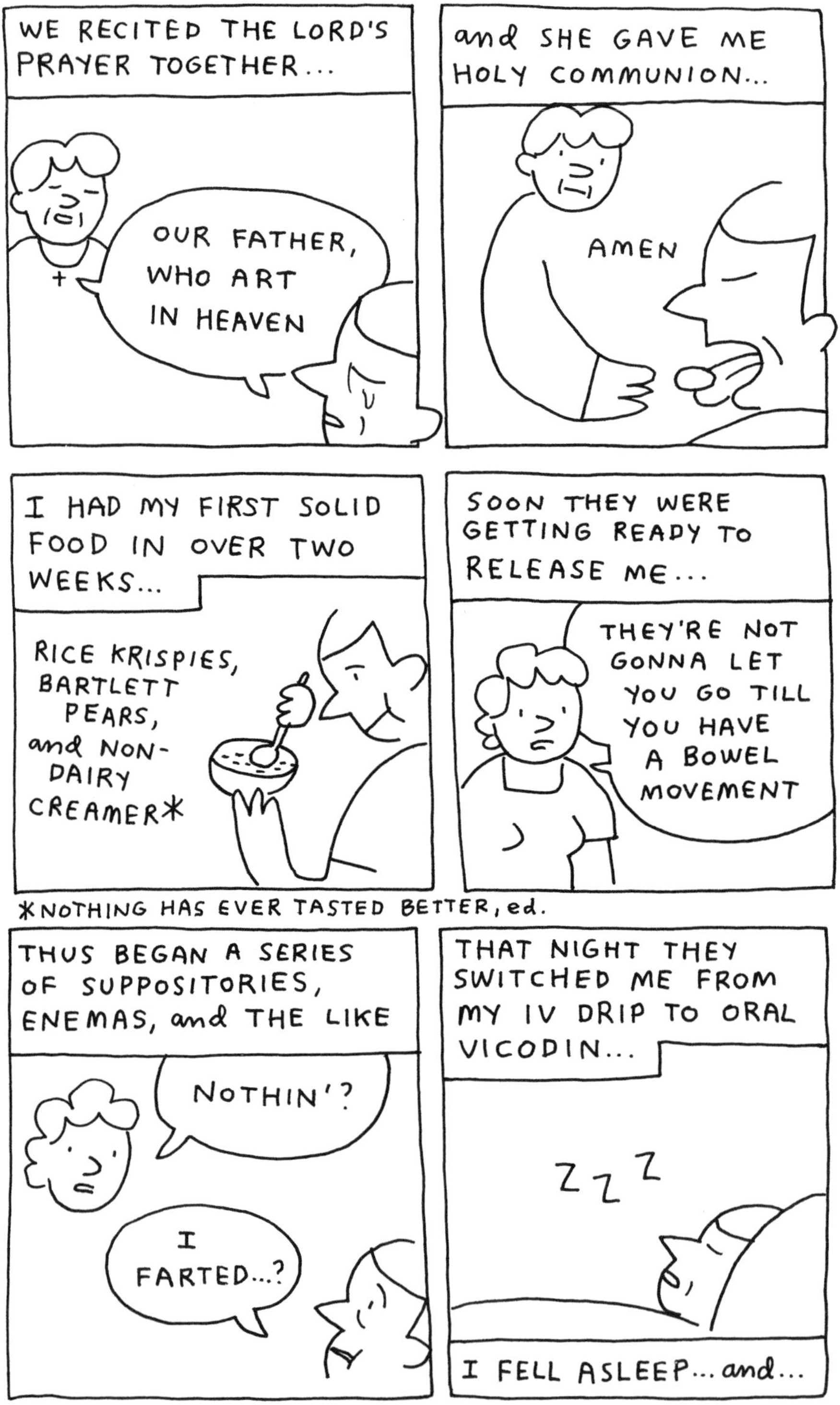
WE RECITED THE LORD'S PRAYER TOGETHER...
OUR FATHER, WHO ART IN HEAVEN
and SHE GAVE ME HOLY COMMUNION...
AMEN
I HAD MY FIRST SOLID FOOD IN OVER TWO WEEKS...
RICE KRISPIES, BARTLETT PEARS, and NON-DAIRY CREAMER*
SOON THEY WERE GETTING READY TO RELEASE ME...
THEY'RE NOT GONNA LET YOU GO TILL YOU HAVE A BOWEL MOVEMENT
*NOTHING HAS EVER TASTED BETTER, ed.
THUS BEGAN A SERIES OF SUPPOSITORIES, ENEMAS, and THE LIKE
NOTHIN'?
I FARTED...?
THAT NIGHT THEY SWITCHED ME FROM MY IV DRIP TO ORAL VICODIN...
Z Z Z
I FELL ASLEEP... and...

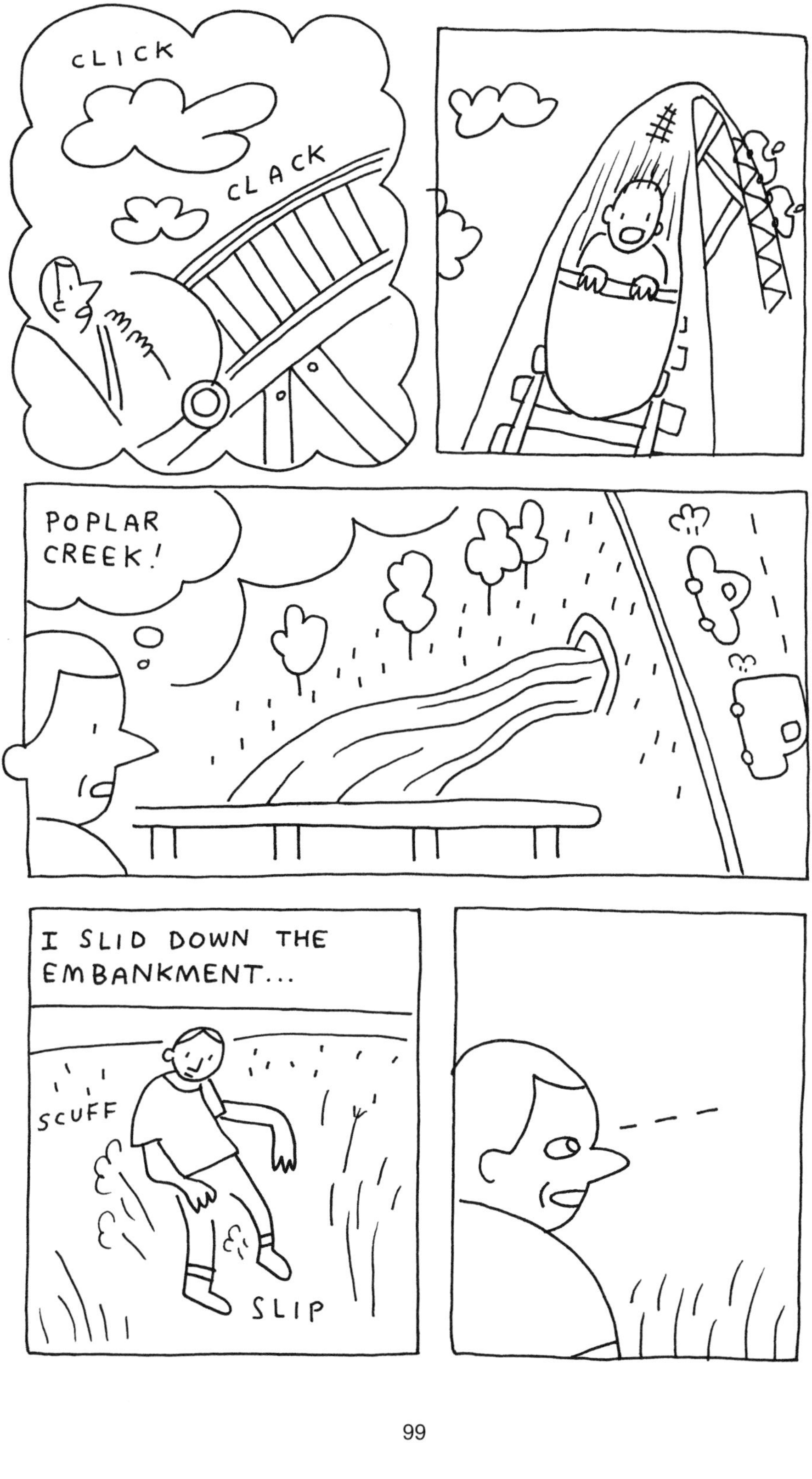
CLICK
CLACK
POPLAR CREEK!
I SLID DOWN THE EMBANKMENT...
SCUFF
SLIP

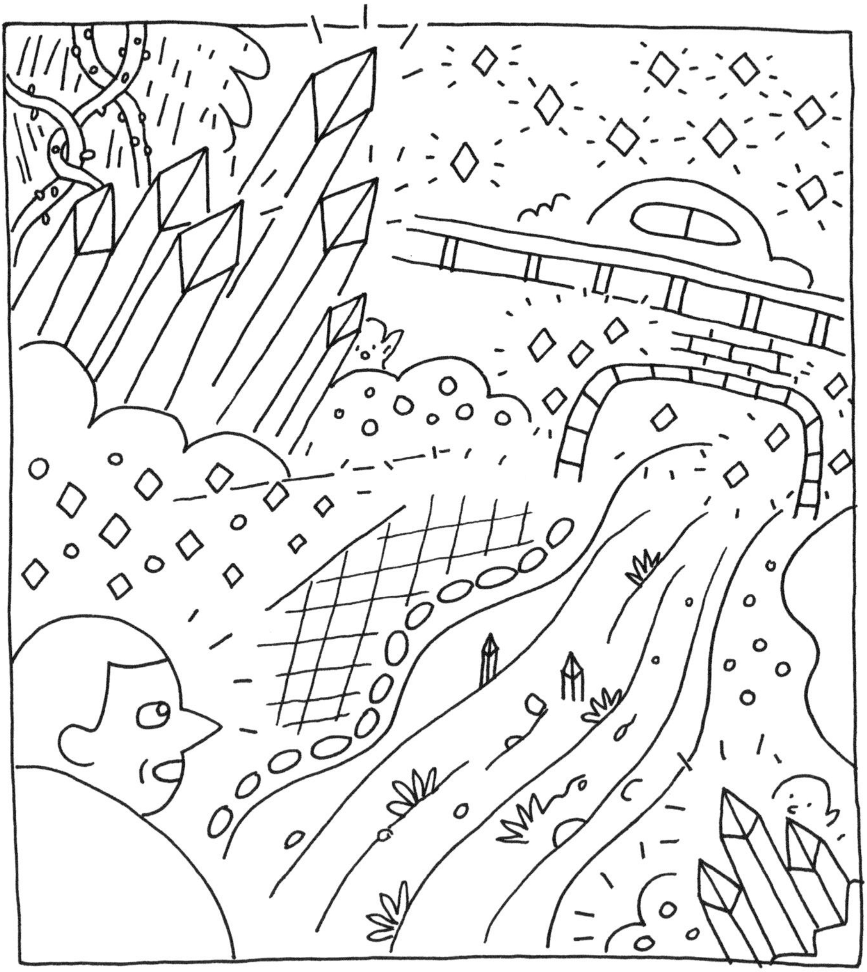

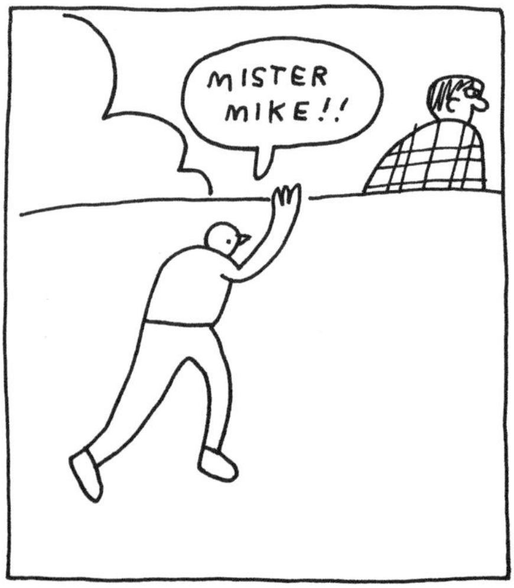
MISTER MIKE!!

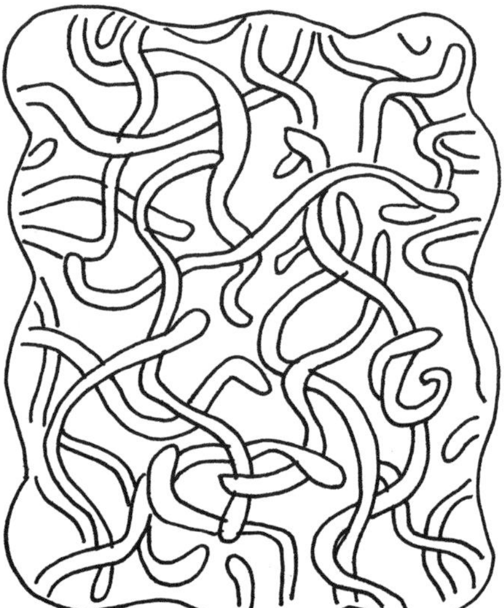

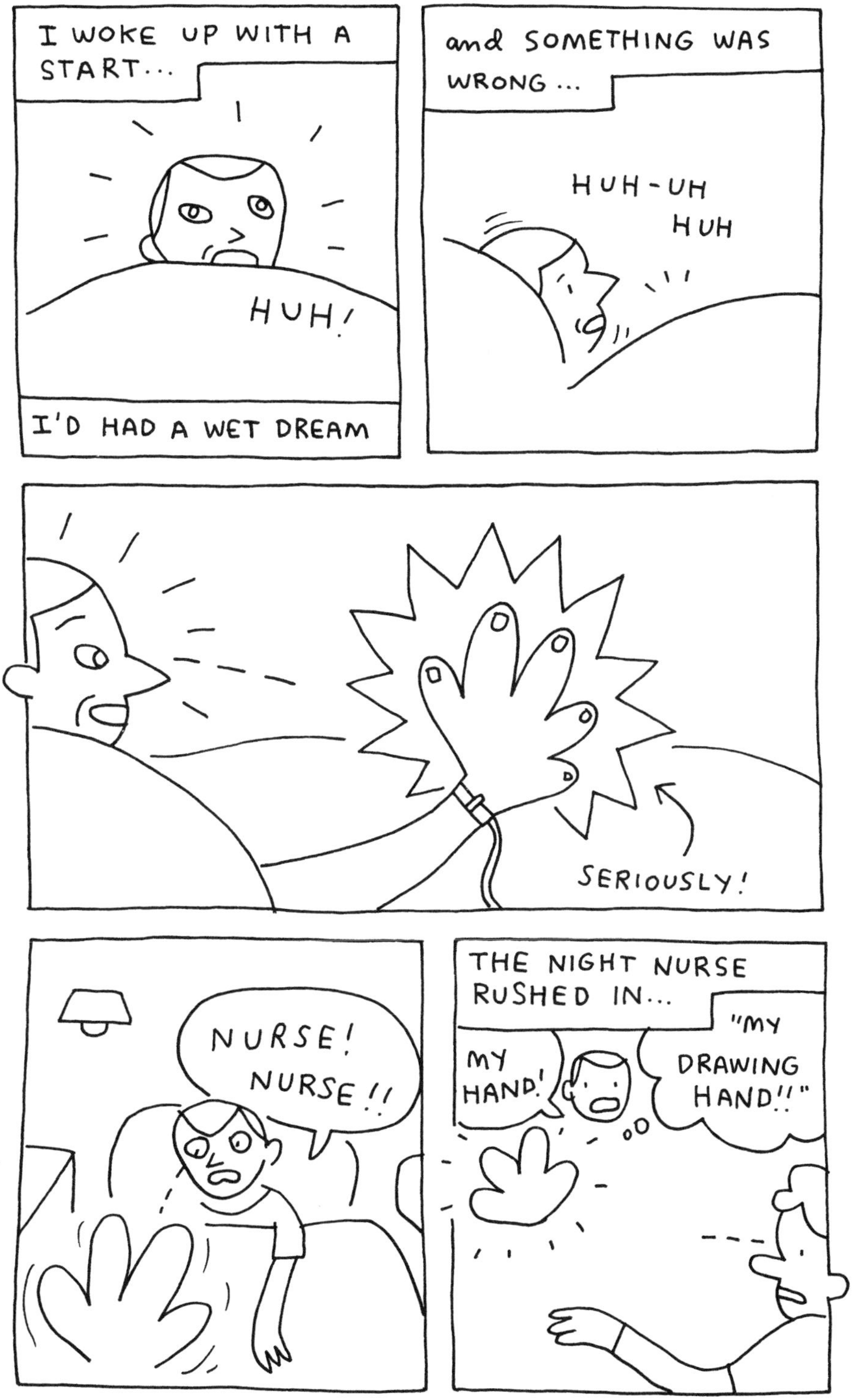
I WOKE UP WITH A START...
HUH!
I'D HAD A WET DREAM
and SOMETHING WAS WRONG...
HUH-UH HUH
SERIOUSLY!
NURSE! NURSE!!
THE NIGHT NURSE RUSHED IN...
MY HAND!
"MY DRAWING HAND!!"

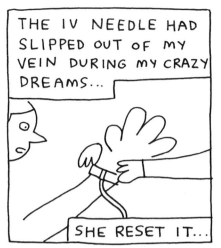

THE IV NEEDLE HAD SLIPPED OUT OF MY VEIN DURING MY CRAZY DREAMS...

SHE RESET IT...

YOU'LL BE FINE! YOUR BODY WILL ABSORB THE EXTRA FLUID OVER TIME...

DON'T WORRY!

I POKED IT...

DOINK

IT FELT LIKE a SQUISHY WARM WATER BALLOON

DEEP

MY ILLNESS HAS GIVEN all THESE PEOPLE A CHANCE TO PRACTICE COMPASSION...

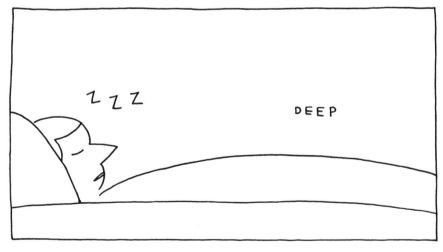

ZZZ

DEEP

Part Five

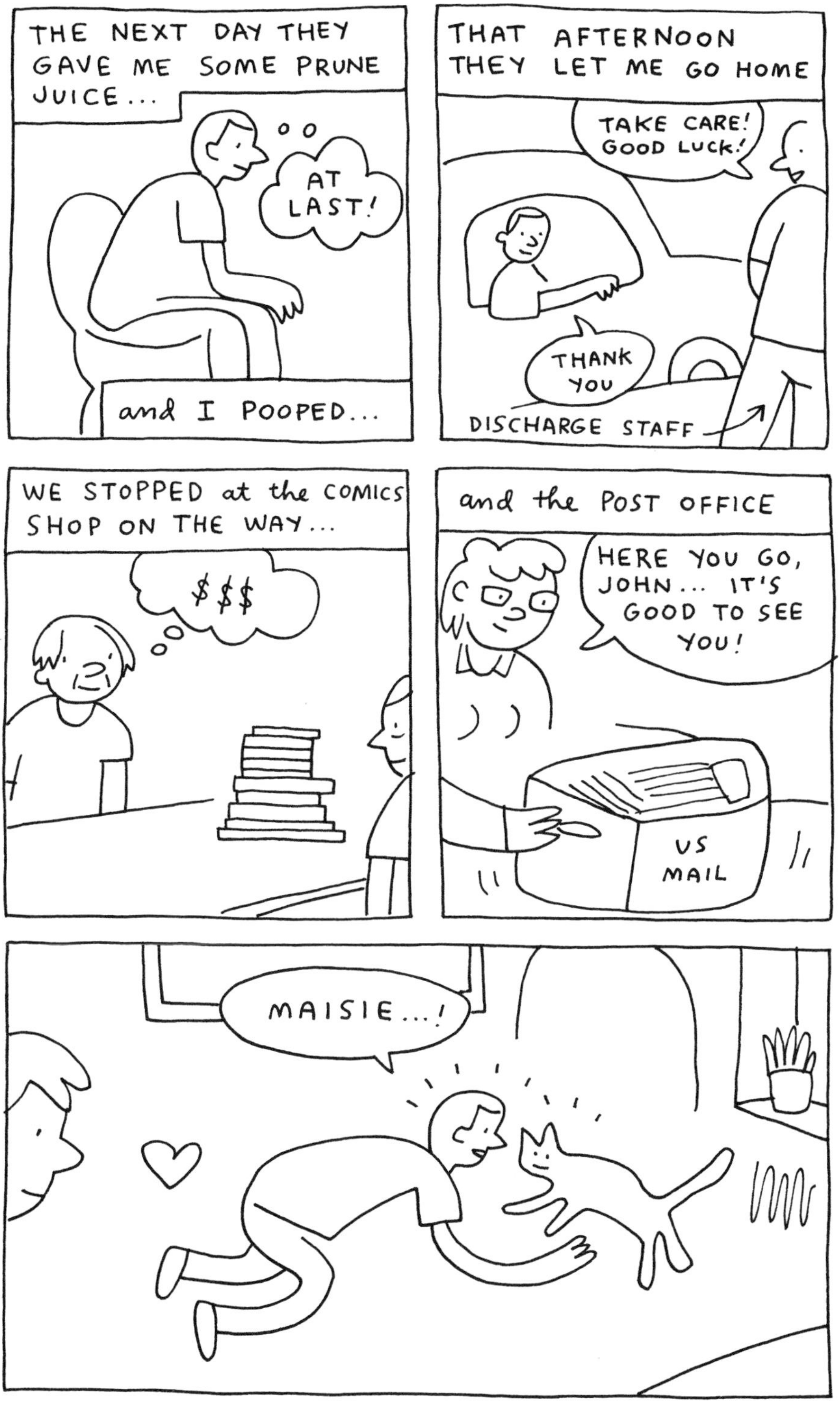
THE NEXT DAY THEY GAVE ME SOME PRUNE JUICE...
AT LAST!
and I POOPED...
THAT AFTERNOON THEY LET ME GO HOME
TAKE CARE! GOOD LUCK!
THANK YOU
DISCHARGE STAFF
WE STOPPED at the COMICS SHOP ON THE WAY...
$$$
and the POST OFFICE
HERE YOU GO, JOHN... IT'S GOOD TO SEE YOU!
US MAIL
MAISIE...!

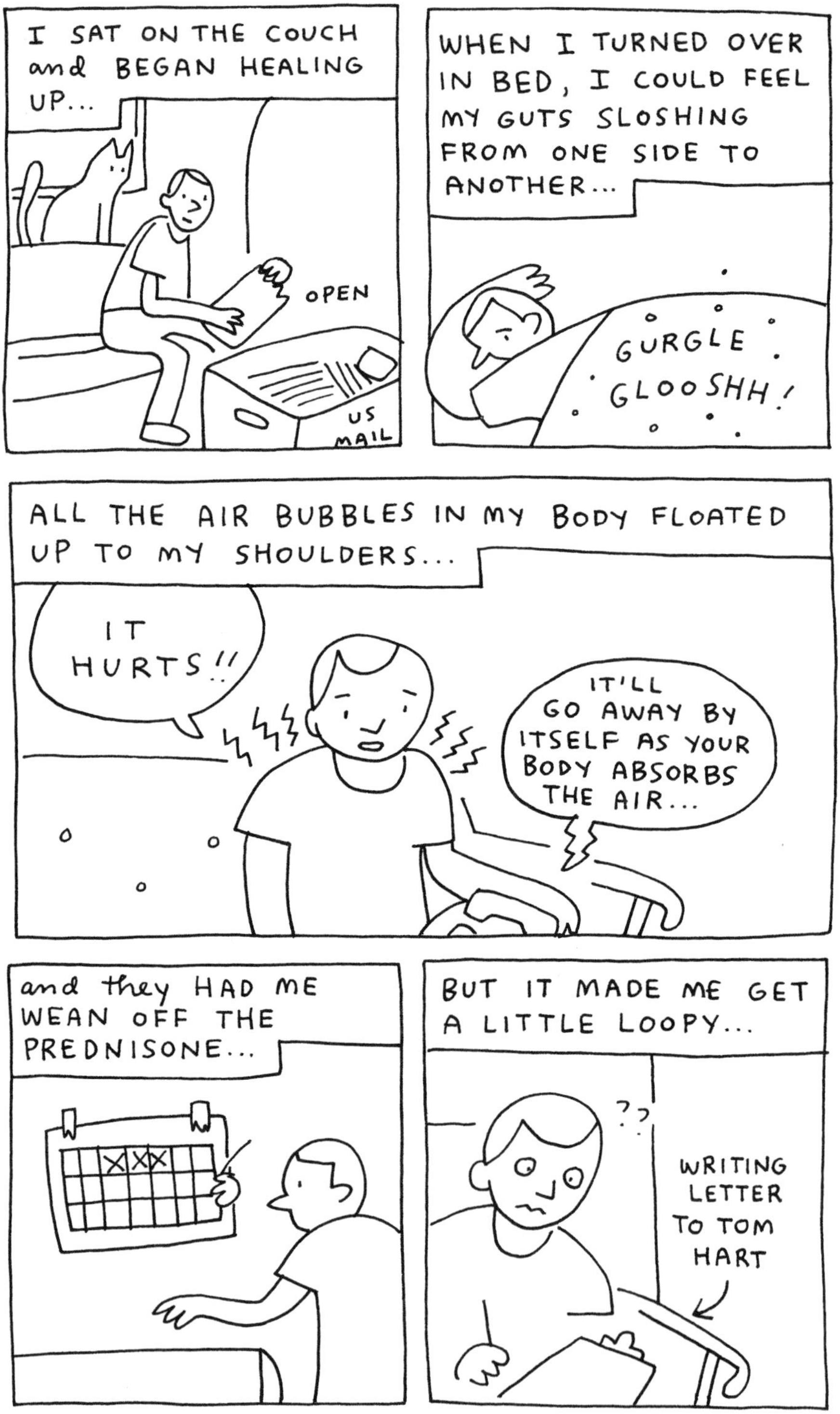
I SAT ON THE COUCH and BEGAN HEALING UP...
OPEN
US MAIL
WHEN I TURNED OVER IN BED, I COULD FEEL MY GUTS SLOSHING FROM ONE SIDE TO ANOTHER...
GURGLE GLOOSHH!
ALL THE AIR BUBBLES IN MY BODY FLOATED UP TO MY SHOULDERS...
IT HURTS!!
IT'LL GO AWAY BY ITSELF AS YOUR BODY ABSORBS THE AIR...
and they HAD ME WEAN OFF THE PREDNISONE...
BUT IT MADE ME GET A LITTLE LOOPY...
??
WRITING LETTER TO TOM HART

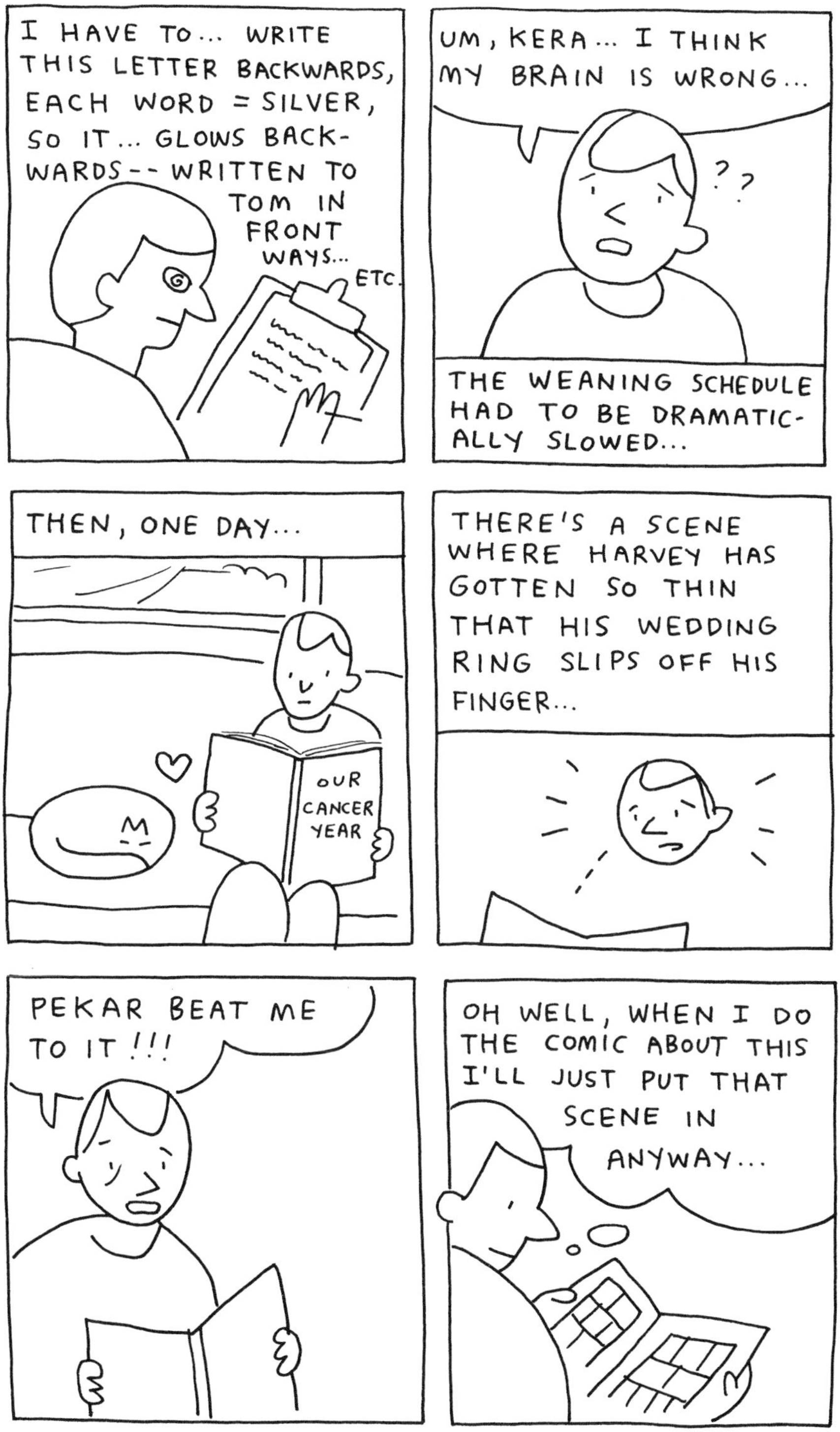
I HAVE TO... WRITE THIS LETTER BACKWARDS, EACH WORD = SILVER, SO IT... GLOWS BACKWARDS -- WRITTEN TO TOM IN FRONT WAYS... ETC.
UM, KERA... I THINK MY BRAIN IS WRONG...
??
THE WEANING SCHEDULE HAD TO BE DRAMATICALLY SLOWED...
THEN, ONE DAY...
OUR CANCER YEAR
THERE'S A SCENE WHERE HARVEY HAS GOTTEN SO THIN THAT HIS WEDDING RING SLIPS OFF HIS FINGER...
PEKAR BEAT ME TO IT!!!
OH WELL, WHEN I DO THE COMIC ABOUT THIS I'LL JUST PUT THAT SCENE IN ANYWAY...

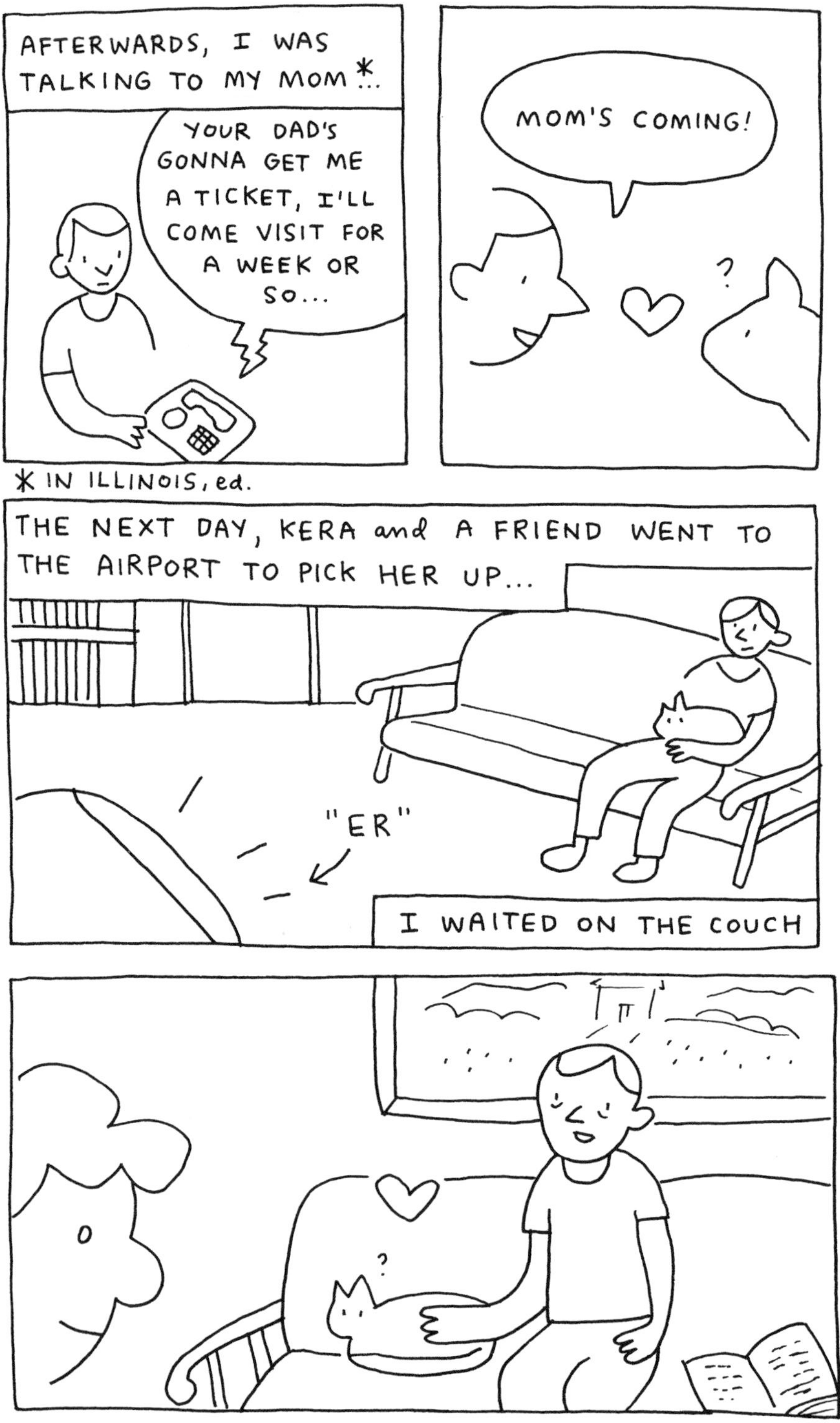

AFTERWARDS, I WAS TALKING TO MY MOM*...
YOUR DAD'S GONNA GET ME A TICKET, I'LL COME VISIT FOR A WEEK OR SO...
MOM'S COMING!
?
* IN ILLINOIS, ed.
THE NEXT DAY, KERA and A FRIEND WENT TO THE AIRPORT TO PICK HER UP...
"ER"
I WAITED ON THE COUCH
?

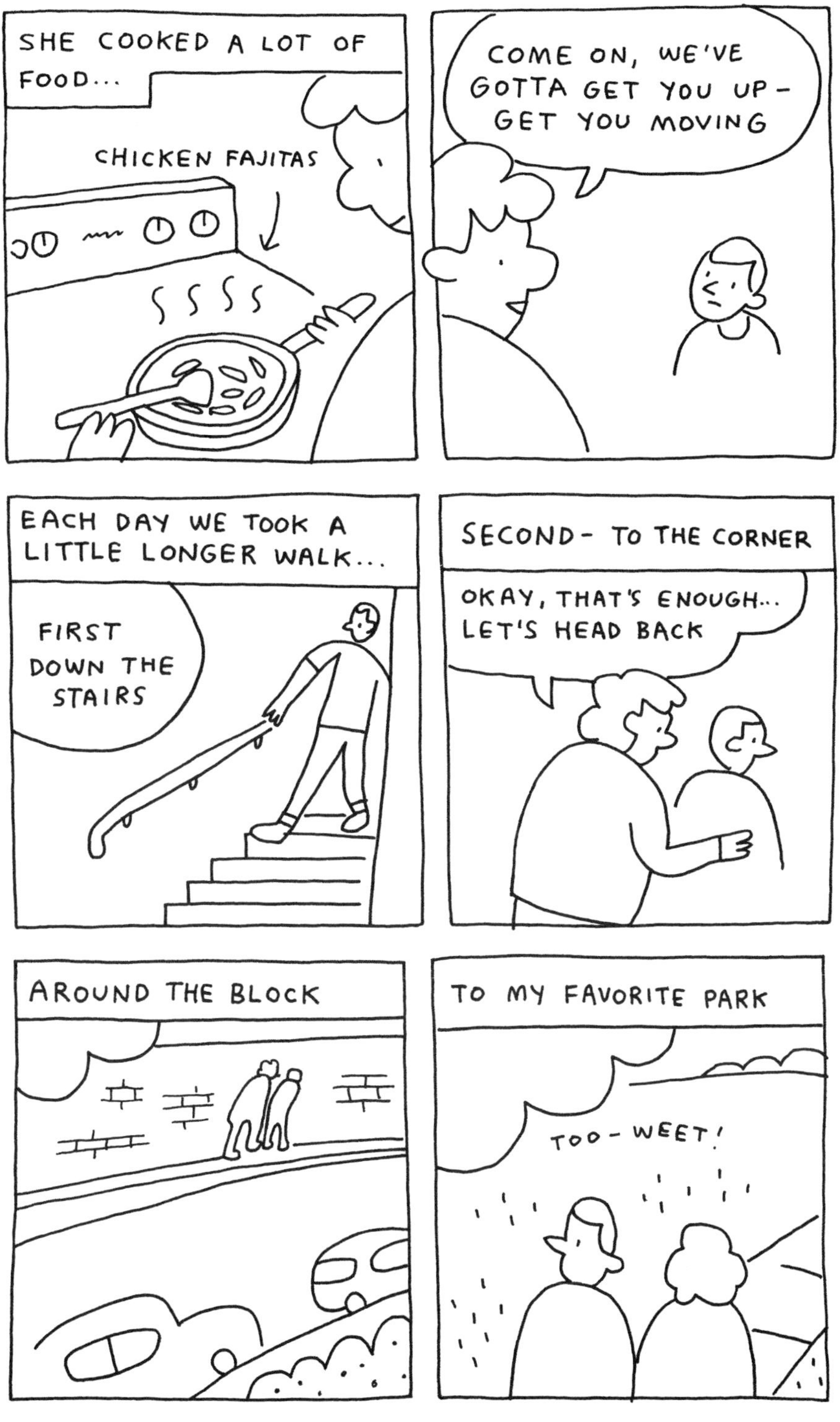
SHE COOKED A LOT OF FOOD...
CHICKEN FAJITAS
COME ON, WE'VE GOTTA GET YOU UP - GET YOU MOVING
EACH DAY WE TOOK A LITTLE LONGER WALK...
FIRST DOWN THE STAIRS
SECOND - TO THE CORNER
OKAY, THAT'S ENOUGH... LET'S HEAD BACK
AROUND THE BLOCK
TO MY FAVORITE PARK
TOO-WEET!

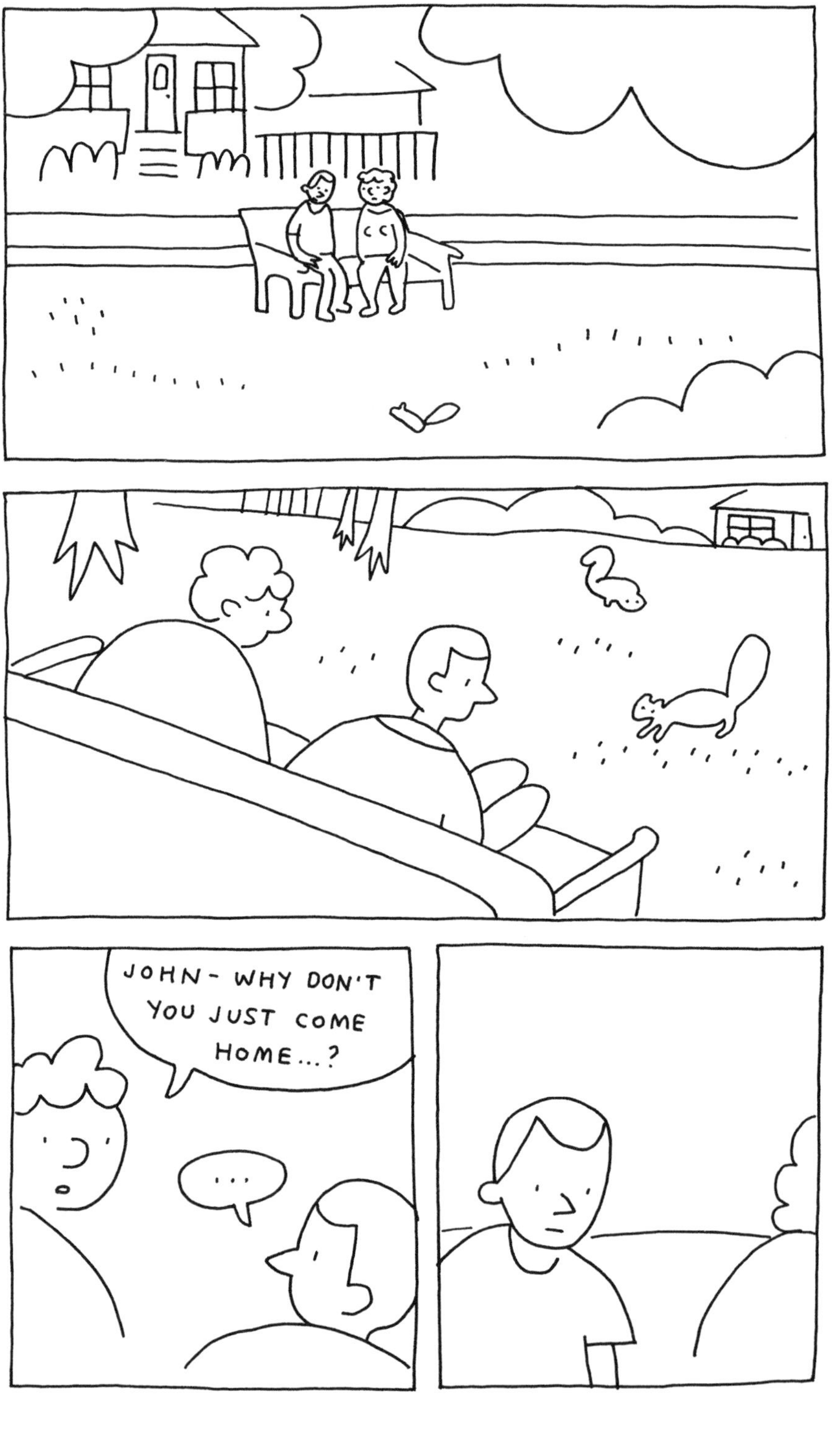
JOHN- WHY DON'T YOU JUST COME HOME...?
...

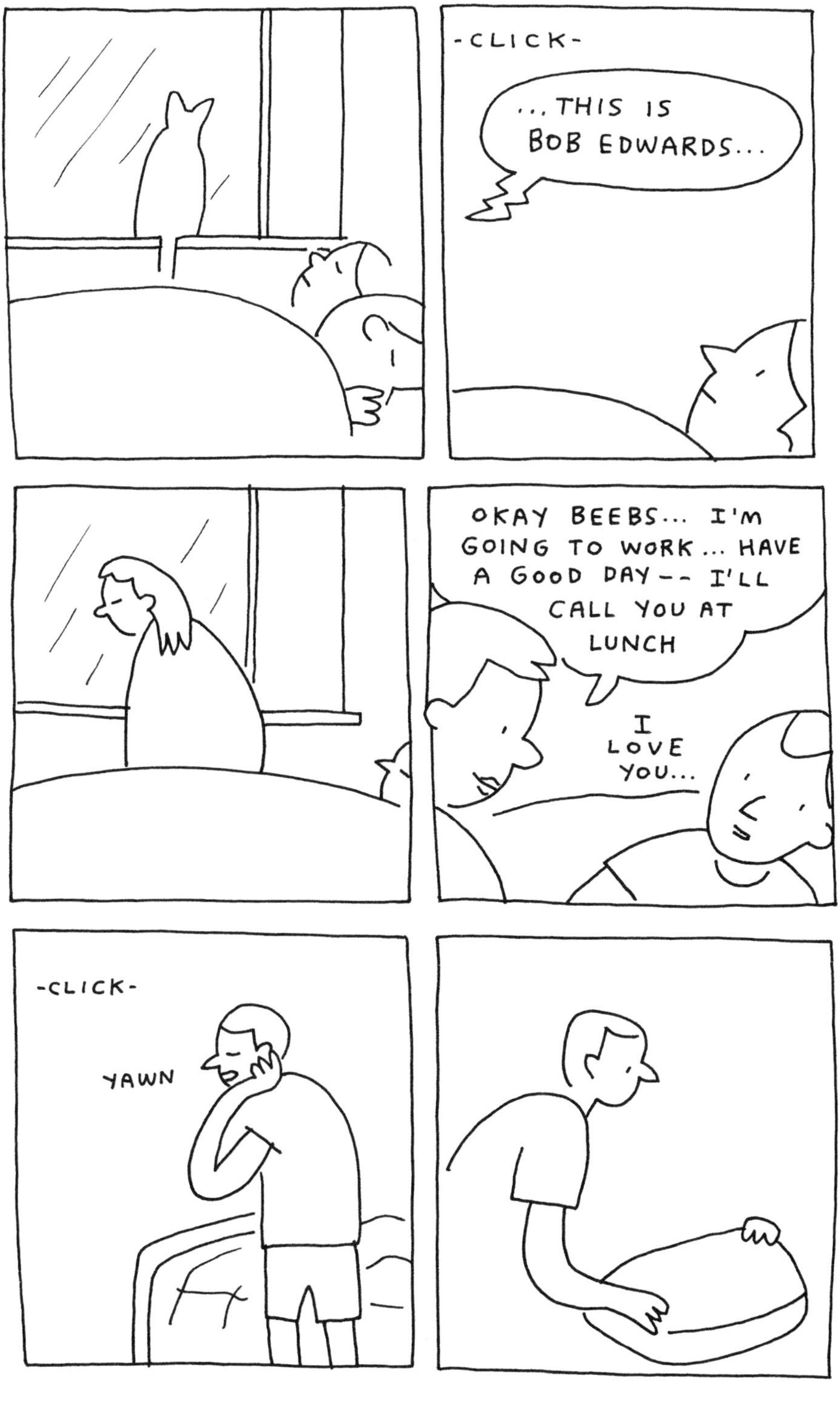
-CLICK-
...THIS IS BOB EDWARDS...
OKAY BEEBS... I'M GOING TO WORK... HAVE A GOOD DAY -- I'LL CALL YOU AT LUNCH
I LOVE YOU...
-CLICK-
YAWN

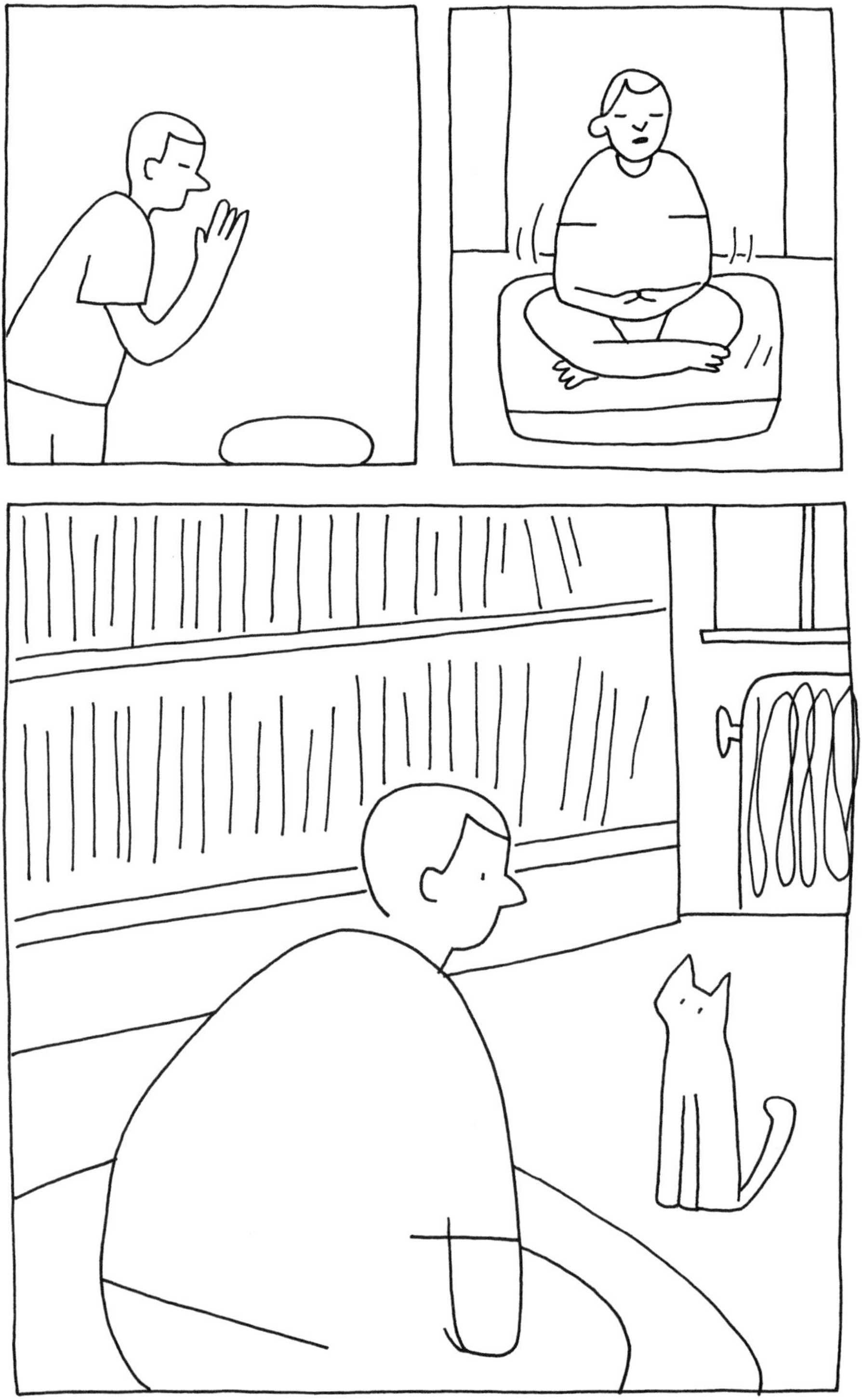

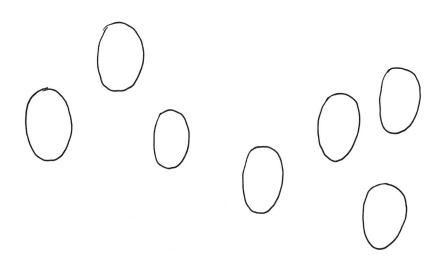

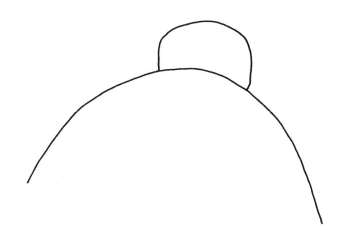

John Porcellino 1997-2014

1998

Part One

IN THE Fall OF '97, I WAS ALIVE.

I EVEN MANAGED TO DRIVE TO THE EAST COAST WITH JOE CHIPS, FOR A COMIX FESTIVAL

SO, JOE -- WHAT'S THE DEAL WITH GALACTUS?

WHEN I GOT BACK TO DENVER, KERA and I STARTED TALKING ABOUT MOVING BACK TO CHICAGO

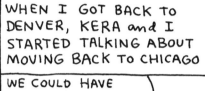

WE COULD HAVE FAMILY THANKSGIVINGS AGAIN!

ZZZ

CHICAGO WAS WHERE OUR ROOTS WERE, WHERE WE GREW UP — FAMILY, FRIENDS, and the BACK OF OUR HAND

I MISS GROUNDHOGS ...

I'D JUST COME THROUGH A MAJOR, LIFE-SAVING SURGERY, and I WAS BEGINNING TO LOOK AT THINGS A LITTLE DIFFERENTLY...

BEAR CREEK GREENBELT ·LAKEWOOD, COLO.·

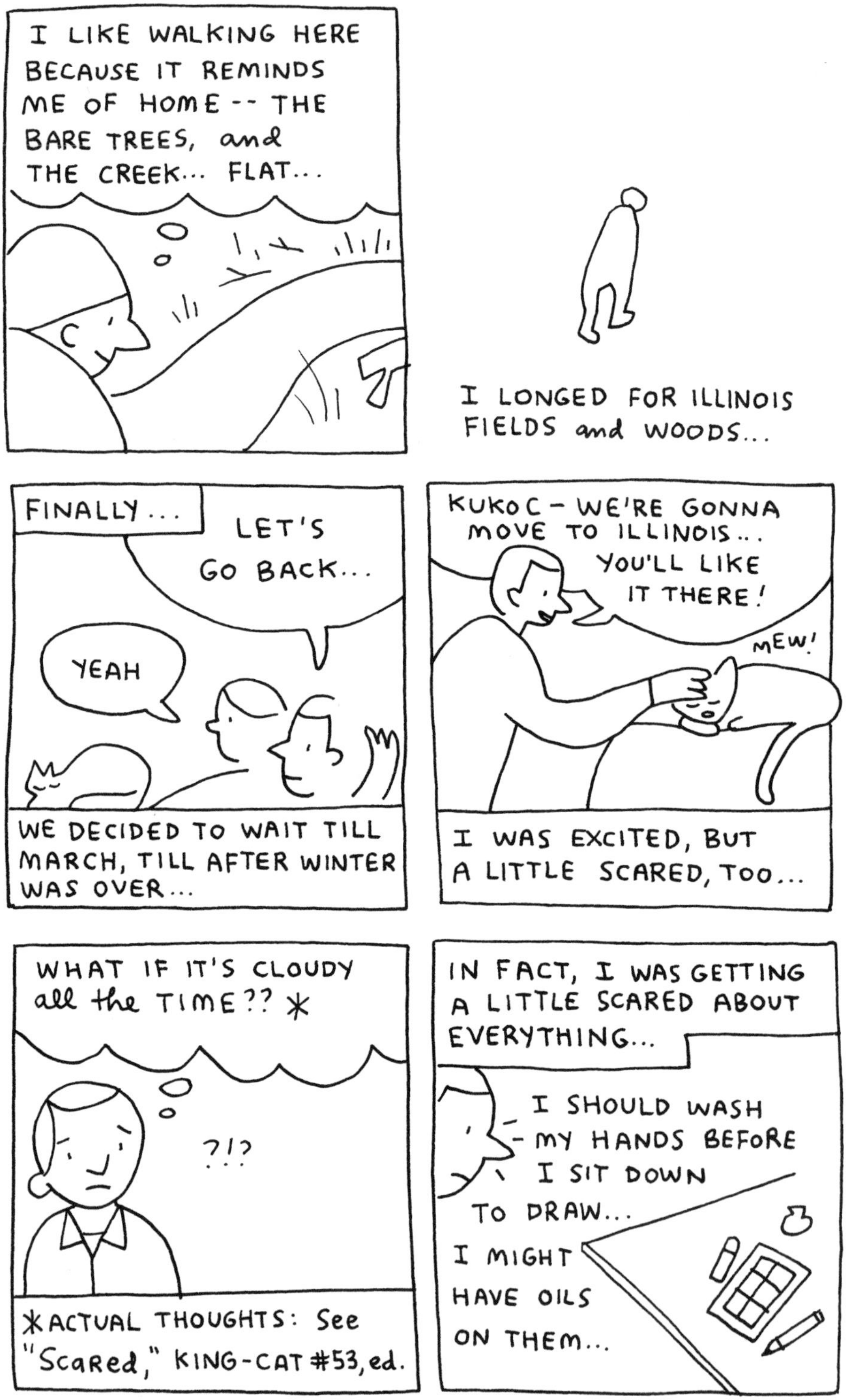
I LIKE WALKING HERE BECAUSE IT REMINDS ME OF HOME -- THE BARE TREES, and THE CREEK... FLAT...
I LONGED FOR ILLINOIS FIELDS and WOODS...
FINALLY...
LET'S GO BACK...
YEAH
WE DECIDED TO WAIT TILL MARCH, TILL AFTER WINTER WAS OVER...
KUKOC - WE'RE GONNA MOVE TO ILLINOIS... YOU'LL LIKE IT THERE!
MEW!
I WAS EXCITED, BUT A LITTLE SCARED, TOO...
WHAT IF IT'S CLOUDY all the TIME?? *
?!?
* ACTUAL THOUGHTS: See "Scared," KING-CAT #53, ed.
IN FACT, I WAS GETTING A LITTLE SCARED ABOUT EVERYTHING...
I SHOULD WASH MY HANDS BEFORE I SIT DOWN TO DRAW...
I MIGHT HAVE OILS ON THEM...

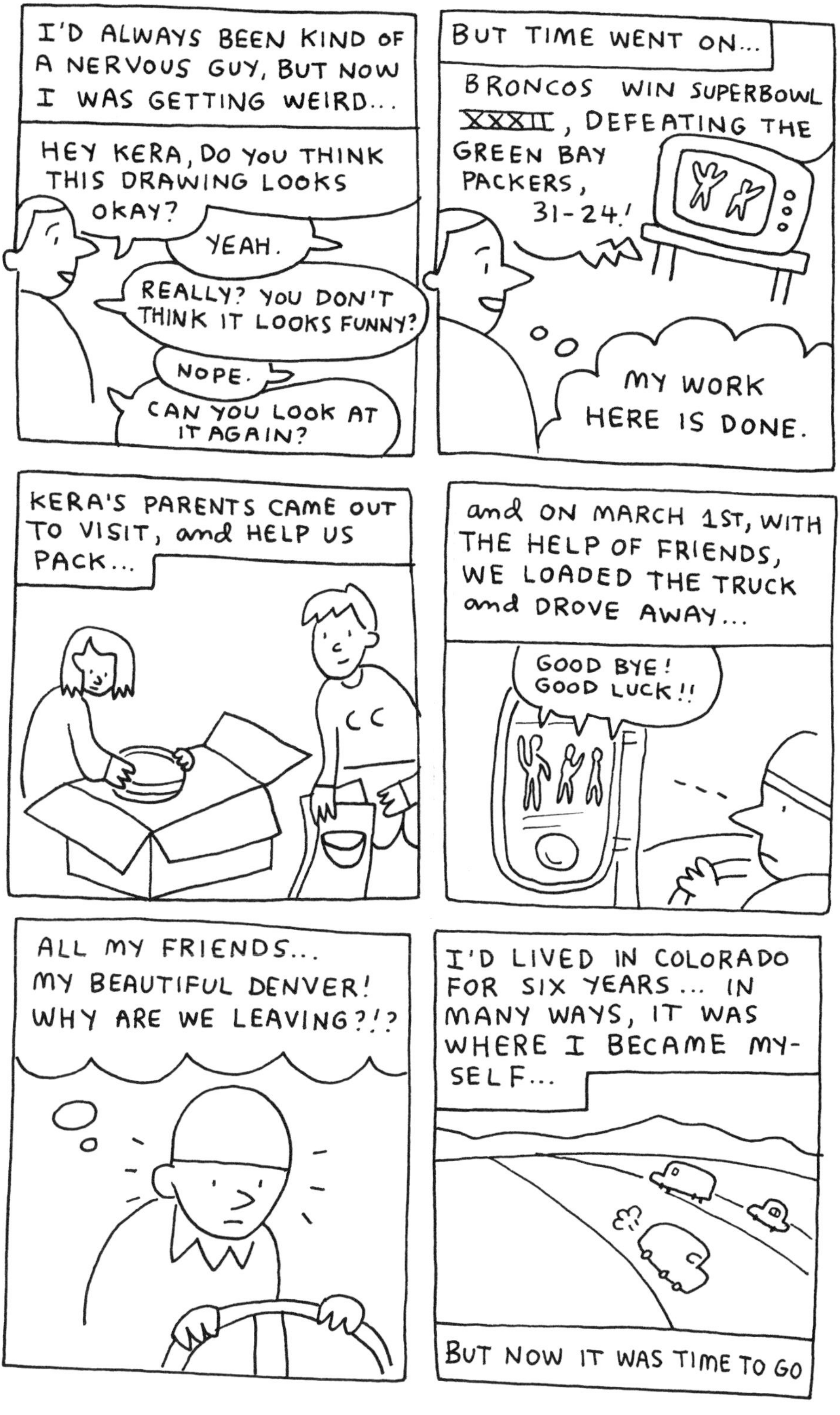
I'D ALWAYS BEEN KIND OF A NERVOUS GUY, BUT NOW I WAS GETTING WEIRD...
HEY KERA, DO YOU THINK THIS DRAWING LOOKS OKAY?
YEAH.
REALLY? YOU DON'T THINK IT LOOKS FUNNY?
NOPE.
CAN YOU LOOK AT IT AGAIN?
BUT TIME WENT ON...
BRONCOS WIN SUPERBOWL XXXII, DEFEATING THE GREEN BAY PACKERS, 31-24!
MY WORK HERE IS DONE.
KERA'S PARENTS CAME OUT TO VISIT, and HELP US PACK...
and ON MARCH 1ST, WITH THE HELP OF FRIENDS, WE LOADED THE TRUCK and DROVE AWAY...
GOOD BYE! GOOD LUCK!!
ALL MY FRIENDS... MY BEAUTIFUL DENVER! WHY ARE WE LEAVING?!?
I'D LIVED IN COLORADO FOR SIX YEARS... IN MANY WAYS, IT WAS WHERE I BECAME MY-SELF...
BUT NOW IT WAS TIME TO GO

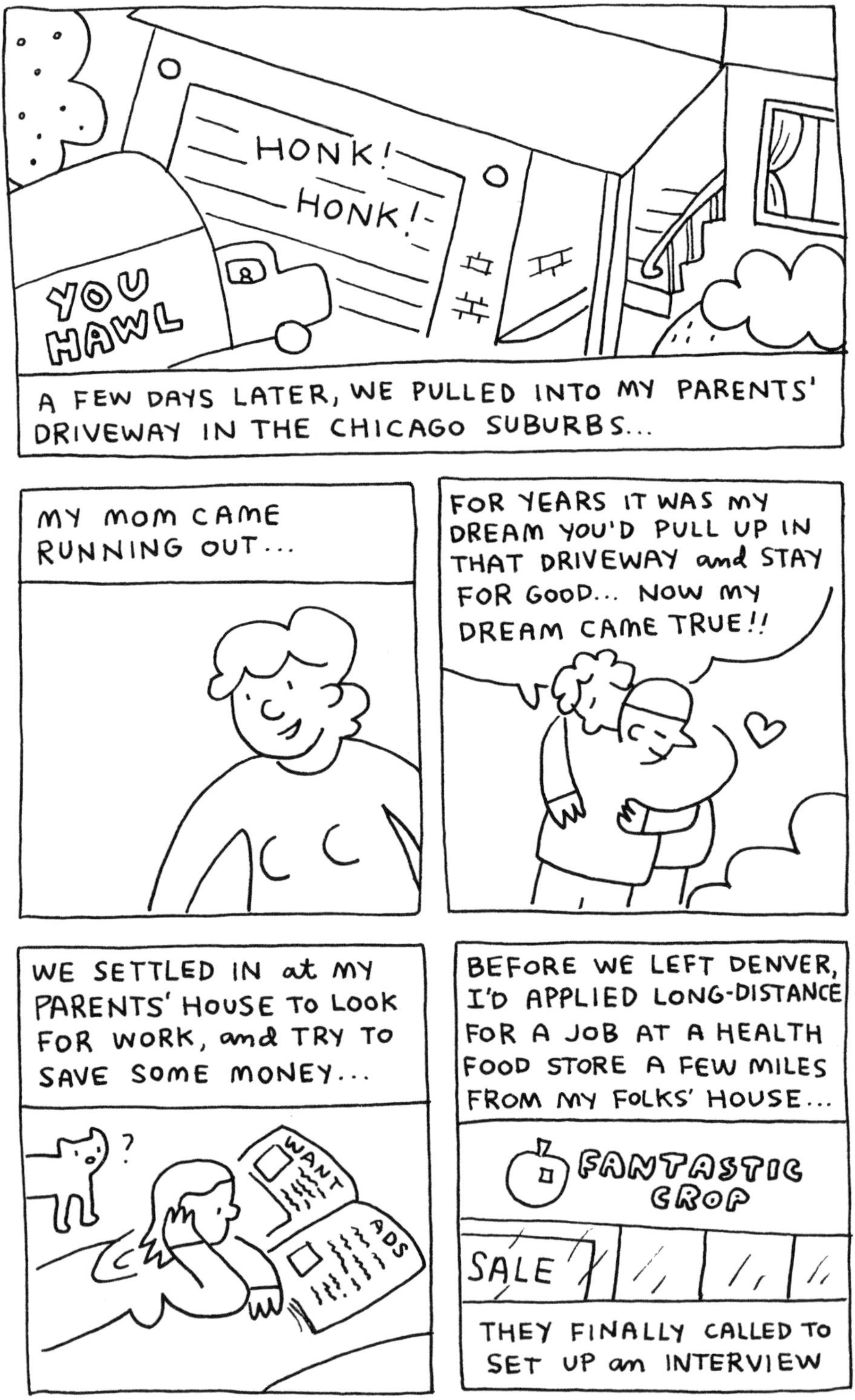
YOU HAWL
HONK! HONK!
A FEW DAYS LATER, WE PULLED INTO MY PARENTS' DRIVEWAY IN THE CHICAGO SUBURBS...
MY MOM CAME RUNNING OUT...
FOR YEARS IT WAS MY DREAM YOU'D PULL UP IN THAT DRIVEWAY and STAY FOR GOOD... NOW MY DREAM CAME TRUE!!
WE SETTLED IN at MY PARENTS' HOUSE TO LOOK FOR WORK, and TRY TO SAVE SOME MONEY...
?
WANT ADS
BEFORE WE LEFT DENVER, I'D APPLIED LONG-DISTANCE FOR A JOB AT A HEALTH FOOD STORE A FEW MILES FROM MY FOLKS' HOUSE...
FANTASTIC CROP
SALE
THEY FINALLY CALLED TO SET UP an INTERVIEW

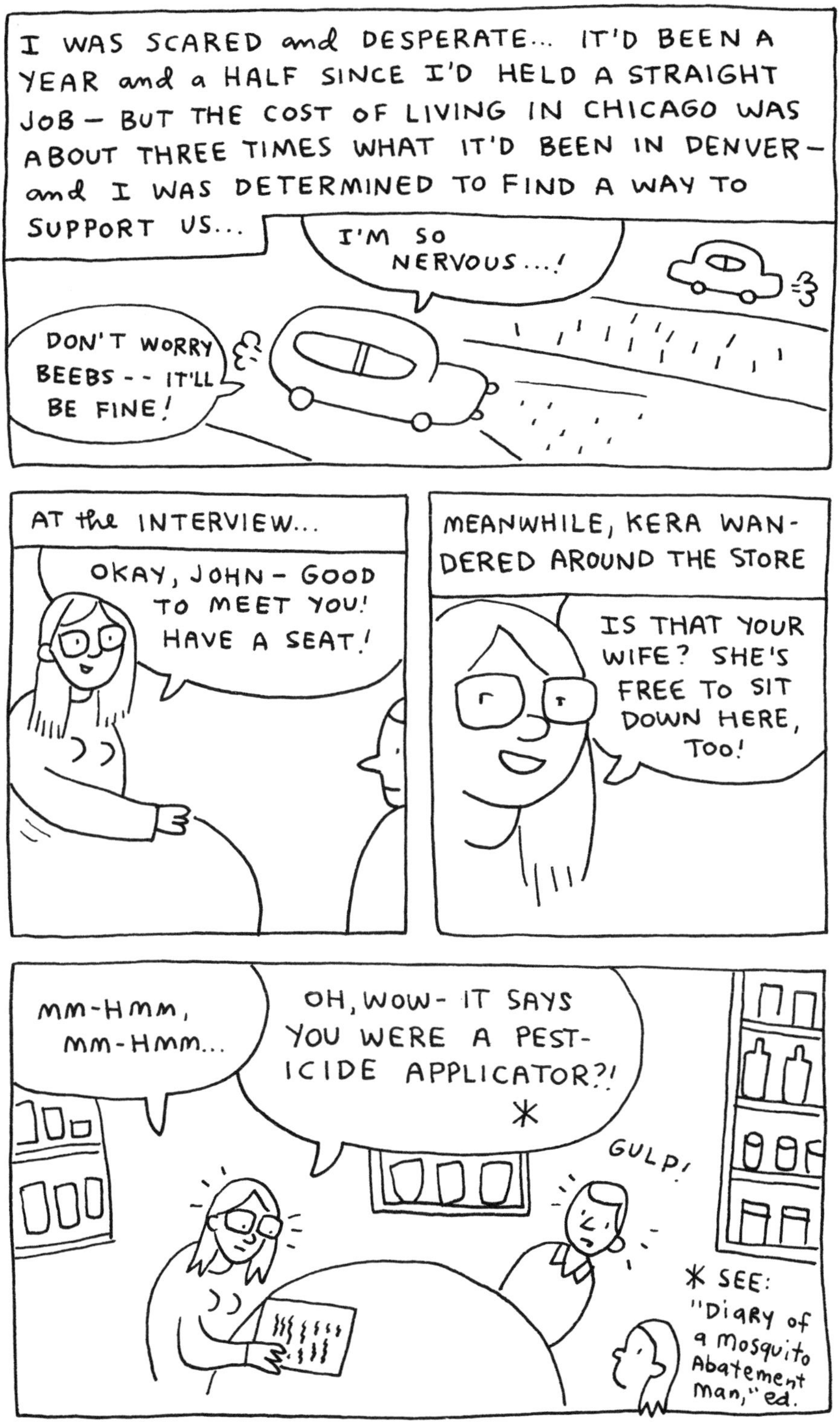
I WAS SCARED and DESPERATE... IT'D BEEN A YEAR and a HALF SINCE I'D HELD A STRAIGHT JOB – BUT THE COST OF LIVING IN CHICAGO WAS ABOUT THREE TIMES WHAT IT'D BEEN IN DENVER – and I WAS DETERMINED TO FIND A WAY TO SUPPORT US...
I'M SO NERVOUS...!
DON'T WORRY BEEBS -- IT'LL BE FINE!
AT the INTERVIEW...
OKAY, JOHN – GOOD TO MEET YOU! HAVE A SEAT!
MEANWHILE, KERA WANDERED AROUND THE STORE
IS THAT YOUR WIFE? SHE'S FREE TO SIT DOWN HERE, TOO!
MM-HMM, MM-HMM...
OH, WOW – IT SAYS YOU WERE A PESTICIDE APPLICATOR?! *
GULP!
* SEE: "Diary of a Mosquito Abatement Man," ed.

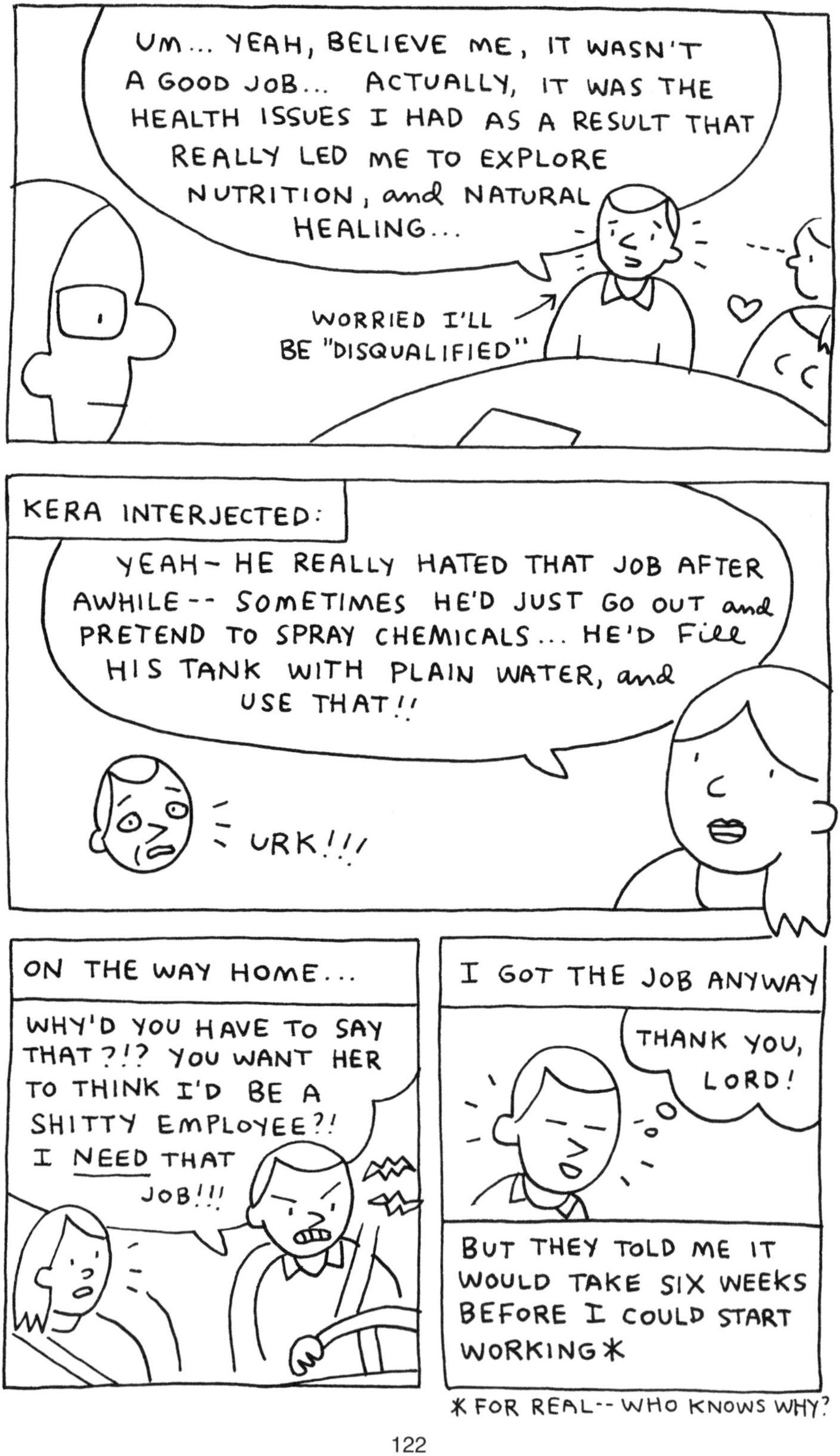
UM... YEAH, BELIEVE ME, IT WASN'T A GOOD JOB... ACTUALLY, IT WAS THE HEALTH ISSUES I HAD AS A RESULT THAT REALLY LED ME TO EXPLORE NUTRITION, and NATURAL HEALING...
WORRIED I'LL BE "DISQUALIFIED"
KERA INTERJECTED:
YEAH- HE REALLY HATED THAT JOB AFTER AWHILE-- SOMETIMES HE'D JUST GO OUT and PRETEND TO SPRAY CHEMICALS... HE'D FILL HIS TANK WITH PLAIN WATER, and USE THAT!!
URK!!!
ON THE WAY HOME...
WHY'D YOU HAVE TO SAY THAT?!? YOU WANT HER TO THINK I'D BE A SHITTY EMPLOYEE?! I NEED THAT JOB!!!
I GOT THE JOB ANYWAY
THANK YOU, LORD!
BUT THEY TOLD ME IT WOULD TAKE SIX WEEKS BEFORE I COULD START WORKING*
* FOR REAL-- WHO KNOWS WHY?

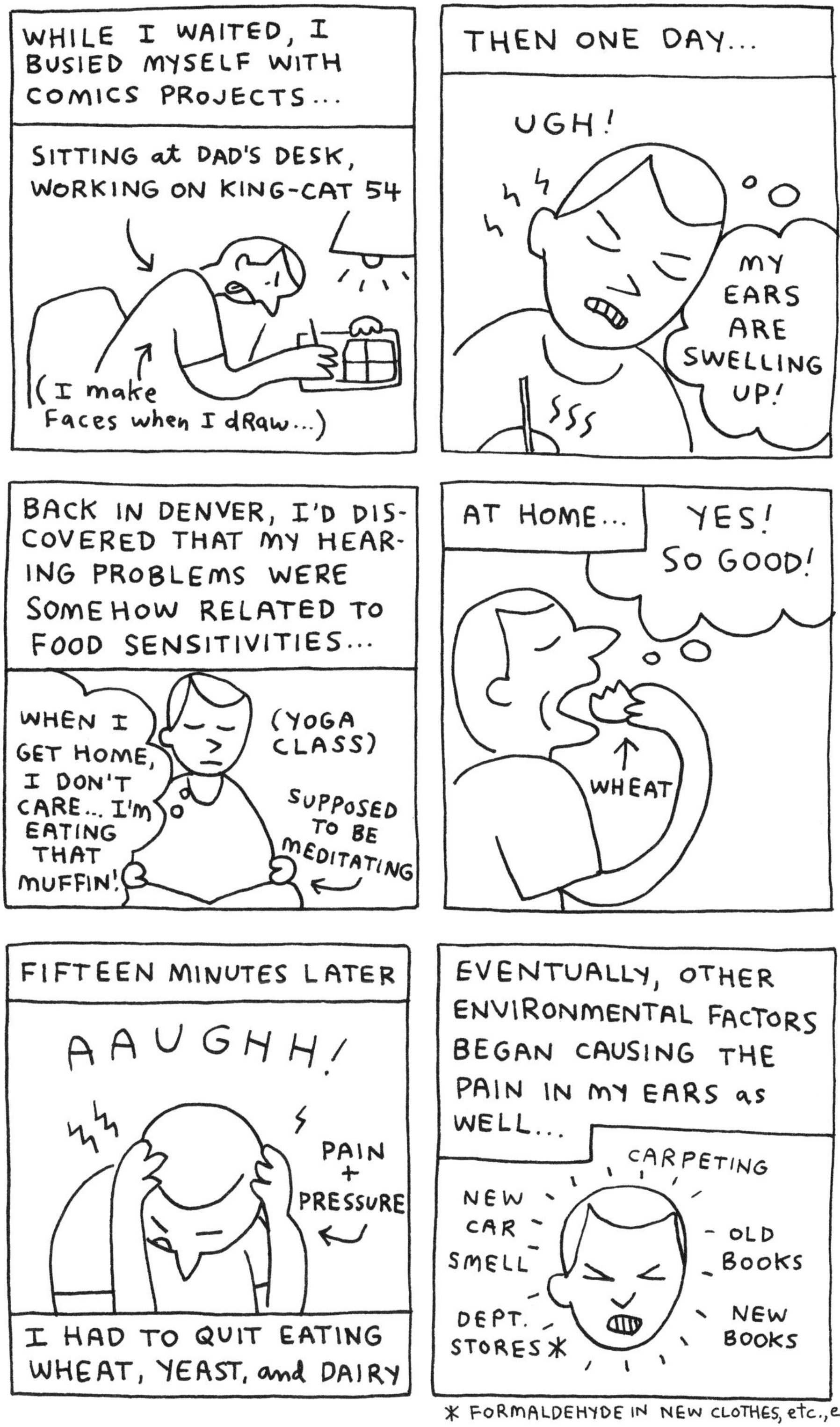
WHILE I WAITED, I BUSIED MYSELF WITH COMICS PROJECTS...
SITTING at DAD'S DESK, WORKING ON KING-CAT 54
(I make Faces when I dRaw...)
THEN ONE DAY...
UGH!
MY EARS ARE SWELLING UP!
BACK IN DENVER, I'D DISCOVERED THAT MY HEARING PROBLEMS WERE SOMEHOW RELATED TO FOOD SENSITIVITIES...
WHEN I GET HOME, I DON'T CARE... I'M EATING THAT MUFFIN!
(YOGA CLASS)
SUPPOSED TO BE MEDITATING
AT HOME...
YES! SO GOOD!
WHEAT
FIFTEEN MINUTES LATER
AAUGHH!
PAIN + PRESSURE
I HAD TO QUIT EATING WHEAT, YEAST, and DAIRY
EVENTUALLY, OTHER ENVIRONMENTAL FACTORS BEGAN CAUSING THE PAIN IN MY EARS as WELL...
CARPETING
NEW CAR SMELL
OLD BOOKS
DEPT. STORES*
NEW BOOKS

* FORMALDEHYDE IN NEW CLOTHES, etc., ed.

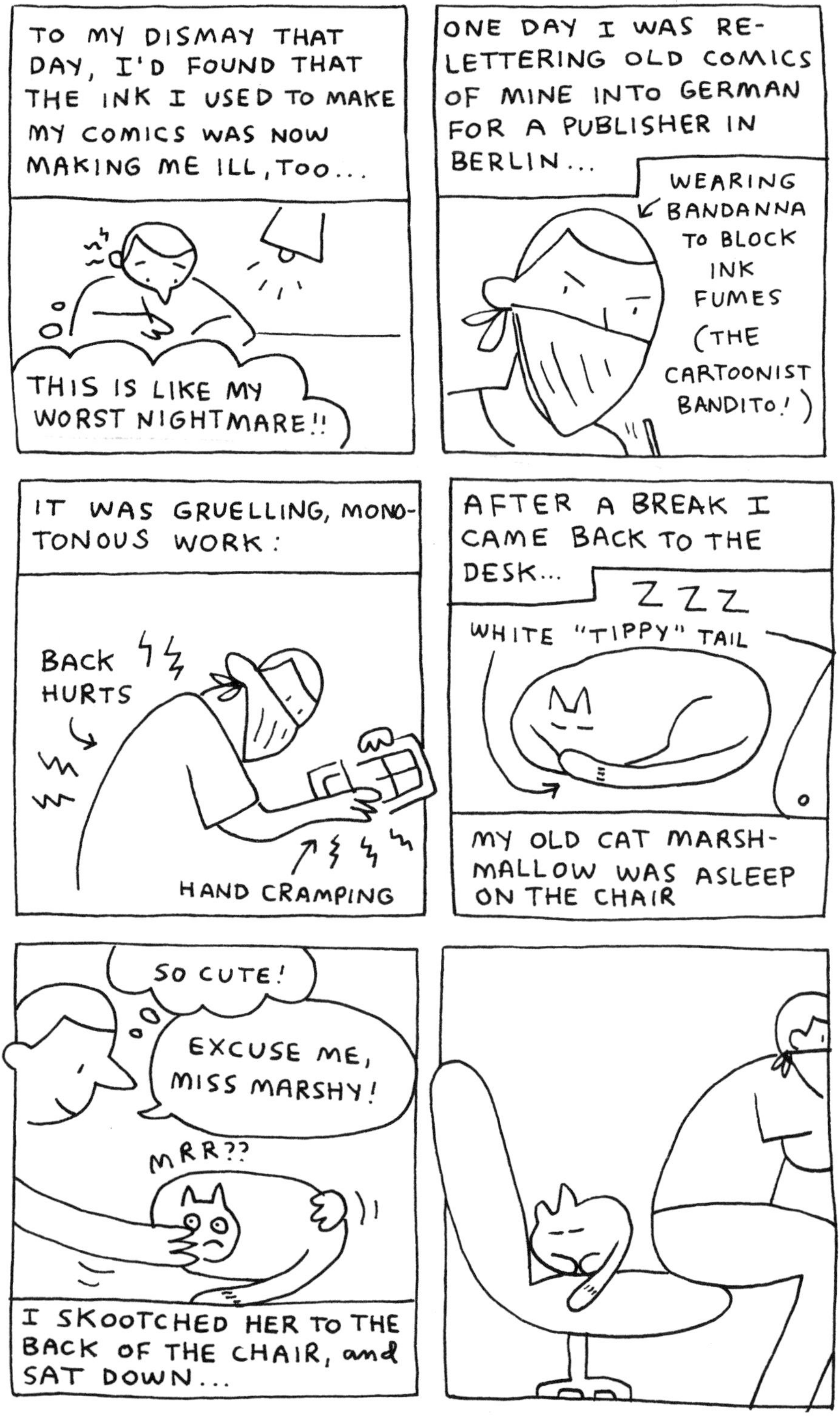
TO MY DISMAY THAT DAY, I'D FOUND THAT THE INK I USED TO MAKE MY COMICS WAS NOW MAKING ME ILL, TOO...
THIS IS LIKE MY WORST NIGHTMARE!!
ONE DAY I WAS RE-LETTERING OLD COMICS OF MINE INTO GERMAN FOR A PUBLISHER IN BERLIN...
WEARING BANDANNA TO BLOCK INK FUMES (THE CARTOONIST BANDITO!)
IT WAS GRUELLING, MONOTONOUS WORK:
BACK HURTS
HAND CRAMPING
AFTER A BREAK I CAME BACK TO THE DESK...
ZZZ
WHITE "TIPPY" TAIL
MY OLD CAT MARSHMALLOW WAS ASLEEP ON THE CHAIR
SO CUTE!
EXCUSE ME, MISS MARSHY!
MRR??
I SKOOTCHED HER TO THE BACK OF THE CHAIR, and SAT DOWN...

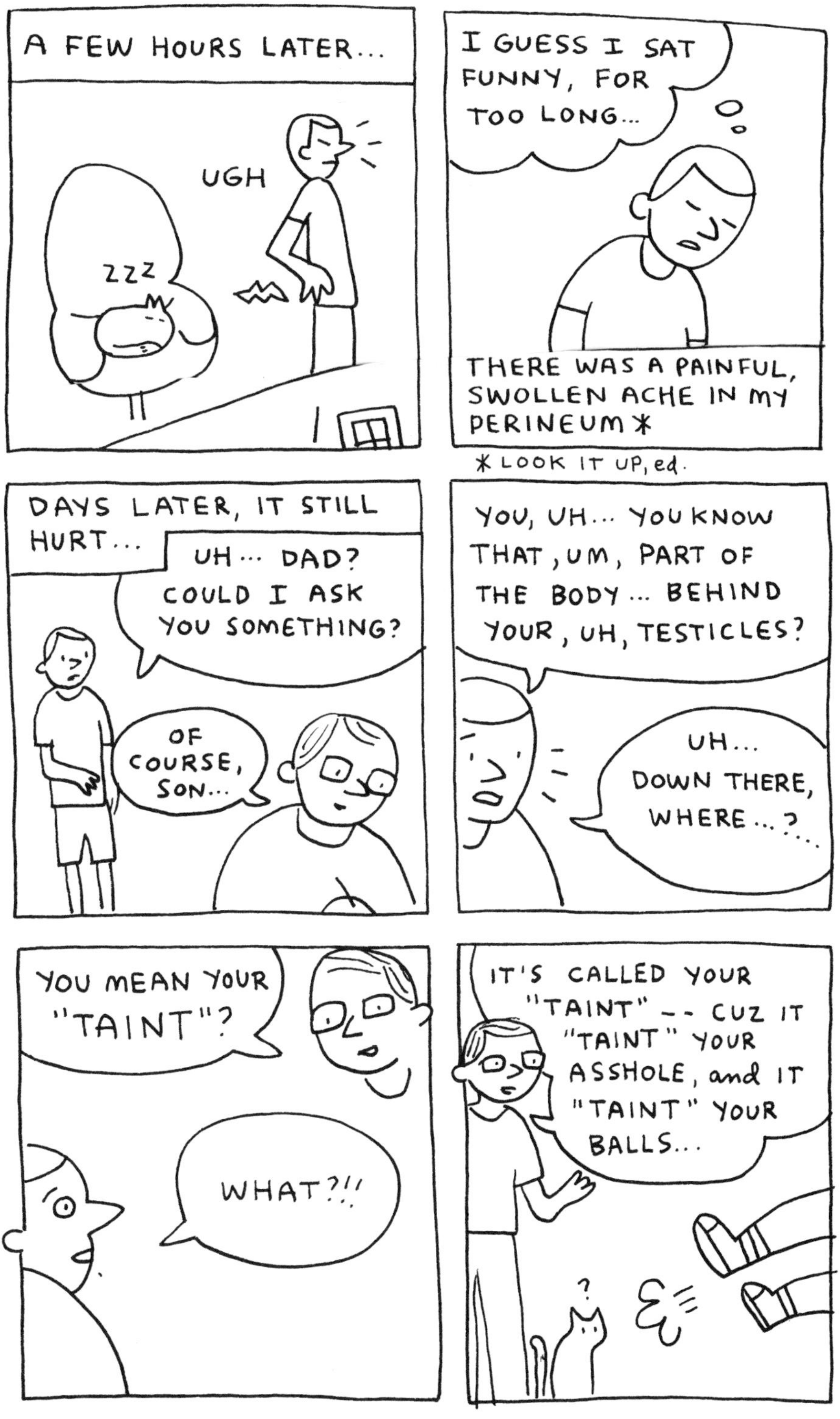
A FEW HOURS LATER...
UGH
ZZZ
I GUESS I SAT FUNNY, FOR TOO LONG...
THERE WAS A PAINFUL, SWOLLEN ACHE IN MY PERINEUM *
* LOOK IT UP, ed.
DAYS LATER, IT STILL HURT...
UH... DAD? COULD I ASK YOU SOMETHING?
OF COURSE, SON...
YOU, UH... YOU KNOW THAT, UM, PART OF THE BODY... BEHIND YOUR, UH, TESTICLES?
UH... DOWN THERE, WHERE...?
YOU MEAN YOUR "TAINT"?
WHAT?!!
IT'S CALLED YOUR "TAINT" -- CUZ IT "TAINT" YOUR ASSHOLE, and IT "TAINT" YOUR BALLS...
?

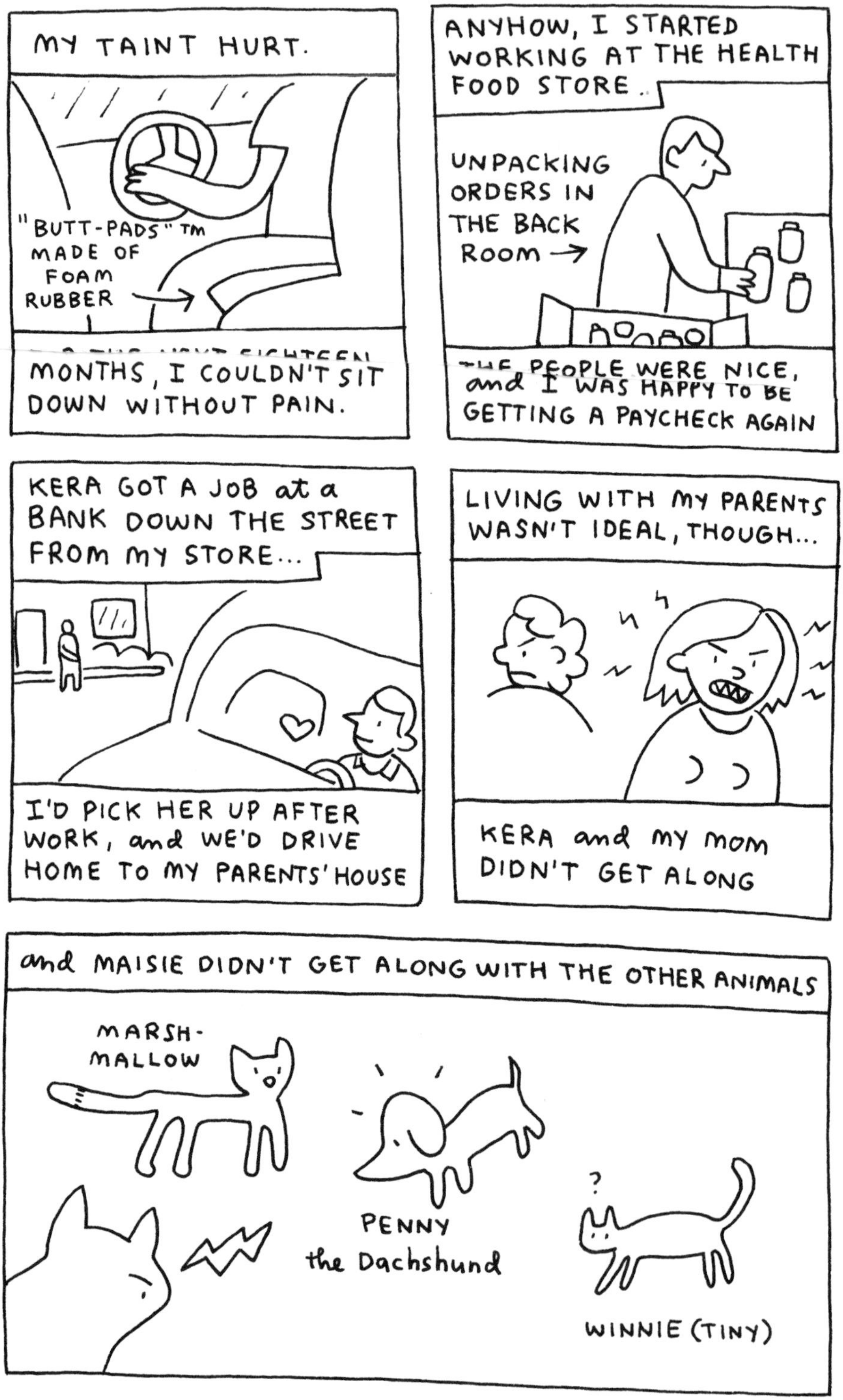
MY TAINT HURT.
"BUTT-PADS" TM MADE OF FOAM RUBBER
MONTHS, I COULDN'T SIT DOWN WITHOUT PAIN.
ANYHOW, I STARTED WORKING AT THE HEALTH FOOD STORE..
UNPACKING ORDERS IN THE BACK ROOM
THE PEOPLE WERE NICE,
and I WAS HAPPY TO BE GETTING A PAYCHECK AGAIN
KERA GOT A JOB at a BANK DOWN THE STREET FROM MY STORE...
I'D PICK HER UP AFTER WORK, and WE'D DRIVE HOME TO MY PARENTS' HOUSE
LIVING WITH MY PARENTS WASN'T IDEAL, THOUGH...
KERA and MY MOM DIDN'T GET ALONG
and MAISIE DIDN'T GET ALONG WITH THE OTHER ANIMALS
MARSH-MALLOW
PENNY the Dachshund
?
WINNIE (TINY)

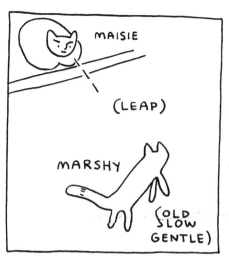

MAISIE

(LEAP)

MARSHY

(OLD SLOW GENTLE)

GOWL! SNAROO!

WE ENDED UP HAVING TO LOCK MAISIE IN OUR LITTLE GUEST ROOM all DAY...

OH KUKOC -- I'M SORRY... THIS IS ONLY TEMPORARY

PURR

I'D COME HOME EVERY DAY WITH MY EARS THRASHED OUT... WE'D EAT DINNER and SIT ON THE BACK PORCH

MY ILLNESSES HAD HUMBLED ME. I WAS JUST HAPPY TO BE THERE...

(SPRING)

and AFTER A FEW YEARS OF SOLITUDE, IT FELT GOOD TO BE OUT IN THE WORLD AGAIN...

PEOPLE ARE UNHAPPY BECAUSE THEY WANT THE THINGS THEY DON'T HAVE and DON'T WANT THE THINGS THEY DO HAVE...

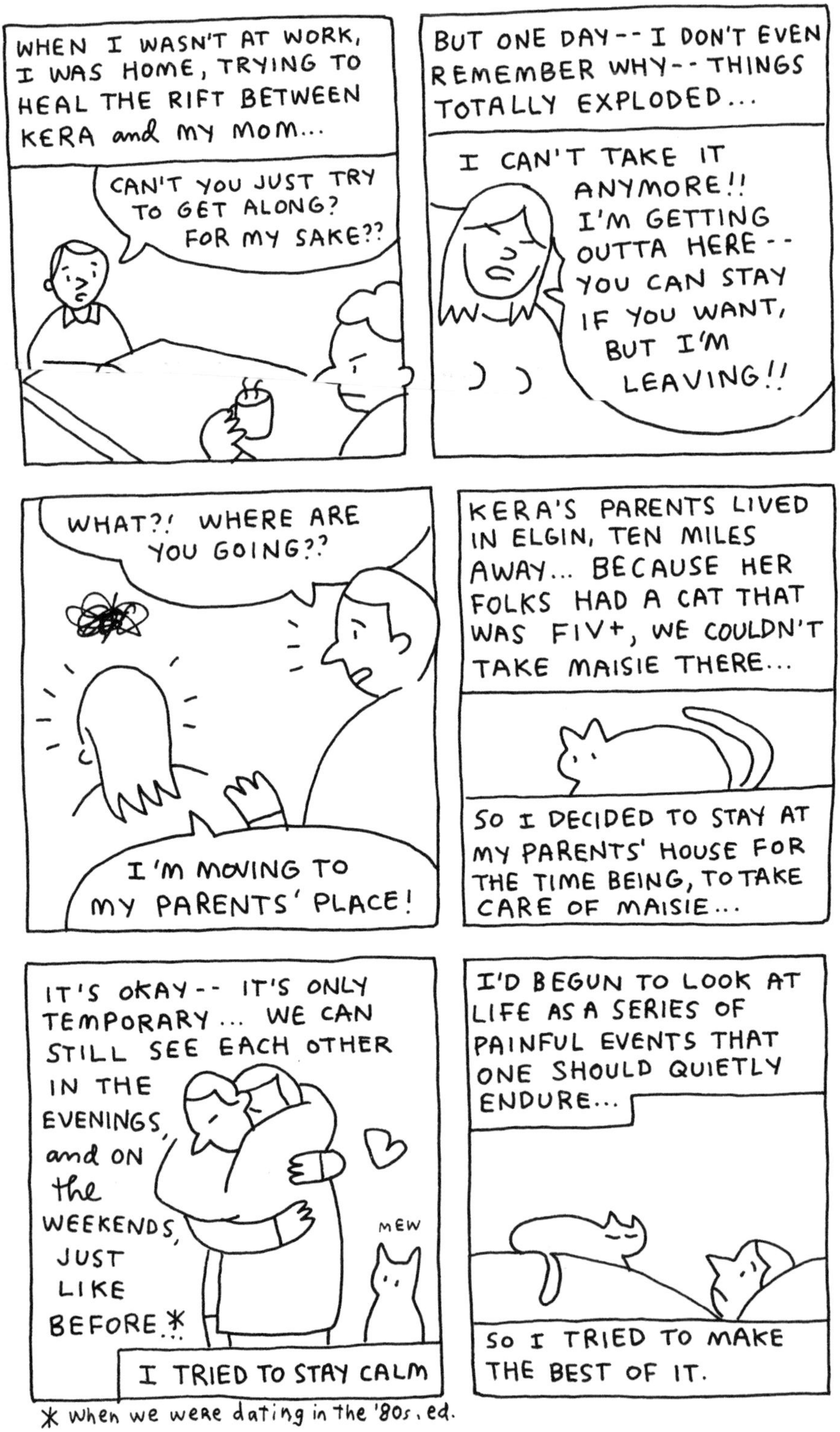
WHEN I WASN'T AT WORK, I WAS HOME, TRYING TO HEAL THE RIFT BETWEEN KERA and MY MOM...
CAN'T YOU JUST TRY TO GET ALONG? FOR MY SAKE??
BUT ONE DAY -- I DON'T EVEN REMEMBER WHY -- THINGS TOTALLY EXPLODED...
I CAN'T TAKE IT ANYMORE!! I'M GETTING OUTTA HERE -- YOU CAN STAY IF YOU WANT, BUT I'M LEAVING!!
WHAT?! WHERE ARE YOU GOING??
I'M MOVING TO MY PARENTS' PLACE!
KERA'S PARENTS LIVED IN ELGIN, TEN MILES AWAY... BECAUSE HER FOLKS HAD A CAT THAT WAS FIV+, WE COULDN'T TAKE MAISIE THERE...
SO I DECIDED TO STAY AT MY PARENTS' HOUSE FOR THE TIME BEING, TO TAKE CARE OF MAISIE...
IT'S OKAY -- IT'S ONLY TEMPORARY... WE CAN STILL SEE EACH OTHER IN THE EVENINGS, and ON the WEEKENDS, JUST LIKE BEFORE*...
MEW
I TRIED TO STAY CALM
I'D BEGUN TO LOOK AT LIFE AS A SERIES OF PAINFUL EVENTS THAT ONE SHOULD QUIETLY ENDURE...
SO I TRIED TO MAKE THE BEST OF IT.

* when we were dating in the '80s. ed.

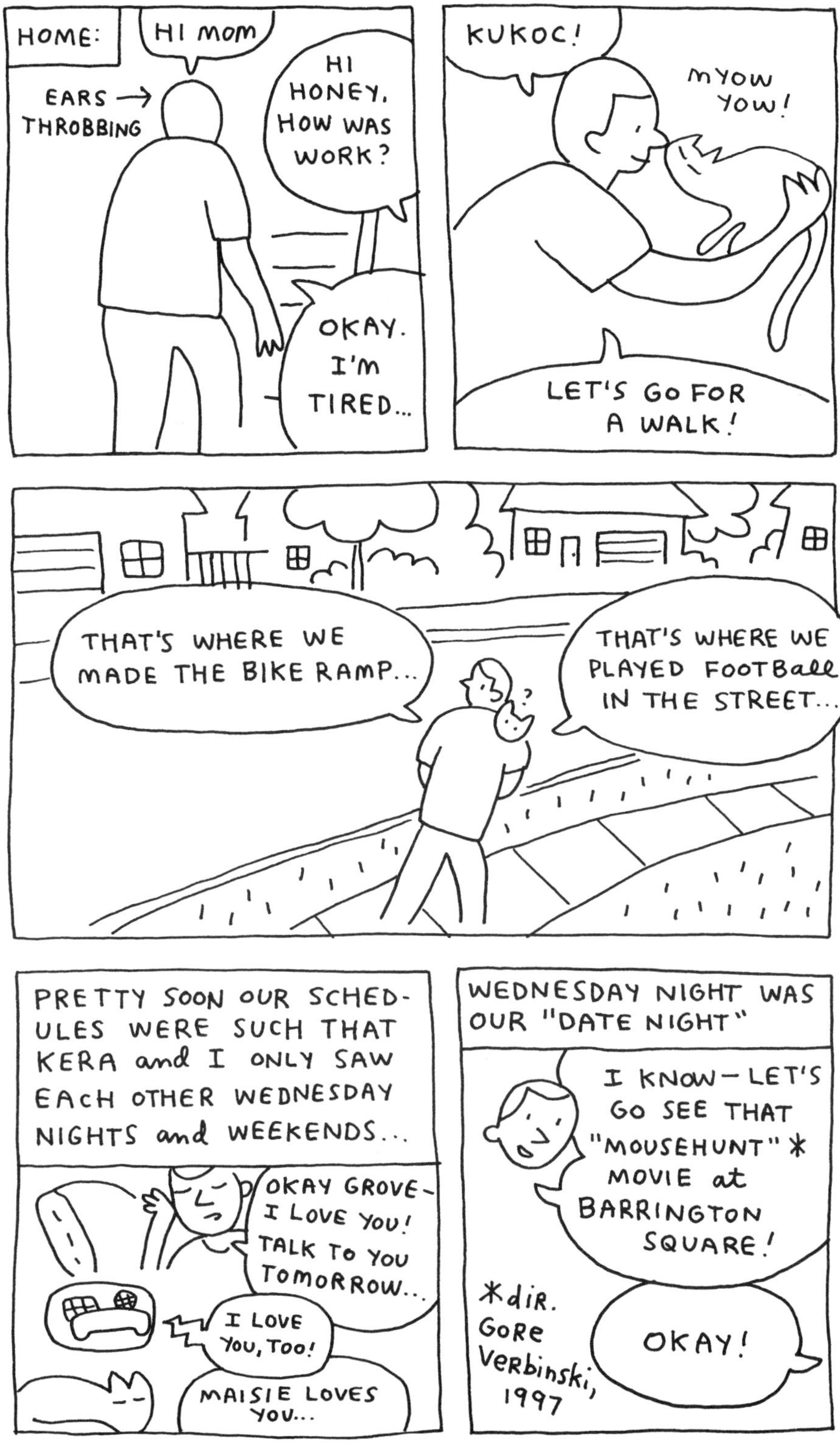
HOME:
HI MOM
EARS → THROBBING
HI HONEY. HOW WAS WORK?
OKAY. I'M TIRED...
KUKOC!
MYOW YOW!
LET'S GO FOR A WALK!
THAT'S WHERE WE MADE THE BIKE RAMP...
?
THAT'S WHERE WE PLAYED FOOTBALL IN THE STREET...
PRETTY SOON OUR SCHEDULES WERE SUCH THAT KERA and I ONLY SAW EACH OTHER WEDNESDAY NIGHTS and WEEKENDS...
OKAY GROVE- I LOVE YOU! TALK TO YOU TOMORROW...
I LOVE YOU, TOO!
MAISIE LOVES YOU...
WEDNESDAY NIGHT WAS OUR "DATE NIGHT"
I KNOW-LET'S GO SEE THAT "MOUSEHUNT"* MOVIE at BARRINGTON SQUARE!
*dir. Gore Verbinski, 1997
OKAY!

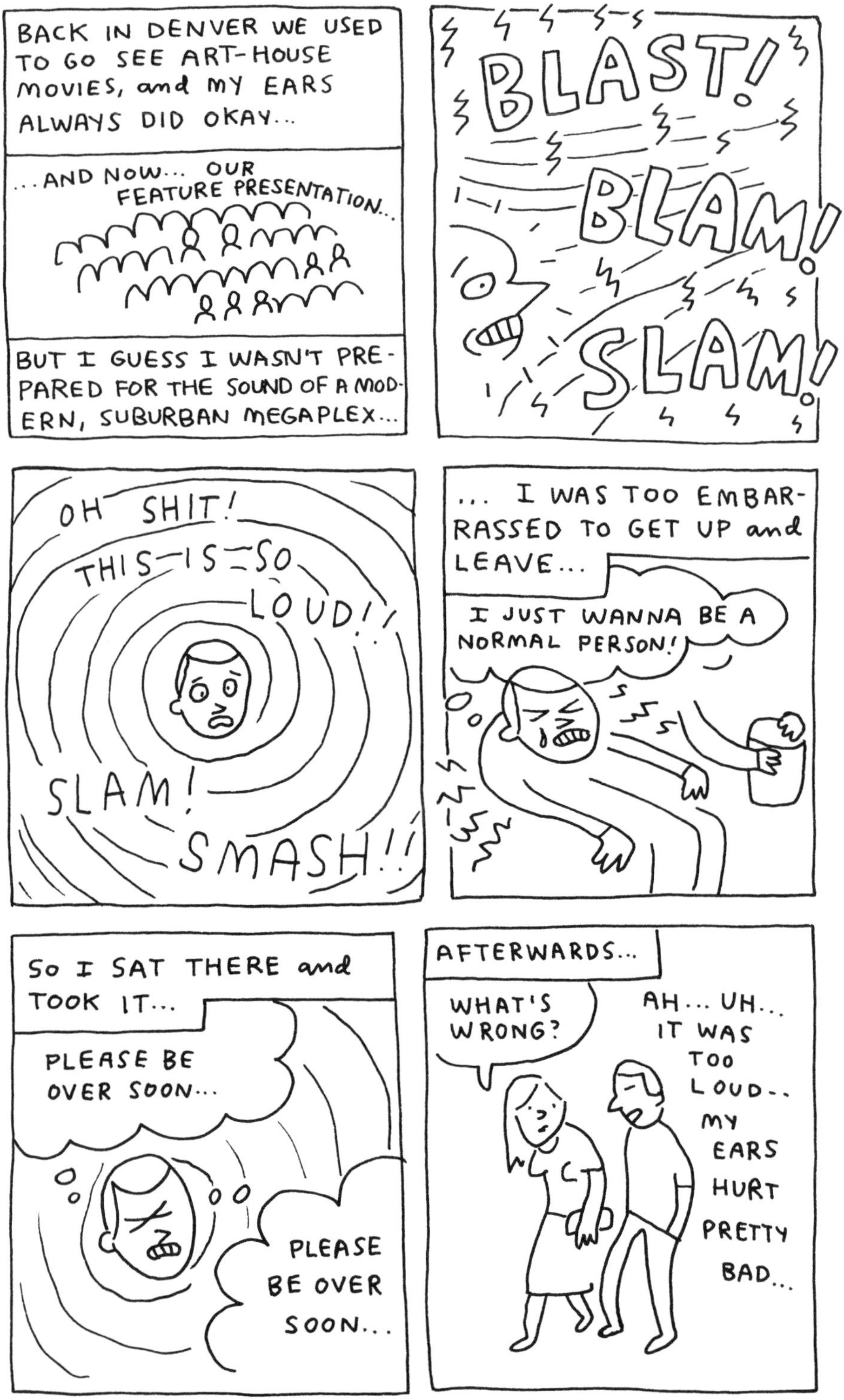
BACK IN DENVER WE USED TO GO SEE ART-HOUSE MOVIES, and MY EARS ALWAYS DID OKAY...
...AND NOW... OUR FEATURE PRESENTATION...
BUT I GUESS I WASN'T PREPARED FOR THE SOUND OF A MODERN, SUBURBAN MEGAPLEX...
BLAST!
BLAM!
SLAM!
OH SHIT! THIS IS SO LOUD!!
SLAM!
SMASH!!
... I WAS TOO EMBARRASSED TO GET UP and LEAVE...
I JUST WANNA BE A NORMAL PERSON!
So I SAT THERE and TOOK IT...
PLEASE BE OVER SOON...
PLEASE BE OVER SOON...
AFTERWARDS...
WHAT'S WRONG?
AH... UH... IT WAS TOO LOUD... MY EARS HURT PRETTY BAD...

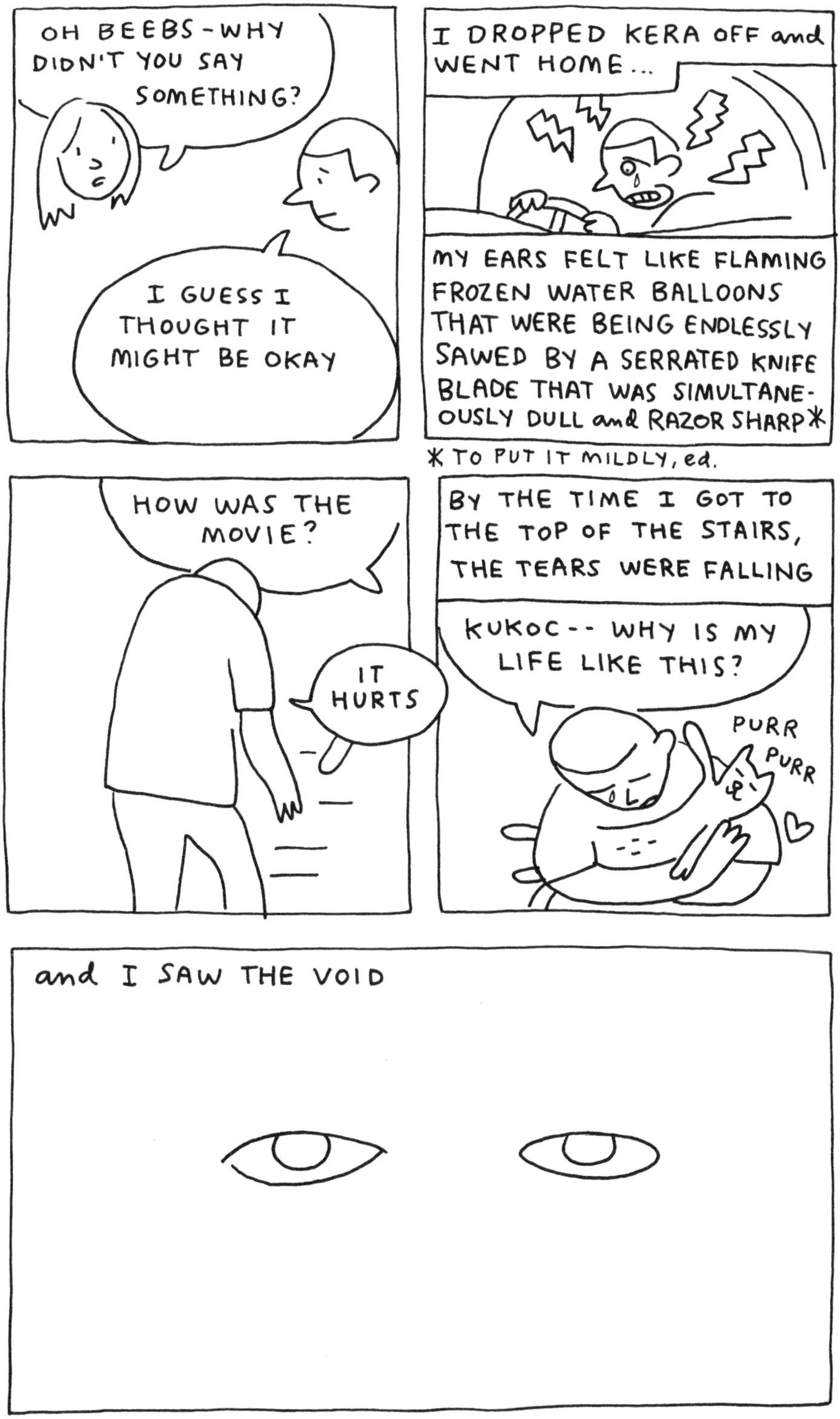

OH BEEBS - WHY DIDN'T YOU SAY SOMETHING?
I GUESS I THOUGHT IT MIGHT BE OKAY
I DROPPED KERA OFF and WENT HOME...
MY EARS FELT LIKE FLAMING FROZEN WATER BALLOONS THAT WERE BEING ENDLESSLY SAWED BY A SERRATED KNIFE BLADE THAT WAS SIMULTANE-OUSLY DULL and RAZOR SHARP*
* TO PUT IT MILDLY, ed.
HOW WAS THE MOVIE?
IT HURTS
BY THE TIME I GOT TO THE TOP OF THE STAIRS, THE TEARS WERE FALLING
KUKOC -- WHY IS MY LIFE LIKE THIS?
PURR
PURR
and I SAW THE VOID

THAT SPRING, MY HEALTH, WHICH HAD BEEN FAIRLY STABLE SINCE THE SURGERY, BEGAN TO TAKE A SERIOUS TURN FOR THE WORSE...

I'D LOST ABOUT 30 LBS DURING MY ILLNESS THE PREVIOUS SUMMER, and I'D NEVER BEEN ABLE TO GAIN THEM BACK, BUT NOW all OF A SUDDEN, I WAS GETTING EVEN THINNER...

FIRST I TURNED GREEN

THEN I TURNED ORANGE

I HAD INSURANCE NOW, SO I WENT TO SEE THE DOCTOR...

WELL... YOU'RE CERTAINLY VERY ORANGE!

THE BLOOD TESTS SHOW YOUR BETA-CAROTENE LEVELS ARE OFF THE CHARTS!

PERHAPS THIS IS WHY YOU'RE ORANGE...

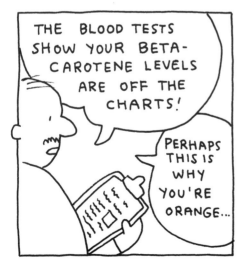

BETA-CAROTENE IS A VITAMIN A PRECURSOR, RIGHT? DO YOU KNOW WHAT ORGAN CONVERTS BETA-CAROTENE TO VITAMIN A? THAT MIGHT BE A CLUE...

NO.

I WENT HOME and LOOKED IT UP. IT WAS THE LIVER.

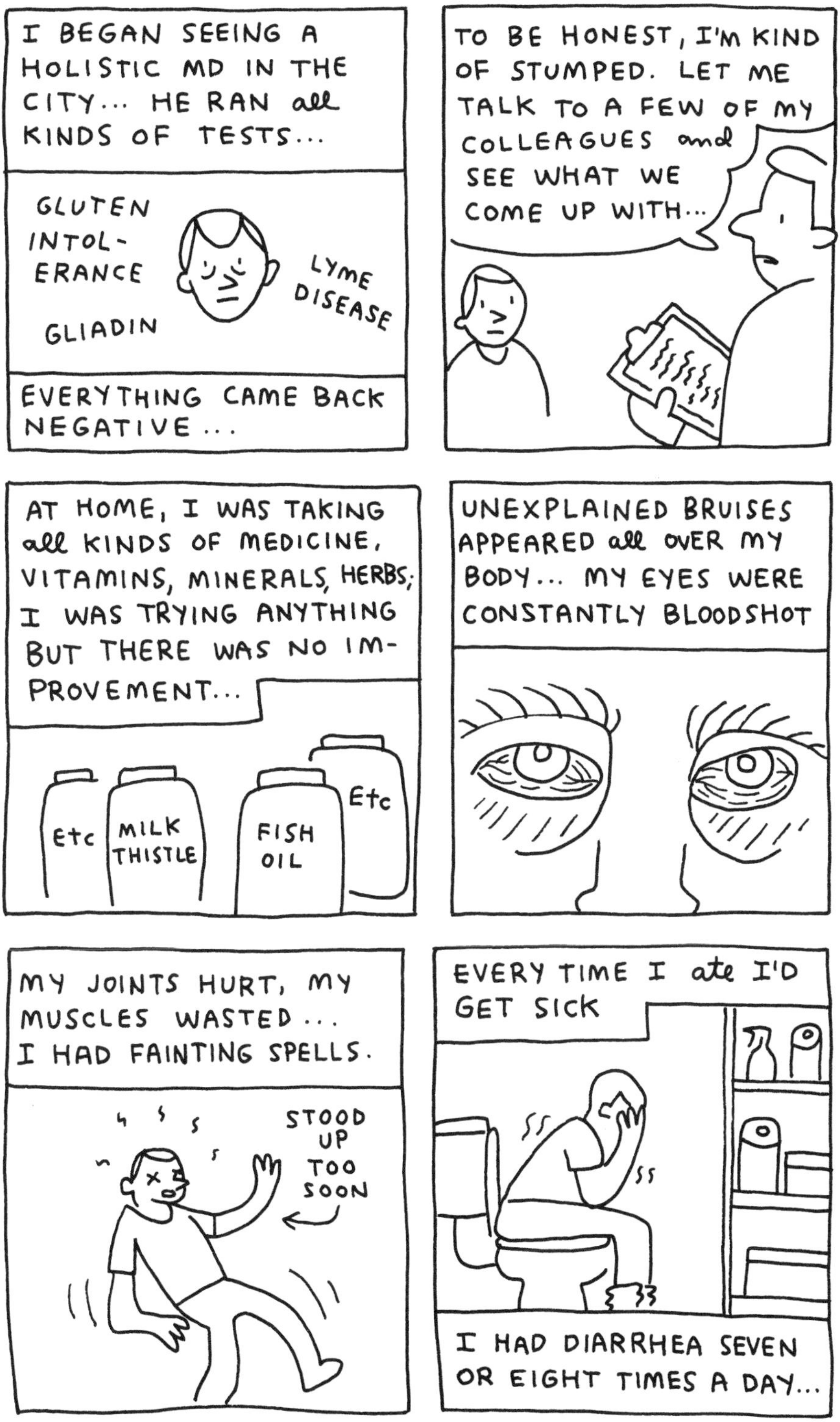
I BEGAN SEEING A HOLISTIC MD IN THE CITY... HE RAN all KINDS OF TESTS...
GLUTEN INTOL-ERANCE
LYME DISEASE
GLIADIN
EVERYTHING CAME BACK NEGATIVE...
TO BE HONEST, I'M KIND OF STUMPED. LET ME TALK TO A FEW OF MY COLLEAGUES and SEE WHAT WE COME UP WITH...
AT HOME, I WAS TAKING all KINDS OF MEDICINE, VITAMINS, MINERALS, HERBS; I WAS TRYING ANYTHING BUT THERE WAS NO IM-PROVEMENT...
Etc
MILK THISTLE
FISH OIL
Etc
UNEXPLAINED BRUISES APPEARED all OVER MY BODY... MY EYES WERE CONSTANTLY BLOODSHOT
MY JOINTS HURT, MY MUSCLES WASTED... I HAD FAINTING SPELLS.
STOOD UP TOO SOON
EVERY TIME I ate I'D GET SICK
I HAD DIARRHEA SEVEN OR EIGHT TIMES A DAY...

WHEN I PICKED UP BOXES at WORK, I RAN THE RISK OF SHITTING MY PANTS...

... and THEN MY EYE-LASHES FELL OUT.

THE DOCTORS I WAS SEEING WERE COMPLETELY BAFFLED... IT OCCURRED TO ME THAT MAYBE I WAS DYING.

...

BUT IN THE MIDST OF all this, I FELT A STRANGE PEACE. IN A WEIRD WAY, I LOOKED FORWARD WITH CURIOSITY TO WHAT WOULD COME NEXT. IF IT WAS MY TIME TO DIE, THEN I WAS OKAY WITH IT.

"IF YOU DIE, JUST DIE." *

* SOYEN SHAKU (1860-1919)

I ONLY HOPED I'D LIVE LONG ENOUGH TO SEE MY BEARS PLAY IN THE Fall...

Part Two

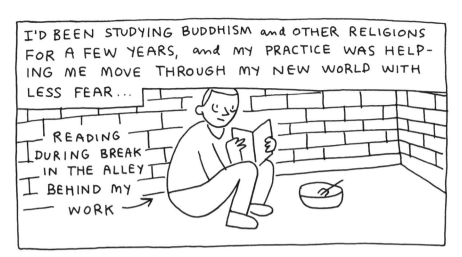

I'D BEEN STUDYING BUDDHISM and OTHER RELIGIONS FOR A FEW YEARS, and MY PRACTICE WAS HELPING ME MOVE THROUGH MY NEW WORLD WITH LESS FEAR...

READING DURING BREAK IN THE ALLEY BEHIND MY WORK →

EVERYWHERE I LOOKED, I SAW BUDDHADHARMA, DIVINITY, GOD'S HAND...

WE EXIST TO REFLECT EACH OTHER...

BUT I WAS ALSO GETTING KIND OF UNNATURALLY MORALISTIC — I WORRIED CONSTANTLY THAT I WOULD SAY OR DO THE WRONG THING...

and I STARTED HAVING WEIRD THOUGHTS ABOUT GOD...

GOD IS SYSTEMATICALLY TAKING all the THINGS I LOVED AWAY FROM ME... FIRST MY EARS WENT BAD, and I COULDN'T PLAY MUSIC; THEN MY PROSTATE WENT BAD, and I COULDN'T HAVE SEX; THEN MY ALLERGIES STARTED, and I COULDN'T EAT FOOD... NEXT I SUPPOSE I'LL LOSE MY WIFE...

BASURA   TRASH ONLY

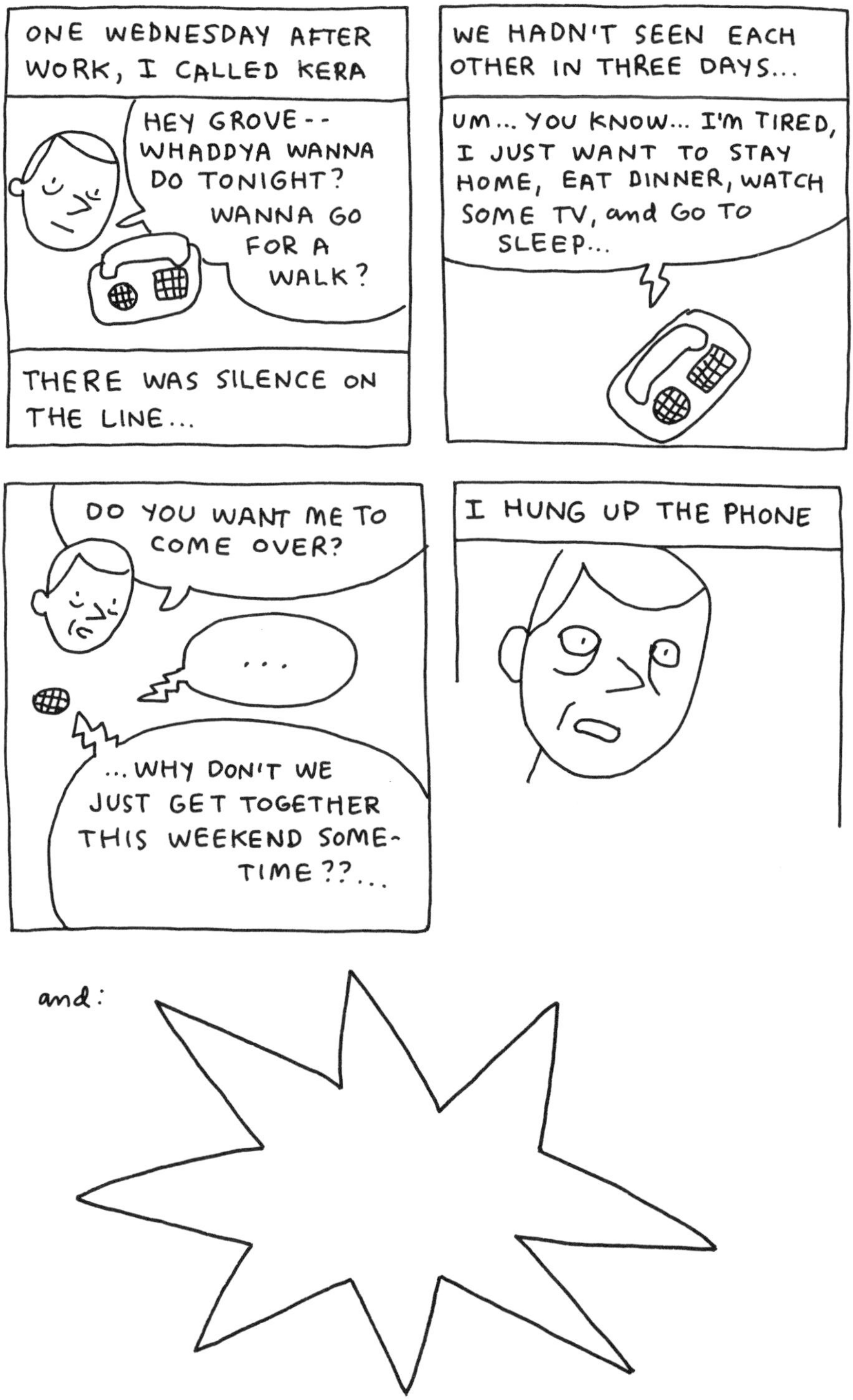
ONE WEDNESDAY AFTER WORK, I CALLED KERA
HEY GROVE-- WHADDYA WANNA DO TONIGHT? WANNA GO FOR A WALK?
THERE WAS SILENCE ON THE LINE...
WE HADN'T SEEN EACH OTHER IN THREE DAYS...
UM... YOU KNOW... I'M TIRED, I JUST WANT TO STAY HOME, EAT DINNER, WATCH SOME TV, and GO TO SLEEP...
DO YOU WANT ME TO COME OVER?
...
...WHY DON'T WE JUST GET TOGETHER THIS WEEKEND SOME-TIME??...
I HUNG UP THE PHONE
and:

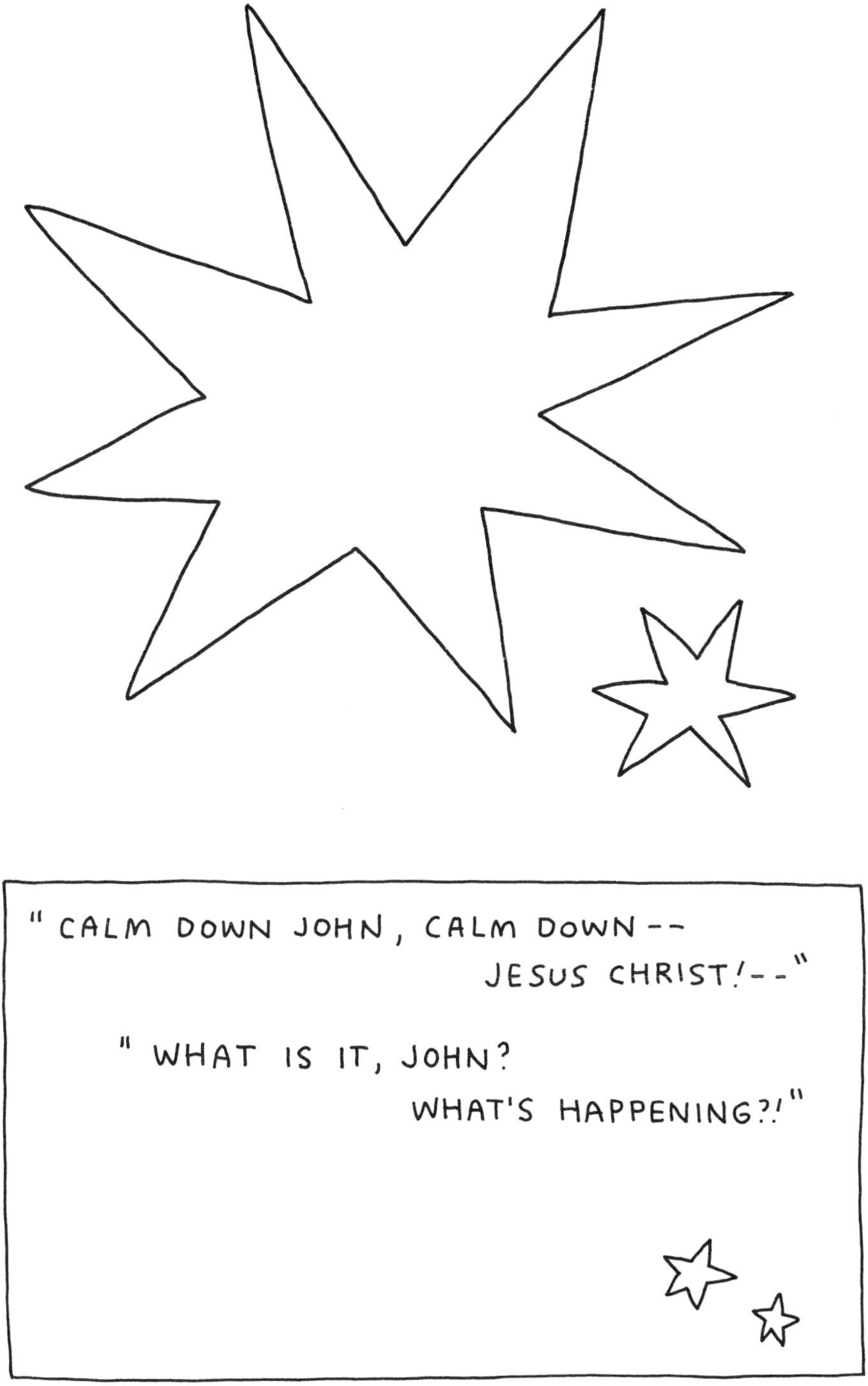
" CALM DOWN JOHN, CALM DOWN --
JESUS CHRIST!--"
" WHAT IS IT, JOHN?
WHAT'S HAPPENING?!"

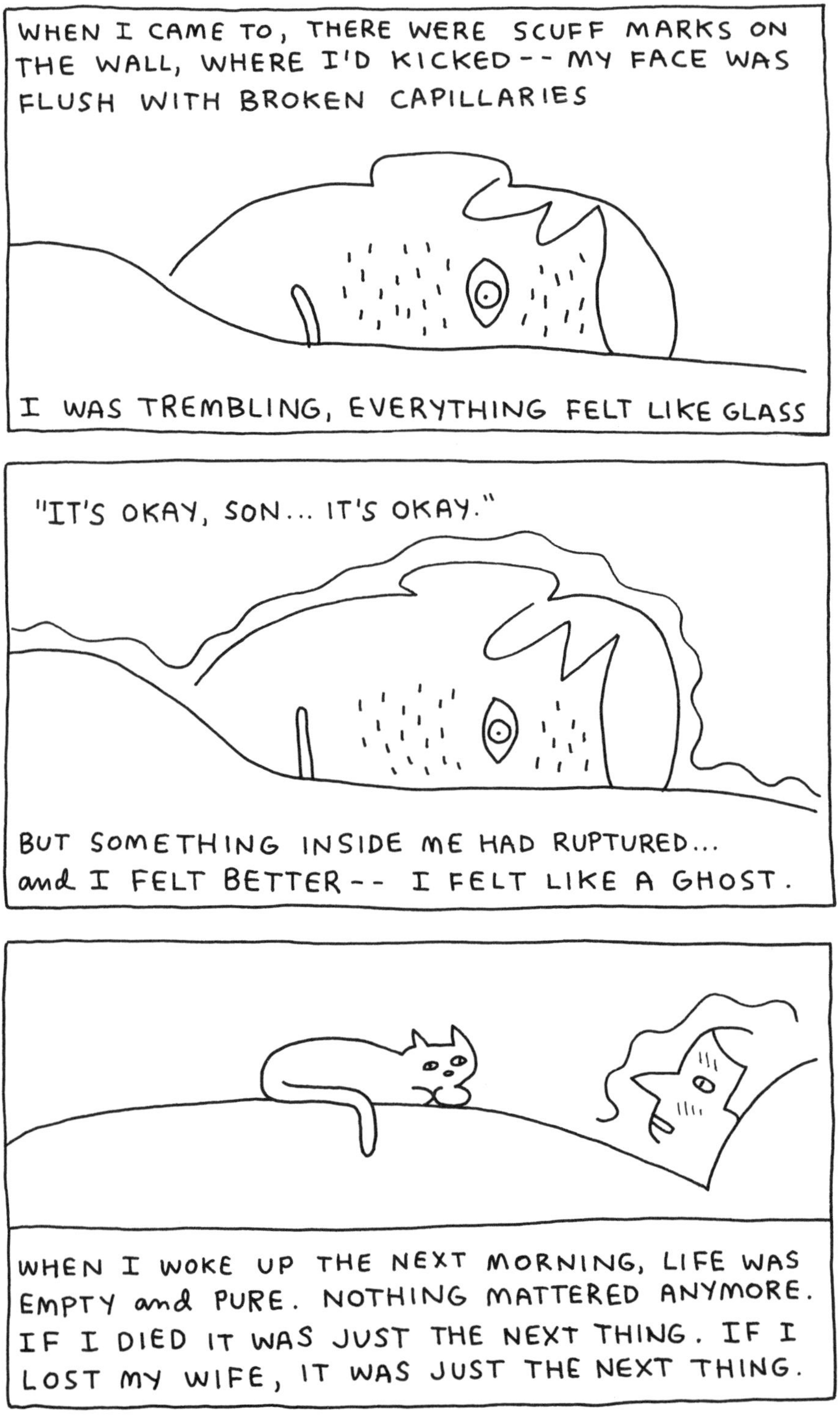
WHEN I CAME TO, THERE WERE SCUFF MARKS ON THE WALL, WHERE I'D KICKED-- MY FACE WAS FLUSH WITH BROKEN CAPILLARIES
I WAS TREMBLING, EVERYTHING FELT LIKE GLASS
"IT'S OKAY, SON... IT'S OKAY."
BUT SOMETHING INSIDE ME HAD RUPTURED... and I FELT BETTER-- I FELT LIKE A GHOST.
WHEN I WOKE UP THE NEXT MORNING, LIFE WAS EMPTY and PURE. NOTHING MATTERED ANYMORE. IF I DIED IT WAS JUST THE NEXT THING. IF I LOST MY WIFE, IT WAS JUST THE NEXT THING.

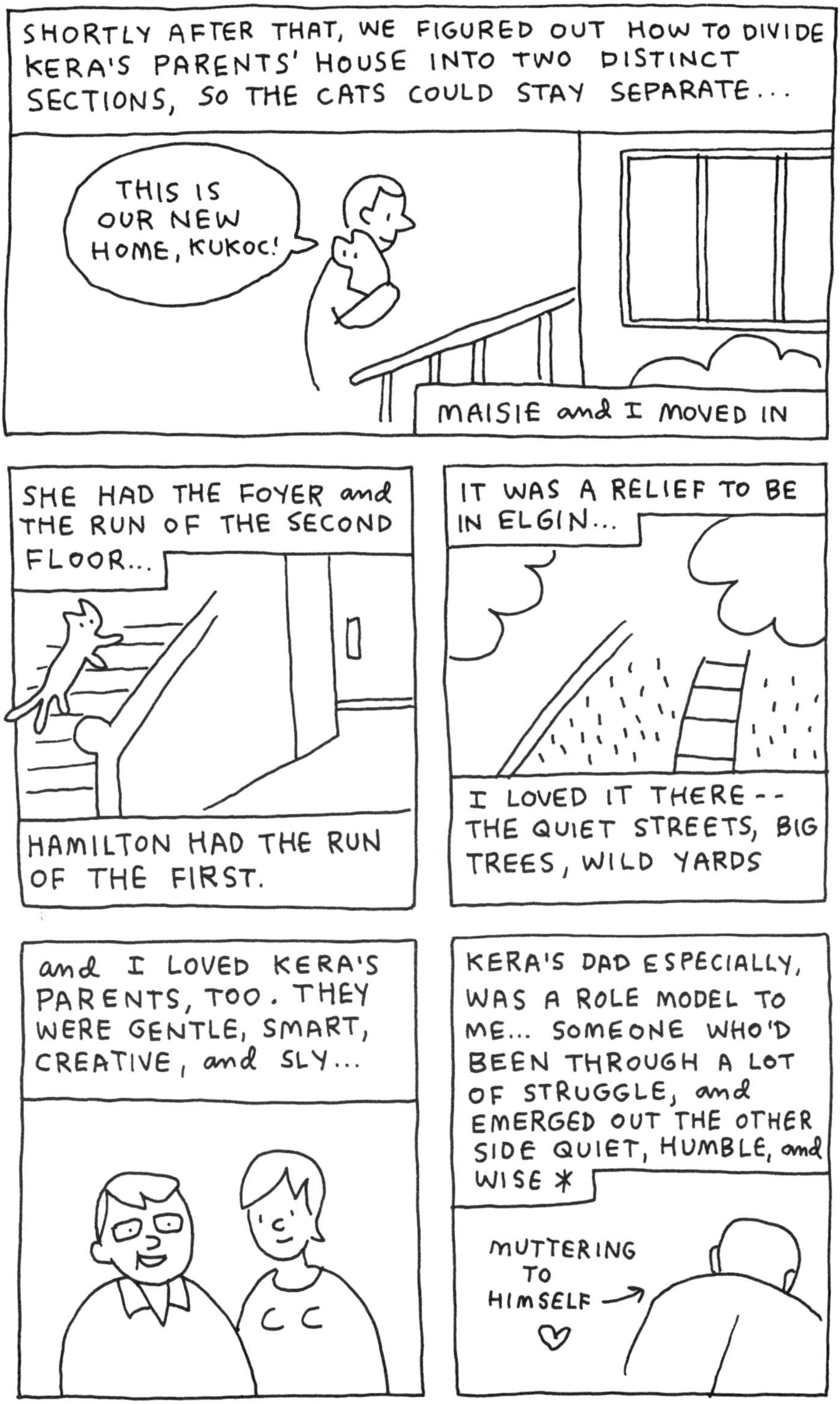
SHORTLY AFTER THAT, WE FIGURED OUT HOW TO DIVIDE KERA'S PARENTS' HOUSE INTO TWO DISTINCT SECTIONS, SO THE CATS COULD STAY SEPARATE...
THIS IS OUR NEW HOME, KUKOC!
MAISIE and I MOVED IN
SHE HAD THE FOYER and THE RUN OF THE SECOND FLOOR...
HAMILTON HAD THE RUN OF THE FIRST.
IT WAS A RELIEF TO BE IN ELGIN...
I LOVED IT THERE-- THE QUIET STREETS, BIG TREES, WILD YARDS
and I LOVED KERA'S PARENTS, TOO. THEY WERE GENTLE, SMART, CREATIVE, and SLY...
C C
KERA'S DAD ESPECIALLY, WAS A ROLE MODEL TO ME... SOMEONE WHO'D BEEN THROUGH A LOT OF STRUGGLE, and EMERGED OUT THE OTHER SIDE QUIET, HUMBLE, and WISE *
MUTTERING TO HIMSELF

*SEE: "A POEM FOR ED," KC 57

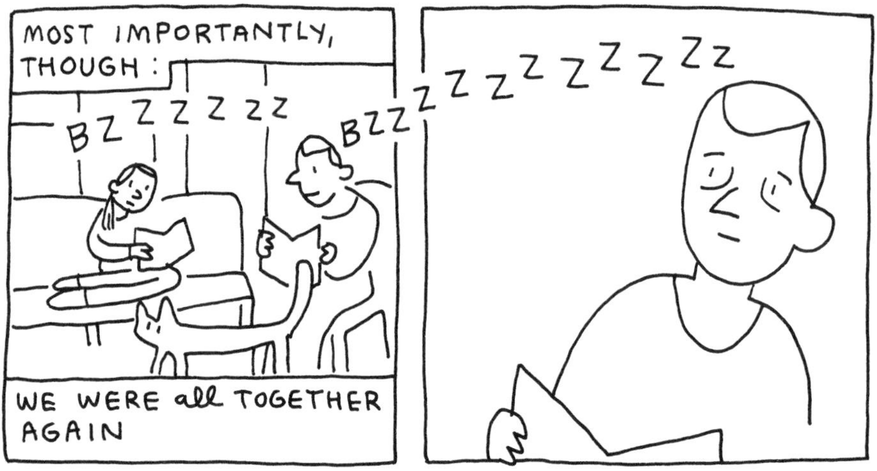
MOST IMPORTANTLY, THOUGH:
BZZZZZZ
WE WERE all TOGETHER AGAIN
BZZZZZZZZZZZ

"CICADAS BURST FORTH
and I RUN FROM THE SOUND.

SEVENTEEN YEARS THEY WAITED--

and SO I WAIT, TOO"

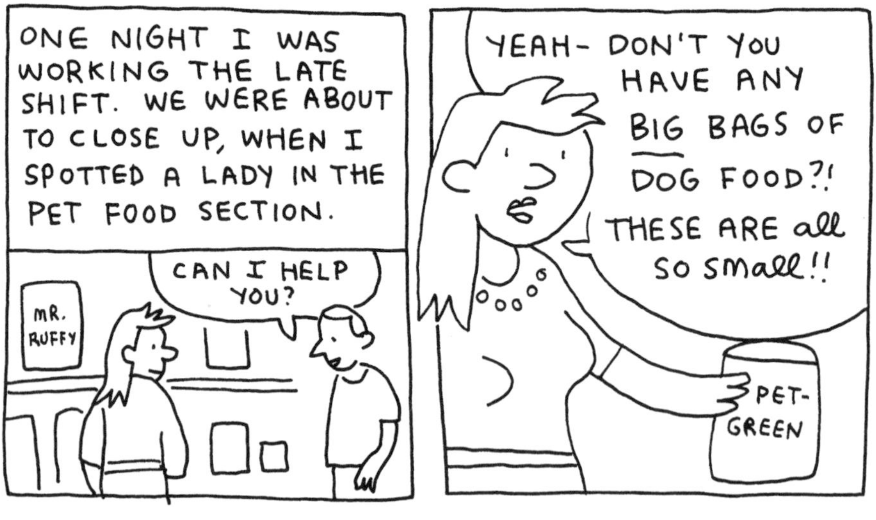
ONE NIGHT I WAS WORKING THE LATE SHIFT. WE WERE ABOUT TO CLOSE UP, WHEN I SPOTTED A LADY IN THE PET FOOD SECTION.
MR. RUFFY
CAN I HELP YOU?
YEAH- DON'T YOU HAVE ANY BIG BAGS OF DOG FOOD?! THESE ARE all SO small!!
PET-GREEN

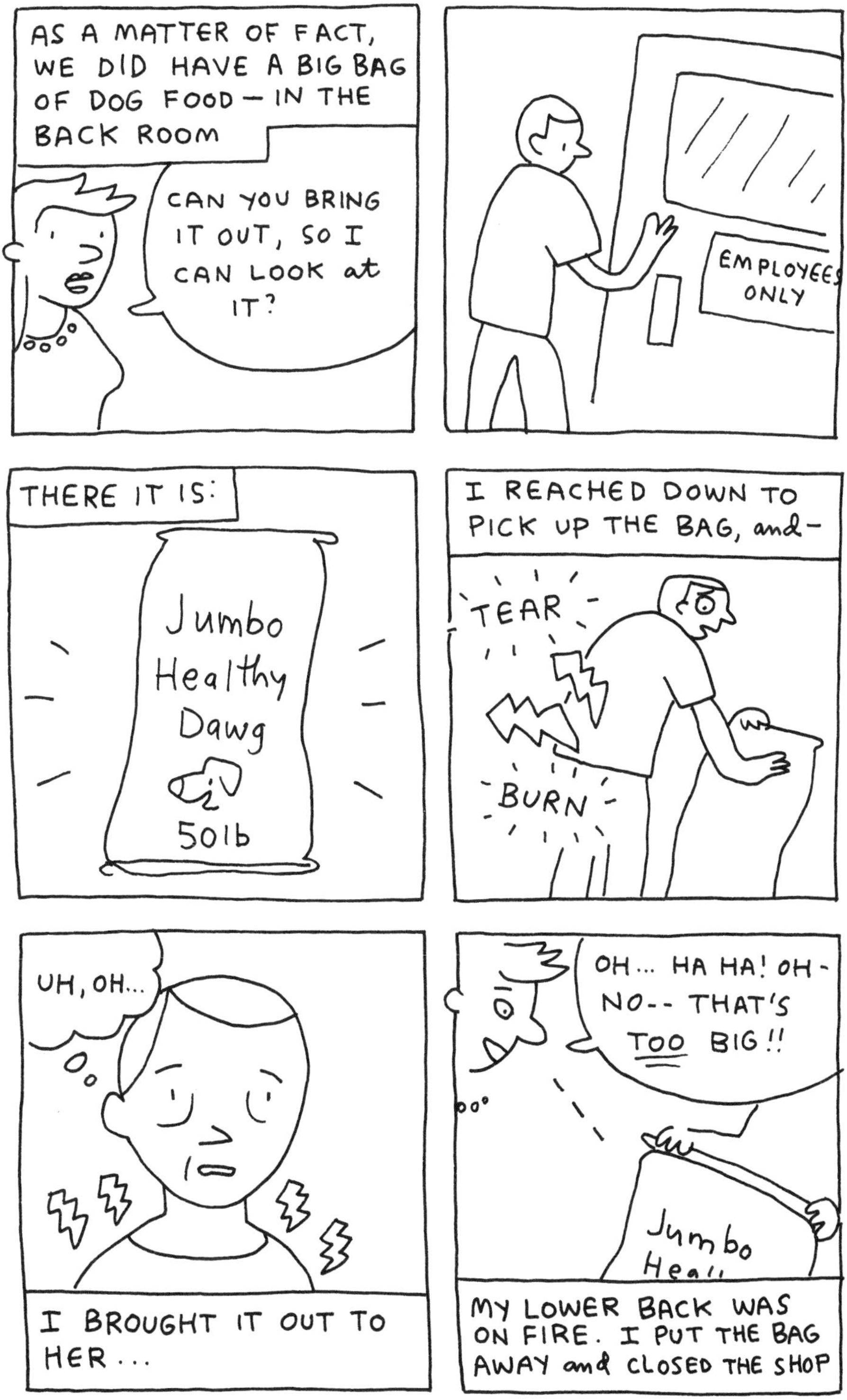
AS A MATTER OF FACT, WE DID HAVE A BIG BAG OF DOG FOOD — IN THE BACK ROOM
CAN YOU BRING IT OUT, SO I CAN LOOK at IT?
EMPLOYEES ONLY
THERE IT IS:
Jumbo Healthy Dawg 50lb
I REACHED DOWN TO PICK UP THE BAG, and—
TEAR
BURN
UH, OH...
I BROUGHT IT OUT TO HER...
OH... HA HA! OH- NO-- THAT'S TOO BIG!!
Jumbo Hea
MY LOWER BACK WAS ON FIRE. I PUT THE BAG AWAY and CLOSED THE SHOP

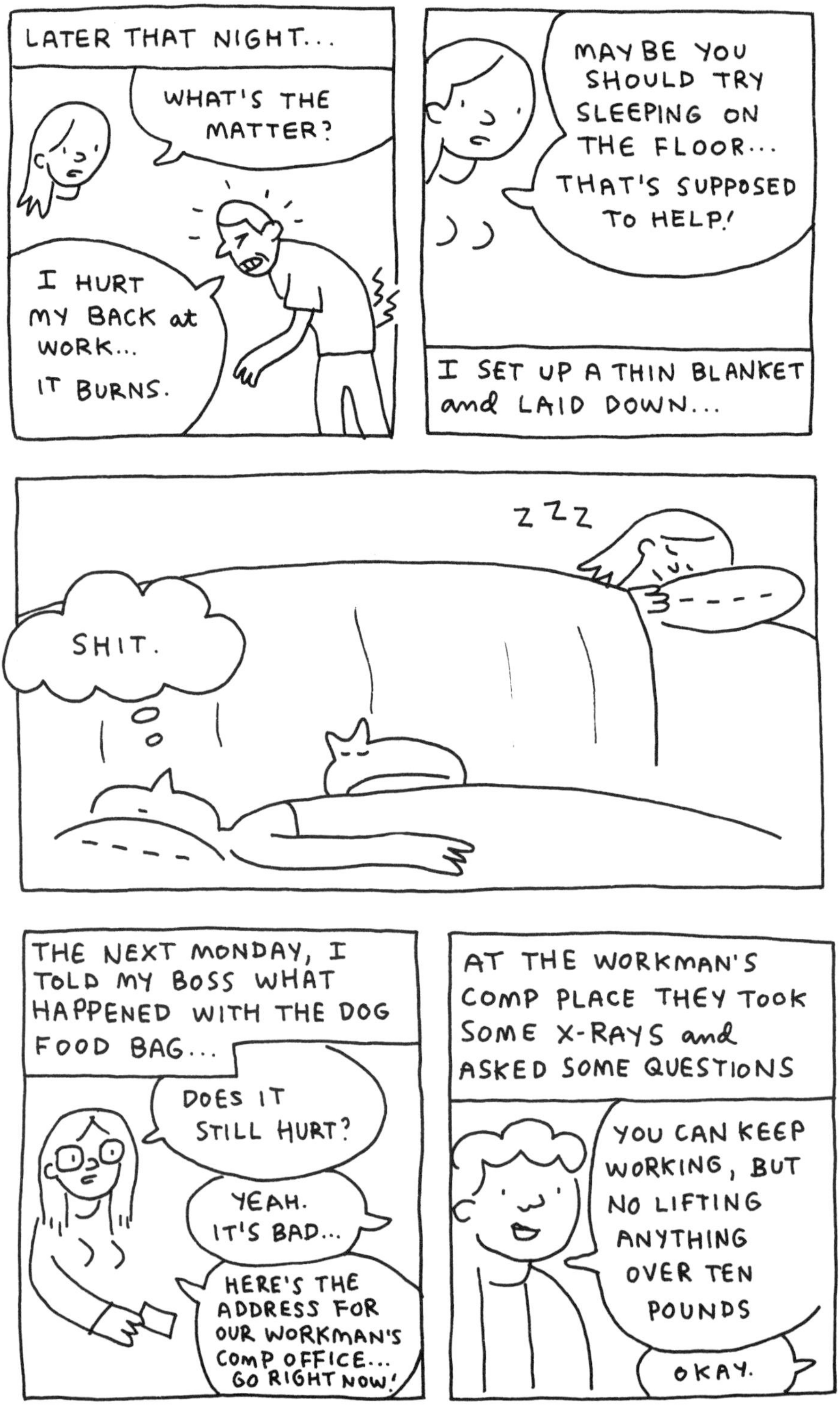
LATER THAT NIGHT...
WHAT'S THE MATTER?
I HURT MY BACK at WORK... IT BURNS.
MAYBE YOU SHOULD TRY SLEEPING ON THE FLOOR... THAT'S SUPPOSED TO HELP!
I SET UP A THIN BLANKET and LAID DOWN...
ZZZ
SHIT.
THE NEXT MONDAY, I TOLD MY BOSS WHAT HAPPENED WITH THE DOG FOOD BAG...
DOES IT STILL HURT?
YEAH. IT'S BAD...
HERE'S THE ADDRESS FOR OUR WORKMAN'S COMP OFFICE... GO RIGHT NOW!
AT THE WORKMAN'S COMP PLACE THEY TOOK SOME X-RAYS and ASKED SOME QUESTIONS
YOU CAN KEEP WORKING, BUT NO LIFTING ANYTHING OVER TEN POUNDS
OKAY.

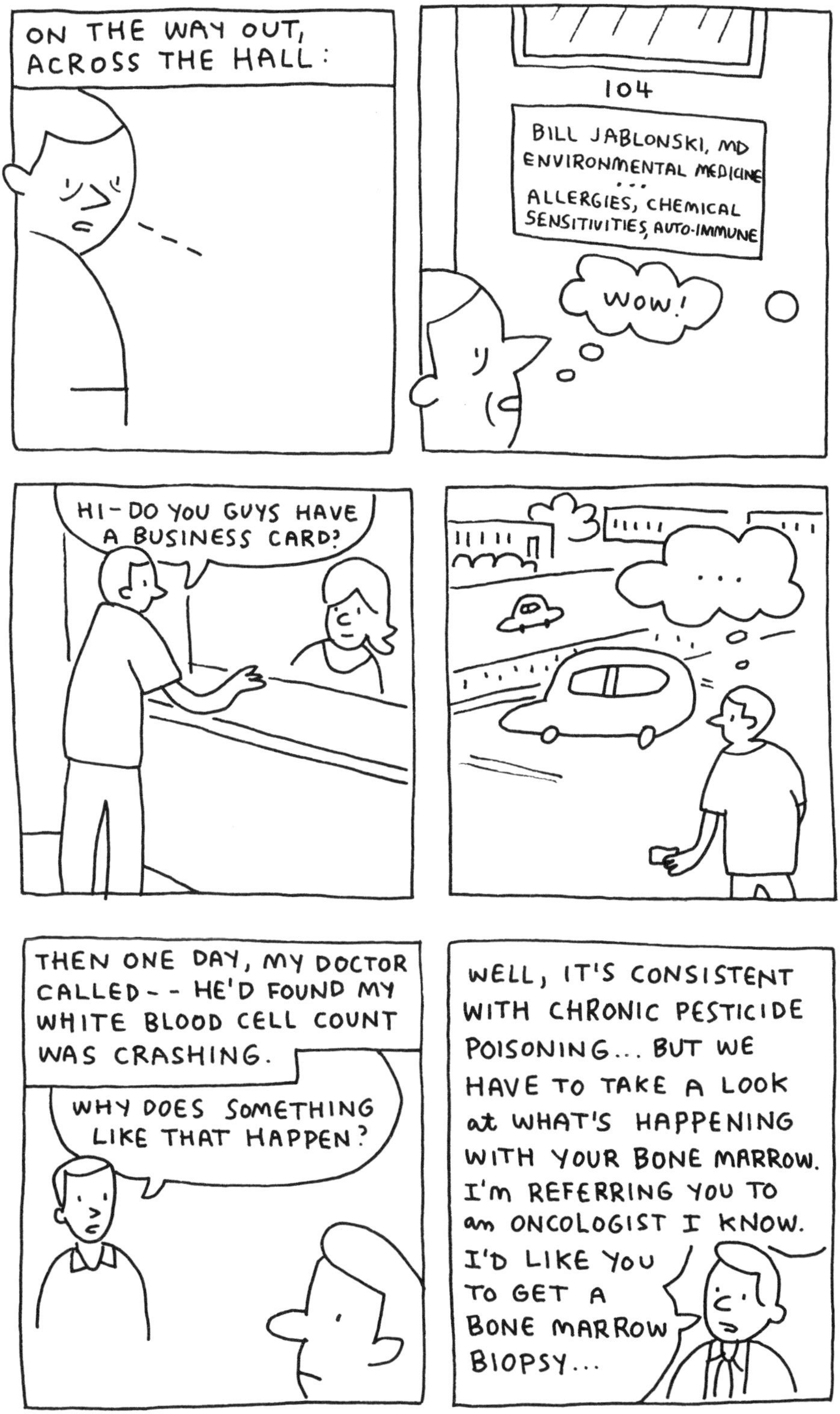
ON THE WAY OUT, ACROSS THE HALL:
104
BILL JABLONSKI, MD
ENVIRONMENTAL MEDICINE
...
ALLERGIES, CHEMICAL SENSITIVITIES, AUTO-IMMUNE
WOW!
HI- DO YOU GUYS HAVE A BUSINESS CARD?
...
THEN ONE DAY, MY DOCTOR CALLED-- HE'D FOUND MY WHITE BLOOD CELL COUNT WAS CRASHING.
WHY DOES SOMETHING LIKE THAT HAPPEN?
WELL, IT'S CONSISTENT WITH CHRONIC PESTICIDE POISONING... BUT WE HAVE TO TAKE A LOOK at WHAT'S HAPPENING WITH YOUR BONE MARROW. I'm REFERRING YOU TO an ONCOLOGIST I KNOW. I'D LIKE YOU TO GET A BONE MARROW BIOPSY...

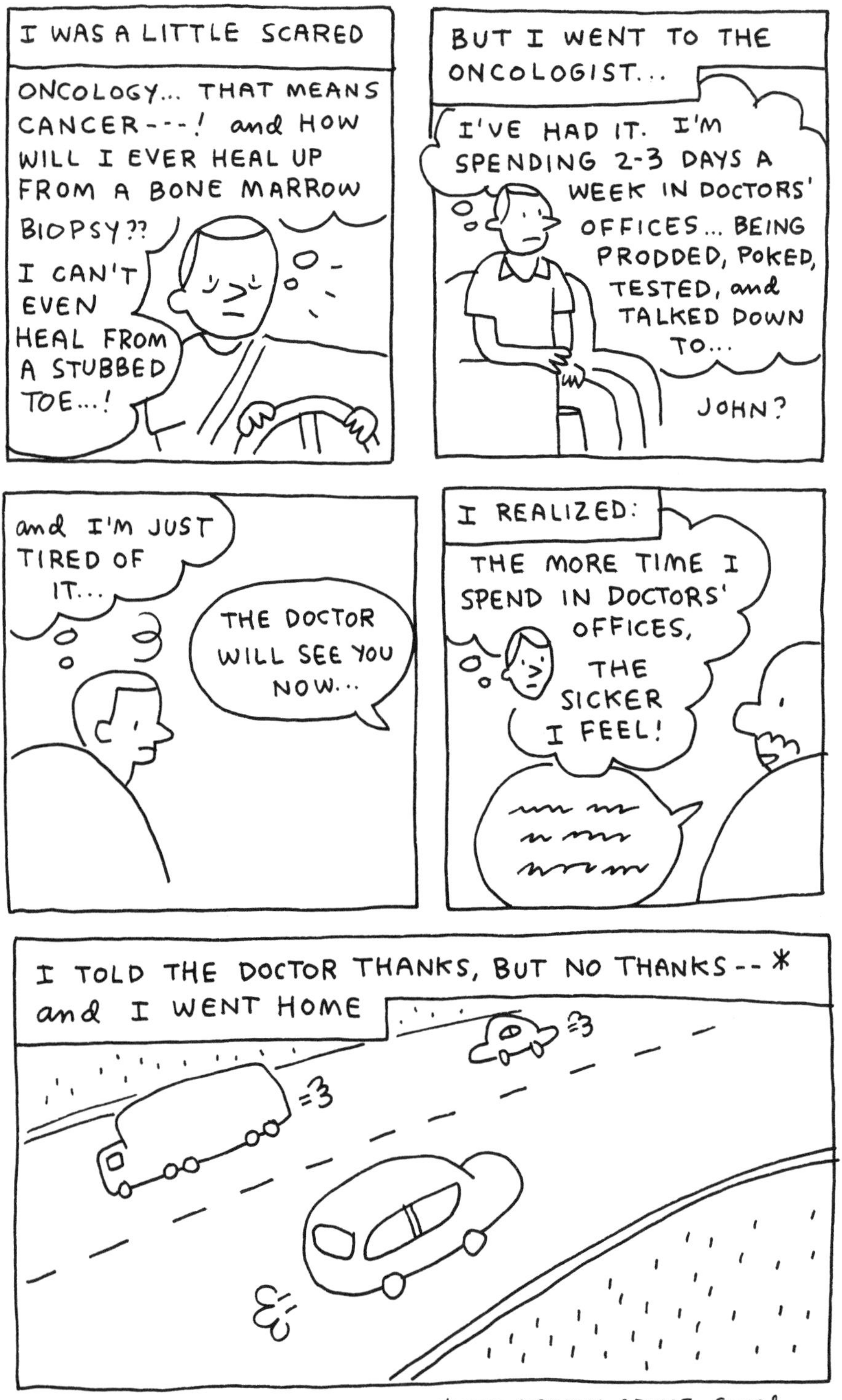
I WAS A LITTLE SCARED
ONCOLOGY... THAT MEANS CANCER---! and HOW WILL I EVER HEAL UP FROM A BONE MARROW BIOPSY??
I CAN'T EVEN HEAL FROM A STUBBED TOE...!
BUT I WENT TO THE ONCOLOGIST...
I'VE HAD IT. I'M SPENDING 2-3 DAYS A WEEK IN DOCTORS' OFFICES... BEING PRODDED, POKED, TESTED, and TALKED DOWN TO...
JOHN?
and I'M JUST TIRED OF IT...
THE DOCTOR WILL SEE YOU NOW...
I REALIZED:
THE MORE TIME I SPEND IN DOCTORS' OFFICES, THE SICKER I FEEL!
I TOLD THE DOCTOR THANKS, BUT NO THANKS--* and I WENT HOME

* NOT MEDICAL ADVICE- Signed, John's Lawyer

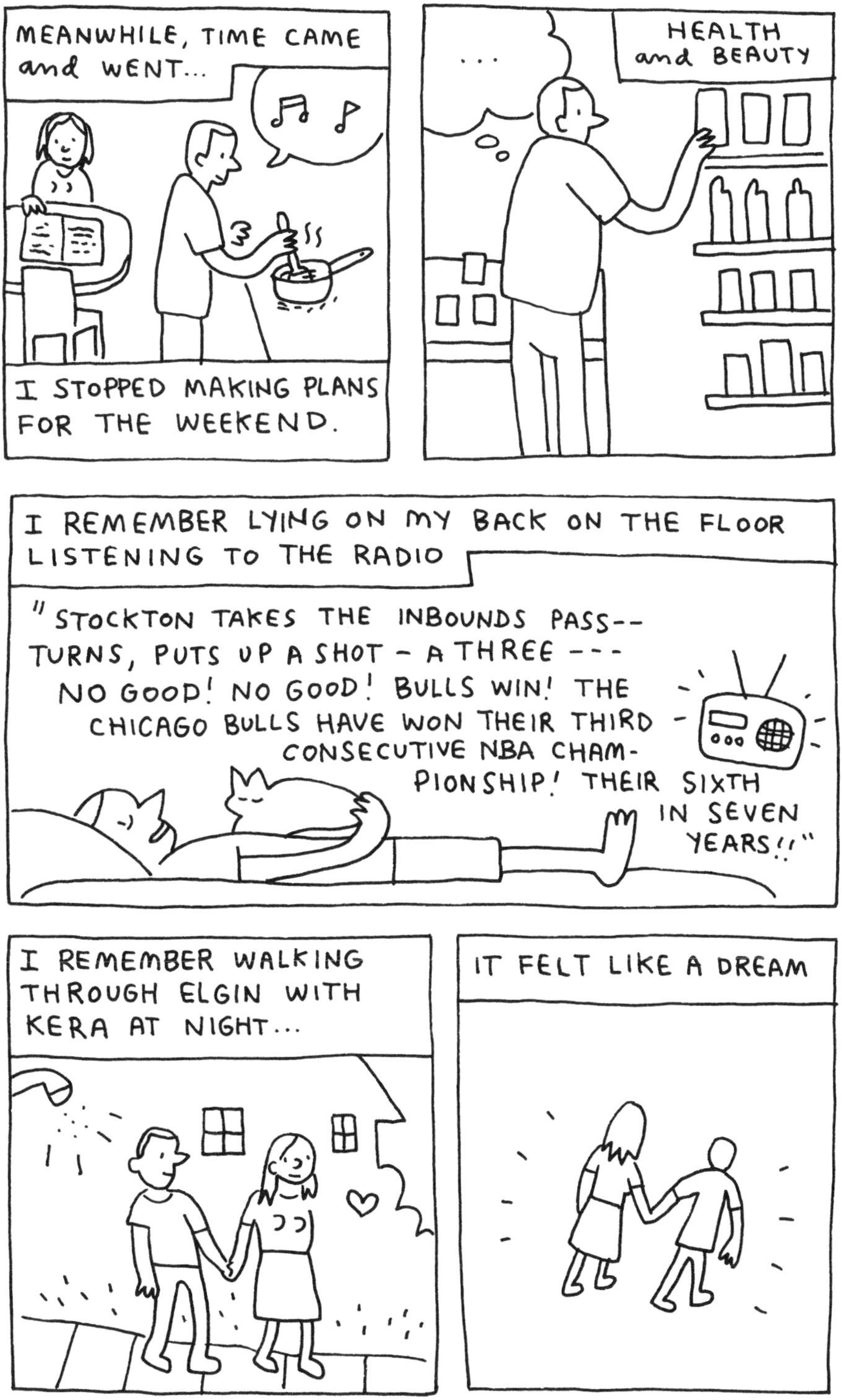
MEANWHILE, TIME CAME and WENT...
I STOPPED MAKING PLANS FOR THE WEEKEND.
...
HEALTH and BEAUTY
I REMEMBER LYING ON MY BACK ON THE FLOOR LISTENING TO THE RADIO
"STOCKTON TAKES THE INBOUNDS PASS-- TURNS, PUTS UP A SHOT - A THREE --- NO GOOD! NO GOOD! BULLS WIN! THE CHICAGO BULLS HAVE WON THEIR THIRD CONSECUTIVE NBA CHAMPIONSHIP! THEIR SIXTH IN SEVEN YEARS!!"
I REMEMBER WALKING THROUGH ELGIN WITH KERA AT NIGHT...
IT FELT LIKE A DREAM

ONE NIGHT WE WERE WALKING DOWN HIGHLAND

LOOK! LOOK!

I SAW THE HOUSE FOR SALE

IT'S A SEARS KIT HOUSE!! *

TAKE ONE

*OBSESSED WITH SEARS, ed.

AND LOOK! THE PERFECT ADDRESS -- 212 N. MELROSE AVENUE.

"...212 N. MELROSE AVENUE..."

MY PARENTS HELPED US WITH A DOWN PAYMENT, and WE GOT A LOAN THROUGH THE BANK KERA WORKED AT...

IT SEEMED ABSURD TO SIGN A 30-YEAR MORTGAGE WHEN I'D STOPPED PLAN- NING FOR THE NEXT WEEK, BUT I DID IT ANYWAY...

AFTERWARDS WE HAD $10 IN OUR BANK ACCOUNT, BUT I WAS HAPPY.

WE WERE TOGETHER... WE HAD A HOME, and a FUTURE.

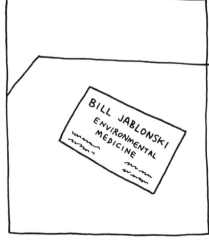

BILL JABLONSKI
ENVIRONMENTAL MEDICINE

Part Three

A FEW WEEKS LATER...

IF YOU COULD HAVE A SEAT, and FILL OUT THIS PAPER-WORK, WE'LL BE WITH YOU SHORTLY...

THEY BROUGHT ME BACK and PREPPED ME FOR MY FIRST ROUND OF "PRICK TESTS"...

WOW!

WIPE

LOOK at THOSE BLACK EYES!

WE CALL THEM "ALLERGIC SHINERS"

ONCE WE GET THIS FIGURED OUT, YOU'RE GONNA FEEL A LOT BETTER!

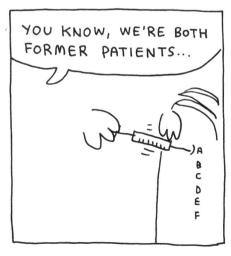

YOU KNOW, WE'RE BOTH FORMER PATIENTS...

A
B
C
D
E
F

WHO KNOWS, ONE DAY WHEN YOU'VE RECOVERED, YOU MIGHT END UP HELPING PEOPLE WITH ALLERGIES, JUST LIKE WE DO!

POKE

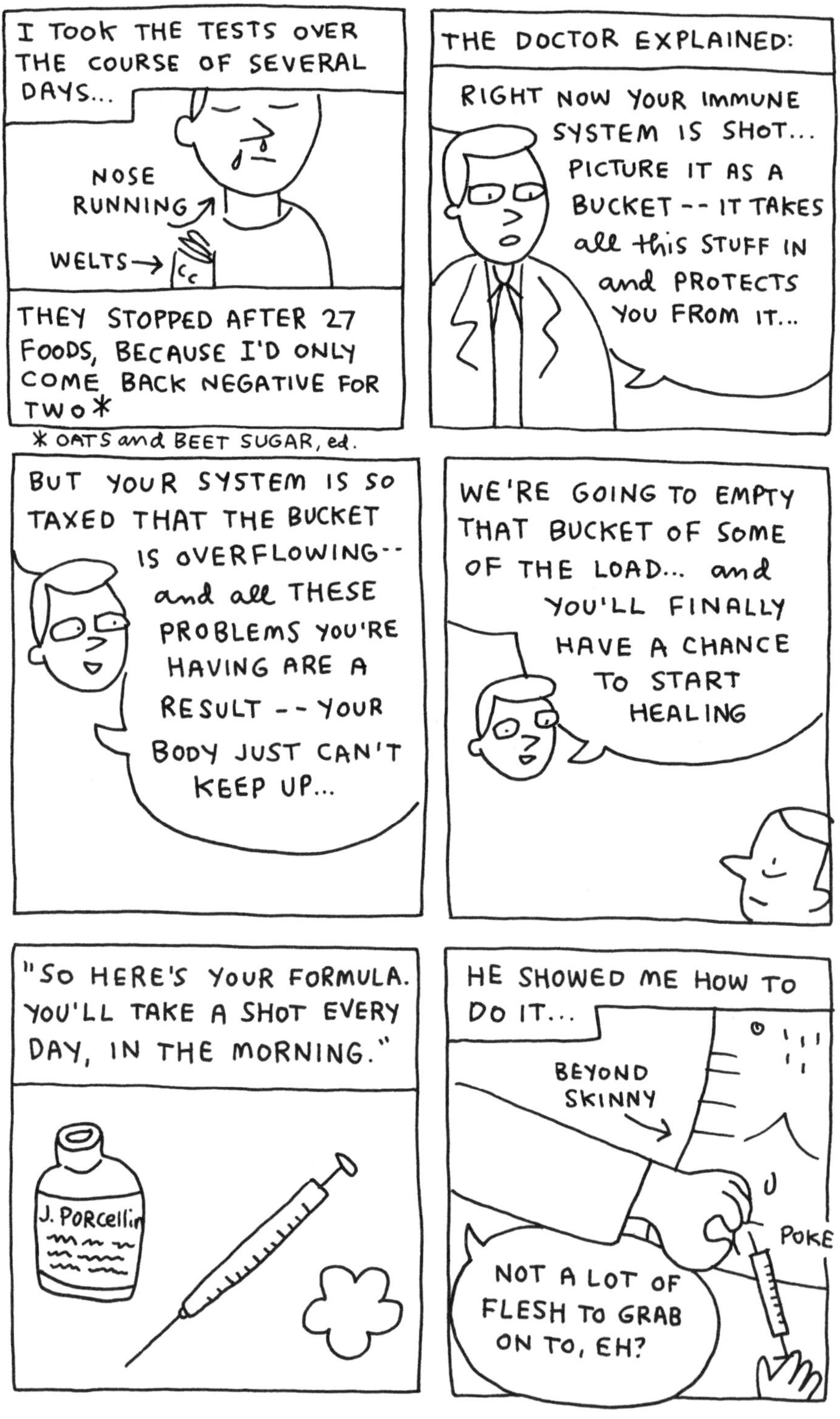
I TOOK THE TESTS OVER THE COURSE OF SEVERAL DAYS...
NOSE RUNNING
WELTS
THEY STOPPED AFTER 27 FOODS, BECAUSE I'D ONLY COME BACK NEGATIVE FOR TWO*
* OATS and BEET SUGAR, ed.
THE DOCTOR EXPLAINED:
RIGHT NOW YOUR IMMUNE SYSTEM IS SHOT... PICTURE IT AS A BUCKET -- IT TAKES all this STUFF IN and PROTECTS YOU FROM IT...
BUT YOUR SYSTEM IS SO TAXED THAT THE BUCKET IS OVERFLOWING-- and all THESE PROBLEMS YOU'RE HAVING ARE A RESULT -- YOUR BODY JUST CAN'T KEEP UP...
WE'RE GOING TO EMPTY THAT BUCKET OF SOME OF THE LOAD... and YOU'LL FINALLY HAVE A CHANCE TO START HEALING
"SO HERE'S YOUR FORMULA. YOU'LL TAKE A SHOT EVERY DAY, IN THE MORNING."
J. PORCELLIN
HE SHOWED ME HOW TO DO IT...
BEYOND SKINNY
POKE
NOT A LOT OF FLESH TO GRAB ON TO, EH?

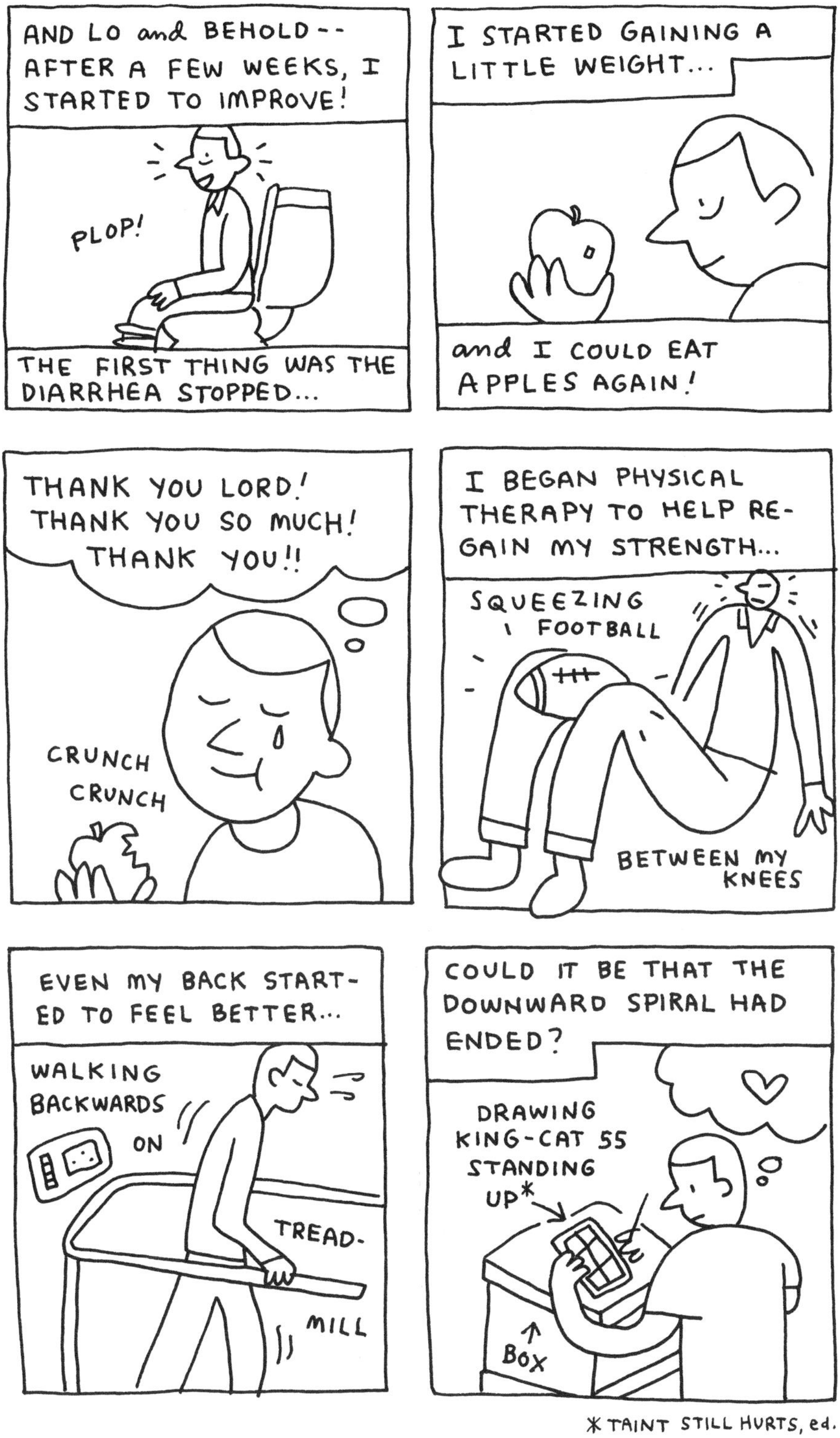
AND LO and BEHOLD--
AFTER A FEW WEEKS, I
STARTED TO IMPROVE!
PLOP!
THE FIRST THING WAS THE
DIARRHEA STOPPED...
I STARTED GAINING A
LITTLE WEIGHT...
and I COULD EAT
APPLES AGAIN!
THANK YOU LORD!
THANK YOU SO MUCH!
THANK YOU!!
CRUNCH
CRUNCH
I BEGAN PHYSICAL
THERAPY TO HELP RE-
GAIN MY STRENGTH...
SQUEEZING
FOOTBALL
BETWEEN MY
KNEES
EVEN MY BACK START-
ED TO FEEL BETTER...
WALKING
BACKWARDS
ON
TREAD-
MILL
COULD IT BE THAT THE
DOWNWARD SPIRAL HAD
ENDED?
DRAWING
KING-CAT 55
STANDING
UP*
BOX
*TAINT STILL HURTS, ed.

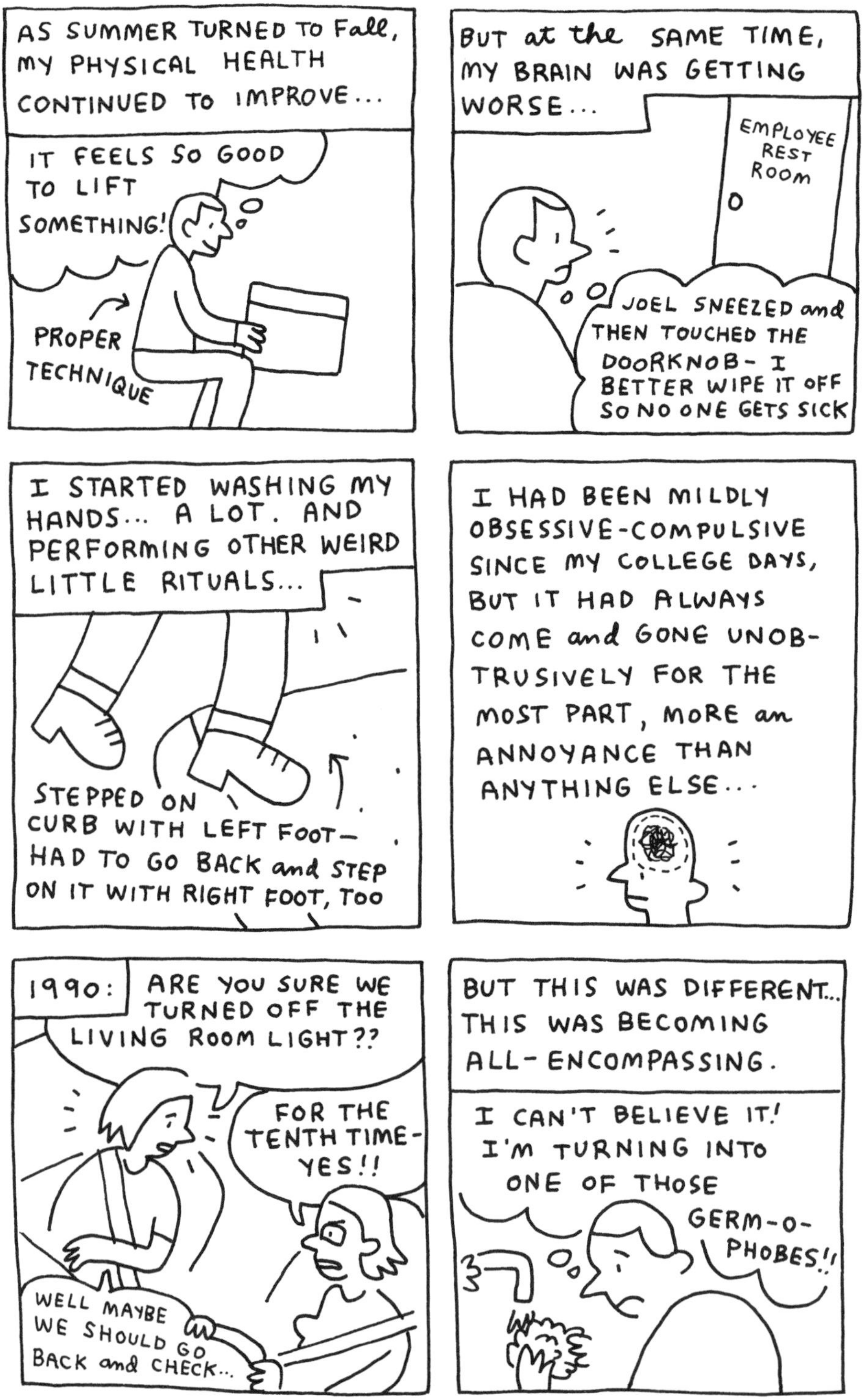
AS SUMMER TURNED TO Fall, MY PHYSICAL HEALTH CONTINUED TO IMPROVE...
IT FEELS SO GOOD TO LIFT SOMETHING!
PROPER TECHNIQUE
BUT at the SAME TIME, MY BRAIN WAS GETTING WORSE...
EMPLOYEE REST ROOM
JOEL SNEEZED and THEN TOUCHED THE DOORKNOB- I BETTER WIPE IT OFF SO NO ONE GETS SICK
I STARTED WASHING MY HANDS... A LOT. AND PERFORMING OTHER WEIRD LITTLE RITUALS...
STEPPED ON CURB WITH LEFT FOOT- HAD TO GO BACK and STEP ON IT WITH RIGHT FOOT, TOO
I HAD BEEN MILDLY OBSESSIVE-COMPULSIVE SINCE MY COLLEGE DAYS, BUT IT HAD ALWAYS COME and GONE UNOB-TRUSIVELY FOR THE MOST PART, MORE an ANNOYANCE THAN ANYTHING ELSE...
1990:
ARE YOU SURE WE TURNED OFF THE LIVING ROOM LIGHT??
FOR THE TENTH TIME- YES!!
WELL MAYBE WE SHOULD GO BACK and CHECK...
BUT THIS WAS DIFFERENT... THIS WAS BECOMING ALL-ENCOMPASSING.
I CAN'T BELIEVE IT! I'M TURNING INTO ONE OF THOSE GERM-O-PHOBES!!

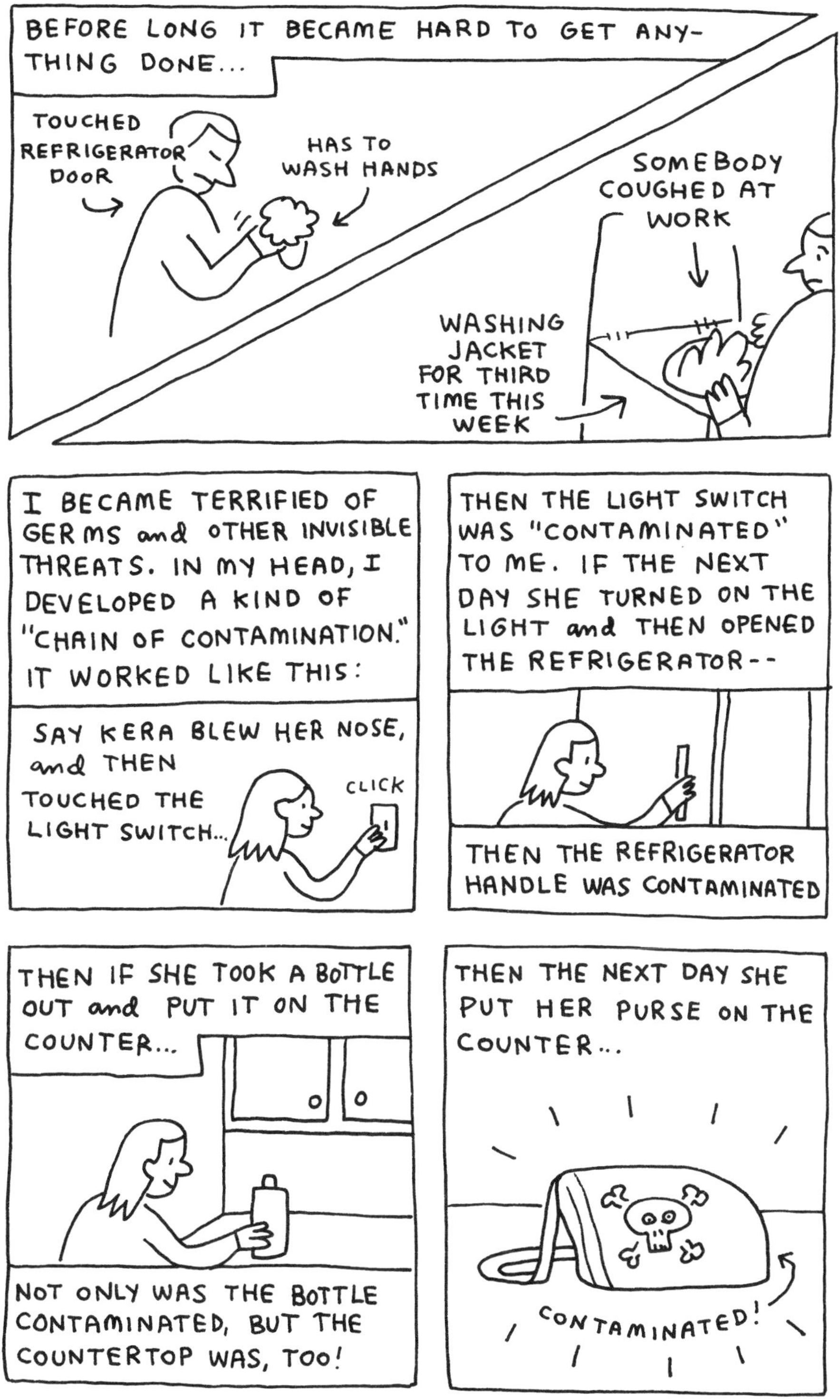
BEFORE LONG IT BECAME HARD TO GET ANYTHING DONE...
TOUCHED REFRIGERATOR DOOR
HAS TO WASH HANDS
SOMEBODY COUGHED AT WORK
WASHING JACKET FOR THIRD TIME THIS WEEK
I BECAME TERRIFIED OF GERMS and OTHER INVISIBLE THREATS. IN MY HEAD, I DEVELOPED A KIND OF "CHAIN OF CONTAMINATION." IT WORKED LIKE THIS:
SAY KERA BLEW HER NOSE, and THEN TOUCHED THE LIGHT SWITCH...
CLICK
THEN THE LIGHT SWITCH WAS "CONTAMINATED" TO ME. IF THE NEXT DAY SHE TURNED ON THE LIGHT and THEN OPENED THE REFRIGERATOR--
THEN THE REFRIGERATOR HANDLE WAS CONTAMINATED
THEN IF SHE TOOK A BOTTLE OUT and PUT IT ON THE COUNTER...
NOT ONLY WAS THE BOTTLE CONTAMINATED, BUT THE COUNTERTOP WAS, TOO!
THEN THE NEXT DAY SHE PUT HER PURSE ON THE COUNTER...
CONTAMINATED!

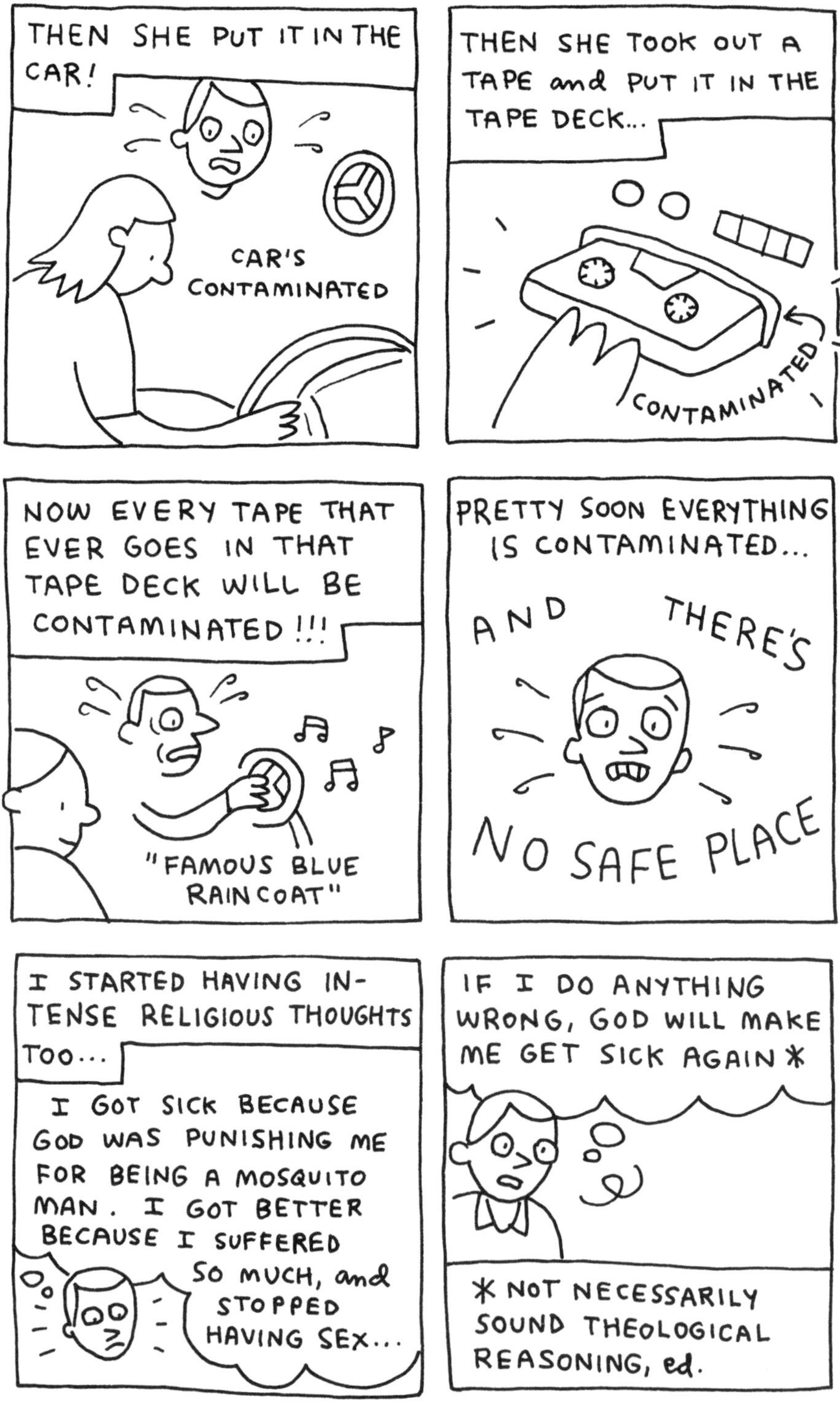
THEN SHE PUT IT IN THE CAR!
CAR'S CONTAMINATED
THEN SHE TOOK OUT A TAPE and PUT IT IN THE TAPE DECK...
CONTAMINATED
NOW EVERY TAPE THAT EVER GOES IN THAT TAPE DECK WILL BE CONTAMINATED!!!
"FAMOUS BLUE RAINCOAT"
PRETTY SOON EVERYTHING IS CONTAMINATED...
AND THERE'S
NO SAFE PLACE
I STARTED HAVING INTENSE RELIGIOUS THOUGHTS TOO...
I GOT SICK BECAUSE GOD WAS PUNISHING ME FOR BEING A MOSQUITO MAN. I GOT BETTER BECAUSE I SUFFERED SO MUCH, and STOPPED HAVING SEX...
IF I DO ANYTHING WRONG, GOD WILL MAKE ME GET SICK AGAIN *
* NOT NECESSARILY SOUND THEOLOGICAL REASONING, ed.

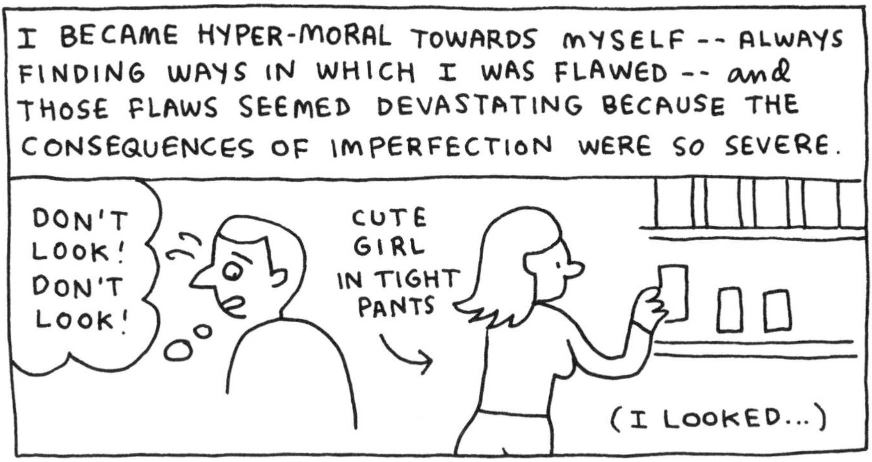
I BECAME HYPER-MORAL TOWARDS MYSELF -- ALWAYS FINDING WAYS IN WHICH I WAS FLAWED -- and THOSE FLAWS SEEMED DEVASTATING BECAUSE THE CONSEQUENCES OF IMPERFECTION WERE SO SEVERE.
DON'T LOOK! DON'T LOOK!
CUTE GIRL IN TIGHT PANTS
(I LOOKED...)

AS A RESULT, MY SPIRITUAL LIFE HAD BECOME SIMULTANEOUSLY COMFORTING and TERRIFYING. I REALIZED I NEEDED SOMEONE I COULD TALK TO ABOUT THIS STUFF... I NEEDED TO FIND A TEACHER...

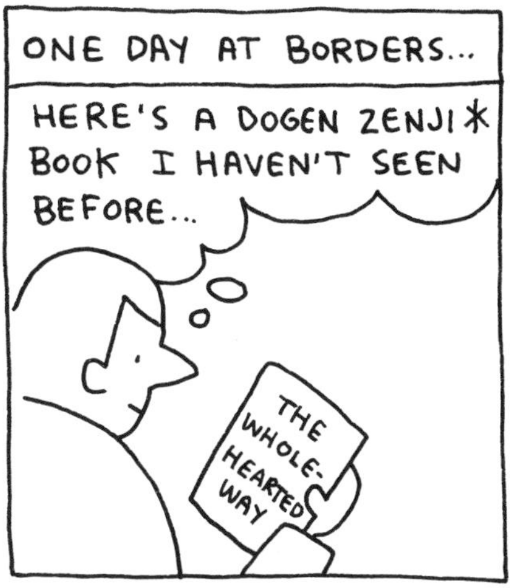
ONE DAY AT BORDERS...
HERE'S A DOGEN ZENJI* BOOK I HAVEN'T SEEN BEFORE...
THE WHOLE-HEARTED WAY

*Founder of Soto Zen in Japan, 1200-1253

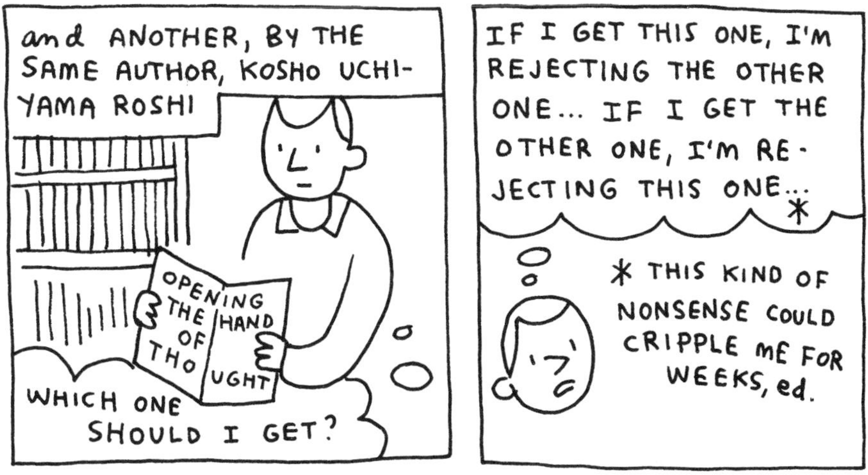
and ANOTHER, BY THE SAME AUTHOR, KOSHO UCHIYAMA ROSHI
OPENING THE HAND OF THOUGHT
WHICH ONE SHOULD I GET?
IF I GET THIS ONE, I'M REJECTING THE OTHER ONE... IF I GET THE OTHER ONE, I'M REJECTING THIS ONE...*
* THIS KIND OF NONSENSE COULD CRIPPLE ME FOR WEEKS, ed.

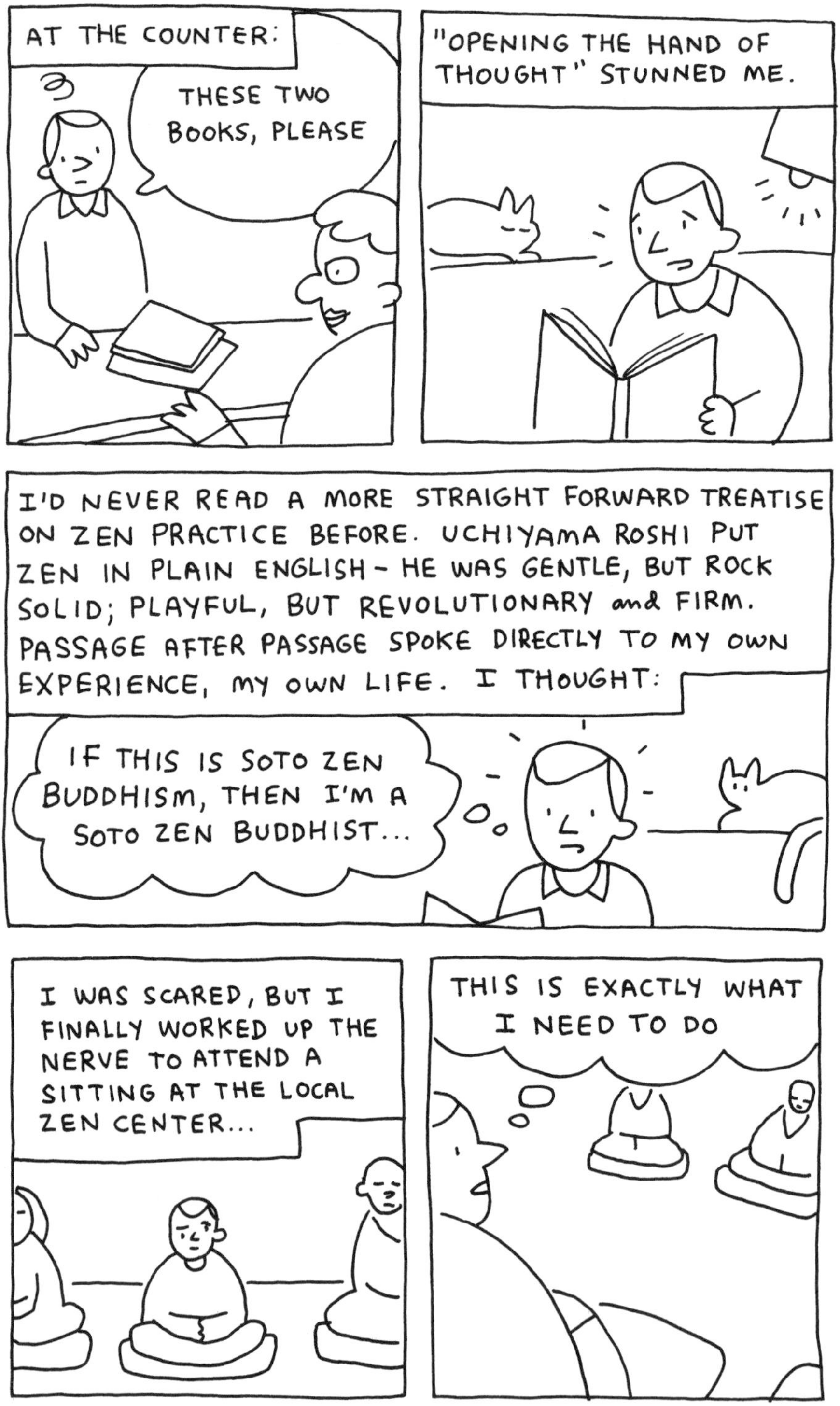
AT THE COUNTER:
THESE TWO BOOKS, PLEASE
"OPENING THE HAND OF THOUGHT" STUNNED ME.
I'D NEVER READ A MORE STRAIGHT FORWARD TREATISE ON ZEN PRACTICE BEFORE. UCHIYAMA ROSHI PUT ZEN IN PLAIN ENGLISH - HE WAS GENTLE, BUT ROCK SOLID; PLAYFUL, BUT REVOLUTIONARY and FIRM. PASSAGE AFTER PASSAGE SPOKE DIRECTLY TO MY OWN EXPERIENCE, MY OWN LIFE. I THOUGHT:
IF THIS IS SOTO ZEN BUDDHISM, THEN I'M A SOTO ZEN BUDDHIST...
I WAS SCARED, BUT I FINALLY WORKED UP THE NERVE TO ATTEND A SITTING AT THE LOCAL ZEN CENTER...
THIS IS EXACTLY WHAT I NEED TO DO

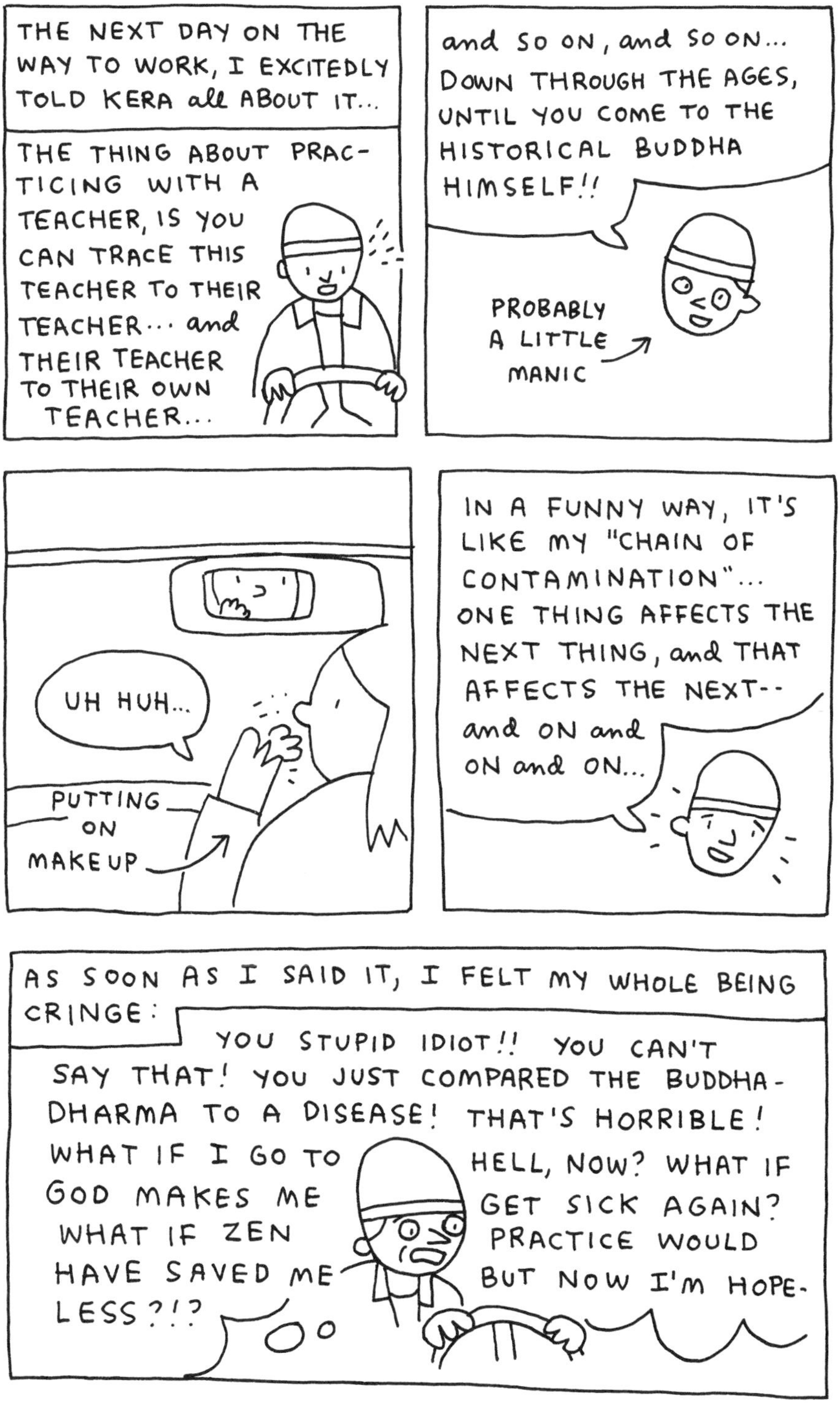
THE NEXT DAY ON THE WAY TO WORK, I EXCITEDLY TOLD KERA all ABOUT IT...
THE THING ABOUT PRACTICING WITH A TEACHER, IS YOU CAN TRACE THIS TEACHER TO THEIR TEACHER... and THEIR TEACHER TO THEIR OWN TEACHER...
and SO ON, and SO ON... DOWN THROUGH THE AGES, UNTIL YOU COME TO THE HISTORICAL BUDDHA HIMSELF!!
PROBABLY A LITTLE MANIC
UH HUH...
PUTTING ON MAKEUP
IN A FUNNY WAY, IT'S LIKE MY "CHAIN OF CONTAMINATION"... ONE THING AFFECTS THE NEXT THING, and THAT AFFECTS THE NEXT-- and ON and ON and ON...
AS SOON AS I SAID IT, I FELT MY WHOLE BEING CRINGE:
YOU STUPID IDIOT!! YOU CAN'T SAY THAT! YOU JUST COMPARED THE BUDDHA-DHARMA TO A DISEASE! THAT'S HORRIBLE! WHAT IF I GO TO HELL, NOW? WHAT IF GOD MAKES ME GET SICK AGAIN? WHAT IF ZEN PRACTICE WOULD HAVE SAVED ME BUT NOW I'M HOPELESS?!?

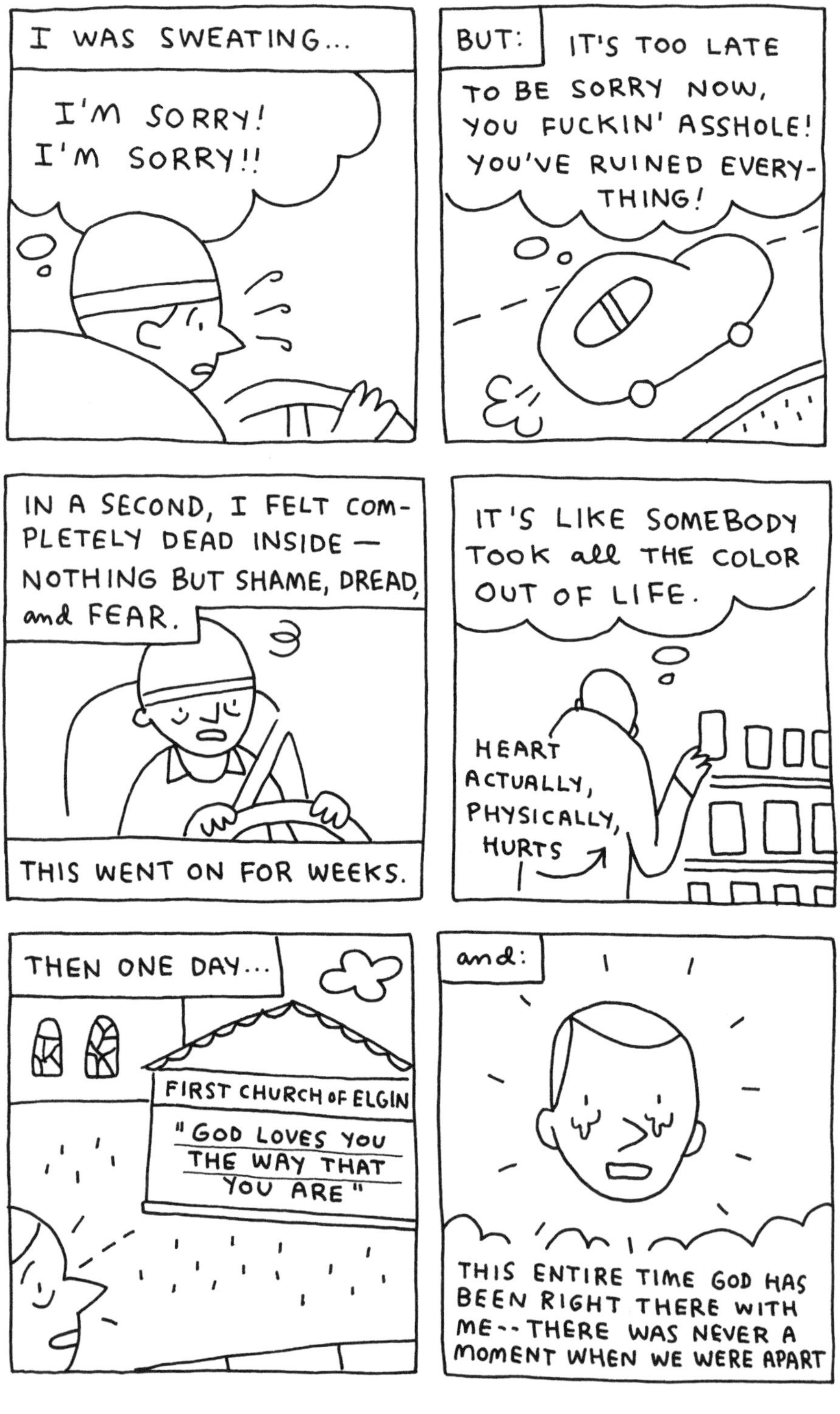
I WAS SWEATING...
I'M SORRY! I'M SORRY!!
BUT:
IT'S TOO LATE TO BE SORRY NOW, YOU FUCKIN' ASSHOLE! YOU'VE RUINED EVERY-THING!
IN A SECOND, I FELT COMPLETELY DEAD INSIDE — NOTHING BUT SHAME, DREAD, and FEAR.
THIS WENT ON FOR WEEKS.
IT'S LIKE SOMEBODY TOOK all THE COLOR OUT OF LIFE.
HEART ACTUALLY, PHYSICALLY, HURTS
THEN ONE DAY...
FIRST CHURCH OF ELGIN
"GOD LOVES YOU THE WAY THAT YOU ARE"
and:
THIS ENTIRE TIME GOD HAS BEEN RIGHT THERE WITH ME -- THERE WAS NEVER A MOMENT WHEN WE WERE APART

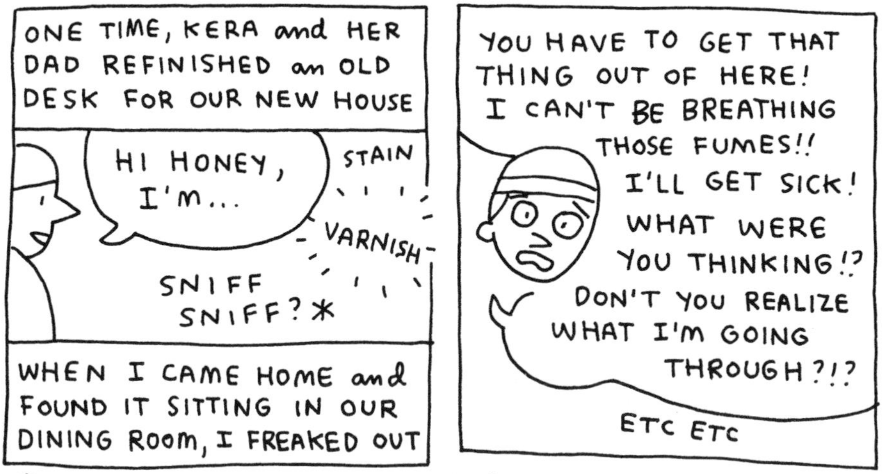
ONE TIME, KERA and HER DAD REFINISHED an OLD DESK FOR OUR NEW HOUSE
HI HONEY, I'M...
STAIN
VARNISH
SNIFF SNIFF? *
WHEN I CAME HOME and FOUND IT SITTING IN OUR DINING ROOM, I FREAKED OUT
YOU HAVE TO GET THAT THING OUT OF HERE! I CAN'T BE BREATHING THOSE FUMES!! I'LL GET SICK! WHAT WERE YOU THINKING!? DON'T YOU REALIZE WHAT I'M GOING THROUGH?!?
ETC ETC

* CHEMICALLY HYPERSENSITIVE NOSE, ed.

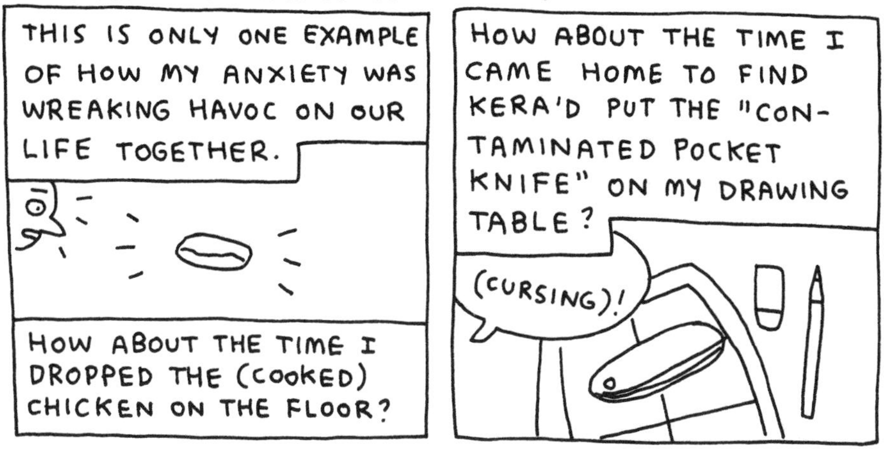
THIS IS ONLY ONE EXAMPLE OF HOW MY ANXIETY WAS WREAKING HAVOC ON OUR LIFE TOGETHER.
HOW ABOUT THE TIME I DROPPED THE (COOKED) CHICKEN ON THE FLOOR?
HOW ABOUT THE TIME I CAME HOME TO FIND KERA'D PUT THE "CONTAMINATED POCKET KNIFE" ON MY DRAWING TABLE?
(CURSING)!

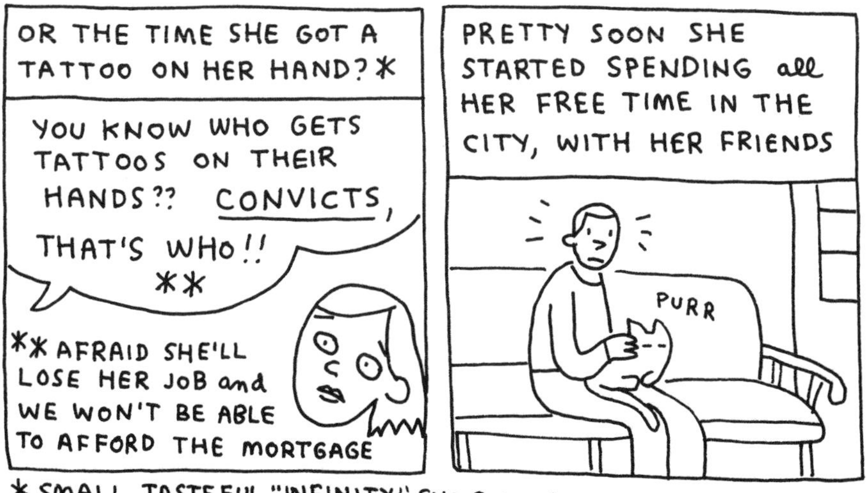
OR THE TIME SHE GOT A TATTOO ON HER HAND? *
YOU KNOW WHO GETS TATTOOS ON THEIR HANDS?? CONVICTS, THAT'S WHO!! **
** AFRAID SHE'LL LOSE HER JOB and WE WON'T BE ABLE TO AFFORD THE MORTGAGE
PRETTY SOON SHE STARTED SPENDING all HER FREE TIME IN THE CITY, WITH HER FRIENDS
PURR

* SMALL, TASTEFUL "INFINITY" SYMBOL, ed.

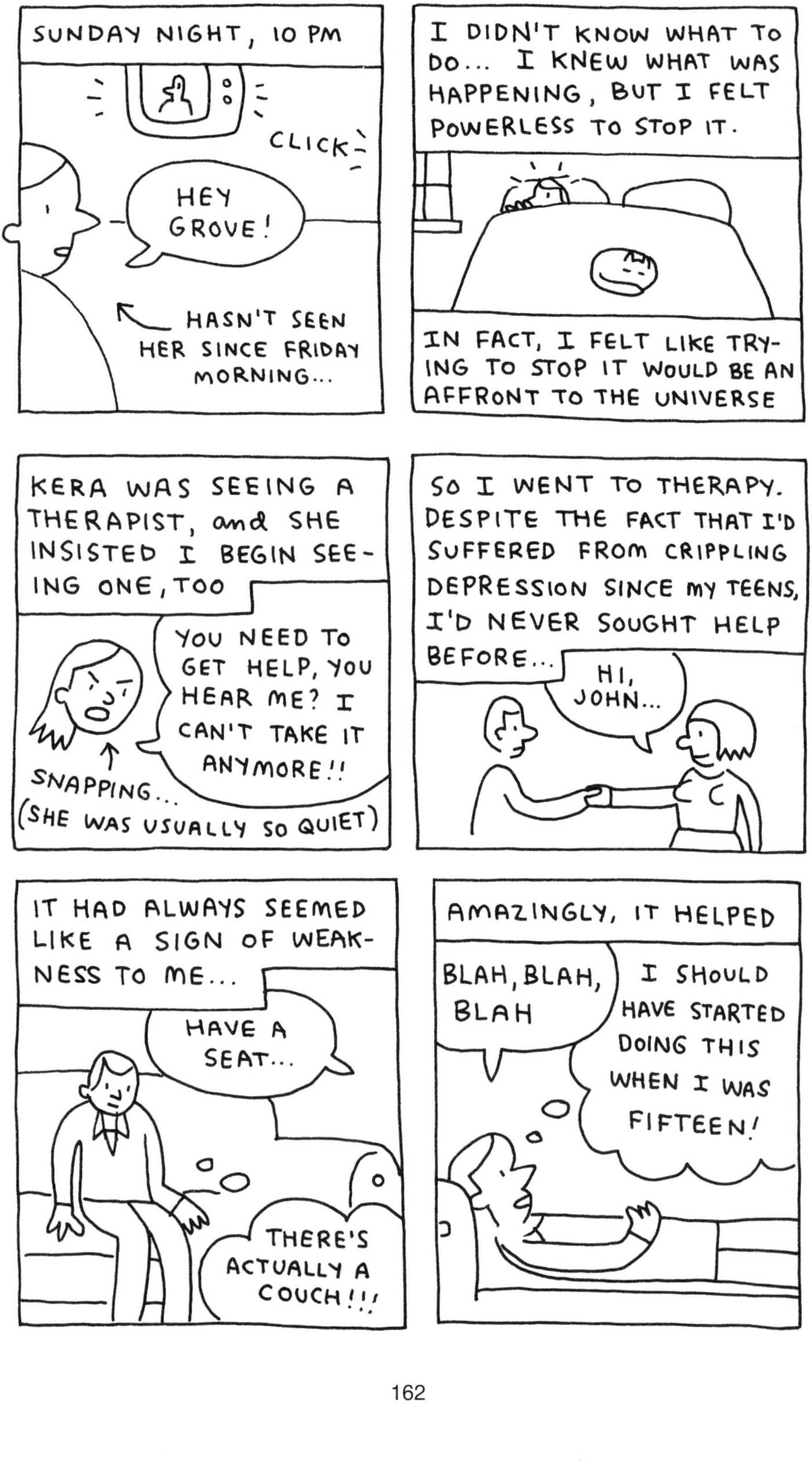
SUNDAY NIGHT, 10 PM
CLICK
HEY GROVE!
HASN'T SEEN HER SINCE FRIDAY MORNING...
I DIDN'T KNOW WHAT TO DO... I KNEW WHAT WAS HAPPENING, BUT I FELT POWERLESS TO STOP IT.
IN FACT, I FELT LIKE TRYING TO STOP IT WOULD BE AN AFFRONT TO THE UNIVERSE
KERA WAS SEEING A THERAPIST, and SHE INSISTED I BEGIN SEEING ONE, TOO
YOU NEED TO GET HELP, YOU HEAR ME? I CAN'T TAKE IT ANYMORE!!
SNAPPING... (SHE WAS USUALLY SO QUIET)
SO I WENT TO THERAPY. DESPITE THE FACT THAT I'D SUFFERED FROM CRIPPLING DEPRESSION SINCE MY TEENS, I'D NEVER SOUGHT HELP BEFORE...
HI, JOHN...
IT HAD ALWAYS SEEMED LIKE A SIGN OF WEAKNESS TO ME...
HAVE A SEAT...
THERE'S ACTUALLY A COUCH!!!
AMAZINGLY, IT HELPED
BLAH, BLAH, BLAH
I SHOULD HAVE STARTED DOING THIS WHEN I WAS FIFTEEN!

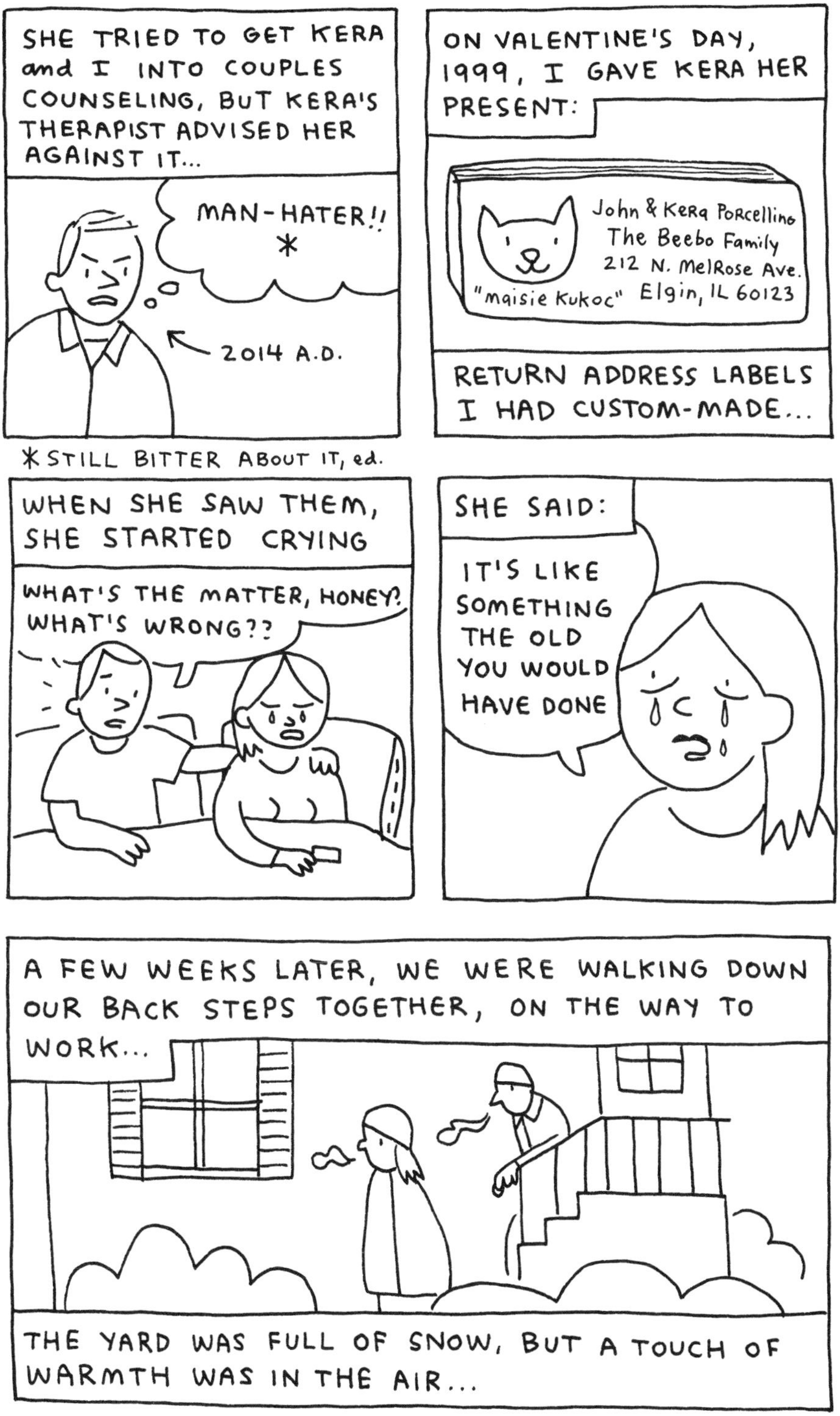
SHE TRIED TO GET KERA and I INTO COUPLES COUNSELING, BUT KERA'S THERAPIST ADVISED HER AGAINST IT...
MAN-HATER!! *
2014 A.D.
* STILL BITTER ABOUT IT, ed.
ON VALENTINE'S DAY, 1999, I GAVE KERA HER PRESENT:
John & Kera Porcellino
The Beebo Family
212 N. MelRose Ave.
Elgin, IL 60123
"maisie Kukoc"
RETURN ADDRESS LABELS I HAD CUSTOM-MADE...
WHEN SHE SAW THEM, SHE STARTED CRYING
WHAT'S THE MATTER, HONEY? WHAT'S WRONG??
SHE SAID:
IT'S LIKE SOMETHING THE OLD YOU WOULD HAVE DONE
A FEW WEEKS LATER, WE WERE WALKING DOWN OUR BACK STEPS TOGETHER, ON THE WAY TO WORK...
THE YARD WAS FULL OF SNOW, BUT A TOUCH OF WARMTH WAS IN THE AIR...

SHE SAID:
I CAN'T WAIT FOR SPRING! WHEN WE CAN COME OUT HERE and DIG AROUND, and PLANT A LITTLE GARDEN!
I WAS BEAMING...
THAT MEANS SHE PLANS TO STAY WITH ME! IT MEANS WE'RE GOING TO BE TOGETHER!!!

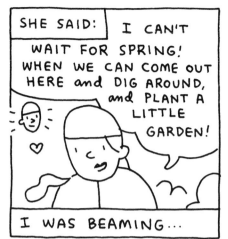

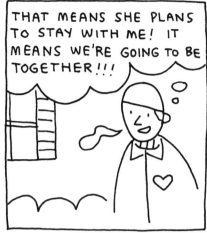

A WEEK LATER, SHE WALKED OUT.

I STOOD THERE AS KERA and HER PARENTS REMOVED all OF HER BELONGINGS FROM OUR HOUSE...

IT WAS THE MOST HUMILIATING MOMENT OF MY LIFE.

TRUE ANXIETY

Part One

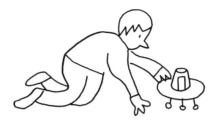

ONE OF MY OLDEST MEMORIES IS A MEMORY OF ANXIOUSNESS...

IT WAS CHRISTMAS, OR A BIRTHDAY — and I'D GOTTEN A MECHANICAL SPACESHIP FOR A PRESENT— WITH A ROBOT INSIDE THAT ROLLED OUT ON A RAMP *

LIGHTS FLASHED—

GEARS WHIRRED...

* STAR HAWK W/ZEROID, IDEAL TOYS - 1977, ed.

BBZZAPP !!!

BUT...

IF I PLAY WITH THIS TOO MUCH, IT'LL WEAR OUT and BREAK !! - and THEN IT'LL BE RUINED !!

8 YEARS OLD

169

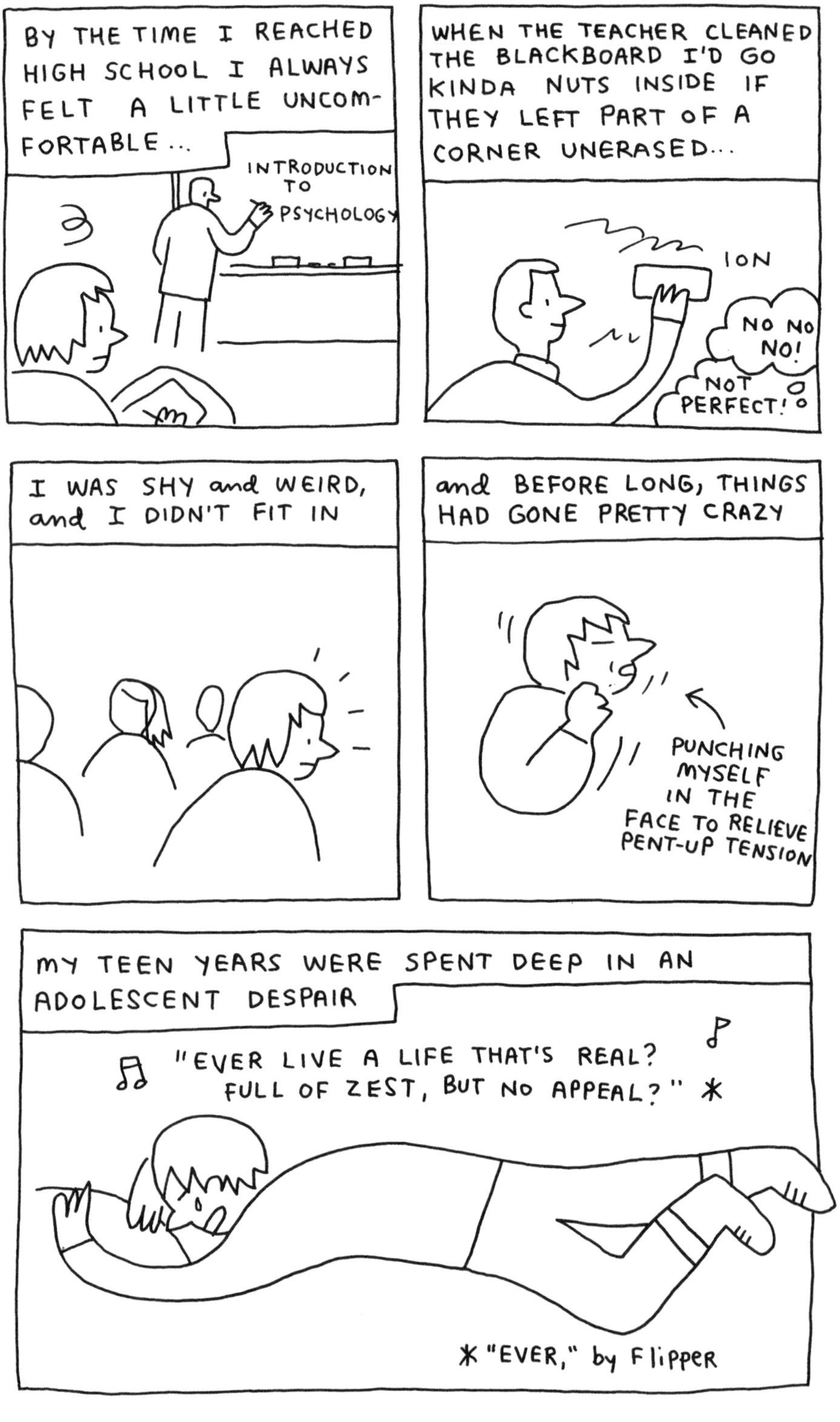
BY THE TIME I REACHED HIGH SCHOOL I ALWAYS FELT A LITTLE UNCOMFORTABLE...
INTRODUCTION TO PSYCHOLOGY
WHEN THE TEACHER CLEANED THE BLACKBOARD I'D GO KINDA NUTS INSIDE IF THEY LEFT PART OF A CORNER UNERASED...
ION
NO NO NO! NOT PERFECT!
I WAS SHY and WEIRD, and I DIDN'T FIT IN
and BEFORE LONG, THINGS HAD GONE PRETTY CRAZY
PUNCHING MYSELF IN THE FACE TO RELIEVE PENT-UP TENSION
MY TEEN YEARS WERE SPENT DEEP IN AN ADOLESCENT DESPAIR
"EVER LIVE A LIFE THAT'S REAL? FULL OF ZEST, BUT NO APPEAL?" *
* "EVER," by Flipper

I WAS PLAGUED BY SUICIDAL THOUGHTS...
"JUST FUCKIN' DIE, JUST KILL YOURSELF, JUST DIE" etc

BUT EARLY ON I DECIDED I WOULDN'T GIVE IN TO THEM*

* RAISED CATHOLIC, ed.

THEY JUST KIND OF BECAME THE BACKGROUND MUSIC TO MY DAY...
"HURL YOURSELF OFF A BRIDGE..."

ANYHOW, WHEN I WAS DEPRESSED THE ANXIETY WASN'T AS BAD — I SIMPLY DIDN'T GIVE A SHIT.

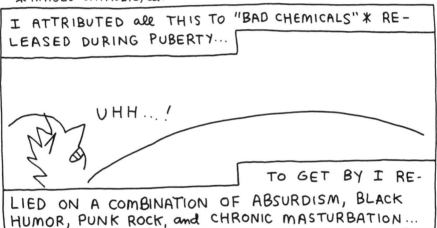

I ATTRIBUTED all THIS TO "BAD CHEMICALS"* RELEASED DURING PUBERTY...

UHH...!

TO GET BY I RELIED ON A COMBINATION OF ABSURDISM, BLACK HUMOR, PUNK ROCK, and CHRONIC MASTURBATION...

* I WAS A BIG KURT VONNEGUT FAN, ed.

IN 1986, I GRADUATED FROM HIGH SCHOOL, LOST MY VIRGINITY (SOMEHOW), and WENT OFF TO COLLEGE TO STUDY ART...

and IT'S HERE THAT OUR STORY BEGINS

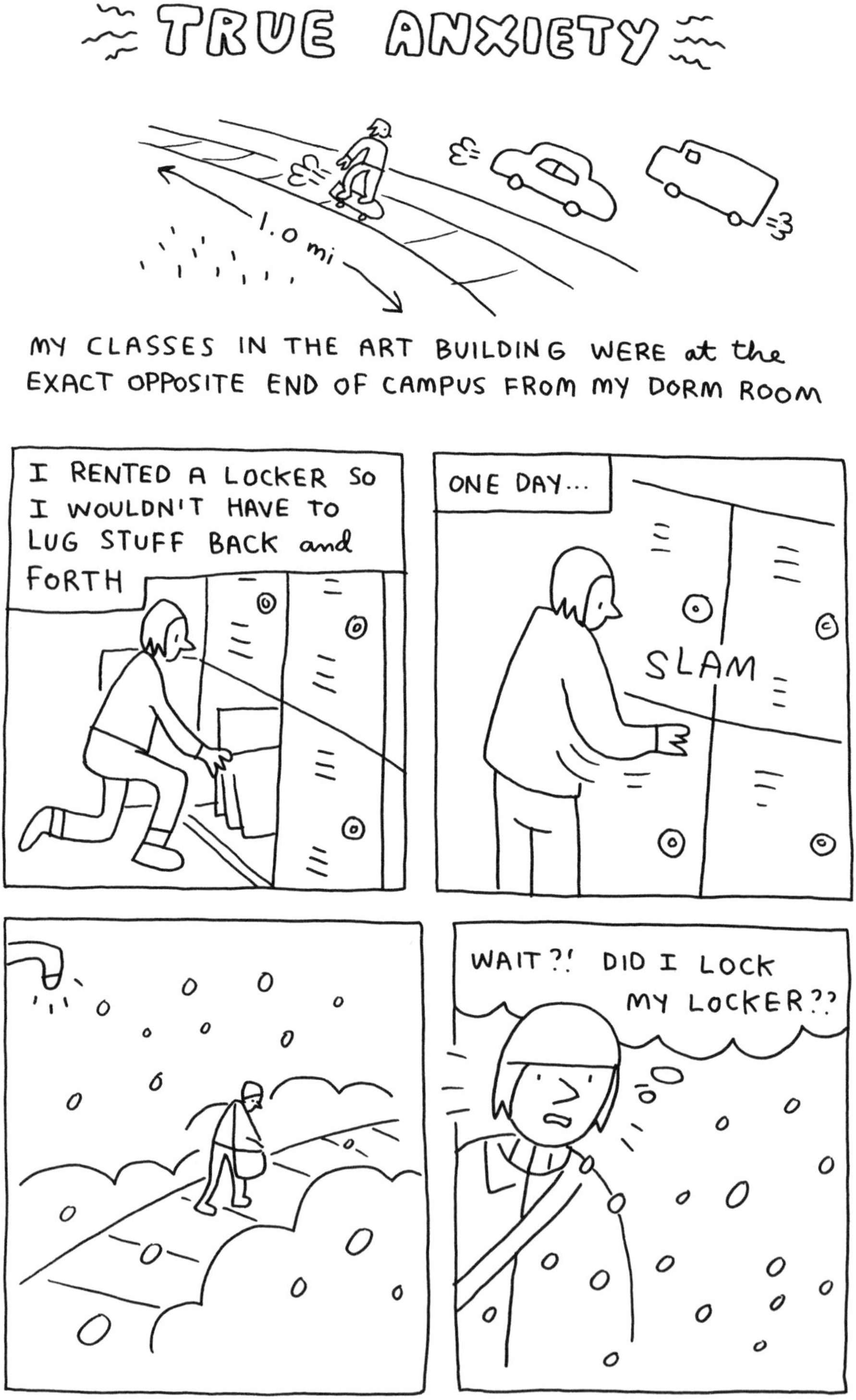
TRUE ANXIETY
1.0 mi
MY CLASSES IN THE ART BUILDING WERE at the EXACT OPPOSITE END OF CAMPUS FROM MY DORM ROOM
I RENTED A LOCKER SO I WOULDN'T HAVE TO LUG STUFF BACK and FORTH
ONE DAY...
SLAM
WAIT?! DID I LOCK MY LOCKER??

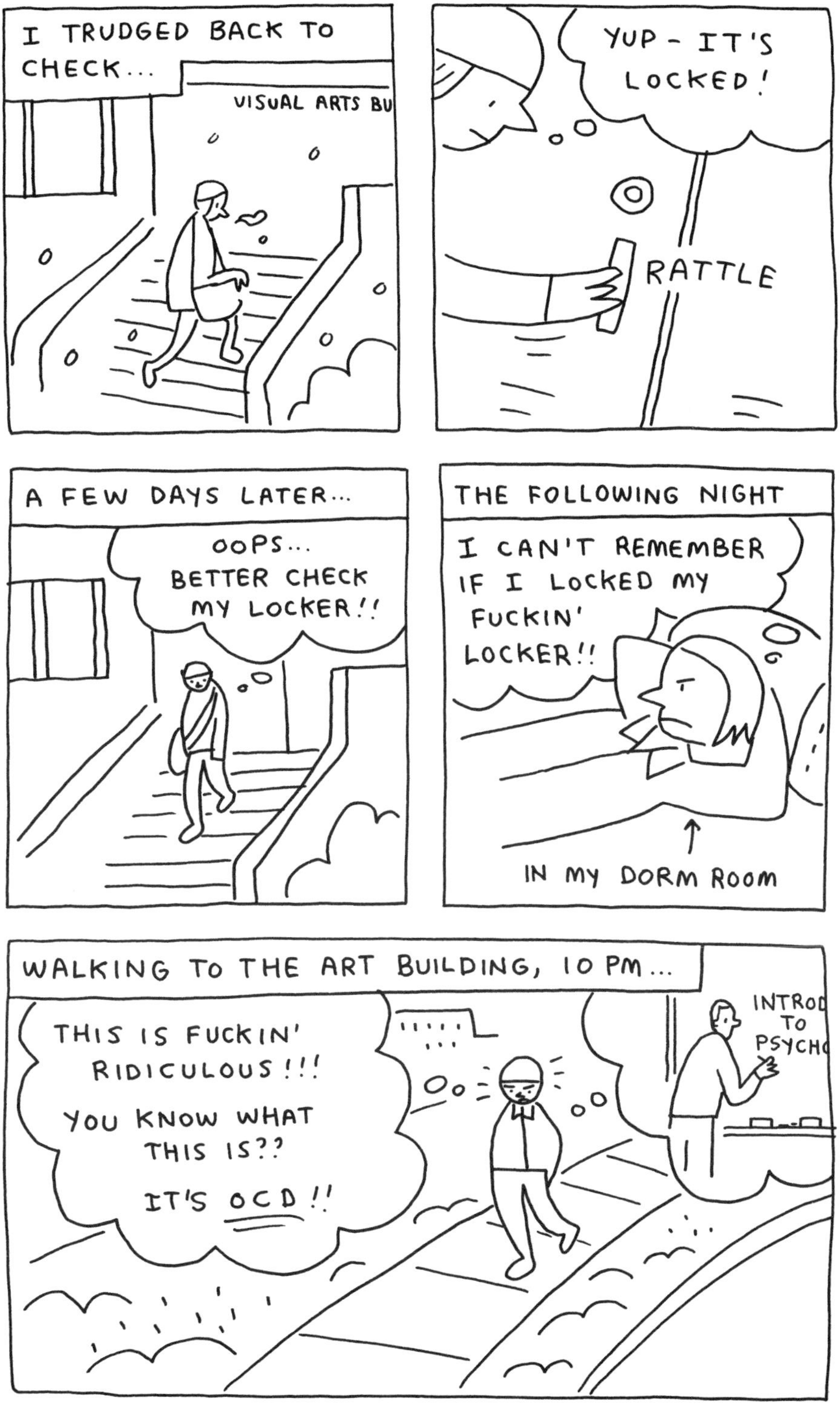
I TRUDGED BACK TO CHECK...
VISUAL ARTS BU
YUP - IT'S LOCKED!
RATTLE
A FEW DAYS LATER...
OOPS... BETTER CHECK MY LOCKER!!
THE FOLLOWING NIGHT
I CAN'T REMEMBER IF I LOCKED MY FUCKIN' LOCKER!!
IN MY DORM ROOM
WALKING TO THE ART BUILDING, 10 PM...
THIS IS FUCKIN' RIDICULOUS!!!
YOU KNOW WHAT THIS IS??
IT'S OCD!!
INTRO TO PSYCH

SO I DEVELOPED A TRICK, WHERE AFTER I LOCKED THE LOCKER I'D KICK IT...

KLANG!

THAT WAY I'D REMEMBER THE SOUND LATER and KNOW THAT IT WAS CLOSED...

KLANG

Peace of mind

ANYHOW, I WENT TO SCHOOL at NIU, MY GIRLFRIEND WENT TO U OF I

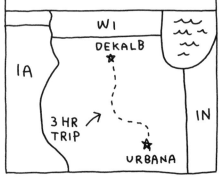

WI
DEKALB
IA
IN
3 HR TRIP
URBANA

I'D GO DOWN THERE ON WEEKENDS, and WE'D HANG OUT and FOOL AROUND

??

A FEW WEEKS LATER...

I MISSED MY PERIOD...

I PANICKED...

OH MY GOD

NO

A FEW YEARS EARLIER I'D HAD THE USUAL REBEL-LIOUS TEENAGE EPIPHANY:

RELIGION IS BULLSHIT... IT'S JUST A MAN-MADE TOOL THAT THE POWERS THAT BE USE TO SCARE THOSE BELOW THEM INTO MAINTAINING THE STATUS QUO...

← 3AM

THEN ONE DAY:

I HAD AN AQUARIUM IN MY ROOM WITH A FEW GOLDFISH IN IT...

and ONE OF THEM DEVELOP-ED FIN ROT

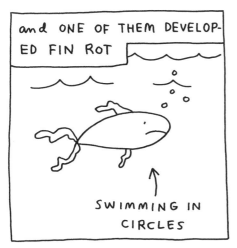

SWIMMING IN CIRCLES

I WAS SHATTERED BY IT

WHY IS THE WORLD SO FULL OF SUFFERING?

I MADE A DEAL WITH GOD...

IF YOU SAVE THIS FISH, I'LL BELIEVE IN YOU...

SOON:

AFTER THAT, I BE-LIEVED IN GOD...

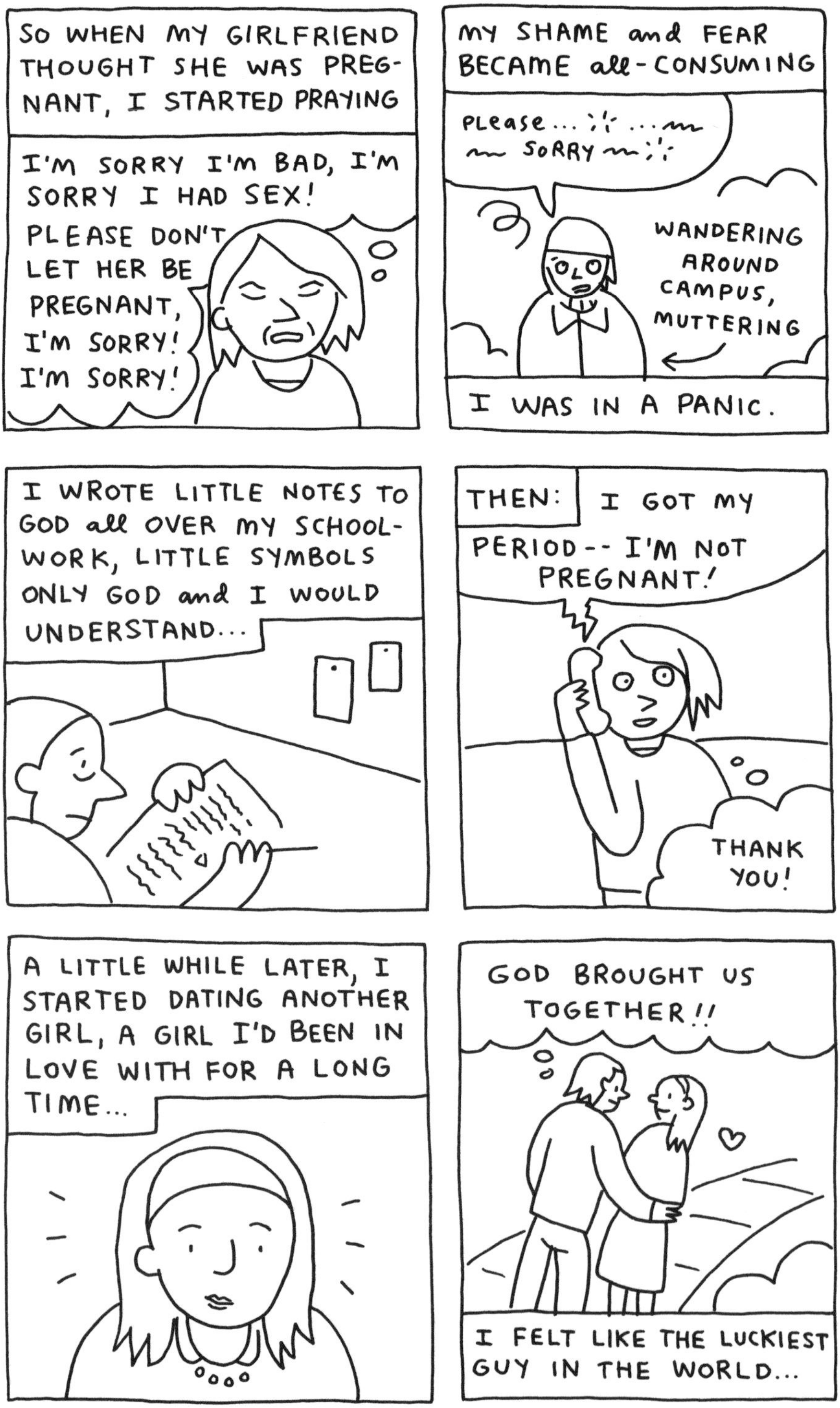
SO WHEN MY GIRLFRIEND THOUGHT SHE WAS PREGNANT, I STARTED PRAYING
I'M SORRY I'M BAD, I'M SORRY I HAD SEX! PLEASE DON'T LET HER BE PREGNANT, I'M SORRY! I'M SORRY!
MY SHAME and FEAR BECAME all-CONSUMING
Please ... SORRY
WANDERING AROUND CAMPUS, MUTTERING
I WAS IN A PANIC.
I WROTE LITTLE NOTES TO GOD all OVER MY SCHOOLWORK, LITTLE SYMBOLS ONLY GOD and I WOULD UNDERSTAND...
THEN:
I GOT MY PERIOD -- I'M NOT PREGNANT!
THANK YOU!
A LITTLE WHILE LATER, I STARTED DATING ANOTHER GIRL, A GIRL I'D BEEN IN LOVE WITH FOR A LONG TIME...
GOD BROUGHT US TOGETHER!!
I FELT LIKE THE LUCKIEST GUY IN THE WORLD...

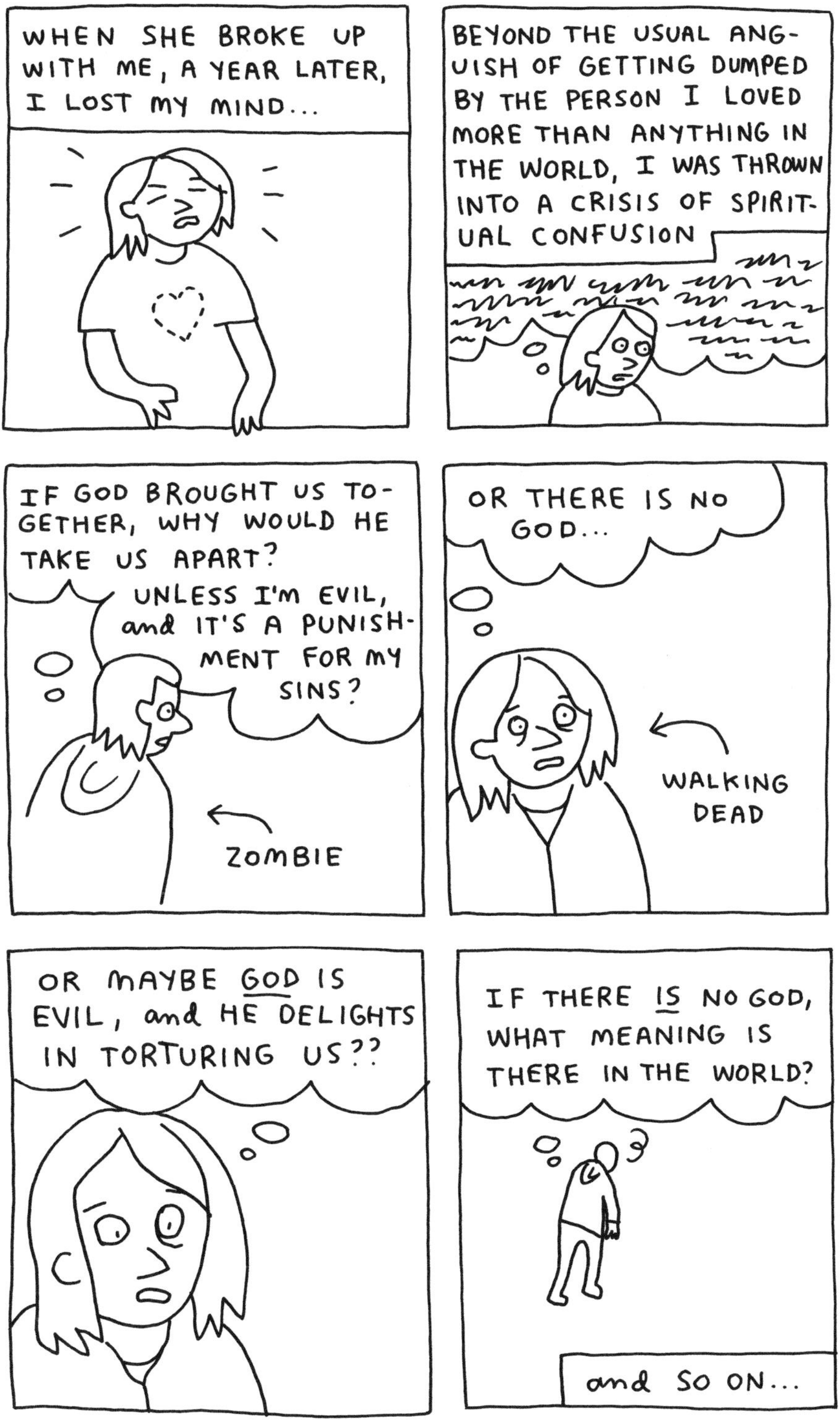
WHEN SHE BROKE UP WITH ME, A YEAR LATER, I LOST MY MIND...
BEYOND THE USUAL ANGUISH OF GETTING DUMPED BY THE PERSON I LOVED MORE THAN ANYTHING IN THE WORLD, I WAS THROWN INTO A CRISIS OF SPIRITUAL CONFUSION
IF GOD BROUGHT US TOGETHER, WHY WOULD HE TAKE US APART?
UNLESS I'M EVIL, and IT'S A PUNISHMENT FOR MY SINS?
ZOMBIE
OR THERE IS NO GOD...
WALKING DEAD
OR MAYBE GOD IS EVIL, and HE DELIGHTS IN TORTURING US??
IF THERE IS NO GOD, WHAT MEANING IS THERE IN THE WORLD?
and SO ON...

THE DREAD and PURE ANGUISH I FELT WAS INSUFFERABLE

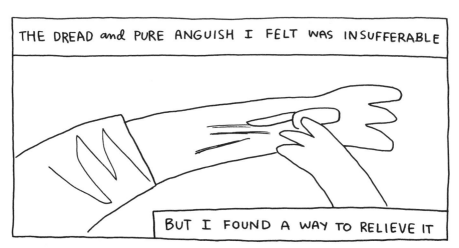

BUT I FOUND A WAY TO RELIEVE IT

CUTTING MYSELF BROUGHT PEACE, SOMEHOW...

SOME NIGHTS IT WAS THE ONLY WAY I COULD Fall ASLEEP...

I WAS DRIFTING AWAY

I'LL ATONE FOR MY SINS... I'LL PROVE TO GOD THAT I'M PURE ENOUGH TO DESERVE HER...

PLEASE TURN TO PAGE 231...

IF I CAN'T HAVE HER, I'LL HAVE NO ONE...

I'LL BE PURE -- and I'LL WAIT FOR HER...

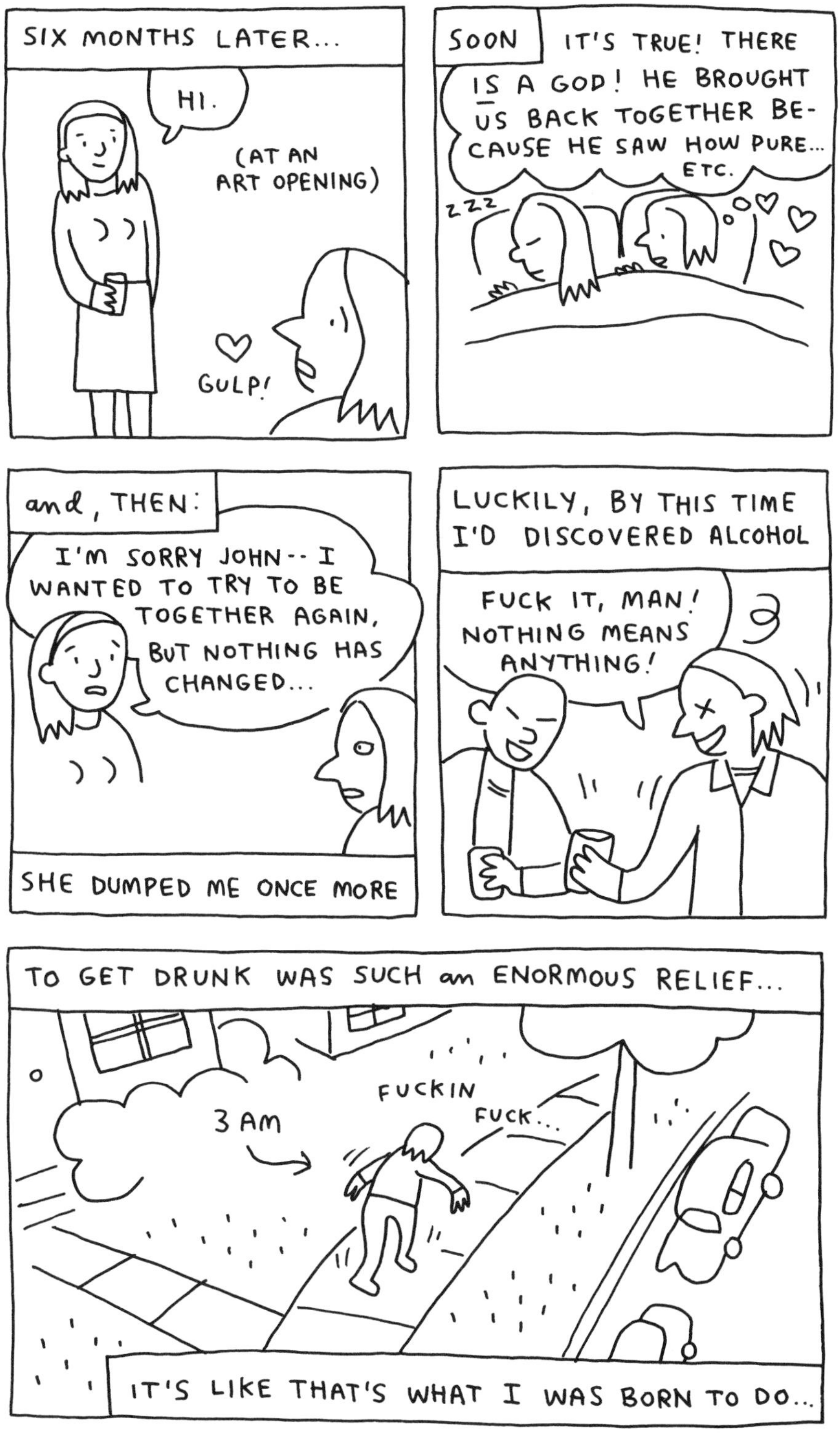
SIX MONTHS LATER...
HI.
(AT AN ART OPENING)
GULP!
SOON
IT'S TRUE! THERE IS A GOD! HE BROUGHT US BACK TOGETHER BECAUSE HE SAW HOW PURE... ETC.
ZZZ
and, THEN:
I'M SORRY JOHN -- I WANTED TO TRY TO BE TOGETHER AGAIN, BUT NOTHING HAS CHANGED...
SHE DUMPED ME ONCE MORE
LUCKILY, BY THIS TIME I'D DISCOVERED ALCOHOL
FUCK IT, MAN! NOTHING MEANS ANYTHING!
TO GET DRUNK WAS SUCH an ENORMOUS RELIEF...
3 AM
FUCKIN
FUCK...
IT'S LIKE THAT'S WHAT I WAS BORN TO DO...

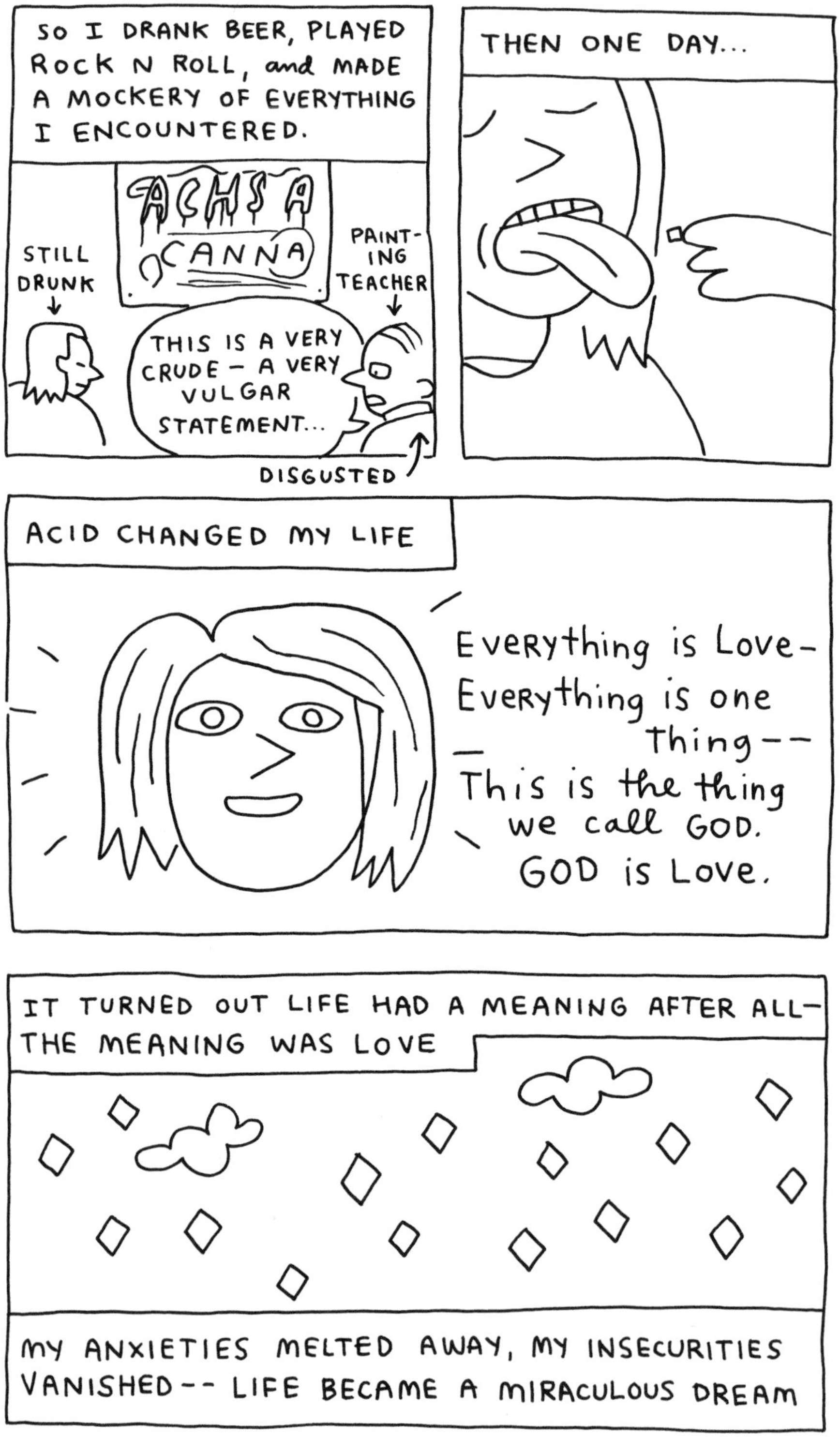
SO I DRANK BEER, PLAYED ROCK N ROLL, and MADE A MOCKERY OF EVERYTHING I ENCOUNTERED.
ACHSA
CANNA
STILL DRUNK
PAINT-ING TEACHER
THIS IS A VERY CRUDE — A VERY VULGAR STATEMENT...
DISGUSTED
THEN ONE DAY...
ACID CHANGED MY LIFE
Everything is Love- Everything is one thing-- This is the thing we call GOD. GOD is Love.
IT TURNED OUT LIFE HAD A MEANING AFTER ALL— THE MEANING WAS LOVE
MY ANXIETIES MELTED AWAY, MY INSECURITIES VANISHED-- LIFE BECAME A MIRACULOUS DREAM

Part Two

AROUND 1992 OR SO, MY ANXIETY BEGAN MAKING A COMEBACK...

DID I TURN THE LIVING ROOM LIGHTS OFF??

DRIVING AROUND BLOCK →

LIGHTS OFF!

IN FACT, IT BEGAN GETTING WORSE THAN EVER

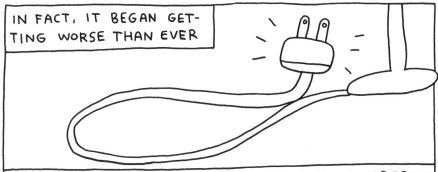

I STARTED TO HAVE TO UNPLUG EVERYTHING ELECTRICAL IN THE APARTMENT BEFORE LEAVING. NOT ONLY THAT, BUT THE PRONGS HAD TO BE ARRANGED SO AS TO NOT BE TOUCHING ANYTHING

THE REFRIGERATOR, IN PARTICULAR, BECAME A PROBLEM...

LEAVING FOR WORK →

DON'T TOUCH IT!!

BUT:

(HAS TO PUSH ON DOOR TO VERIFY IT'S CLOSED) →

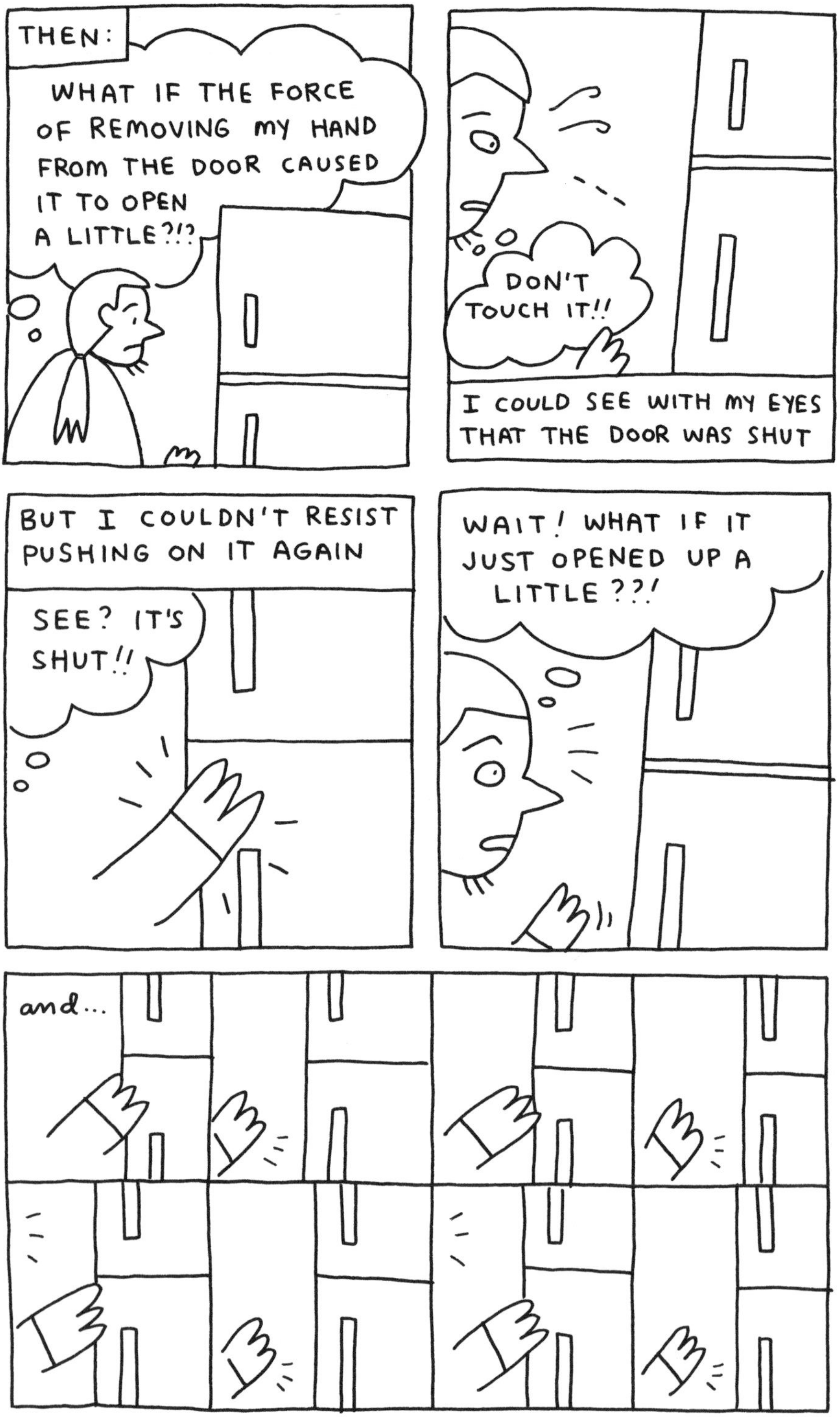

THEN:
WHAT IF THE FORCE OF REMOVING MY HAND FROM THE DOOR CAUSED IT TO OPEN A LITTLE?!?
DON'T TOUCH IT!!
I COULD SEE WITH MY EYES THAT THE DOOR WAS SHUT
BUT I COULDN'T RESIST PUSHING ON IT AGAIN
SEE? IT'S SHUT!!
WAIT! WHAT IF IT JUST OPENED UP A LITTLE??!
and...

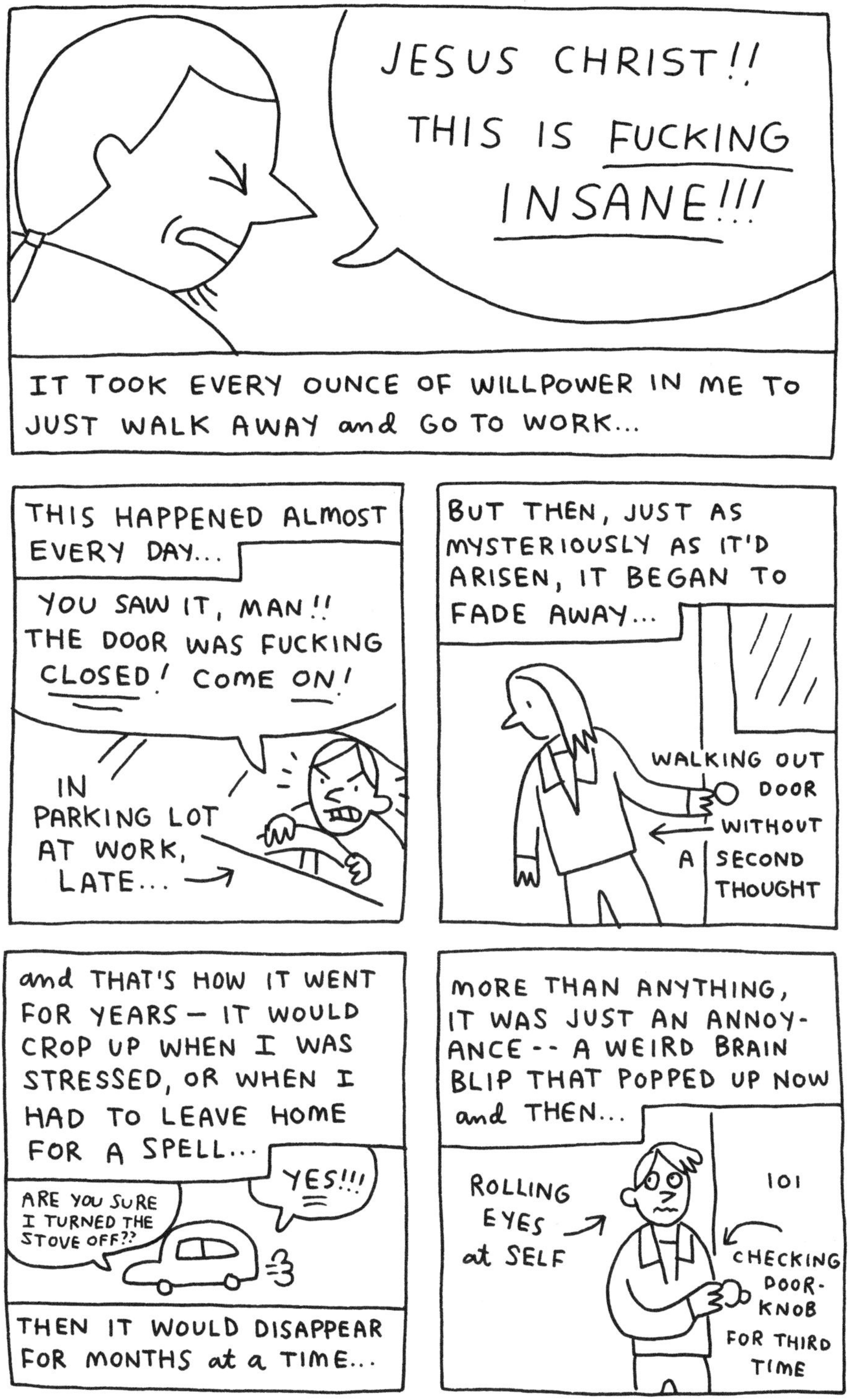
JESUS CHRIST!! THIS IS FUCKING INSANE!!!
IT TOOK EVERY OUNCE OF WILLPOWER IN ME TO JUST WALK AWAY and GO TO WORK...
THIS HAPPENED ALMOST EVERY DAY...
YOU SAW IT, MAN!! THE DOOR WAS FUCKING CLOSED! COME ON!
IN PARKING LOT AT WORK, LATE...
BUT THEN, JUST AS MYSTERIOUSLY AS IT'D ARISEN, IT BEGAN TO FADE AWAY...
WALKING OUT DOOR WITHOUT A SECOND THOUGHT
and THAT'S HOW IT WENT FOR YEARS — IT WOULD CROP UP WHEN I WAS STRESSED, OR WHEN I HAD TO LEAVE HOME FOR A SPELL...
ARE YOU SURE I TURNED THE STOVE OFF??
YES!!!
THEN IT WOULD DISAPPEAR FOR MONTHS at a TIME...
MORE THAN ANYTHING, IT WAS JUST AN ANNOY-ANCE -- A WEIRD BRAIN BLIP THAT POPPED UP NOW and THEN...
ROLLING EYES at SELF
101
CHECKING DOOR-KNOB FOR THIRD TIME

THEN, IN THE SUMMER OF 1997, I GOT REALLY SICK...

DURING A LIFE-SAVING SURGERY, DOCTORS REMOVED A (BENIGN) TUMOR FROM MY SMALL INTESTINES and SENT ME HOME TO CONVALESCE

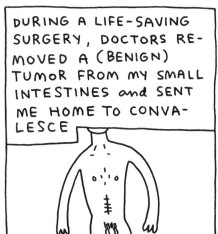

BUT THE TRUTH IS I NEVER FULLY RECOVERED

STILL SUPER-SKINNY SIX MONTHS LATER →

IN FACT, I SPENT MOST OF 1998 IN and OUT OF DOCTORS' OFFICES, STRUGGLING WITH DOZENS OF MYSTERIOUS SYMPTOMS...

DERMATOLOGIST →

MY WARTS HAVE WARTS...

JESUS CHRIST!*

* ACTUAL QUOTE, ed.

FINALLY, THAT Fall, I FOUND A DOCTOR WHO WAS ABLE TO HELP ME -- and I STARTED TO IMPROVE.

DAILY ALLERGY SHOTS

BUT AS MY PHYSICAL HEALTH GOT BETTER, MY MENTAL HEALTH COLLAPSED

DID I LOCK THE DOORS at WORK BEFORE COMING HOME???

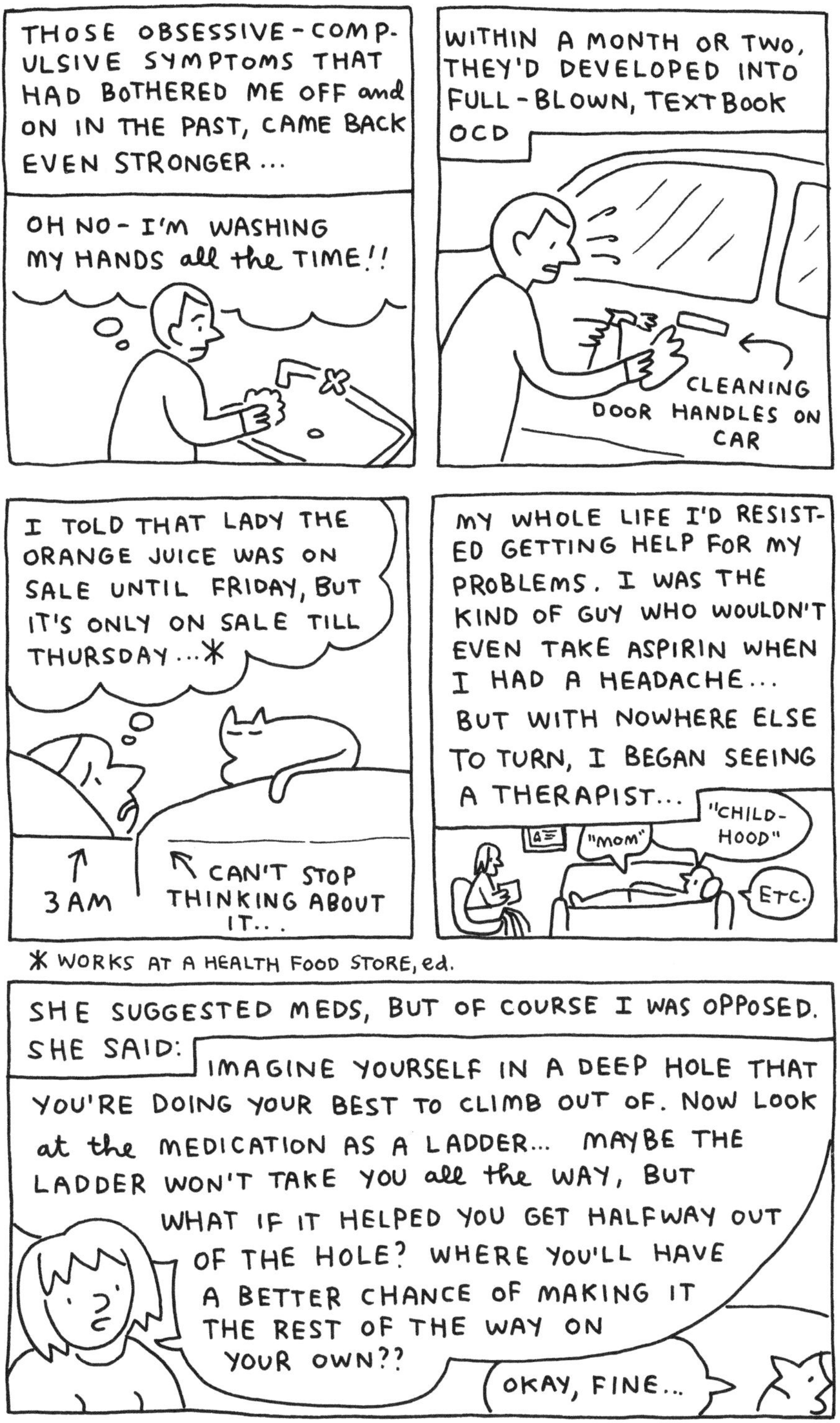
THOSE OBSESSIVE-COMPULSIVE SYMPTOMS THAT HAD BOTHERED ME OFF and ON IN THE PAST, CAME BACK EVEN STRONGER...
OH NO - I'M WASHING MY HANDS all the TIME!!
WITHIN A MONTH OR TWO, THEY'D DEVELOPED INTO FULL-BLOWN, TEXTBOOK OCD
CLEANING DOOR HANDLES ON CAR
I TOLD THAT LADY THE ORANGE JUICE WAS ON SALE UNTIL FRIDAY, BUT IT'S ONLY ON SALE TILL THURSDAY...*
3 AM
CAN'T STOP THINKING ABOUT IT...
MY WHOLE LIFE I'D RESISTED GETTING HELP FOR MY PROBLEMS. I WAS THE KIND OF GUY WHO WOULDN'T EVEN TAKE ASPIRIN WHEN I HAD A HEADACHE... BUT WITH NOWHERE ELSE TO TURN, I BEGAN SEEING A THERAPIST...
"MOM"
"CHILDHOOD"
ETC.
* WORKS AT A HEALTH FOOD STORE, ed.
SHE SUGGESTED MEDS, BUT OF COURSE I WAS OPPOSED. SHE SAID:
IMAGINE YOURSELF IN A DEEP HOLE THAT YOU'RE DOING YOUR BEST TO CLIMB OUT OF. NOW LOOK at the MEDICATION AS A LADDER... MAYBE THE LADDER WON'T TAKE YOU all the WAY, BUT WHAT IF IT HELPED YOU GET HALFWAY OUT OF THE HOLE? WHERE YOU'LL HAVE A BETTER CHANCE OF MAKING IT THE REST OF THE WAY ON YOUR OWN??
OKAY, FINE...

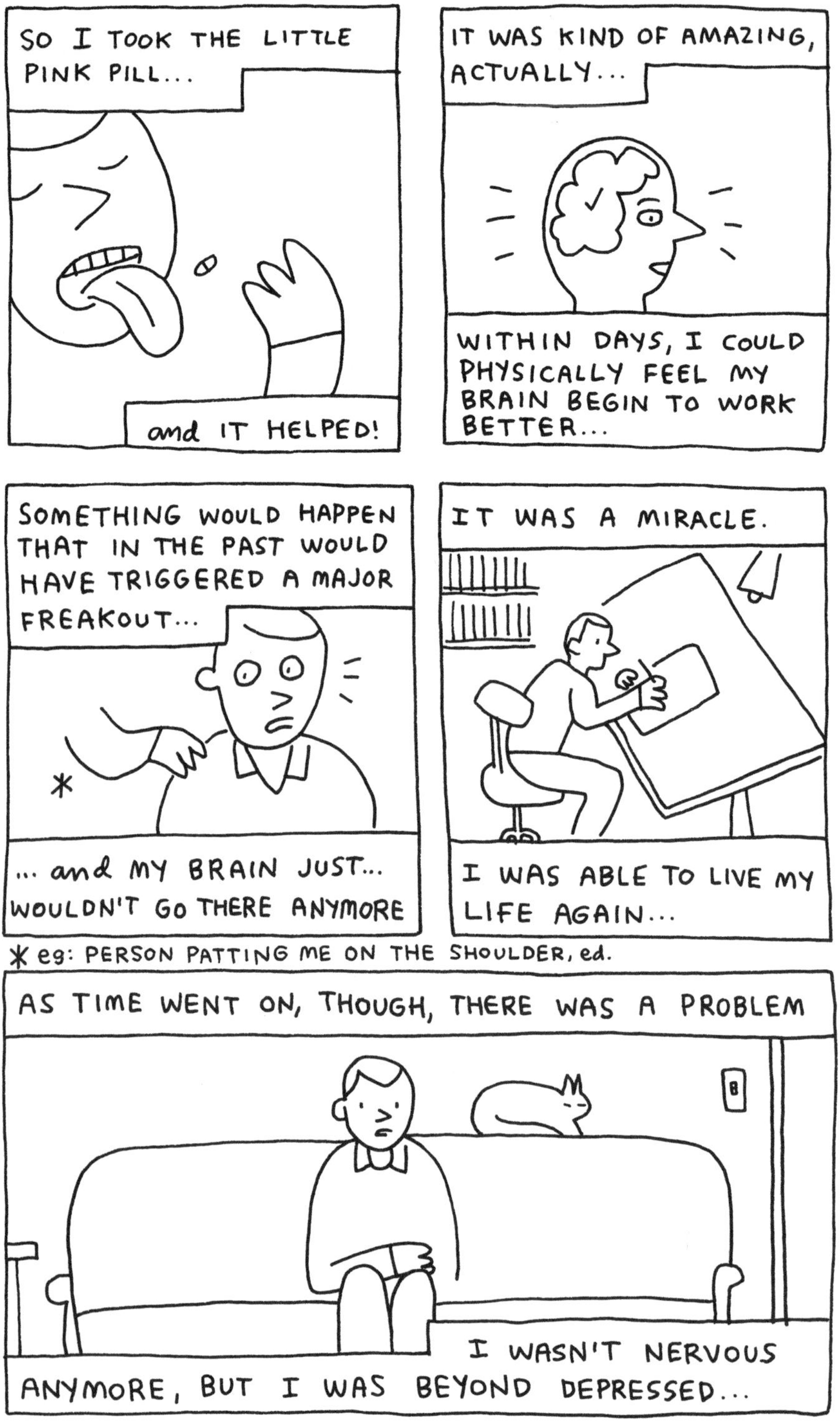
SO I TOOK THE LITTLE PINK PILL...
and IT HELPED!
IT WAS KIND OF AMAZING, ACTUALLY...
WITHIN DAYS, I COULD PHYSICALLY FEEL MY BRAIN BEGIN TO WORK BETTER...
SOMETHING WOULD HAPPEN THAT IN THE PAST WOULD HAVE TRIGGERED A MAJOR FREAKOUT...
*
... and MY BRAIN JUST... WOULDN'T GO THERE ANYMORE
IT WAS A MIRACLE.
I WAS ABLE TO LIVE MY LIFE AGAIN...
* eg: PERSON PATTING ME ON THE SHOULDER, ed.
AS TIME WENT ON, THOUGH, THERE WAS A PROBLEM
I WASN'T NERVOUS ANYMORE, BUT I WAS BEYOND DEPRESSED...

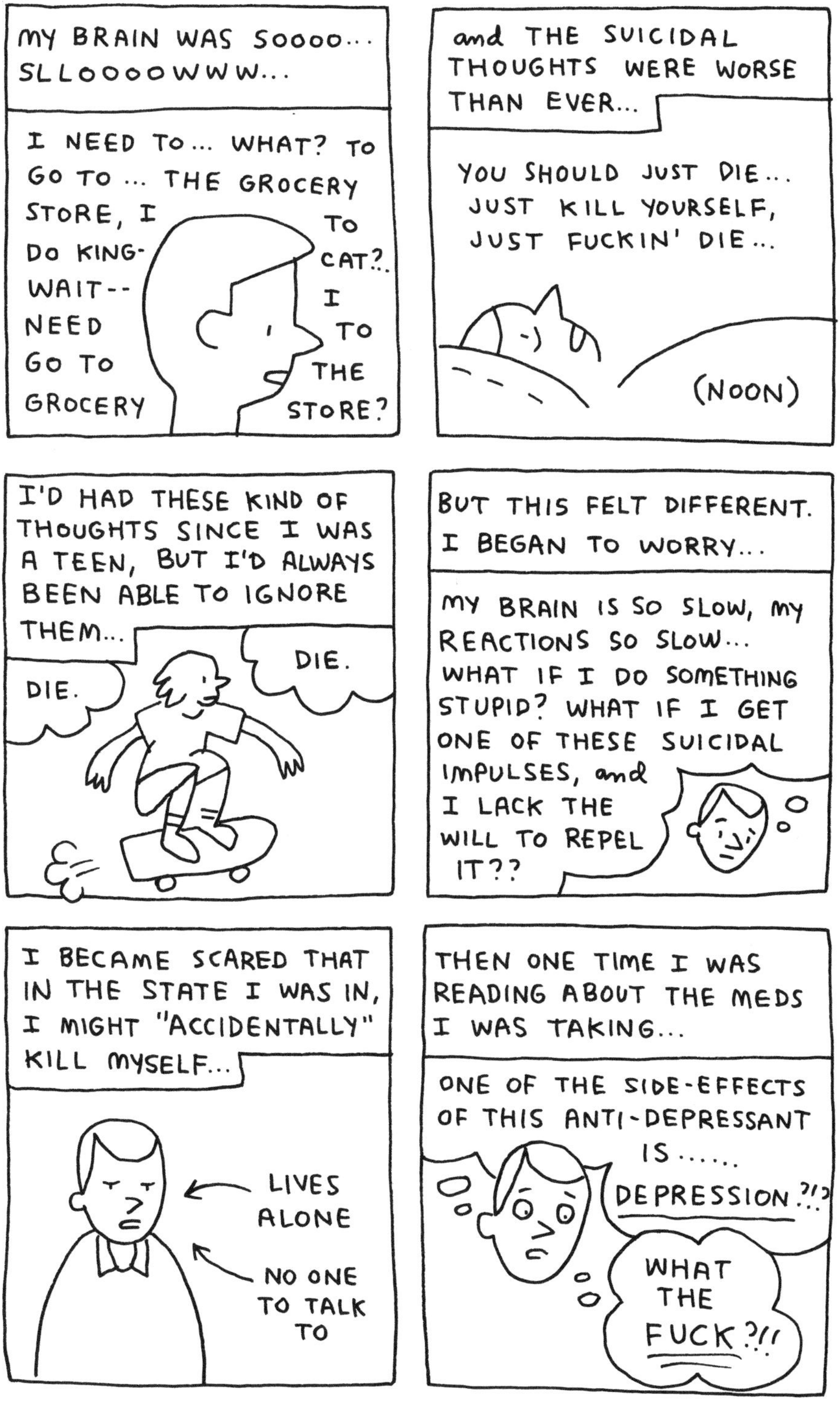
MY BRAIN WAS SOOOO... SLLOOOOWWW...
I NEED TO... WHAT? TO GO TO... THE GROCERY STORE, I DO KING- WAIT-- NEED GO TO GROCERY
TO CAT?.. I TO THE STORE?
and THE SUICIDAL THOUGHTS WERE WORSE THAN EVER...
YOU SHOULD JUST DIE... JUST KILL YOURSELF, JUST FUCKIN' DIE...
(NOON)
I'D HAD THESE KIND OF THOUGHTS SINCE I WAS A TEEN, BUT I'D ALWAYS BEEN ABLE TO IGNORE THEM...
DIE.
DIE.
BUT THIS FELT DIFFERENT. I BEGAN TO WORRY...
MY BRAIN IS SO SLOW, MY REACTIONS SO SLOW... WHAT IF I DO SOMETHING STUPID? WHAT IF I GET ONE OF THESE SUICIDAL IMPULSES, and I LACK THE WILL TO REPEL IT??
I BECAME SCARED THAT IN THE STATE I WAS IN, I MIGHT "ACCIDENTALLY" KILL MYSELF...
LIVES ALONE
NO ONE TO TALK TO
THEN ONE TIME I WAS READING ABOUT THE MEDS I WAS TAKING...
ONE OF THE SIDE-EFFECTS OF THIS ANTI-DEPRESSANT IS...... DEPRESSION?!?
WHAT THE FUCK?!!

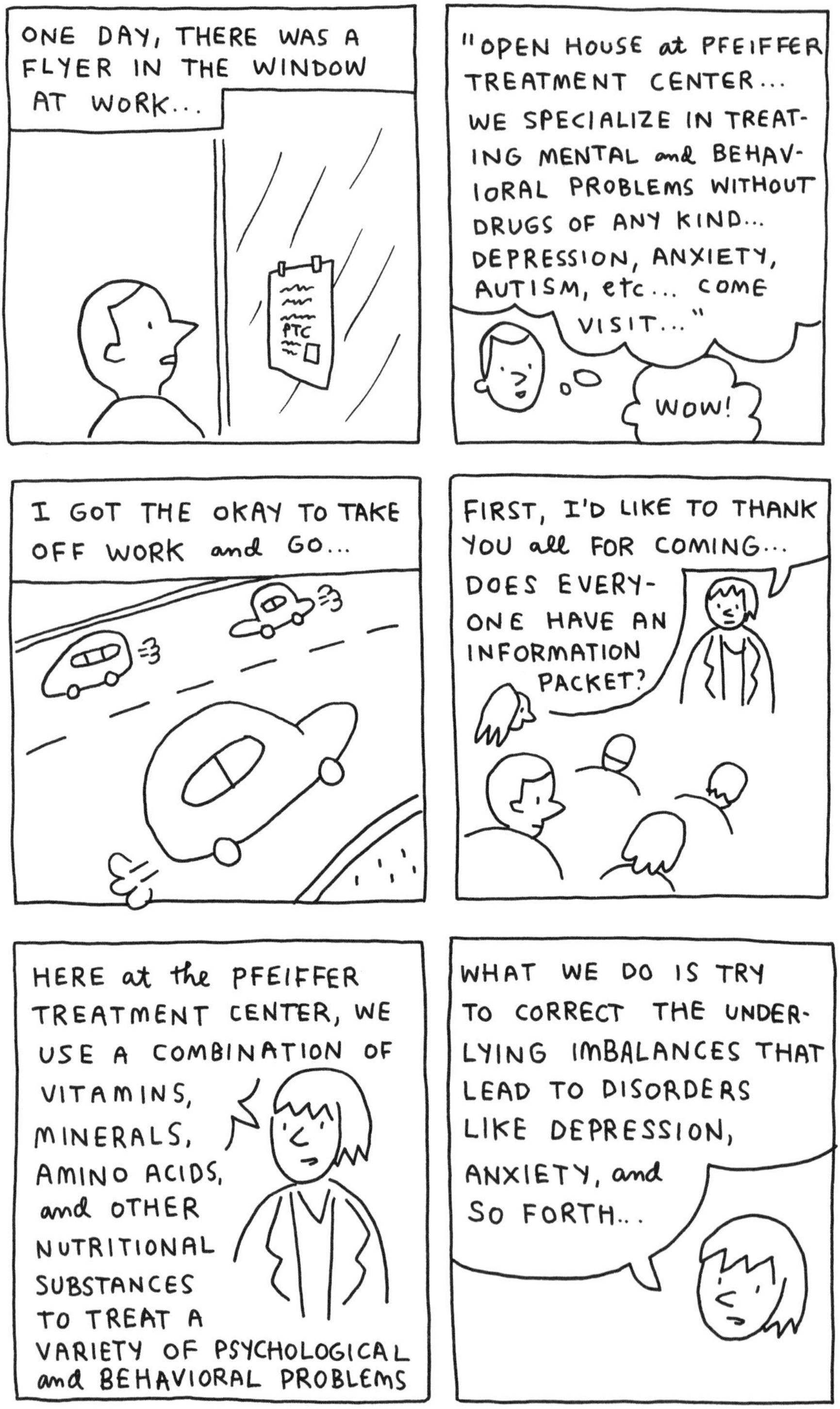
ONE DAY, THERE WAS A FLYER IN THE WINDOW AT WORK...
PTC
"OPEN HOUSE at PFEIFFER TREATMENT CENTER... WE SPECIALIZE IN TREATING MENTAL and BEHAVIORAL PROBLEMS WITHOUT DRUGS OF ANY KIND... DEPRESSION, ANXIETY, AUTISM, etc... COME VISIT..."
WOW!
I GOT THE OKAY TO TAKE OFF WORK and GO...
FIRST, I'D LIKE TO THANK YOU all FOR COMING... DOES EVERYONE HAVE AN INFORMATION PACKET?
HERE at the PFEIFFER TREATMENT CENTER, WE USE A COMBINATION OF VITAMINS, MINERALS, AMINO ACIDS, and OTHER NUTRITIONAL SUBSTANCES TO TREAT A VARIETY OF PSYCHOLOGICAL and BEHAVIORAL PROBLEMS
WHAT WE DO IS TRY TO CORRECT THE UNDERLYING IMBALANCES THAT LEAD TO DISORDERS LIKE DEPRESSION, ANXIETY, and SO FORTH...

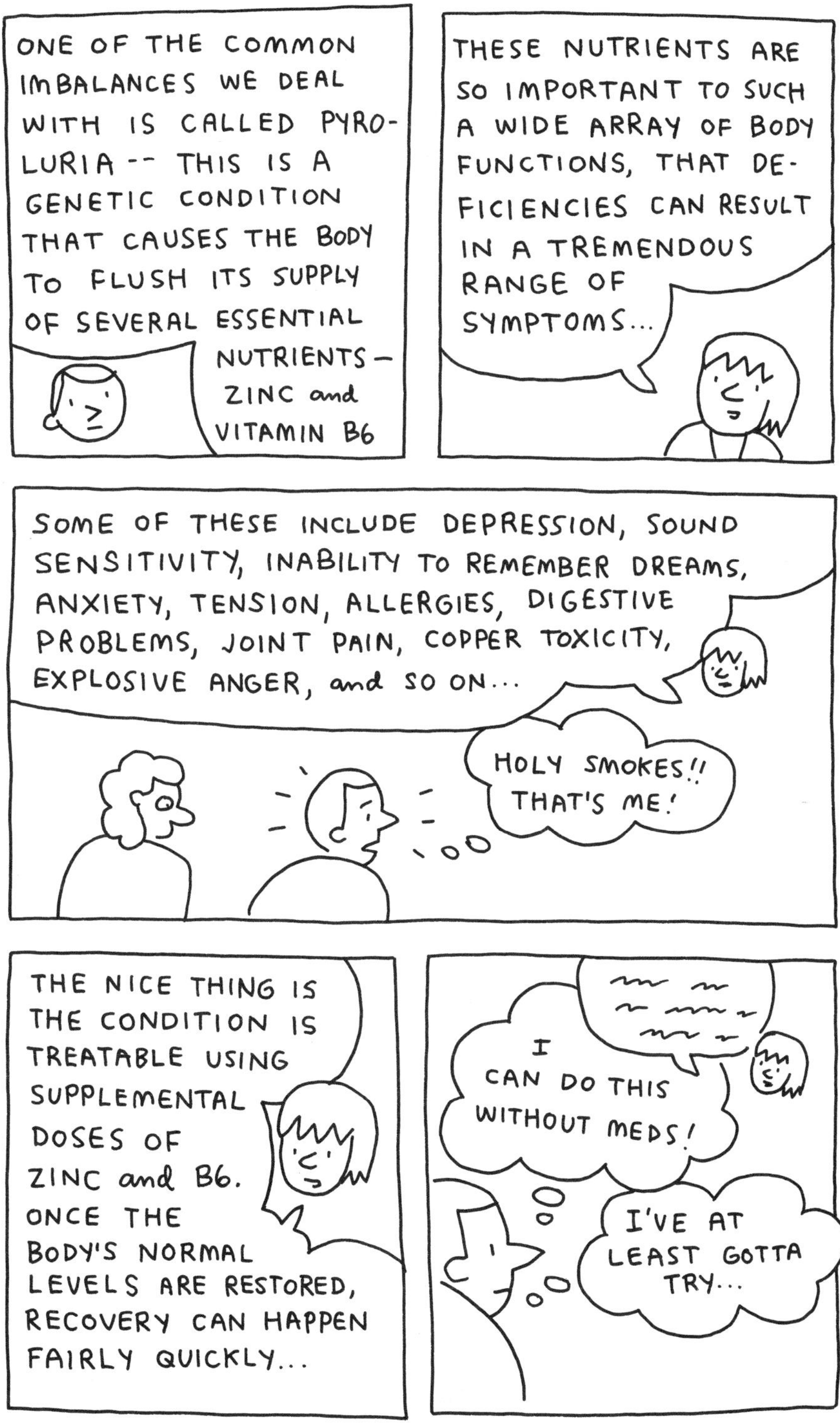
ONE OF THE COMMON IMBALANCES WE DEAL WITH IS CALLED PYRO-LURIA -- THIS IS A GENETIC CONDITION THAT CAUSES THE BODY TO FLUSH ITS SUPPLY OF SEVERAL ESSENTIAL NUTRIENTS — ZINC and VITAMIN B6
THESE NUTRIENTS ARE SO IMPORTANT TO SUCH A WIDE ARRAY OF BODY FUNCTIONS, THAT DE-FICIENCIES CAN RESULT IN A TREMENDOUS RANGE OF SYMPTOMS...
SOME OF THESE INCLUDE DEPRESSION, SOUND SENSITIVITY, INABILITY TO REMEMBER DREAMS, ANXIETY, TENSION, ALLERGIES, DIGESTIVE PROBLEMS, JOINT PAIN, COPPER TOXICITY, EXPLOSIVE ANGER, and SO ON...
HOLY SMOKES!! THAT'S ME!
THE NICE THING IS THE CONDITION IS TREATABLE USING SUPPLEMENTAL DOSES OF ZINC and B6. ONCE THE BODY'S NORMAL LEVELS ARE RESTORED, RECOVERY CAN HAPPEN FAIRLY QUICKLY...
I CAN DO THIS WITHOUT MEDS!
I'VE AT LEAST GOTTA TRY...

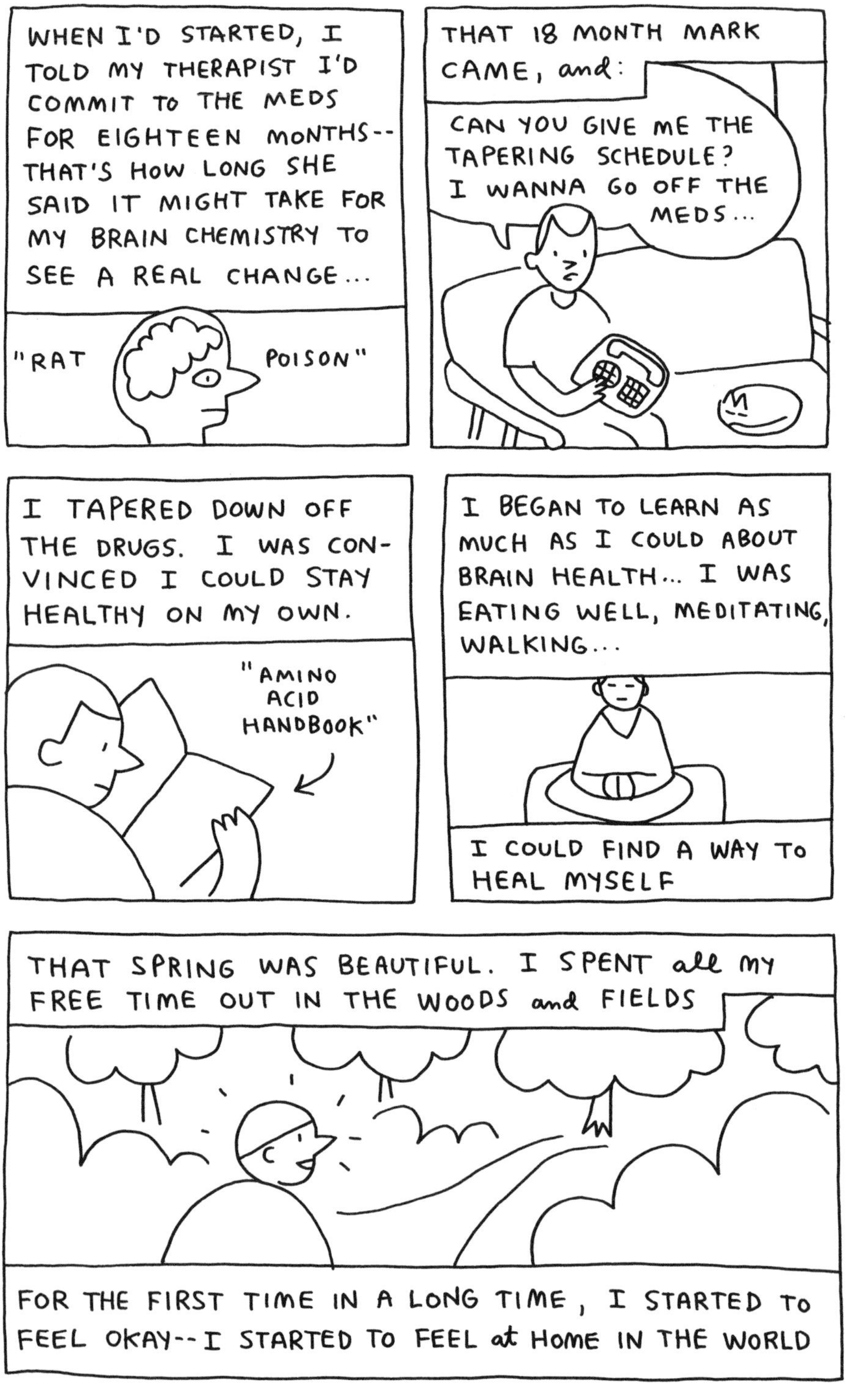
WHEN I'D STARTED, I TOLD MY THERAPIST I'D COMMIT TO THE MEDS FOR EIGHTEEN MONTHS-- THAT'S HOW LONG SHE SAID IT MIGHT TAKE FOR MY BRAIN CHEMISTRY TO SEE A REAL CHANGE...
"RAT POISON"
THAT 18 MONTH MARK CAME, and:
CAN YOU GIVE ME THE TAPERING SCHEDULE? I WANNA GO OFF THE MEDS...
I TAPERED DOWN OFF THE DRUGS. I WAS CONVINCED I COULD STAY HEALTHY ON MY OWN.
"AMINO ACID HANDBOOK"
I BEGAN TO LEARN AS MUCH AS I COULD ABOUT BRAIN HEALTH... I WAS EATING WELL, MEDITATING, WALKING...
I COULD FIND A WAY TO HEAL MYSELF
THAT SPRING WAS BEAUTIFUL. I SPENT all MY FREE TIME OUT IN THE WOODS and FIELDS
FOR THE FIRST TIME IN A LONG TIME, I STARTED TO FEEL OKAY--I STARTED TO FEEL at HOME IN THE WORLD

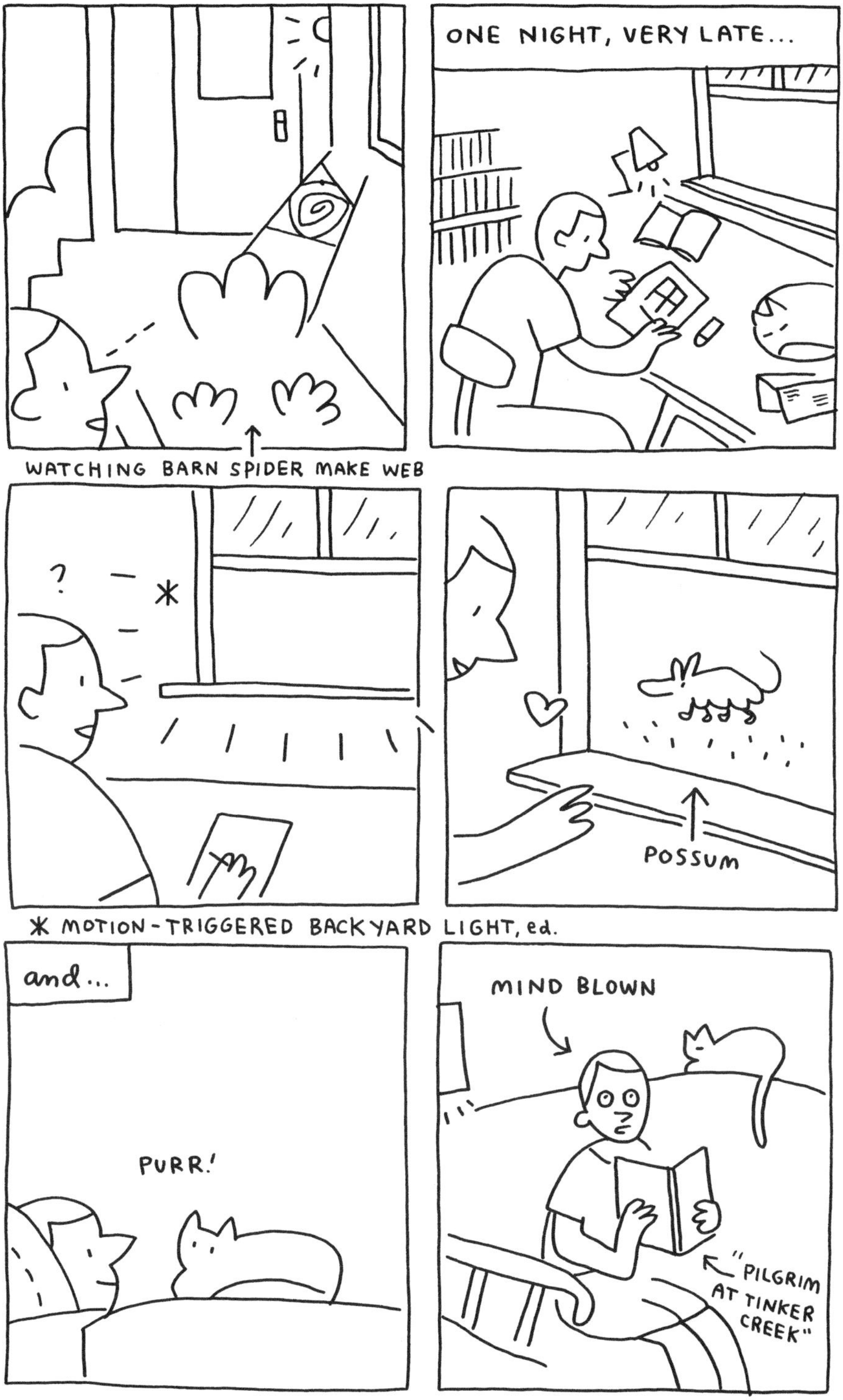
ONE NIGHT, VERY LATE...
WATCHING BARN SPIDER MAKE WEB
?
*
POSSUM
* MOTION-TRIGGERED BACKYARD LIGHT, ed.
and...
PURR!
MIND BLOWN
"PILGRIM AT TINKER CREEK"

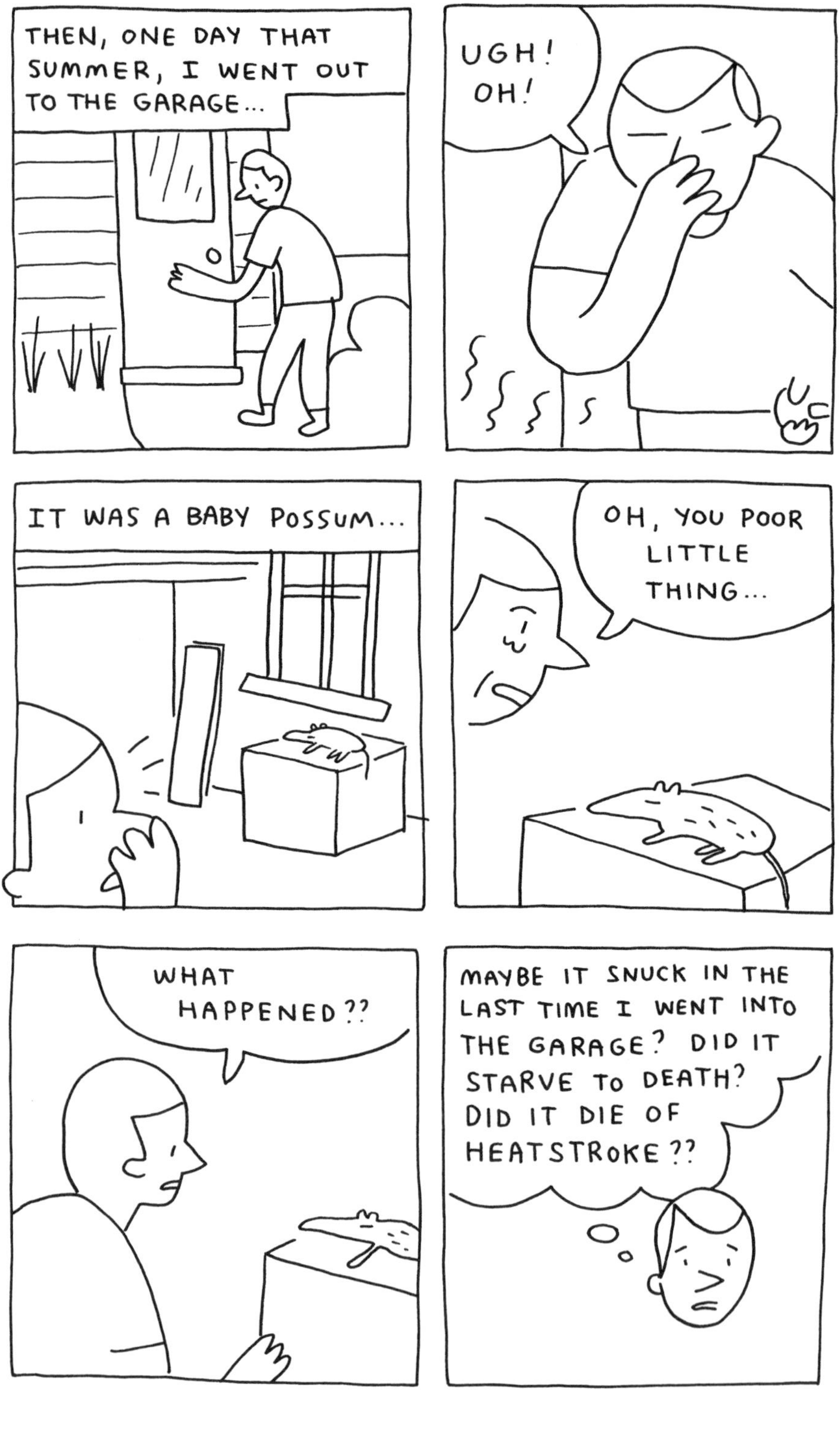
THEN, ONE DAY THAT SUMMER, I WENT OUT TO THE GARAGE...
UGH! OH!
IT WAS A BABY POSSUM...
OH, YOU POOR LITTLE THING...
WHAT HAPPENED??
MAYBE IT SNUCK IN THE LAST TIME I WENT INTO THE GARAGE? DID IT STARVE TO DEATH? DID IT DIE OF HEATSTROKE??

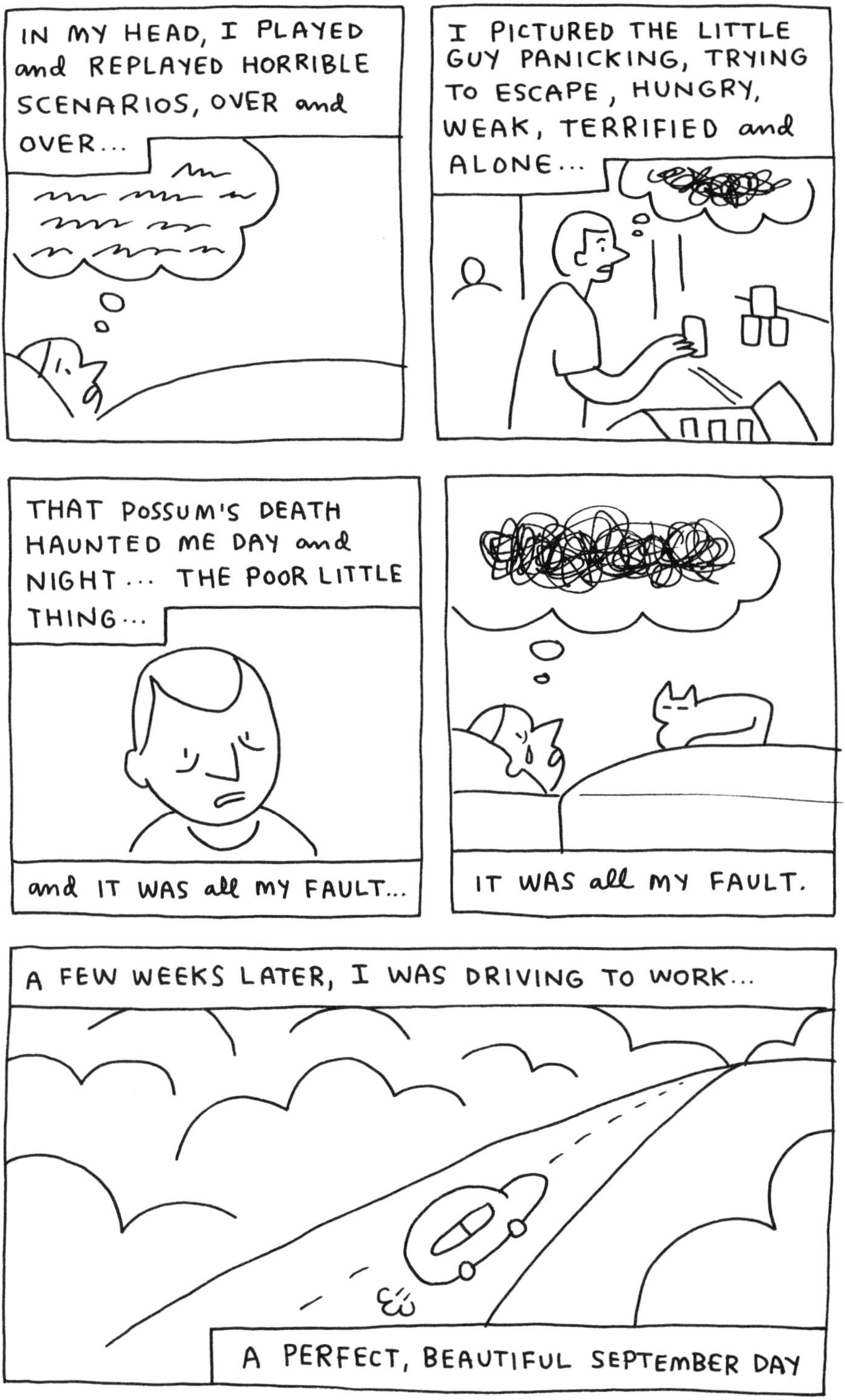
IN MY HEAD, I PLAYED and REPLAYED HORRIBLE SCENARIOS, OVER and OVER...
I PICTURED THE LITTLE GUY PANICKING, TRYING TO ESCAPE, HUNGRY, WEAK, TERRIFIED and ALONE...
THAT POSSUM'S DEATH HAUNTED ME DAY and NIGHT... THE POOR LITTLE THING...
and IT WAS all MY FAULT...
IT WAS all MY FAULT.
A FEW WEEKS LATER, I WAS DRIVING TO WORK...
A PERFECT, BEAUTIFUL SEPTEMBER DAY

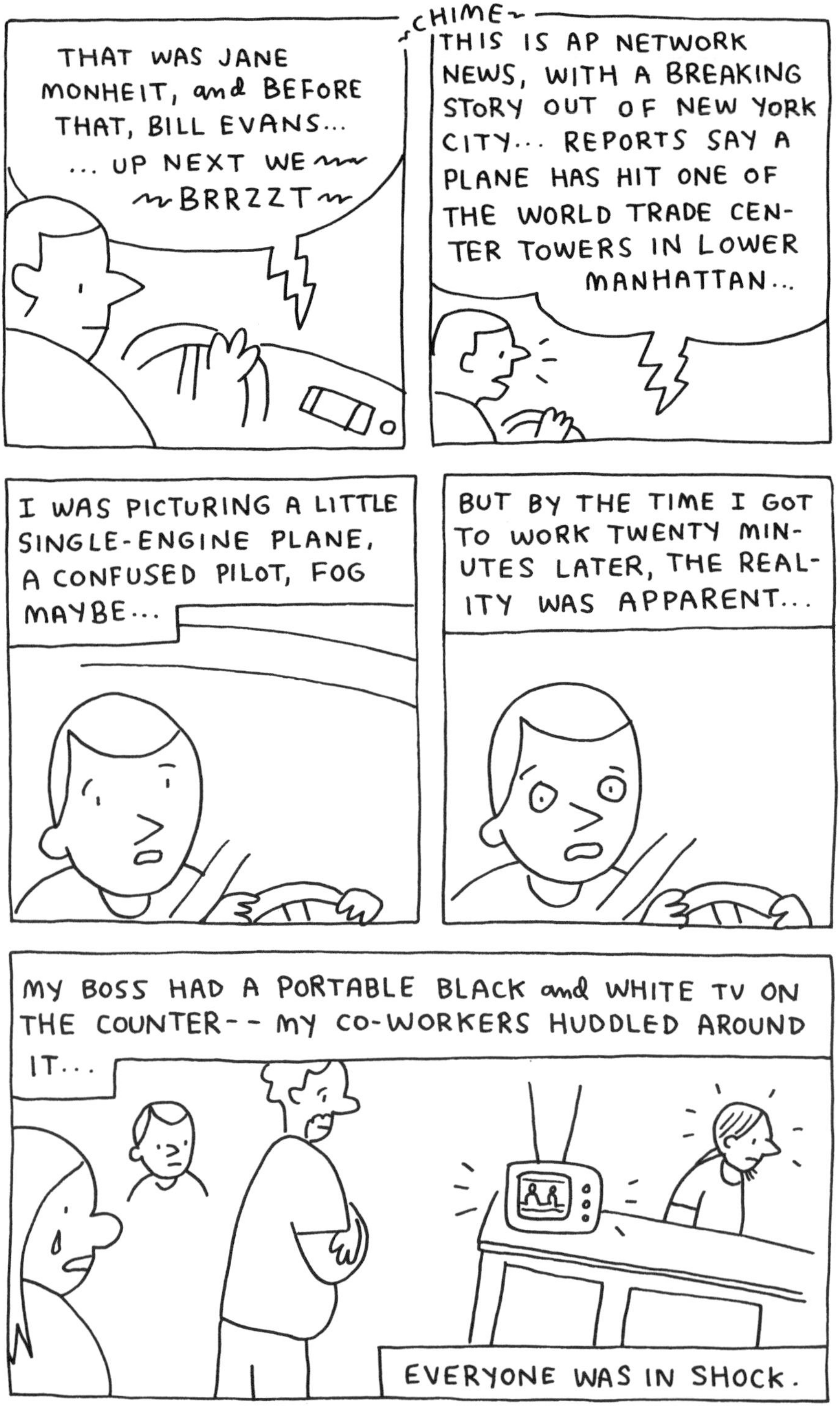
THAT WAS JANE MONHEIT, and BEFORE THAT, BILL EVANS... ...UP NEXT WE
BRRZZT
CHIME
THIS IS AP NETWORK NEWS, WITH A BREAKING STORY OUT OF NEW YORK CITY... REPORTS SAY A PLANE HAS HIT ONE OF THE WORLD TRADE CENTER TOWERS IN LOWER MANHATTAN...
I WAS PICTURING A LITTLE SINGLE-ENGINE PLANE, A CONFUSED PILOT, FOG MAYBE...
BUT BY THE TIME I GOT TO WORK TWENTY MINUTES LATER, THE REALITY WAS APPARENT...
MY BOSS HAD A PORTABLE BLACK and WHITE TV ON THE COUNTER-- MY CO-WORKERS HUDDLED AROUND IT...
EVERYONE WAS IN SHOCK.

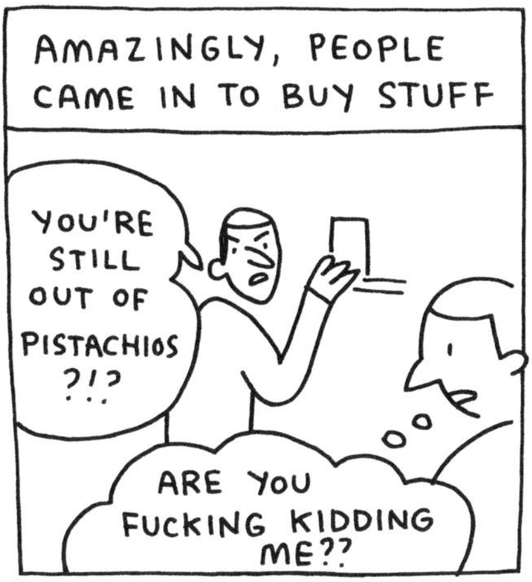
AMAZINGLY, PEOPLE CAME IN TO BUY STUFF
YOU'RE STILL OUT OF PISTACHIOS ?!?
ARE YOU FUCKING KIDDING ME??

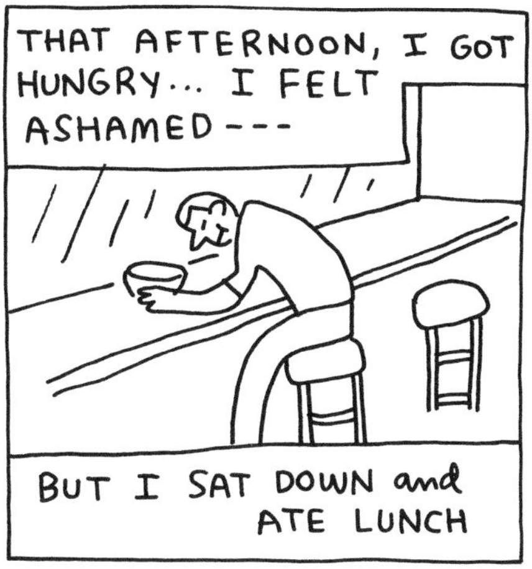
THAT AFTERNOON, I GOT HUNGRY... I FELT ASHAMED---
BUT I SAT DOWN and ATE LUNCH

Part Three

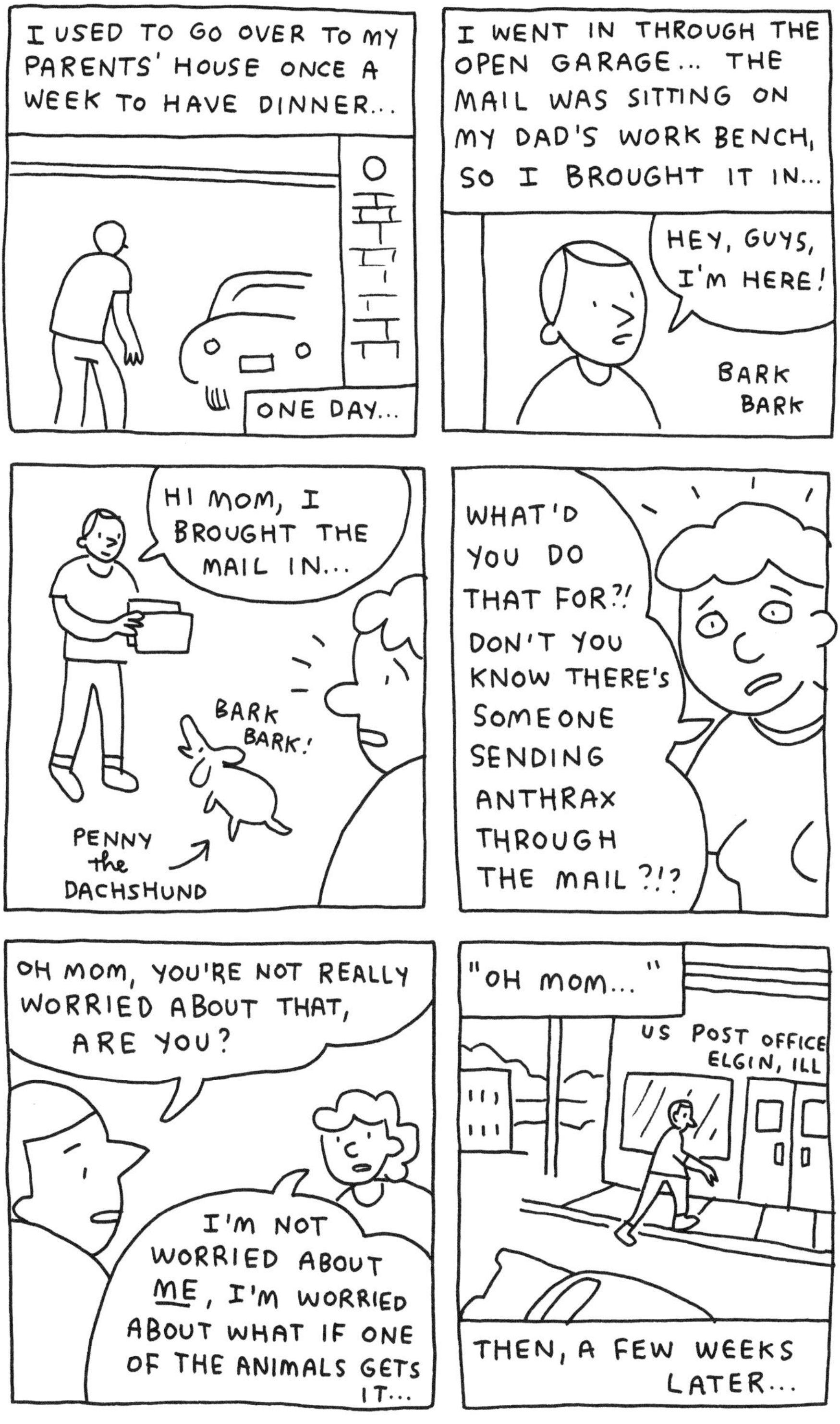
I USED TO GO OVER TO MY PARENTS' HOUSE ONCE A WEEK TO HAVE DINNER...
ONE DAY...
I WENT IN THROUGH THE OPEN GARAGE... THE MAIL WAS SITTING ON MY DAD'S WORK BENCH, SO I BROUGHT IT IN...
HEY, GUYS, I'M HERE!
BARK BARK
HI MOM, I BROUGHT THE MAIL IN...
BARK BARK!
PENNY the DACHSHUND
WHAT'D YOU DO THAT FOR?! DON'T YOU KNOW THERE'S SOMEONE SENDING ANTHRAX THROUGH THE MAIL?!?
OH MOM, YOU'RE NOT REALLY WORRIED ABOUT THAT, ARE YOU?
I'M NOT WORRIED ABOUT ME, I'M WORRIED ABOUT WHAT IF ONE OF THE ANIMALS GETS IT...
"OH MOM..."
US POST OFFICE ELGIN, ILL
THEN, A FEW WEEKS LATER...

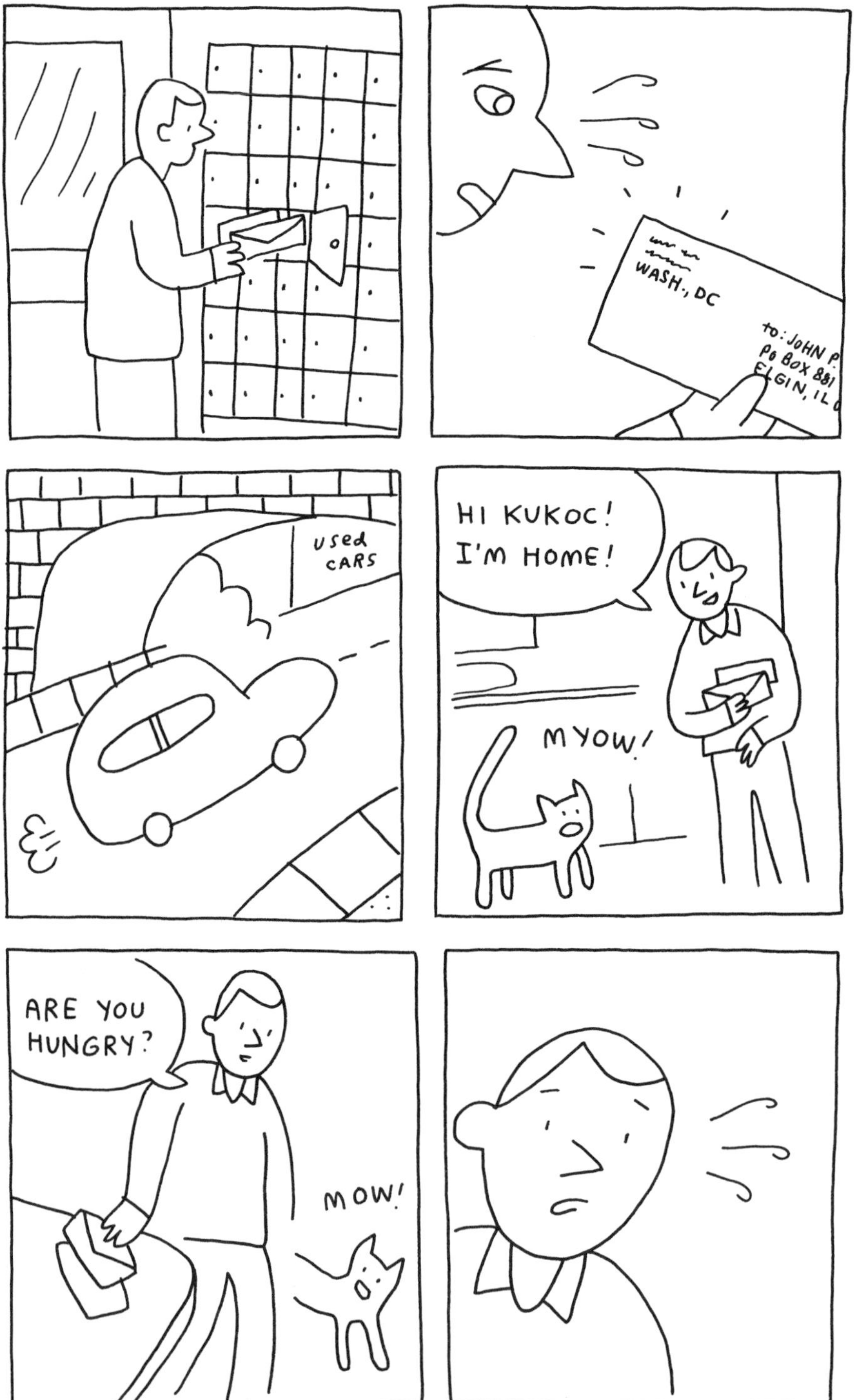
WASH., DC
to: JOHN P.
PO BOX 881
ELGIN, IL
used CARS
HI KUKOC! I'M HOME!
MYOW!
ARE YOU HUNGRY?
MOW!

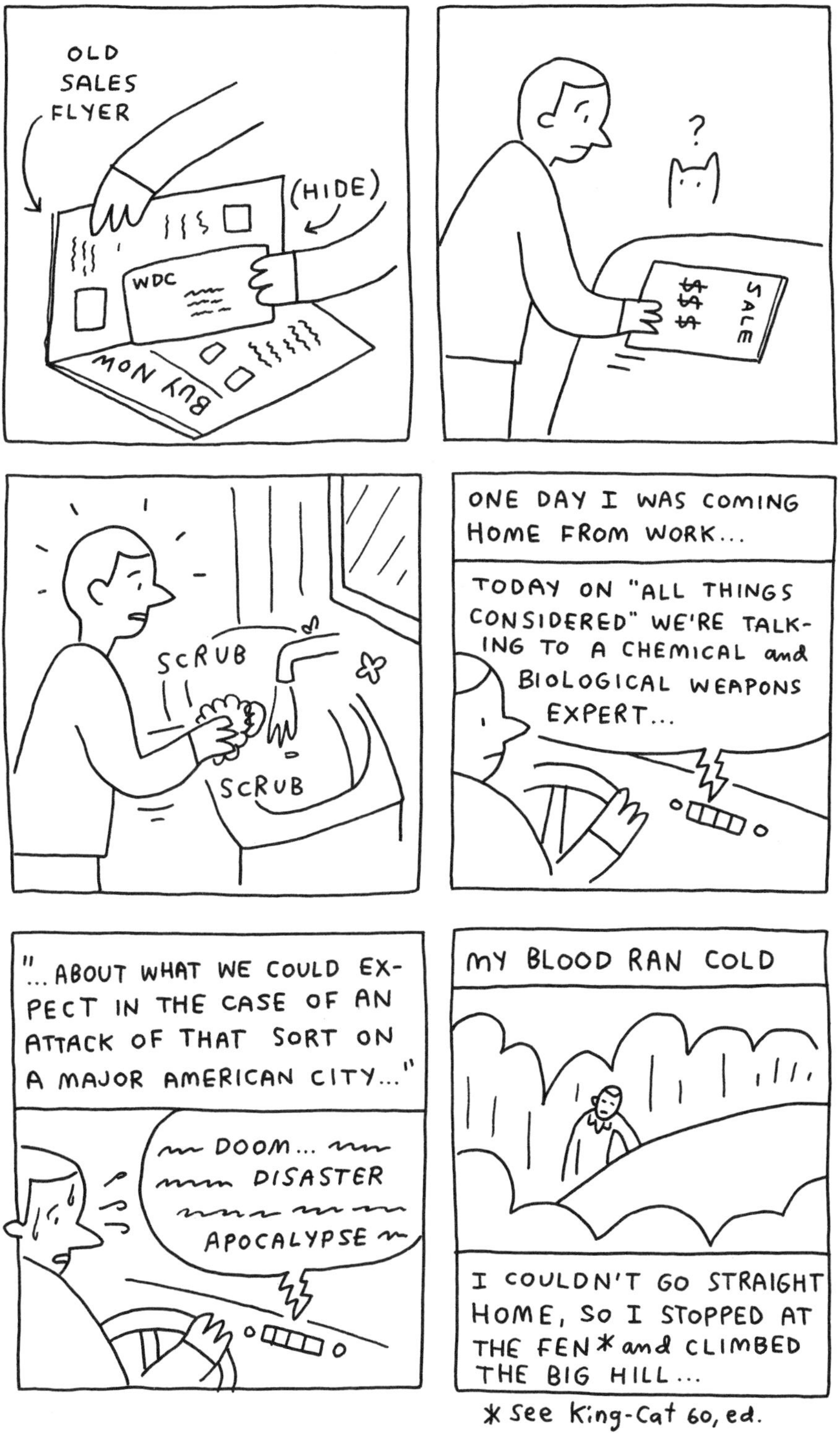
OLD SALES FLYER
(HIDE)
WDC
BUY NOW
?
$$$
SALE
SCRUB
SCRUB
ONE DAY I WAS COMING HOME FROM WORK...
TODAY ON "ALL THINGS CONSIDERED" WE'RE TALKING TO A CHEMICAL and BIOLOGICAL WEAPONS EXPERT...
"...ABOUT WHAT WE COULD EXPECT IN THE CASE OF AN ATTACK OF THAT SORT ON A MAJOR AMERICAN CITY..."
DOOM... DISASTER APOCALYPSE
MY BLOOD RAN COLD
I COULDN'T GO STRAIGHT HOME, SO I STOPPED AT THE FEN* and CLIMBED THE BIG HILL...

* see King-Cat 60, ed.

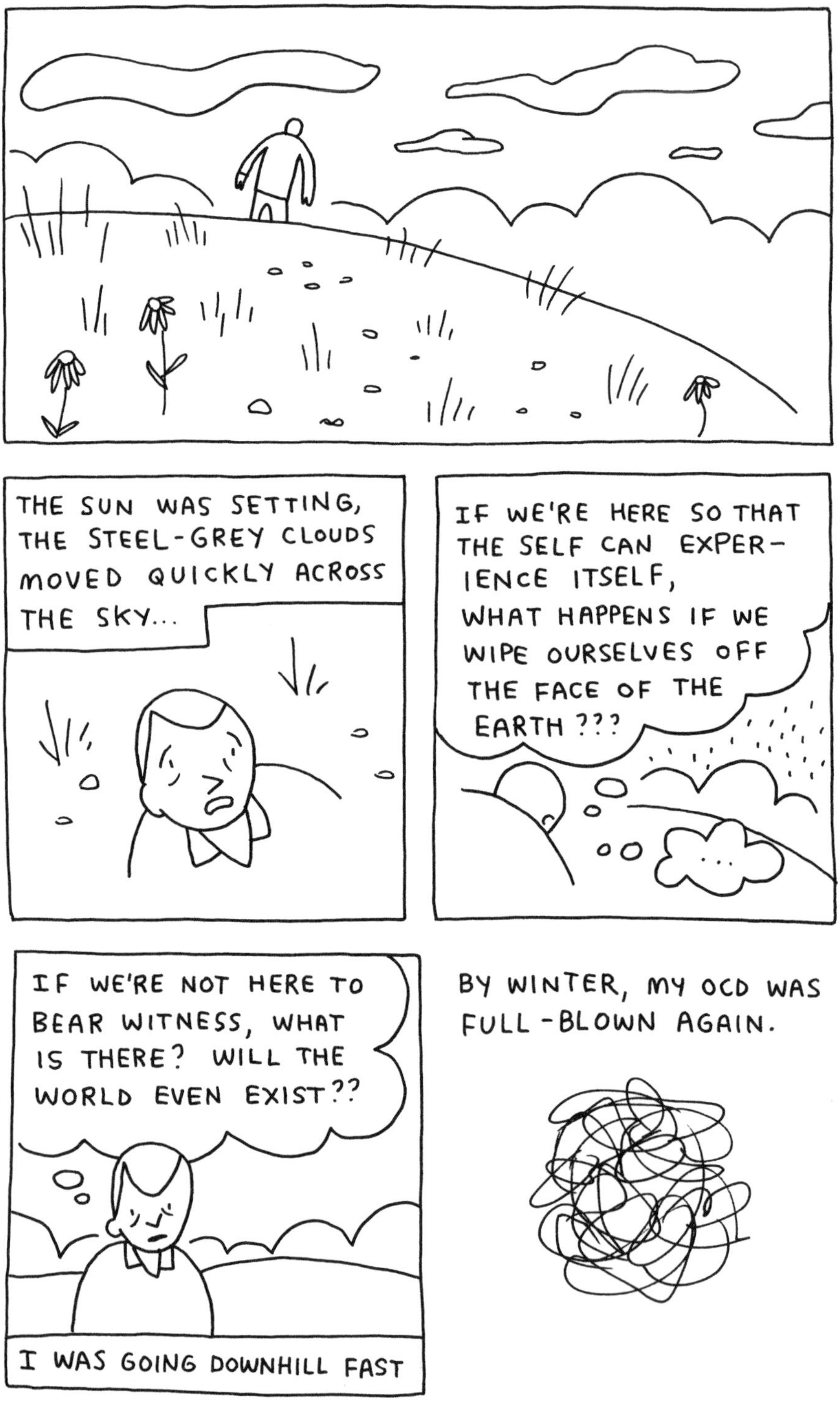
THE SUN WAS SETTING, THE STEEL-GREY CLOUDS MOVED QUICKLY ACROSS THE SKY...
IF WE'RE HERE SO THAT THE SELF CAN EXPER-IENCE ITSELF, WHAT HAPPENS IF WE WIPE OURSELVES OFF THE FACE OF THE EARTH???
IF WE'RE NOT HERE TO BEAR WITNESS, WHAT IS THERE? WILL THE WORLD EVEN EXIST??
I WAS GOING DOWNHILL FAST
BY WINTER, MY OCD WAS FULL-BLOWN AGAIN.

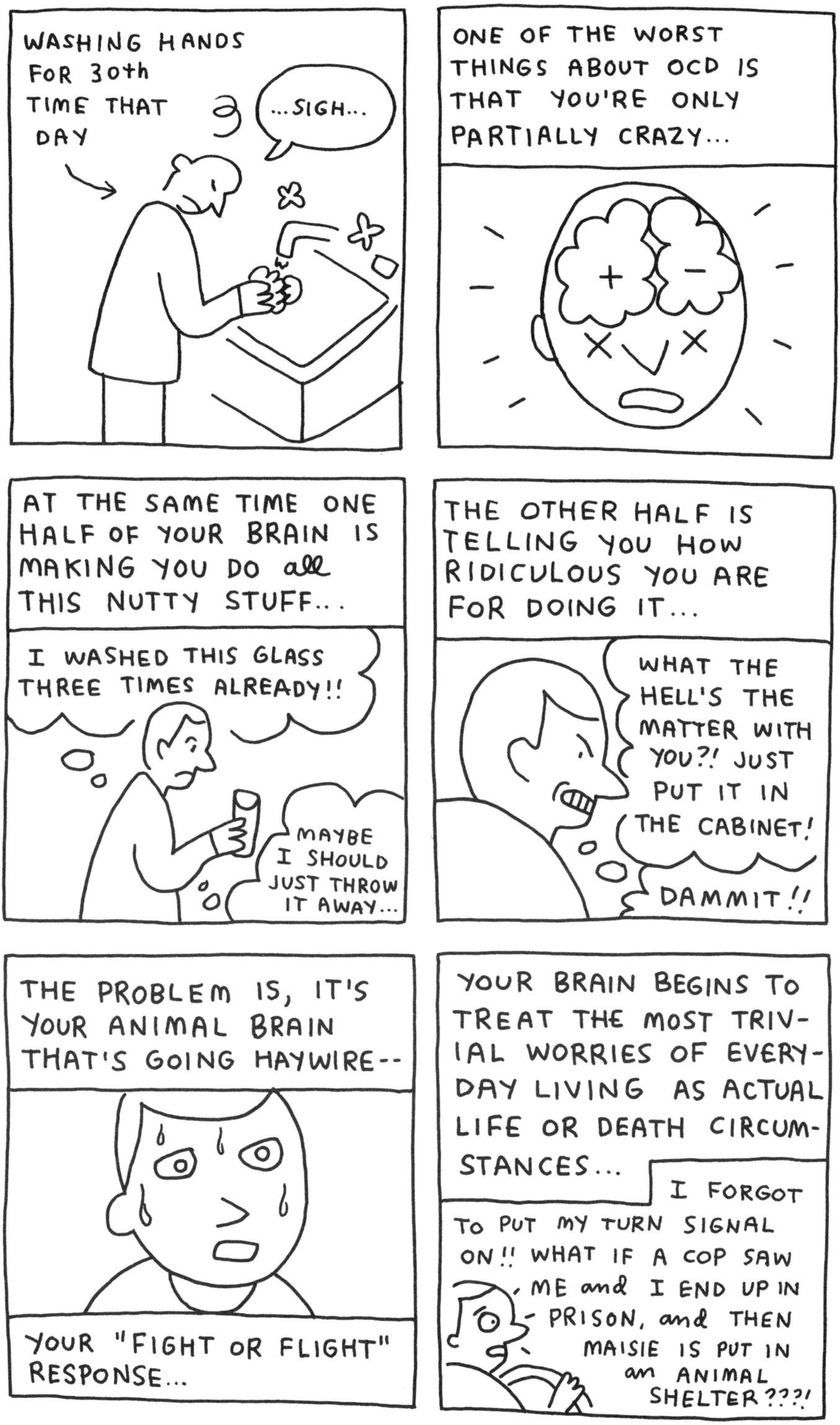
WASHING HANDS FOR 30th TIME THAT DAY
...SIGH...
ONE OF THE WORST THINGS ABOUT OCD IS THAT YOU'RE ONLY PARTIALLY CRAZY...
AT THE SAME TIME ONE HALF OF YOUR BRAIN IS MAKING YOU DO all THIS NUTTY STUFF...
I WASHED THIS GLASS THREE TIMES ALREADY!!
MAYBE I SHOULD JUST THROW IT AWAY...
THE OTHER HALF IS TELLING YOU HOW RIDICULOUS YOU ARE FOR DOING IT...
WHAT THE HELL'S THE MATTER WITH YOU?! JUST PUT IT IN THE CABINET!
DAMMIT!!
THE PROBLEM IS, IT'S YOUR ANIMAL BRAIN THAT'S GOING HAYWIRE--
YOUR "FIGHT OR FLIGHT" RESPONSE...
YOUR BRAIN BEGINS TO TREAT THE MOST TRIV-IAL WORRIES OF EVERY-DAY LIVING AS ACTUAL LIFE OR DEATH CIRCUM-STANCES...
I FORGOT TO PUT MY TURN SIGNAL ON!! WHAT IF A COP SAW ME and I END UP IN PRISON, and THEN MAISIE IS PUT IN an ANIMAL SHELTER???!

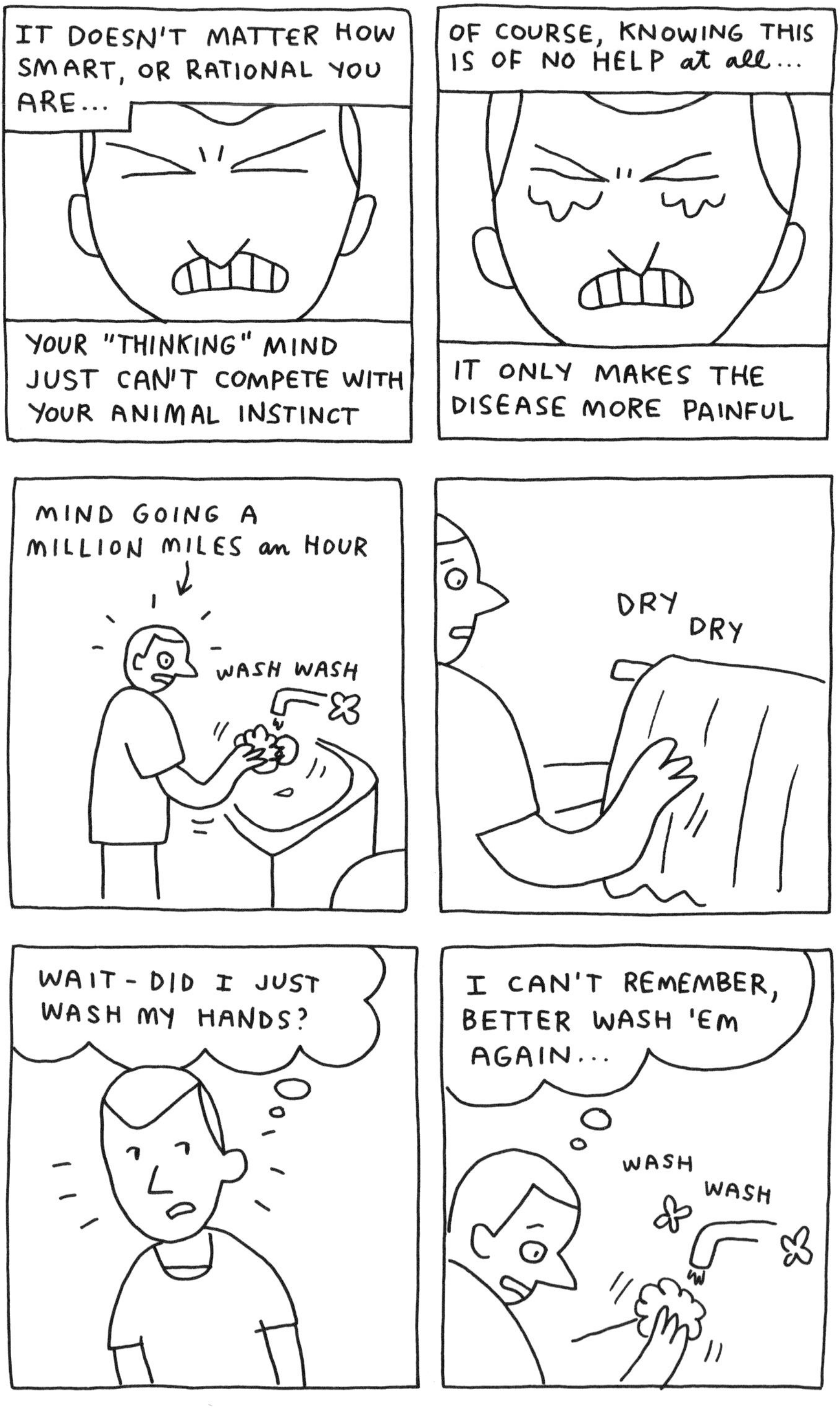
IT DOESN'T MATTER HOW SMART, OR RATIONAL YOU ARE...
YOUR "THINKING" MIND JUST CAN'T COMPETE WITH YOUR ANIMAL INSTINCT
OF COURSE, KNOWING THIS IS OF NO HELP at all...
IT ONLY MAKES THE DISEASE MORE PAINFUL
MIND GOING A MILLION MILES an HOUR
WASH WASH
DRY DRY
WAIT - DID I JUST WASH MY HANDS?
I CAN'T REMEMBER, BETTER WASH 'EM AGAIN...
WASH WASH

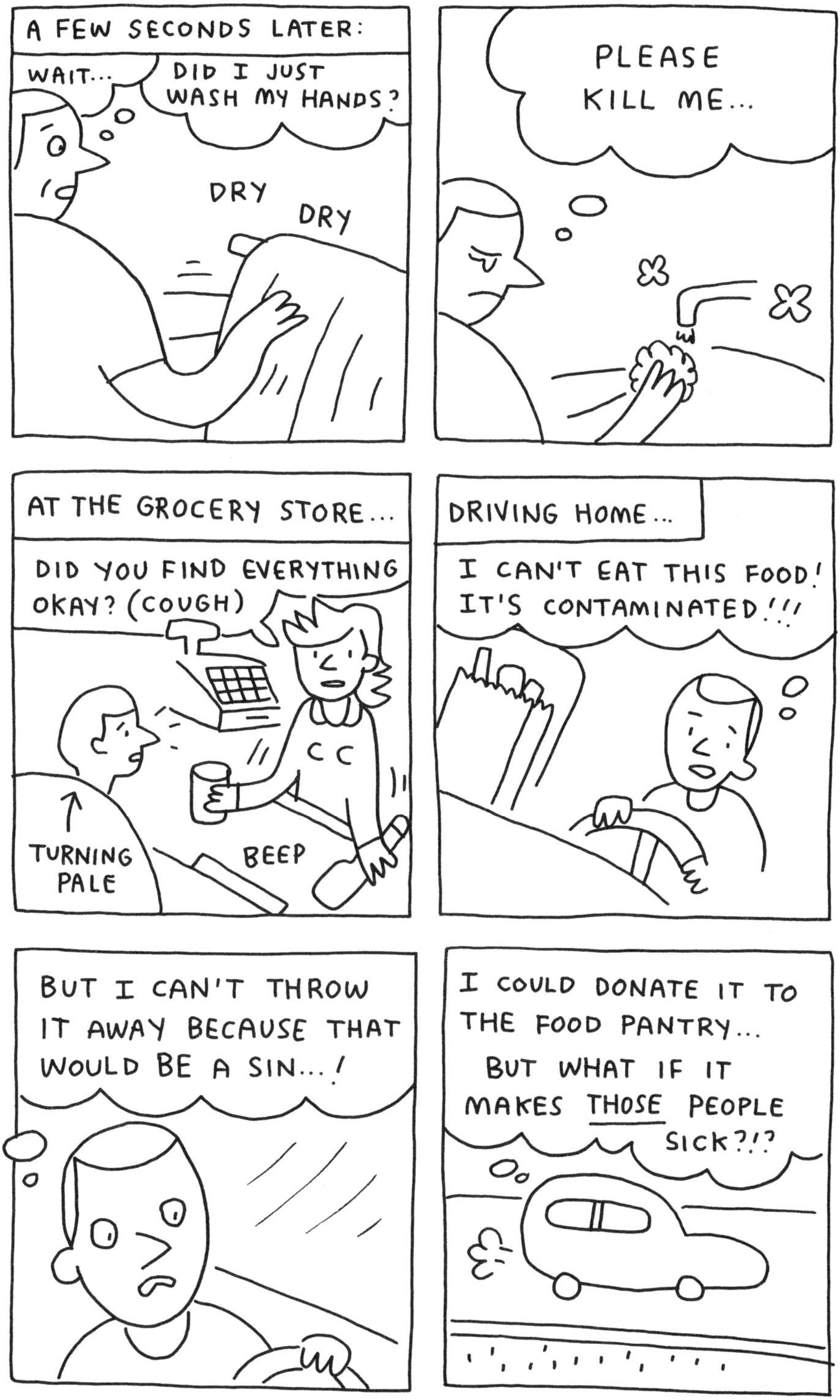
A FEW SECONDS LATER:
WAIT...
DID I JUST WASH MY HANDS?
DRY
DRY
PLEASE KILL ME...
AT THE GROCERY STORE...
DID YOU FIND EVERYTHING OKAY? (COUGH)
TURNING PALE
BEEP
DRIVING HOME...
I CAN'T EAT THIS FOOD! IT'S CONTAMINATED!!!
BUT I CAN'T THROW IT AWAY BECAUSE THAT WOULD BE A SIN...!
I COULD DONATE IT TO THE FOOD PANTRY...
BUT WHAT IF IT MAKES THOSE PEOPLE SICK?!?

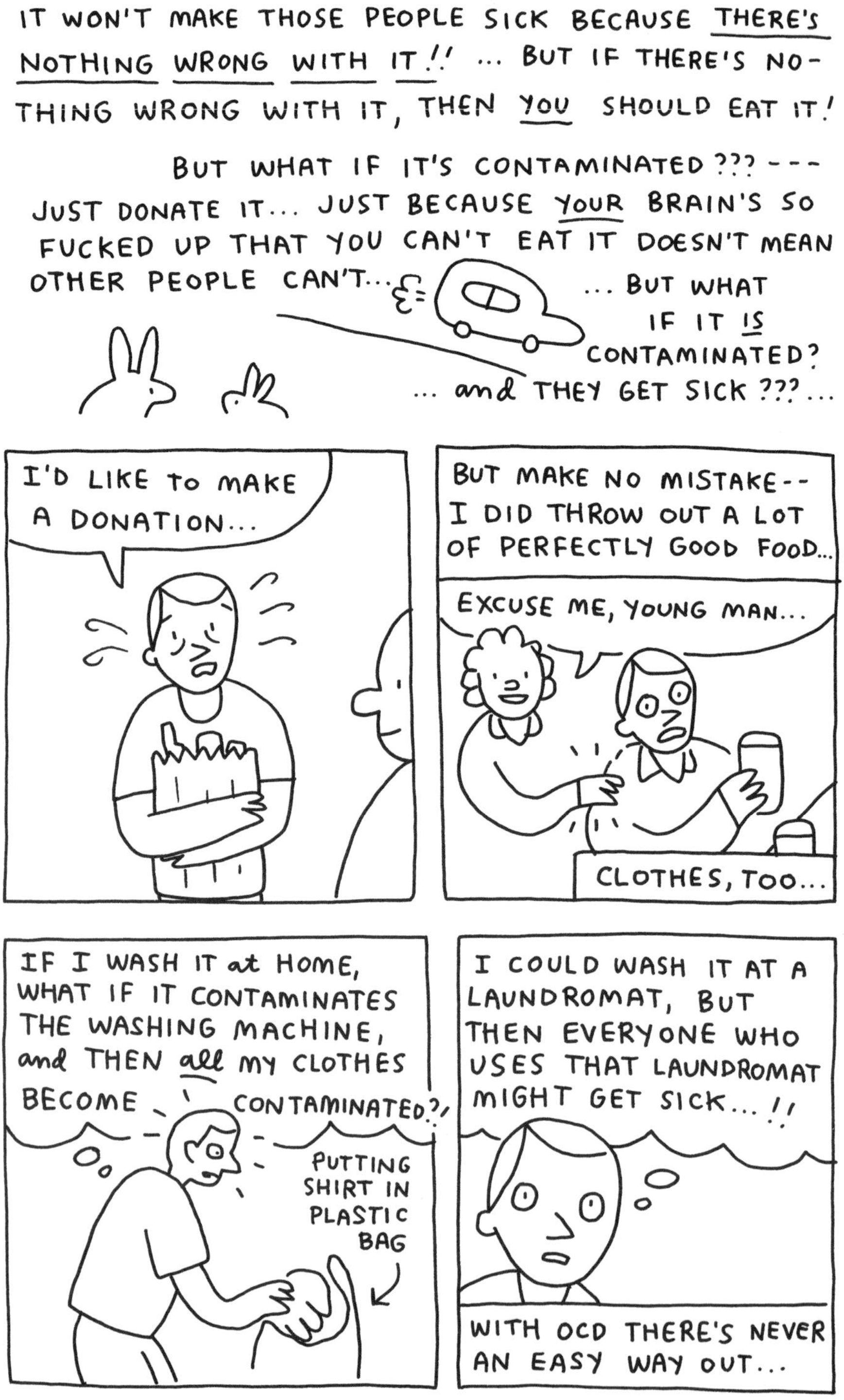
IT WON'T MAKE THOSE PEOPLE SICK BECAUSE THERE'S NOTHING WRONG WITH IT!! ... BUT IF THERE'S NOTHING WRONG WITH IT, THEN YOU SHOULD EAT IT!
BUT WHAT IF IT'S CONTAMINATED??? ---
JUST DONATE IT... JUST BECAUSE YOUR BRAIN'S SO FUCKED UP THAT YOU CAN'T EAT IT DOESN'T MEAN OTHER PEOPLE CAN'T...
... BUT WHAT IF IT IS CONTAMINATED?
... and THEY GET SICK???...
I'D LIKE TO MAKE A DONATION...
BUT MAKE NO MISTAKE-- I DID THROW OUT A LOT OF PERFECTLY GOOD FOOD...
EXCUSE ME, YOUNG MAN...
CLOTHES, TOO...
IF I WASH IT at HOME, WHAT IF IT CONTAMINATES THE WASHING MACHINE, and THEN all MY CLOTHES BECOME CONTAMINATED?!
PUTTING SHIRT IN PLASTIC BAG
I COULD WASH IT AT A LAUNDROMAT, BUT THEN EVERYONE WHO USES THAT LAUNDROMAT MIGHT GET SICK...!!
WITH OCD THERE'S NEVER AN EASY WAY OUT...

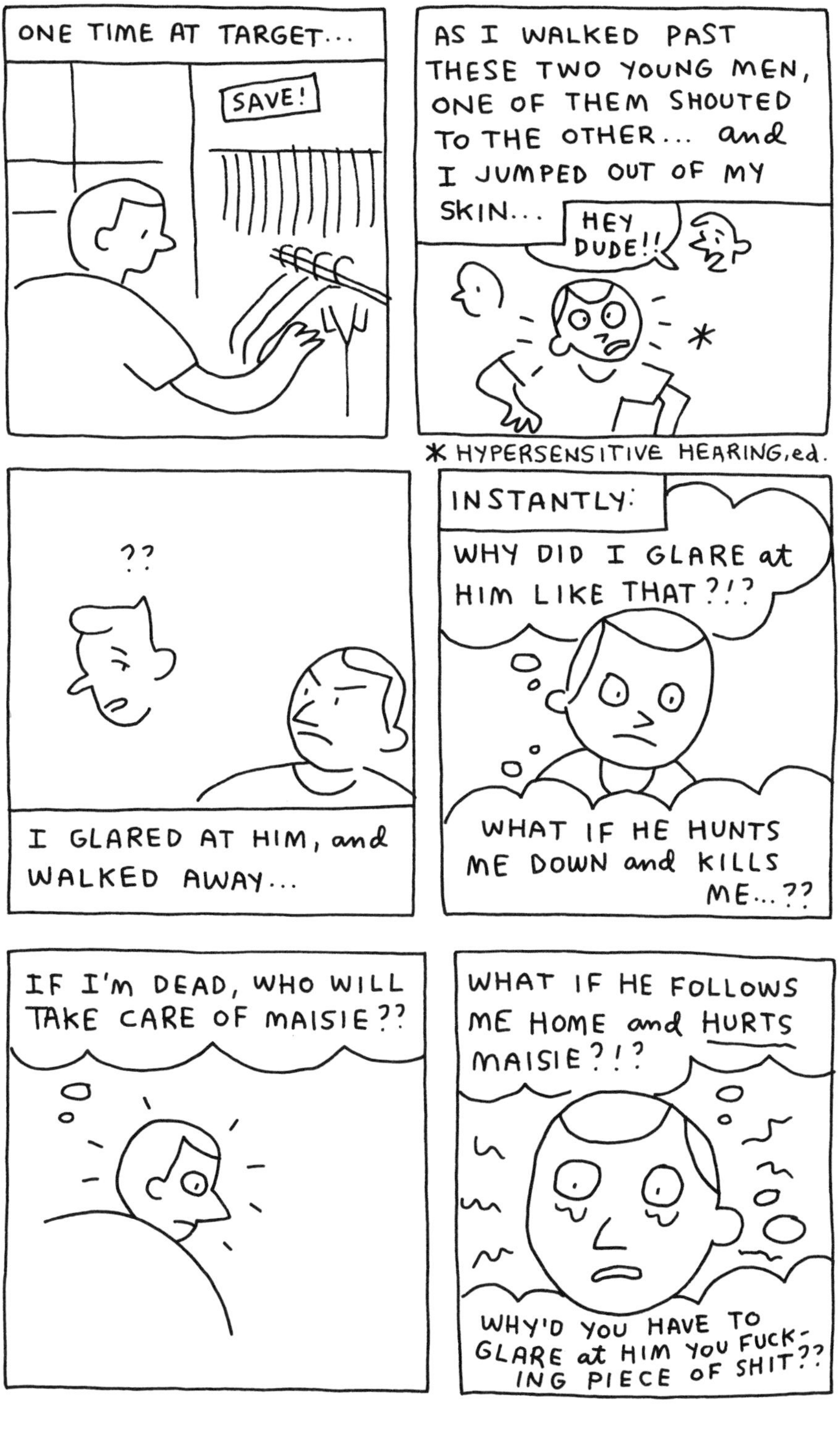
ONE TIME AT TARGET...
SAVE!
AS I WALKED PAST THESE TWO YOUNG MEN, ONE OF THEM SHOUTED TO THE OTHER... and I JUMPED OUT OF MY SKIN...
HEY DUDE!!
*
* HYPERSENSITIVE HEARING, ed.
??
I GLARED AT HIM, and WALKED AWAY...
INSTANTLY:
WHY DID I GLARE at HIM LIKE THAT?!?
WHAT IF HE HUNTS ME DOWN and KILLS ME...??
IF I'm DEAD, WHO WILL TAKE CARE OF MAISIE??
WHAT IF HE FOLLOWS ME HOME and HURTS MAISIE?!?
WHY'D YOU HAVE TO GLARE at HIM YOU FUCK-ING PIECE OF SHIT??

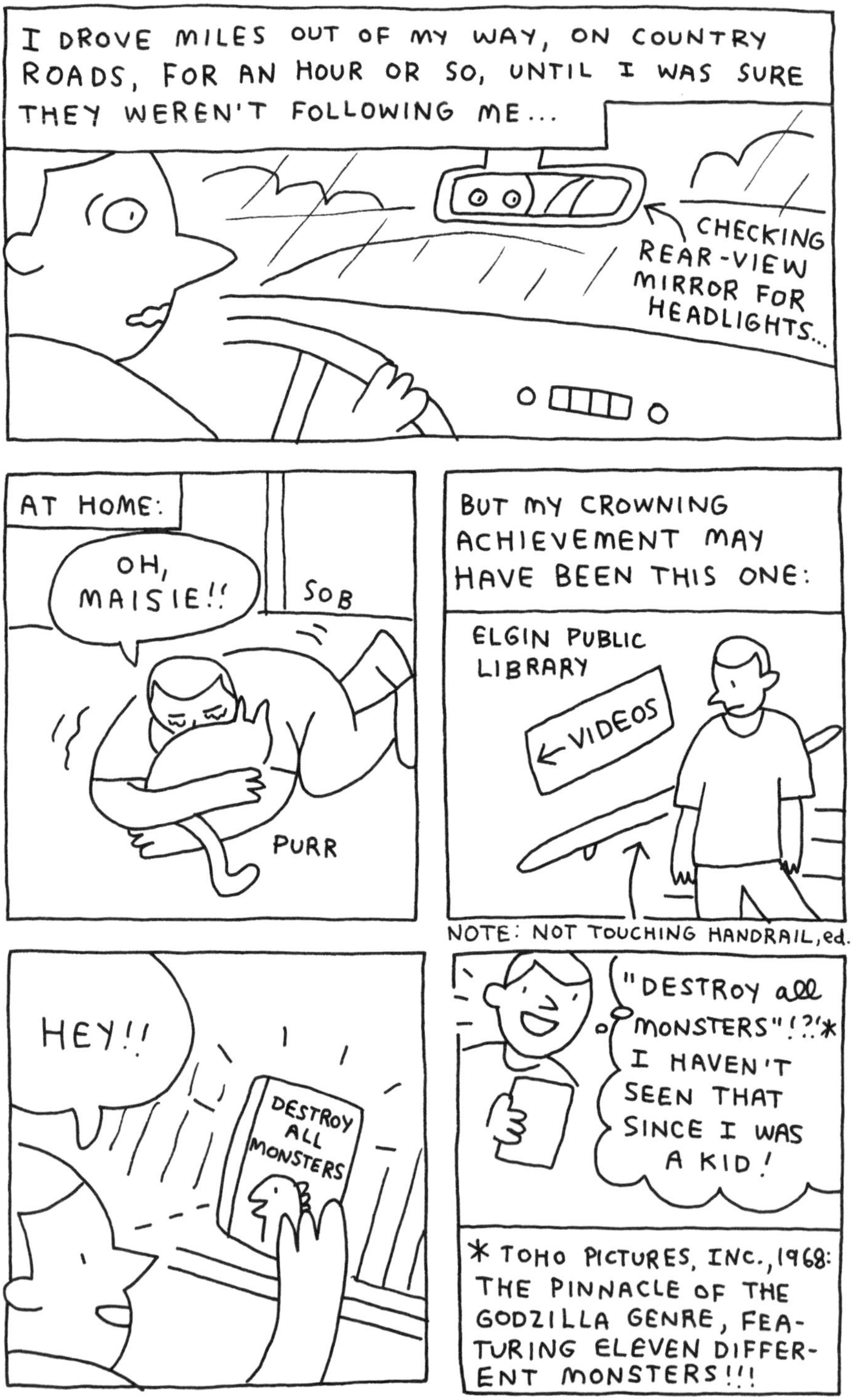
I DROVE MILES OUT OF MY WAY, ON COUNTRY ROADS, FOR AN HOUR OR SO, UNTIL I WAS SURE THEY WEREN'T FOLLOWING ME...
CHECKING REAR-VIEW MIRROR FOR HEADLIGHTS...
AT HOME:
OH, MAISIE!!
SOB
PURR
BUT MY CROWNING ACHIEVEMENT MAY HAVE BEEN THIS ONE:
ELGIN PUBLIC LIBRARY
← VIDEOS
NOTE: NOT TOUCHING HANDRAIL, ed.
HEY!!
DESTROY ALL MONSTERS
"DESTROY all MONSTERS"!?!* I HAVEN'T SEEN THAT SINCE I WAS A KID!
* TOHO PICTURES, INC., 1968: THE PINNACLE OF THE GODZILLA GENRE, FEATURING ELEVEN DIFFERENT MONSTERS!!!

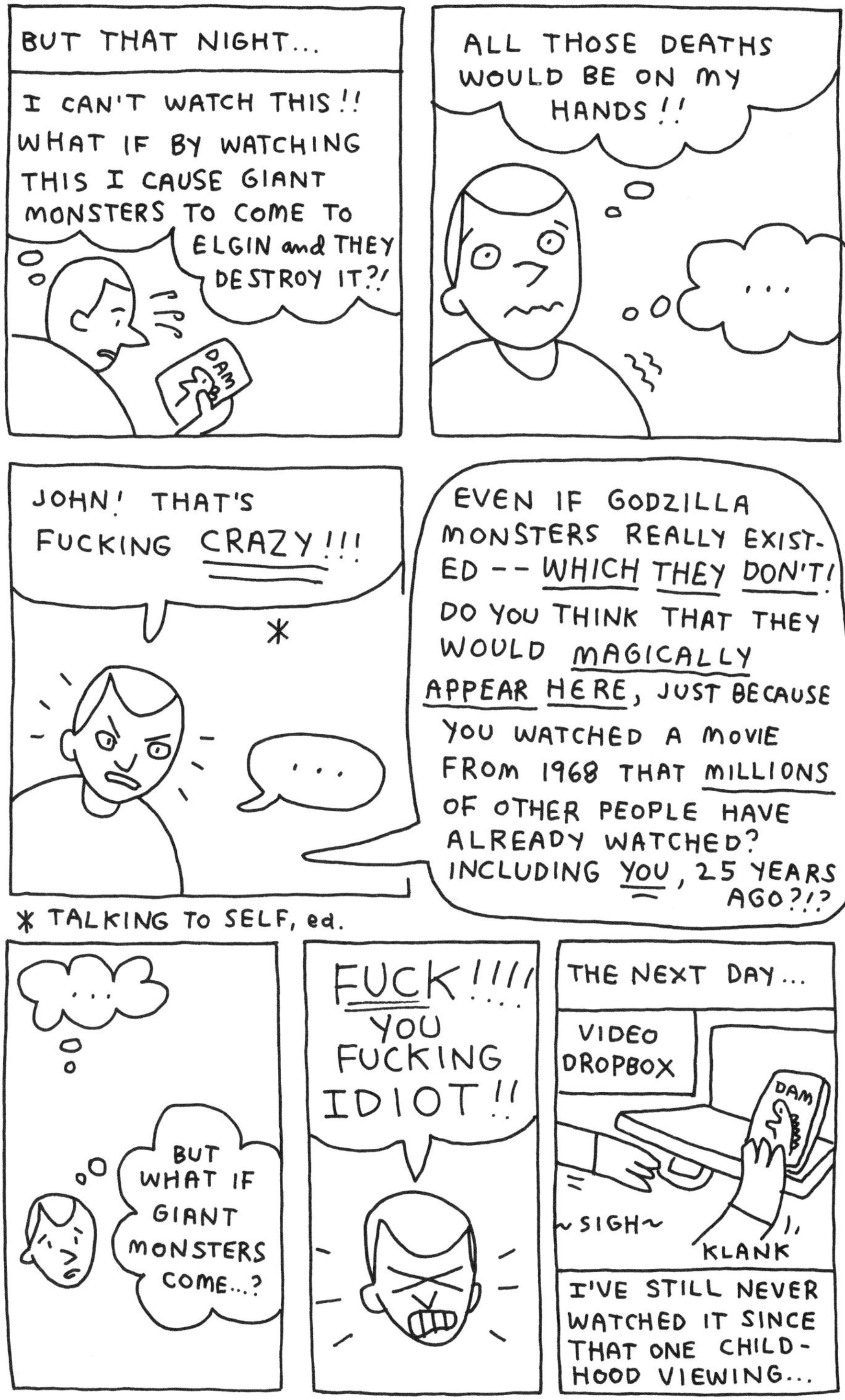
BUT THAT NIGHT...
I CAN'T WATCH THIS!! WHAT IF BY WATCHING THIS I CAUSE GIANT MONSTERS TO COME TO ELGIN and THEY DESTROY IT?!
DAM
ALL THOSE DEATHS WOULD BE ON MY HANDS!!
...
JOHN! THAT'S FUCKING CRAZY!!!
*
...
EVEN IF GODZILLA MONSTERS REALLY EXISTED -- WHICH THEY DON'T! DO YOU THINK THAT THEY WOULD MAGICALLY APPEAR HERE, JUST BECAUSE YOU WATCHED A MOVIE FROM 1968 THAT MILLIONS OF OTHER PEOPLE HAVE ALREADY WATCHED? INCLUDING YOU, 25 YEARS AGO?!?
* TALKING TO SELF, ed.
...
BUT WHAT IF GIANT MONSTERS COME...?
FUCK!!!! YOU FUCKING IDIOT!!
THE NEXT DAY...
VIDEO DROPBOX
DAM
~SIGH~
KLANK
I'VE STILL NEVER WATCHED IT SINCE THAT ONE CHILDHOOD VIEWING...

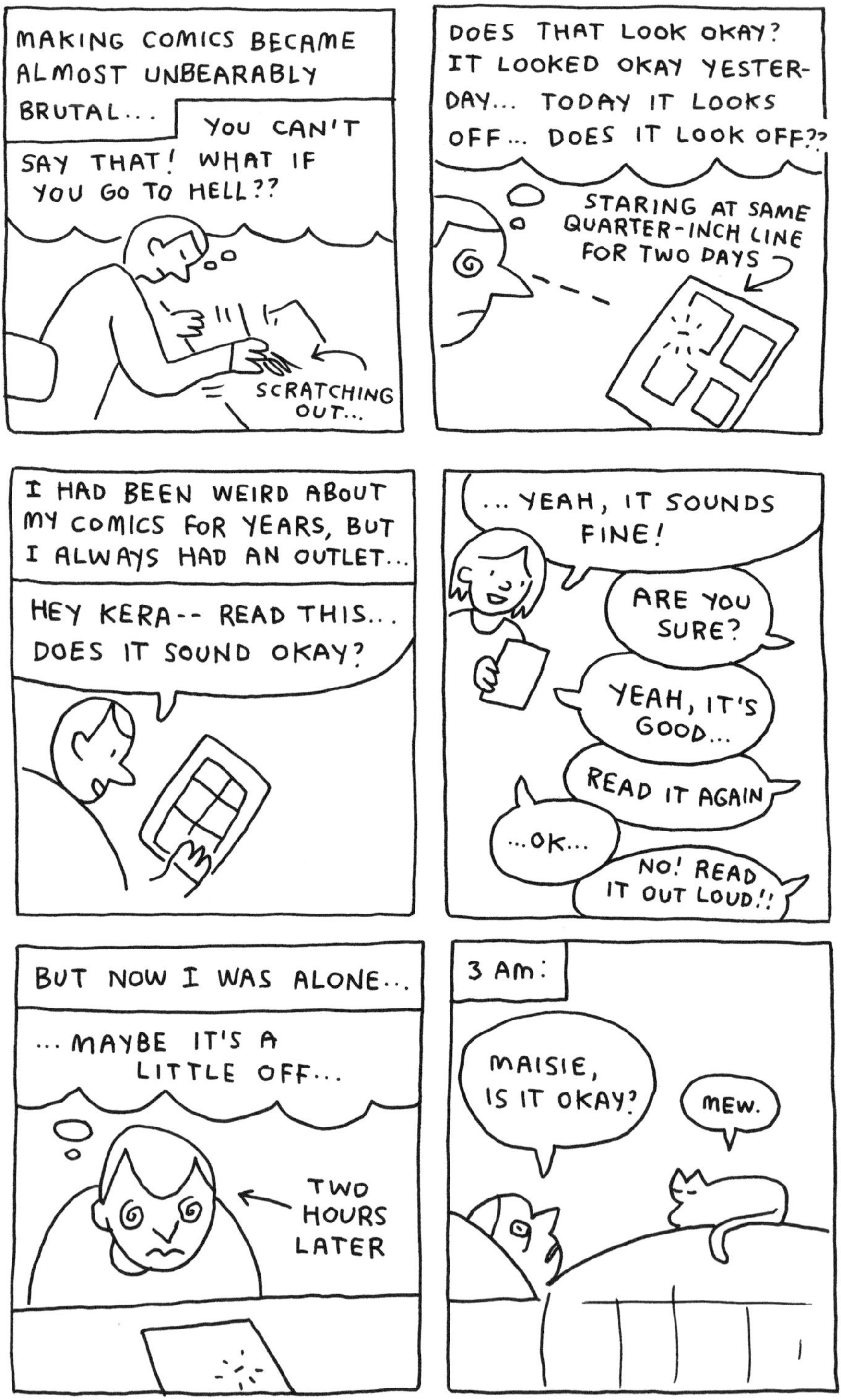
MAKING COMICS BECAME ALMOST UNBEARABLY BRUTAL...
YOU CAN'T SAY THAT! WHAT IF YOU GO TO HELL??
SCRATCHING OUT...
DOES THAT LOOK OKAY? IT LOOKED OKAY YESTER-DAY... TODAY IT LOOKS OFF... DOES IT LOOK OFF??
STARING AT SAME QUARTER-INCH LINE FOR TWO DAYS
I HAD BEEN WEIRD ABOUT MY COMICS FOR YEARS, BUT I ALWAYS HAD AN OUTLET...
HEY KERA-- READ THIS... DOES IT SOUND OKAY?
...YEAH, IT SOUNDS FINE!
ARE YOU SURE?
YEAH, IT'S GOOD...
READ IT AGAIN
...OK...
NO! READ IT OUT LOUD!!
BUT NOW I WAS ALONE...
...MAYBE IT'S A LITTLE OFF...
TWO HOURS LATER
3 AM:
MAISIE, IS IT OKAY?
MEW.

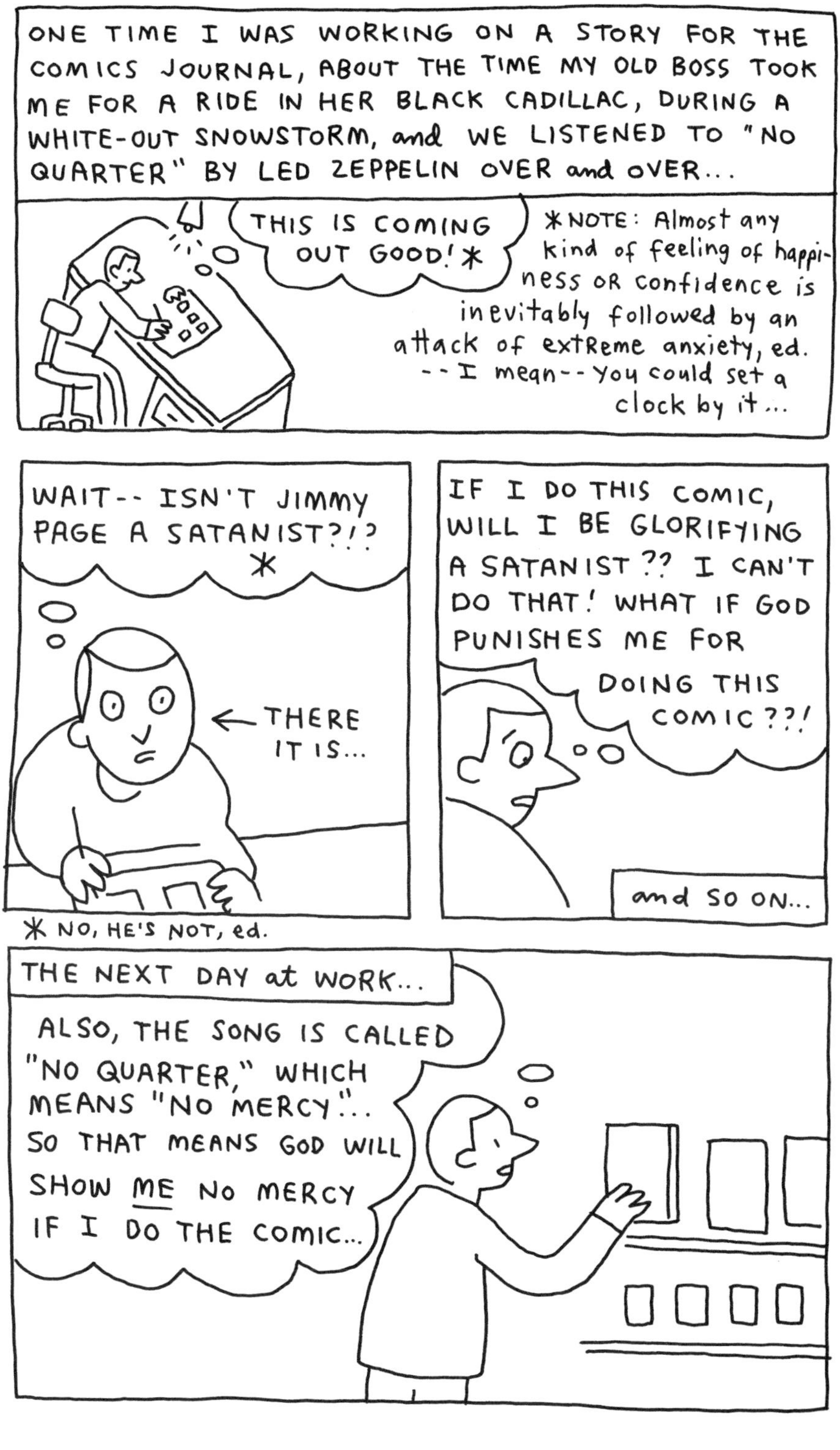
ONE TIME I WAS WORKING ON A STORY FOR THE COMICS JOURNAL, ABOUT THE TIME MY OLD BOSS TOOK ME FOR A RIDE IN HER BLACK CADILLAC, DURING A WHITE-OUT SNOWSTORM, and WE LISTENED TO "NO QUARTER" BY LED ZEPPELIN OVER and OVER...
THIS IS COMING OUT GOOD! *
* NOTE: Almost any kind of feeling of happiness or confidence is inevitably followed by an attack of extreme anxiety, ed. --I mean--You could set a clock by it...
WAIT-- ISN'T JIMMY PAGE A SATANIST?!? *
THERE IT IS...
* NO, HE'S NOT, ed.
IF I DO THIS COMIC, WILL I BE GLORIFYING A SATANIST?? I CAN'T DO THAT! WHAT IF GOD PUNISHES ME FOR DOING THIS COMIC??!
and SO ON...
THE NEXT DAY at WORK...
ALSO, THE SONG IS CALLED "NO QUARTER," WHICH MEANS "NO MERCY"... SO THAT MEANS GOD WILL SHOW ME NO MERCY IF I DO THE COMIC...

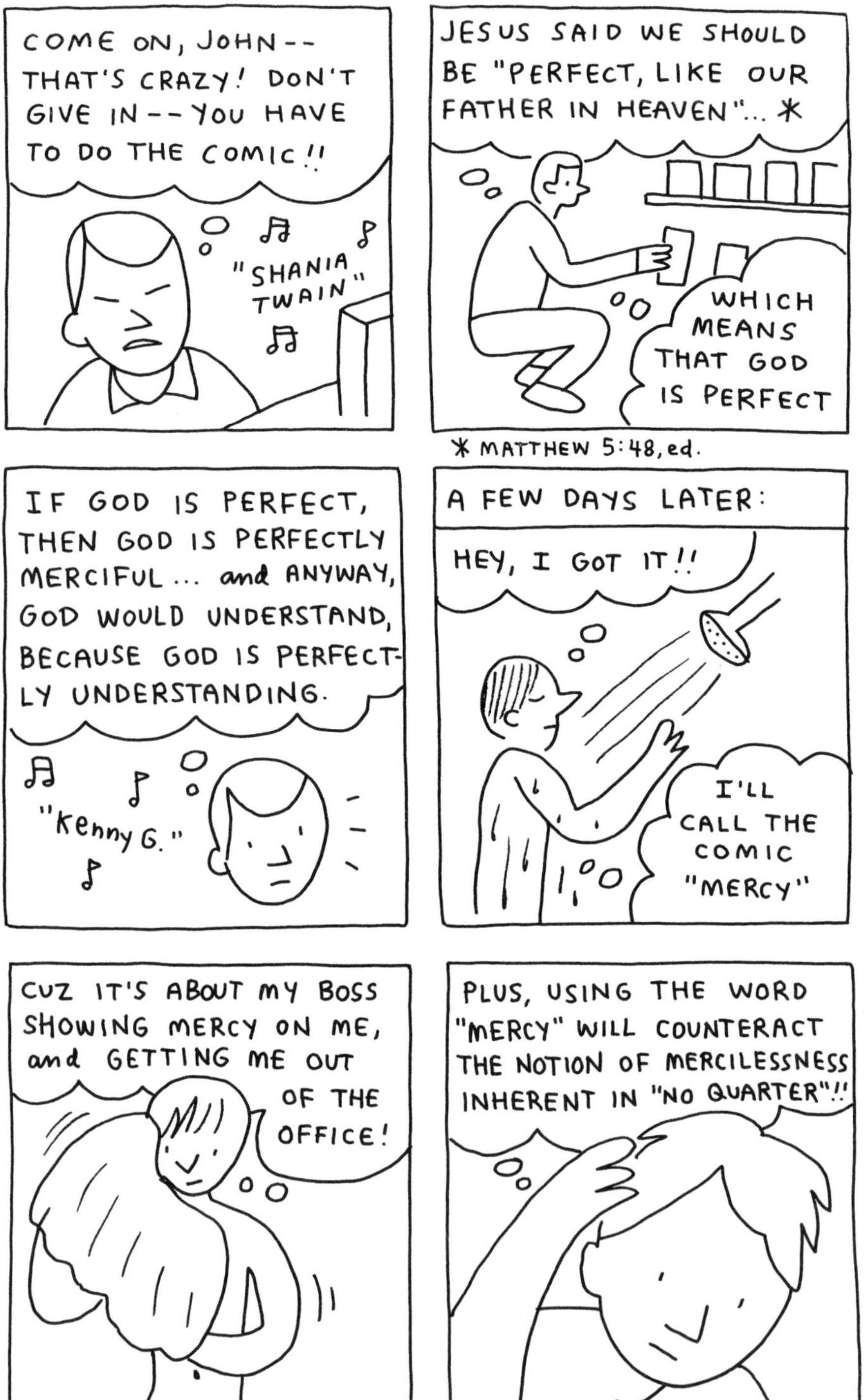
COME ON, JOHN-- THAT'S CRAZY! DON'T GIVE IN -- YOU HAVE TO DO THE COMIC!!
"SHANIA TWAIN"
JESUS SAID WE SHOULD BE "PERFECT, LIKE OUR FATHER IN HEAVEN"... *
WHICH MEANS THAT GOD IS PERFECT
* MATTHEW 5:48, ed.
IF GOD IS PERFECT, THEN GOD IS PERFECTLY MERCIFUL... and ANYWAY, GOD WOULD UNDERSTAND, BECAUSE GOD IS PERFECTLY UNDERSTANDING.
"Kenny G."
A FEW DAYS LATER:
HEY, I GOT IT!!
I'LL CALL THE COMIC "MERCY"
CUZ IT'S ABOUT MY BOSS SHOWING MERCY ON ME, and GETTING ME OUT OF THE OFFICE!
PLUS, USING THE WORD "MERCY" WILL COUNTERACT THE NOTION OF MERCILESSNESS INHERENT IN "NO QUARTER"!!

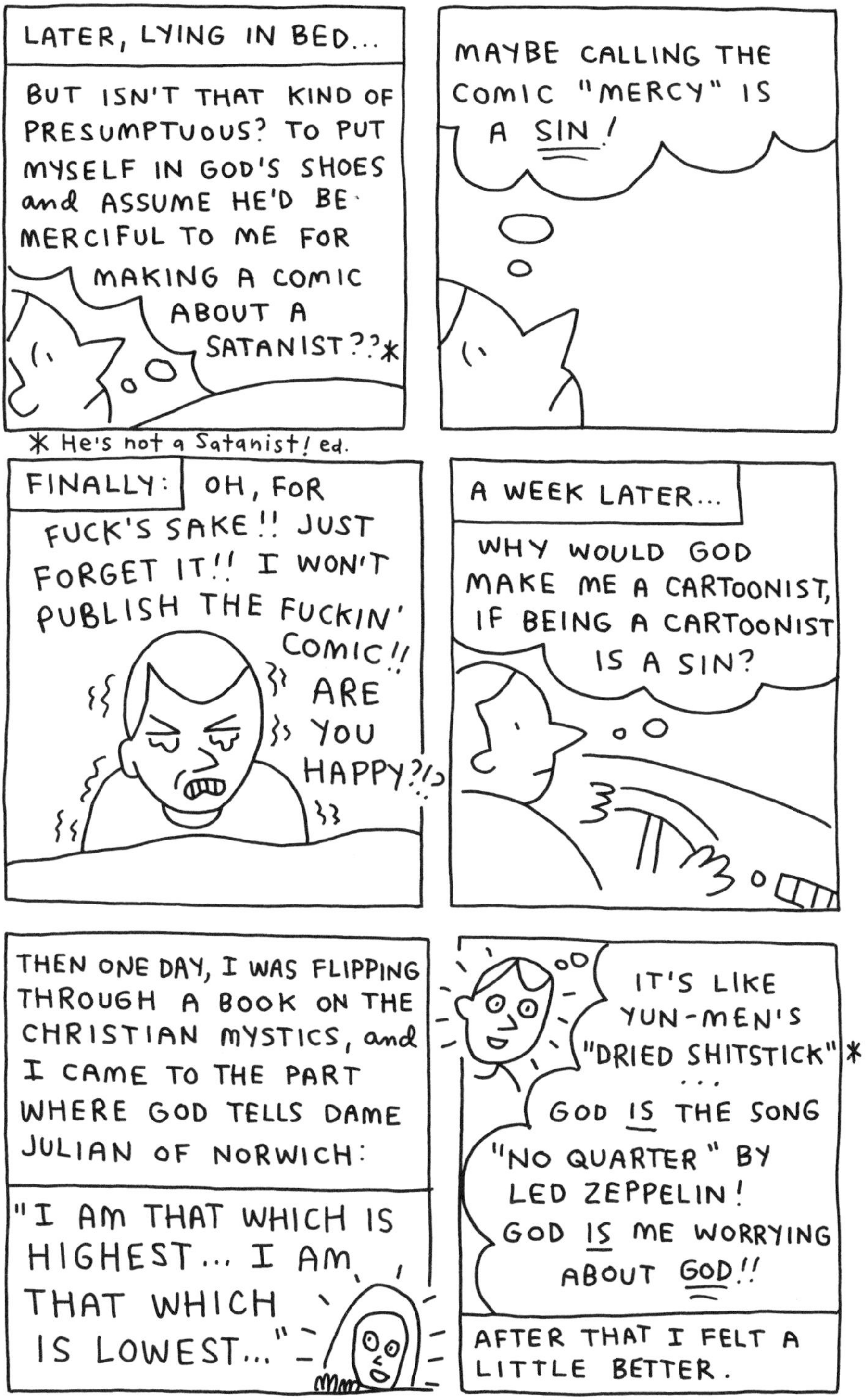
LATER, LYING IN BED...
BUT ISN'T THAT KIND OF PRESUMPTUOUS? TO PUT MYSELF IN GOD'S SHOES and ASSUME HE'D BE MERCIFUL TO ME FOR MAKING A COMIC ABOUT A SATANIST??*
* He's not a Satanist! ed.
MAYBE CALLING THE COMIC "MERCY" IS A SIN!
FINALLY:
OH, FOR FUCK'S SAKE!! JUST FORGET IT!! I WON'T PUBLISH THE FUCKIN' COMIC!! ARE YOU HAPPY?!?
A WEEK LATER...
WHY WOULD GOD MAKE ME A CARTOONIST, IF BEING A CARTOONIST IS A SIN?
THEN ONE DAY, I WAS FLIPPING THROUGH A BOOK ON THE CHRISTIAN MYSTICS, and I CAME TO THE PART WHERE GOD TELLS DAME JULIAN OF NORWICH:
"I AM THAT WHICH IS HIGHEST... I AM THAT WHICH IS LOWEST..."
IT'S LIKE YUN-MEN'S "DRIED SHITSTICK"* ... GOD IS THE SONG "NO QUARTER" BY LED ZEPPELIN! GOD IS ME WORRYING ABOUT GOD!!
AFTER THAT I FELT A LITTLE BETTER.
* SEE APPENDIX, ed.

Part Four

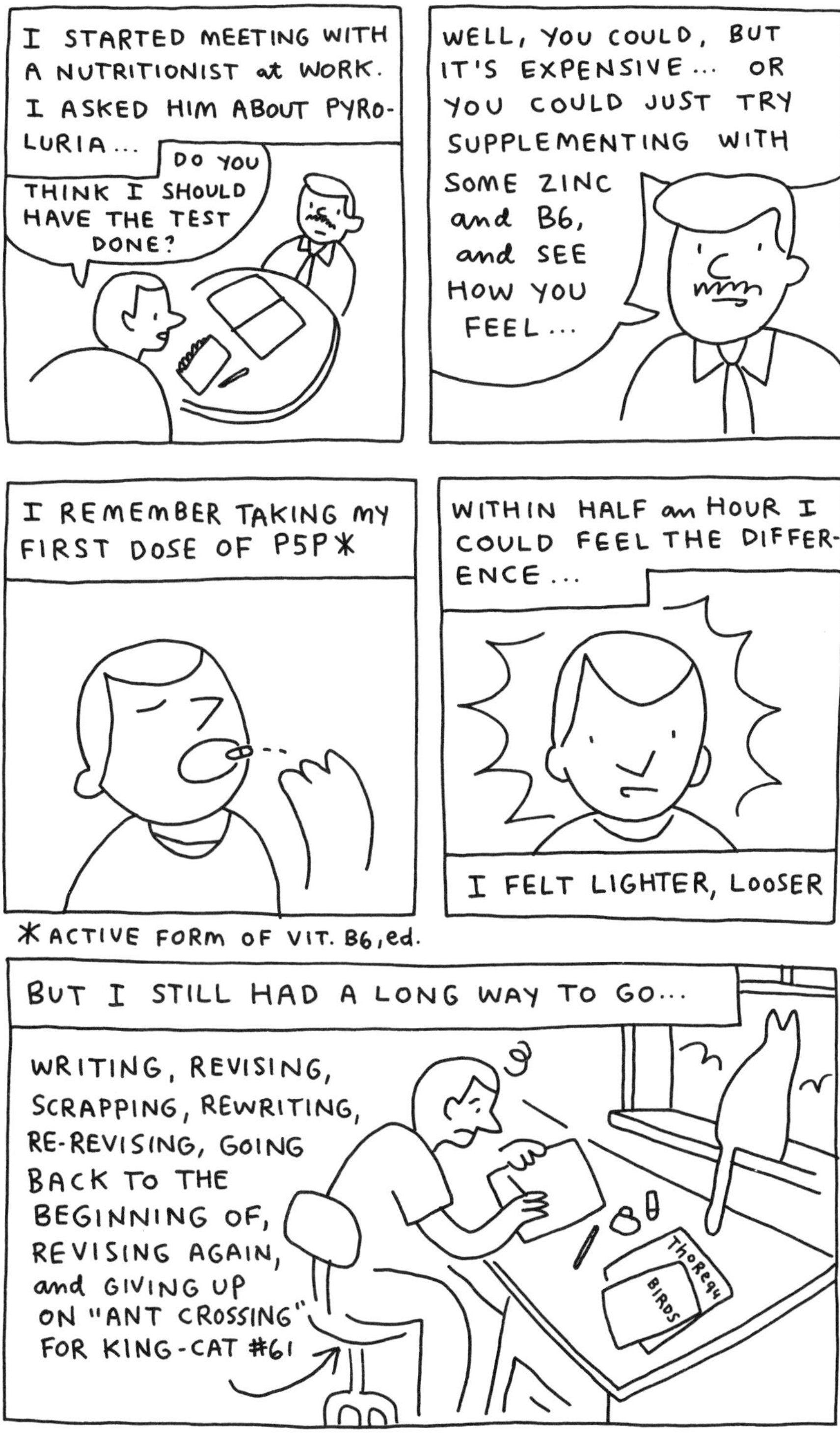
I STARTED MEETING WITH A NUTRITIONIST at WORK. I ASKED HIM ABOUT PYRO-LURIA...
DO YOU THINK I SHOULD HAVE THE TEST DONE?
WELL, YOU COULD, BUT IT'S EXPENSIVE... OR YOU COULD JUST TRY SUPPLEMENTING WITH
SOME ZINC and B6, and SEE HOW YOU FEEL...
I REMEMBER TAKING MY FIRST DOSE OF P5P*
WITHIN HALF an HOUR I COULD FEEL THE DIFFER-ENCE...
I FELT LIGHTER, LOOSER
*ACTIVE FORM OF VIT. B6, ed.
BUT I STILL HAD A LONG WAY TO GO...
WRITING, REVISING, SCRAPPING, REWRITING, RE-REVISING, GOING BACK TO THE BEGINNING OF, REVISING AGAIN, and GIVING UP ON "ANT CROSSING" FOR KING-CAT #61
THOREAU
BIRDS

ONE DAY: I'M TAKING all this EXTRA ZINC—MAYBE I SHOULD TAKE SOME COPPER, TO BALANCE IT OUT...

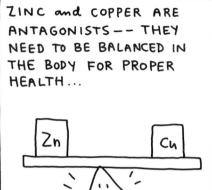

ZINC and COPPER ARE ANTAGONISTS—THEY NEED TO BE BALANCED IN THE BODY FOR PROPER HEALTH...

IF ZINC IS TOO HIGH, COPPER GOES WAY DOWN, and VICE VERSA...

SO I TOOK A SMALL DOSE OF COPPER... and MOMENTS LATER...

BLEAUGHH!

IT WAS ANOTHER CLUE: I HAD COPPER TOXICITY

THEN MY ZINC LEVELS MUST BE REALLY LOW... MAYBE I DO HAVE PYROLURIA...

WIPE WIPE

I WROTE TO THE PFEIFFER CENTER TO GET THEIR NEW PATIENT PACKET... BUT I WAS TOO AFRAID TO TURN IT IN...

WHAT IF THEY THROW ME IN THE LOONEY BIN?? *

I WAS GOING TO HAVE TO GO IT ALONE...

*ACTUAL THOUGHTS, ed.

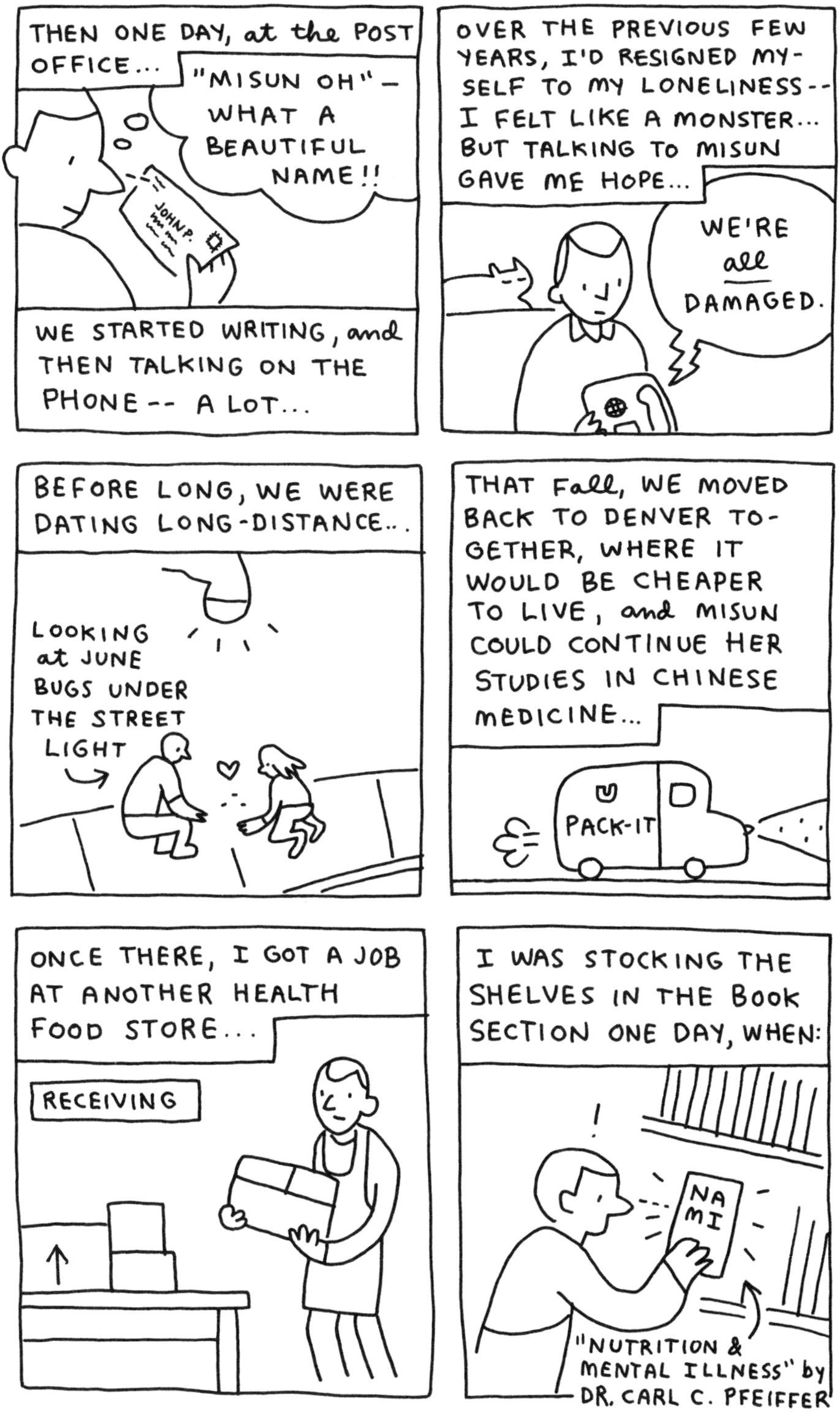
THEN ONE DAY, at the POST OFFICE...
"MISUN OH" — WHAT A BEAUTIFUL NAME!!
JOHN P.
WE STARTED WRITING, and THEN TALKING ON THE PHONE -- A LOT...
OVER THE PREVIOUS FEW YEARS, I'D RESIGNED MY-SELF TO MY LONELINESS -- I FELT LIKE A MONSTER... BUT TALKING TO MISUN GAVE ME HOPE...
WE'RE all DAMAGED.
BEFORE LONG, WE WERE DATING LONG-DISTANCE...
LOOKING at JUNE BUGS UNDER THE STREET LIGHT
THAT Fall, WE MOVED BACK TO DENVER TO-GETHER, WHERE IT WOULD BE CHEAPER TO LIVE, and MISUN COULD CONTINUE HER STUDIES IN CHINESE MEDICINE...
PACK-IT
ONCE THERE, I GOT A JOB AT ANOTHER HEALTH FOOD STORE...
RECEIVING
I WAS STOCKING THE SHELVES IN THE BOOK SECTION ONE DAY, WHEN:
!
NAMI
"NUTRITION & MENTAL ILLNESS" by DR. CARL C. PFEIFFER

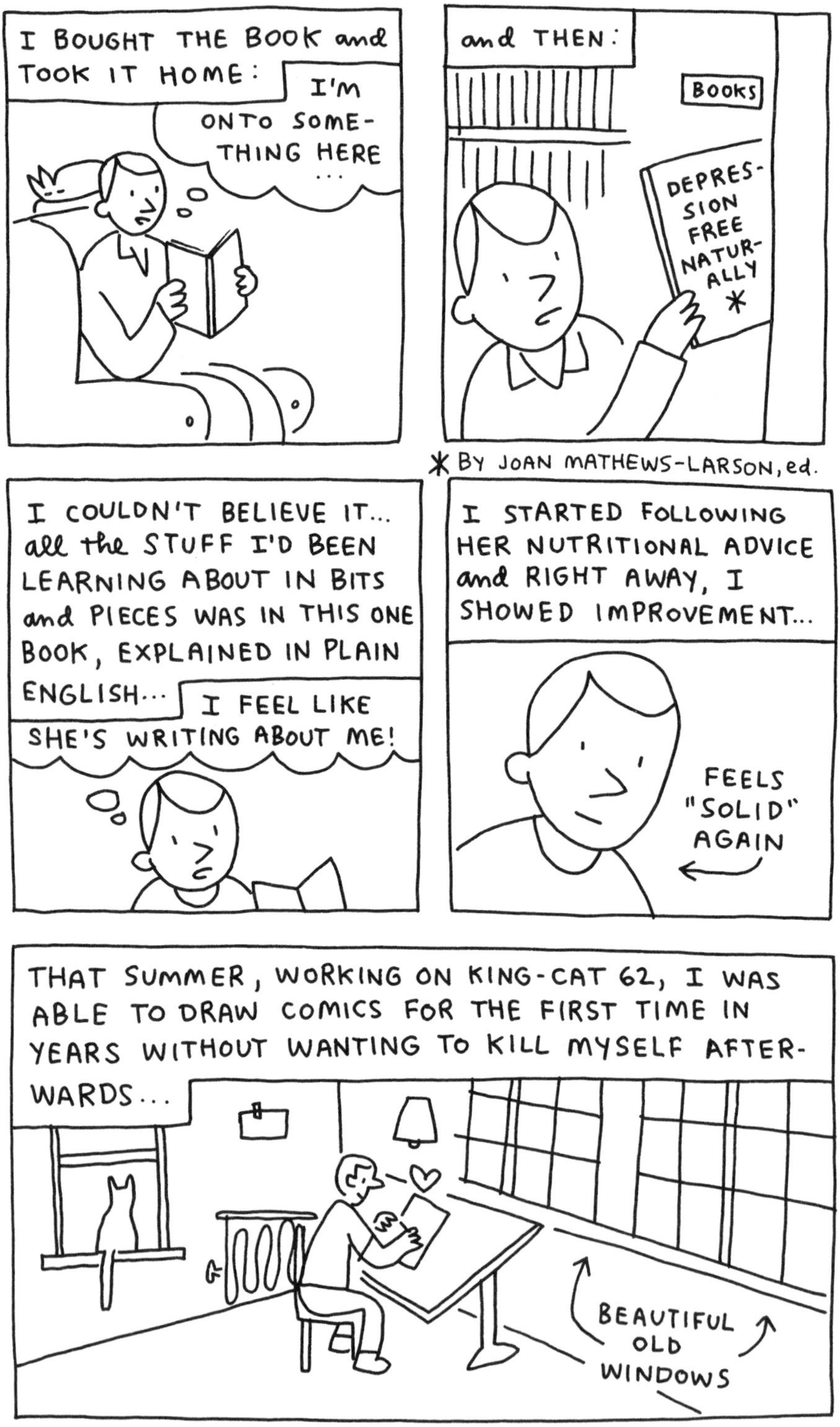
I BOUGHT THE BOOK and TOOK IT HOME:
I'M ONTO SOMETHING HERE . . .
and THEN:
BOOKS
DEPRESSION FREE NATURALLY *
* BY JOAN MATHEWS-LARSON, ed.
I COULDN'T BELIEVE IT... all the STUFF I'D BEEN LEARNING ABOUT IN BITS and PIECES WAS IN THIS ONE BOOK, EXPLAINED IN PLAIN ENGLISH...
I FEEL LIKE SHE'S WRITING ABOUT ME!
I STARTED FOLLOWING HER NUTRITIONAL ADVICE and RIGHT AWAY, I SHOWED IMPROVEMENT...
FEELS "SOLID" AGAIN
THAT SUMMER, WORKING ON KING-CAT 62, I WAS ABLE TO DRAW COMICS FOR THE FIRST TIME IN YEARS WITHOUT WANTING TO KILL MYSELF AFTERWARDS...
BEAUTIFUL OLD WINDOWS

ALL MY NUTRITIONAL STUDIES WERE COMING TOGETHER...

ZINC IS USED IN ABUNDANCE NOT ONLY IN SEROTONIN CONVERSION, BUT also IN THE EARS and PROSTATE...*

PYROLURIC MALES TYPICALLY START SHOWING SYMPTOMS at PUBERTY, BECAUSE THAT'S WHEN WHAT LITTLE ZINC THEY HAVE IS MAXED OUT BY SEXUAL DEVELOPMENT...

* HAS HAD PROSTATE PROBLEMS SINCE AGE 18, ed.

NOT TO MENTION THAT EVERY TIME I MASTURBATED, I WAS LOSING ZINC WITH EACH ORGASM...

BEAT OFF EVERY DAY FOR ALMOST FOURTEEN YEARS

NO WONDER I GOT SO FUCKED UP AS A TEENAGER!!

LOSS OF ZINC and B6 ALSO LEADS TO ENZYME DYSFUNCTION and DIGESTIVE and IMMUNE SYSTEM ABNORMALITIES...

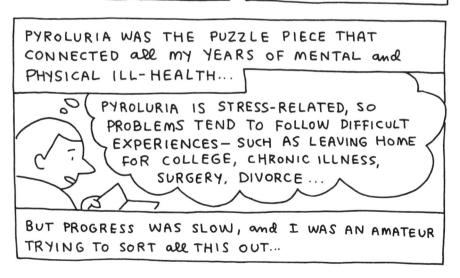

PYROLURIA WAS THE PUZZLE PIECE THAT CONNECTED all MY YEARS OF MENTAL and PHYSICAL ILL-HEALTH...

PYROLURIA IS STRESS-RELATED, SO PROBLEMS TEND TO FOLLOW DIFFICULT EXPERIENCES— SUCH AS LEAVING HOME FOR COLLEGE, CHRONIC ILLNESS, SURGERY, DIVORCE...

BUT PROGRESS WAS SLOW, and I WAS AN AMATEUR TRYING TO SORT all THIS OUT...

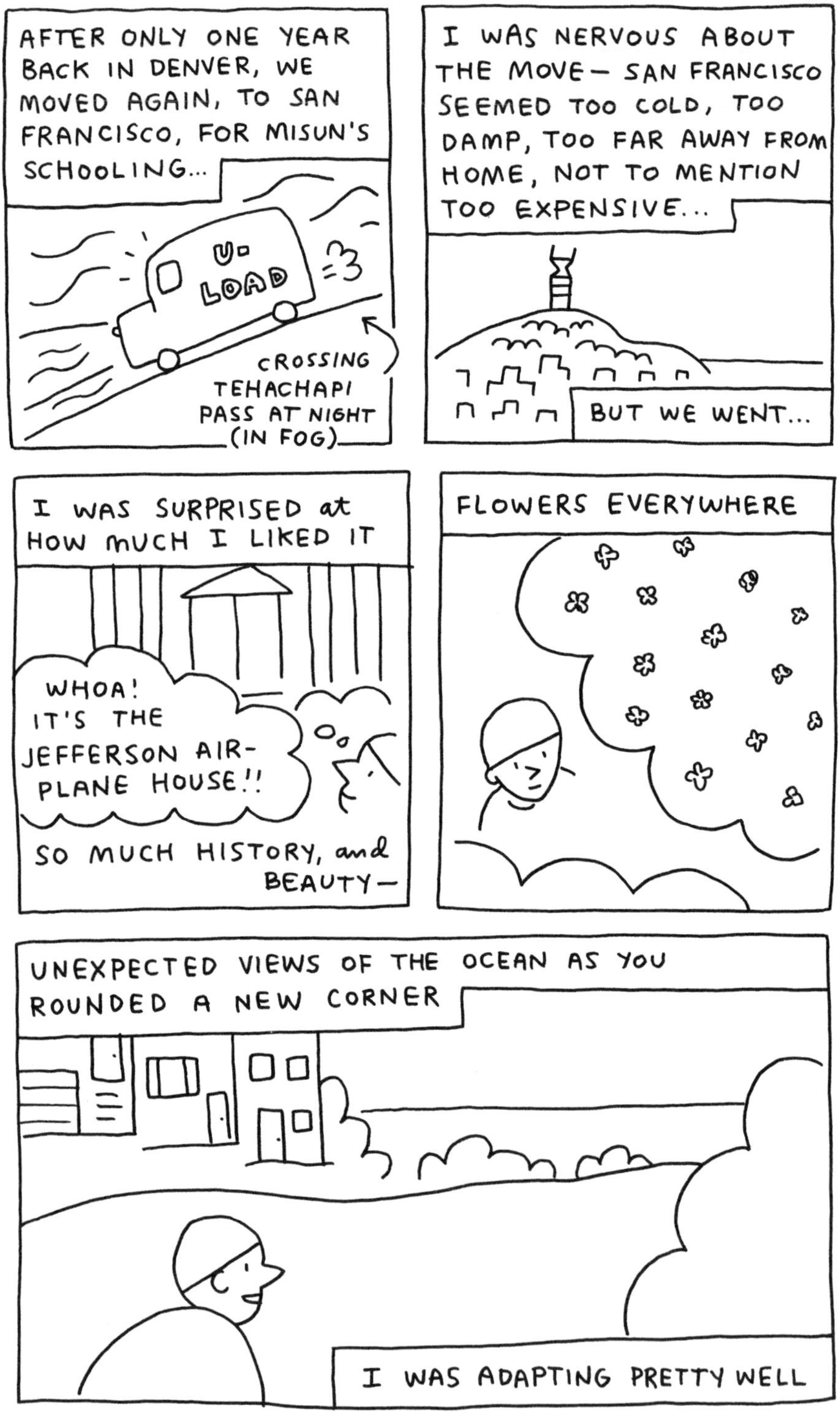

AFTER ONLY ONE YEAR BACK IN DENVER, WE MOVED AGAIN, TO SAN FRANCISCO, FOR MISUN'S SCHOOLING...
U-LOAD
CROSSING TEHACHAPI PASS AT NIGHT (IN FOG)
I WAS NERVOUS ABOUT THE MOVE— SAN FRANCISCO SEEMED TOO COLD, TOO DAMP, TOO FAR AWAY FROM HOME, NOT TO MENTION TOO EXPENSIVE...
BUT WE WENT...
I WAS SURPRISED at HOW MUCH I LIKED IT
WHOA! IT'S THE JEFFERSON AIRPLANE HOUSE!!
SO MUCH HISTORY, and BEAUTY—
FLOWERS EVERYWHERE
UNEXPECTED VIEWS OF THE OCEAN AS YOU ROUNDED A NEW CORNER
I WAS ADAPTING PRETTY WELL

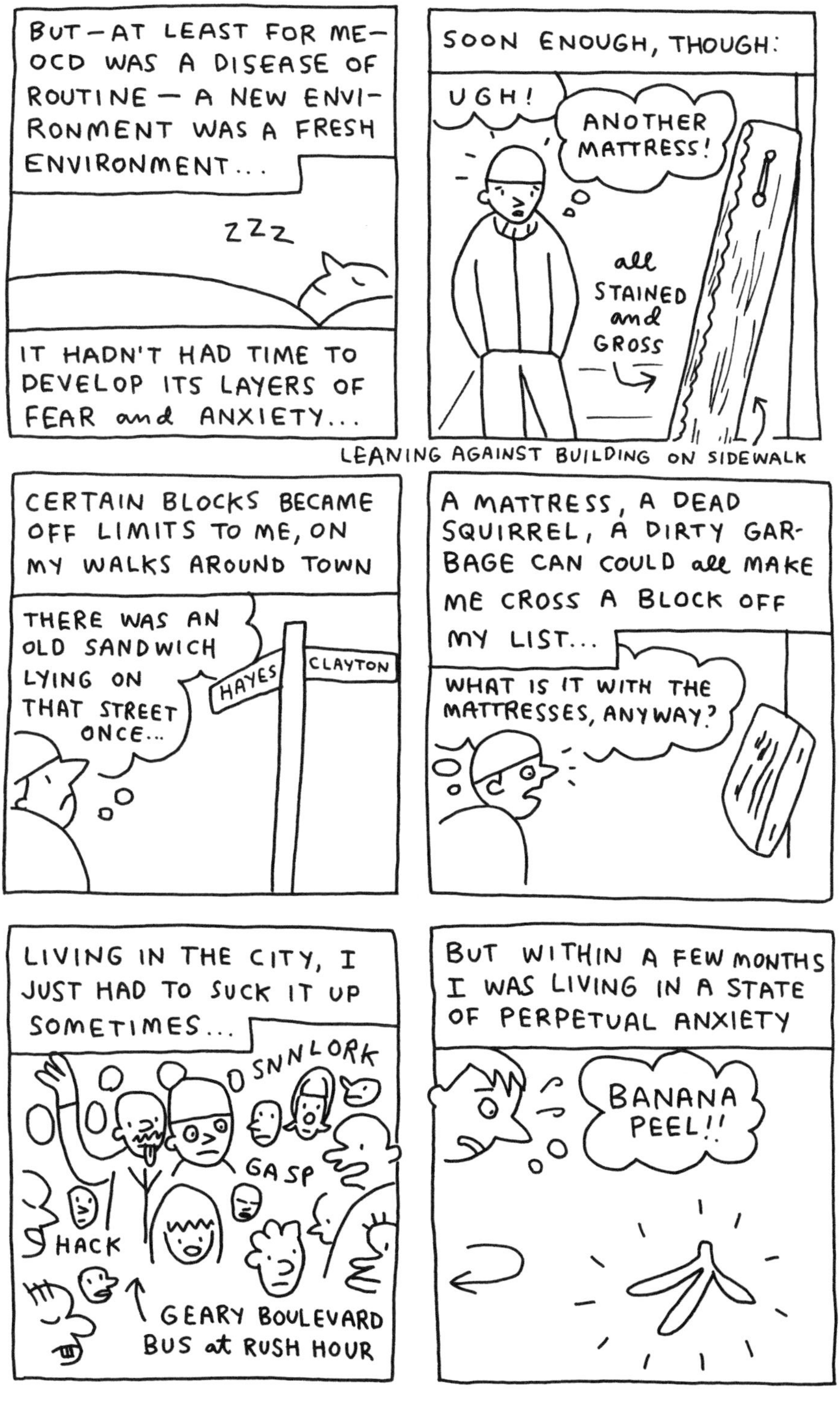
BUT—AT LEAST FOR ME—OCD WAS A DISEASE OF ROUTINE—A NEW ENVIRONMENT WAS A FRESH ENVIRONMENT...
ZZZ
IT HADN'T HAD TIME TO DEVELOP ITS LAYERS OF FEAR and ANXIETY...
SOON ENOUGH, THOUGH:
UGH!
ANOTHER MATTRESS!
all STAINED and GROSS
LEANING AGAINST BUILDING ON SIDEWALK
CERTAIN BLOCKS BECAME OFF LIMITS TO ME, ON MY WALKS AROUND TOWN
THERE WAS AN OLD SANDWICH LYING ON THAT STREET ONCE...
HAYES
CLAYTON
A MATTRESS, A DEAD SQUIRREL, A DIRTY GARBAGE CAN COULD all MAKE ME CROSS A BLOCK OFF MY LIST...
WHAT IS IT WITH THE MATTRESSES, ANYWAY?
LIVING IN THE CITY, I JUST HAD TO SUCK IT UP SOMETIMES...
SNNLORK
GASP
HACK
GEARY BOULEVARD BUS at RUSH HOUR
BUT WITHIN A FEW MONTHS I WAS LIVING IN A STATE OF PERPETUAL ANXIETY
BANANA PEEL!!

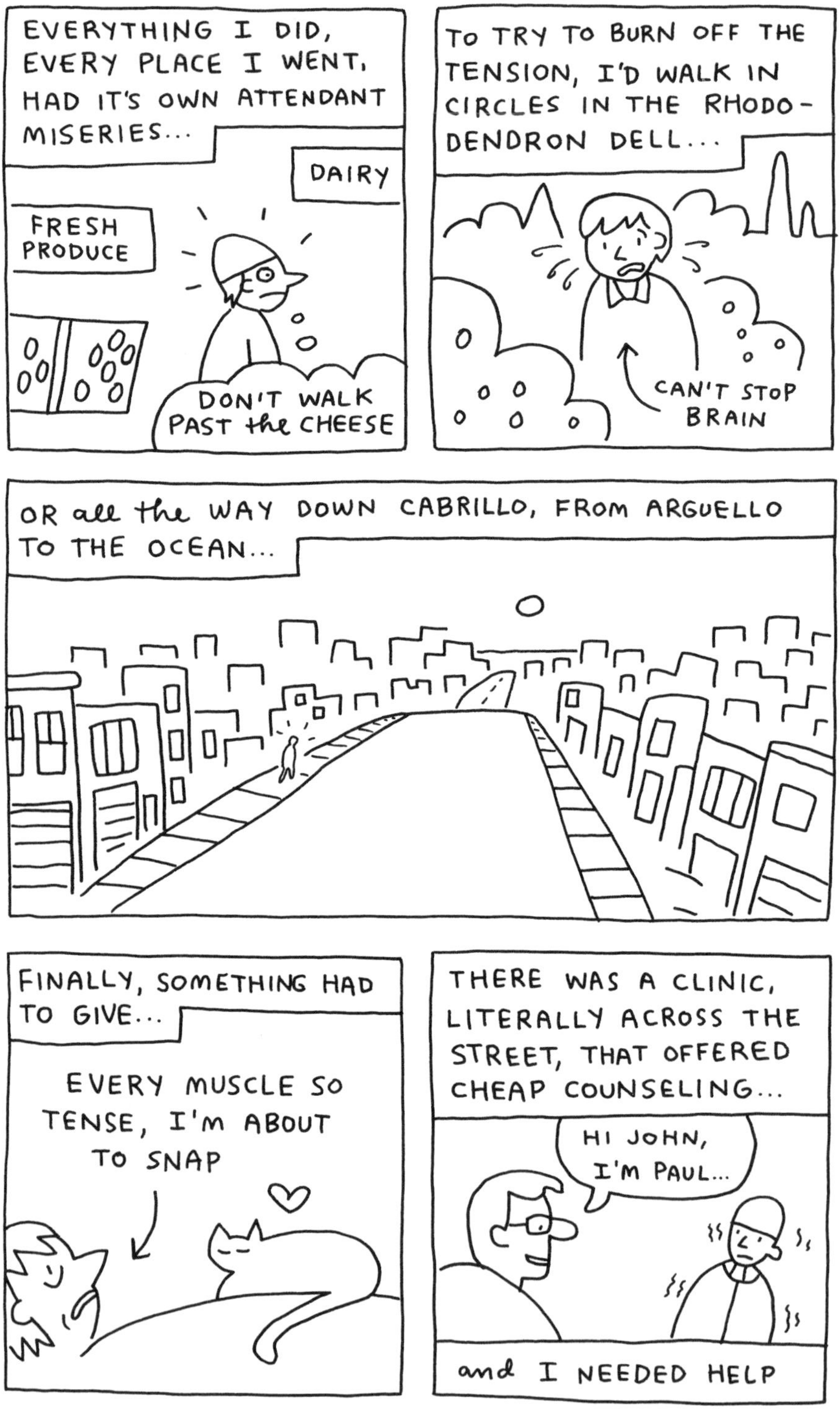
EVERYTHING I DID, EVERY PLACE I WENT, HAD IT'S OWN ATTENDANT MISERIES...
DAIRY
FRESH PRODUCE
DON'T WALK PAST the CHEESE
TO TRY TO BURN OFF THE TENSION, I'D WALK IN CIRCLES IN THE RHODODENDRON DELL...
CAN'T STOP BRAIN
OR all the WAY DOWN CABRILLO, FROM ARGUELLO TO THE OCEAN...
FINALLY, SOMETHING HAD TO GIVE...
EVERY MUSCLE SO TENSE, I'M ABOUT TO SNAP
THERE WAS A CLINIC, LITERALLY ACROSS THE STREET, THAT OFFERED CHEAP COUNSELING...
HI JOHN, I'M PAUL...
and I NEEDED HELP

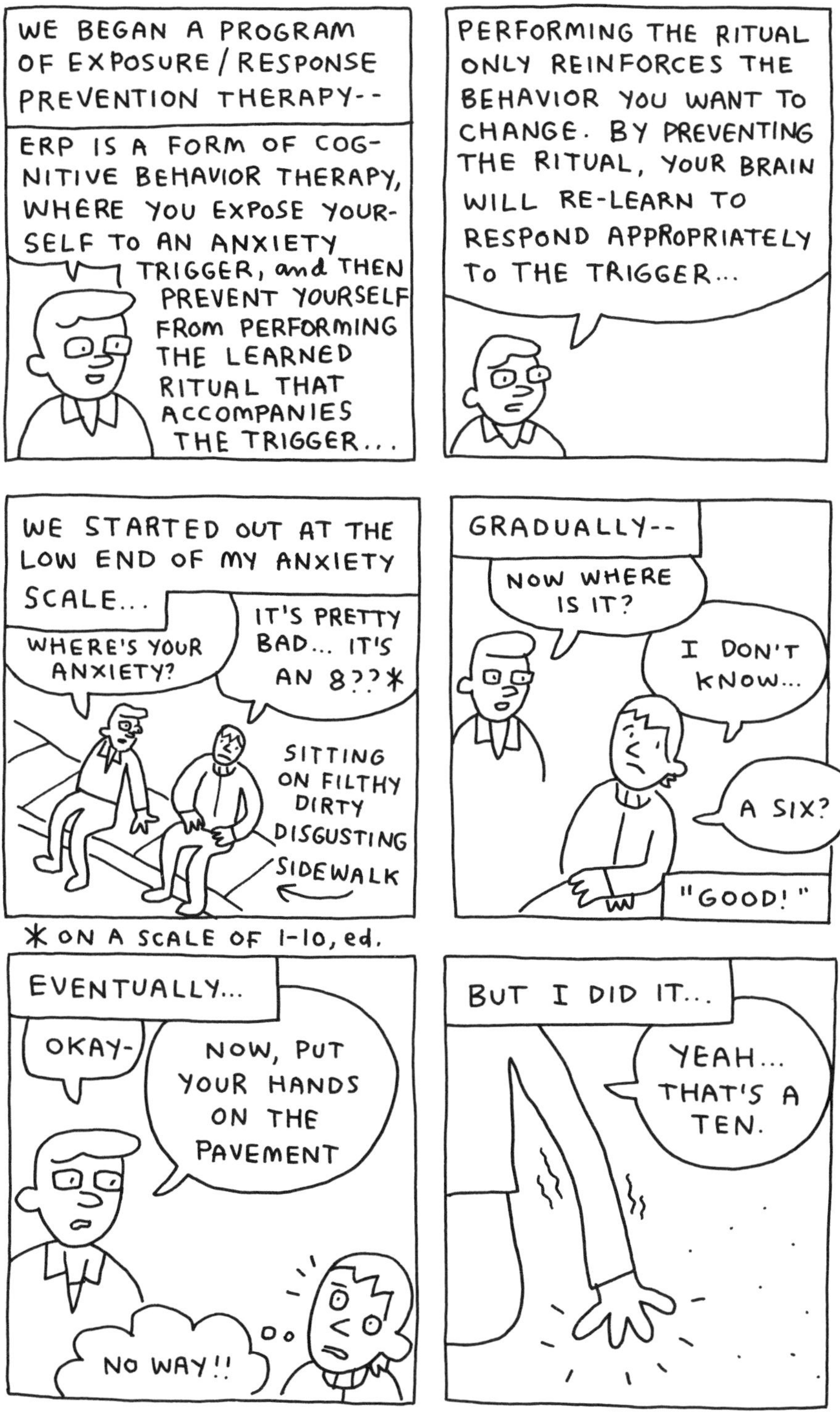
WE BEGAN A PROGRAM OF EXPOSURE/RESPONSE PREVENTION THERAPY--
ERP IS A FORM OF COGNITIVE BEHAVIOR THERAPY, WHERE YOU EXPOSE YOURSELF TO AN ANXIETY TRIGGER, and THEN PREVENT YOURSELF FROM PERFORMING THE LEARNED RITUAL THAT ACCOMPANIES THE TRIGGER...
PERFORMING THE RITUAL ONLY REINFORCES THE BEHAVIOR YOU WANT TO CHANGE. BY PREVENTING THE RITUAL, YOUR BRAIN WILL RE-LEARN TO RESPOND APPROPRIATELY TO THE TRIGGER...
WE STARTED OUT AT THE LOW END OF MY ANXIETY SCALE...
WHERE'S YOUR ANXIETY?
IT'S PRETTY BAD... IT'S AN 8??*
SITTING ON FILTHY DIRTY DISGUSTING SIDEWALK
GRADUALLY--
NOW WHERE IS IT?
I DON'T KNOW...
A SIX?
"GOOD!"
* ON A SCALE OF 1-10, ed.
EVENTUALLY...
OKAY-
NOW, PUT YOUR HANDS ON THE PAVEMENT
NO WAY!!
BUT I DID IT...
YEAH... THAT'S A TEN.

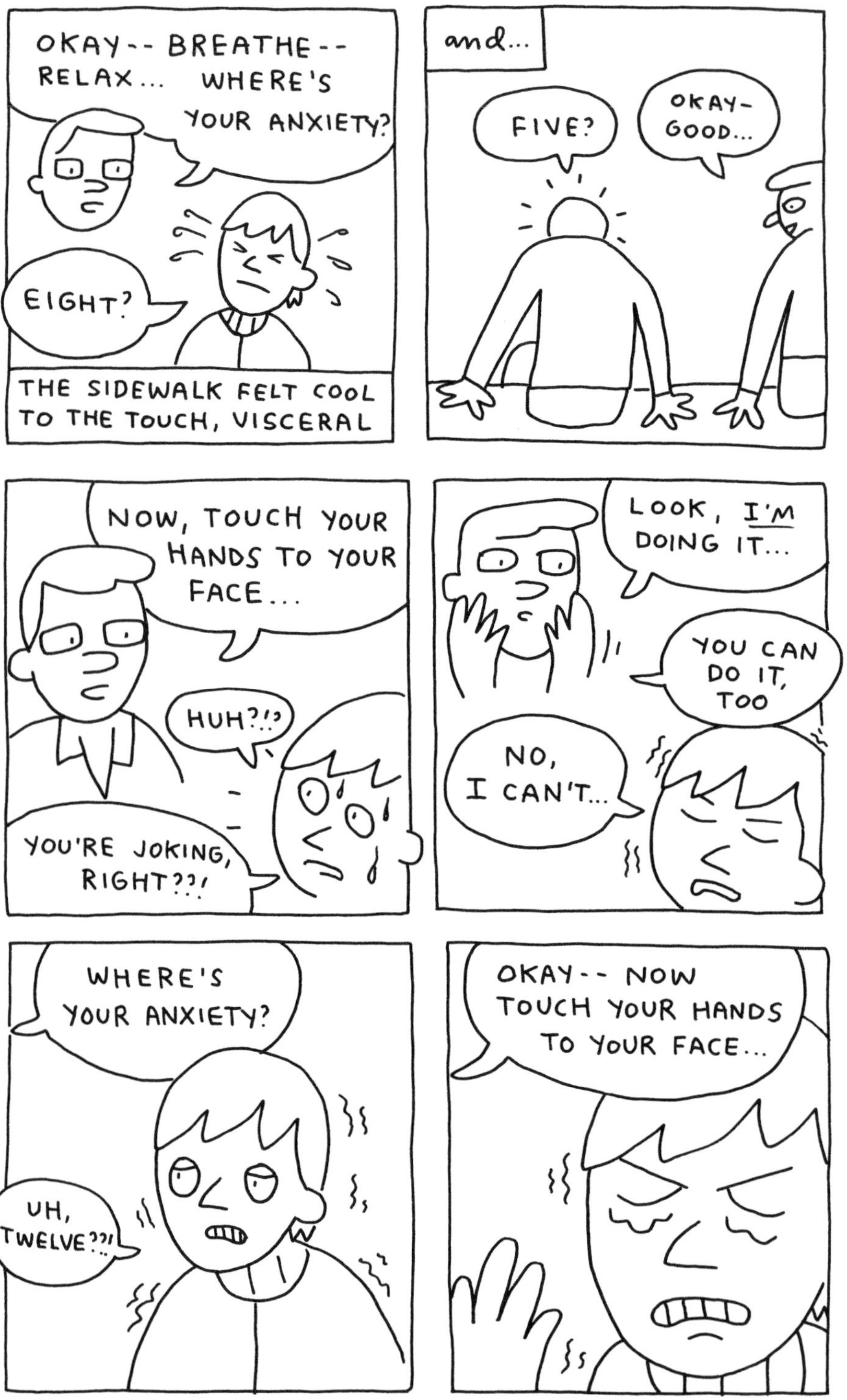
OKAY-- BREATHE-- RELAX... WHERE'S YOUR ANXIETY?
EIGHT?
THE SIDEWALK FELT COOL TO THE TOUCH, VISCERAL
and...
FIVE?
OKAY- GOOD...
NOW, TOUCH YOUR HANDS TO YOUR FACE...
HUH?!?
YOU'RE JOKING, RIGHT??!
LOOK, I'M DOING IT...
YOU CAN DO IT, TOO
NO, I CAN'T...
WHERE'S YOUR ANXIETY?
UH, TWELVE??!
OKAY-- NOW TOUCH YOUR HANDS TO YOUR FACE...

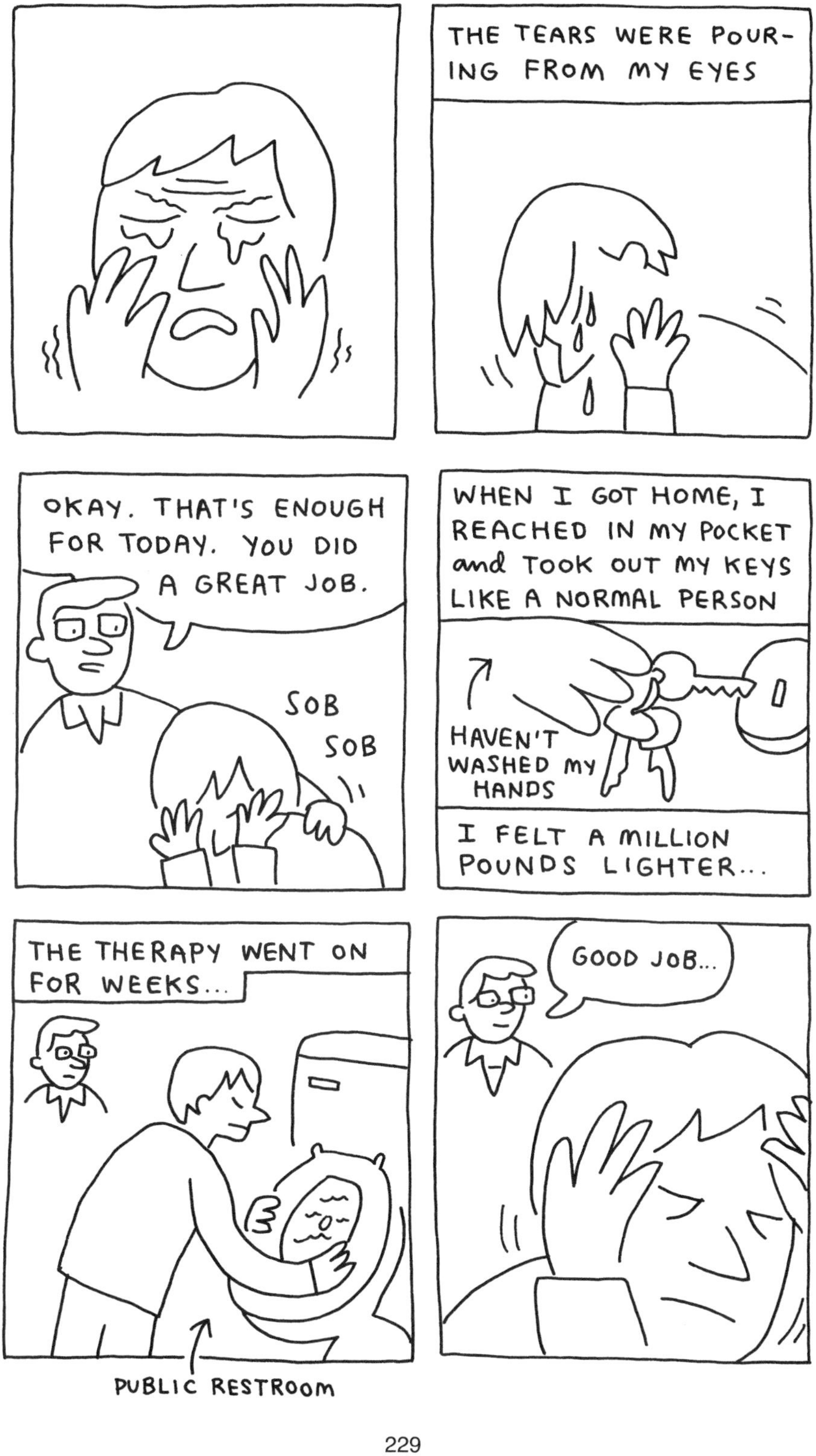
THE TEARS WERE POURING FROM MY EYES
OKAY. THAT'S ENOUGH FOR TODAY. YOU DID A GREAT JOB.
SOB
SOB
WHEN I GOT HOME, I REACHED IN MY POCKET and TOOK OUT MY KEYS LIKE A NORMAL PERSON
HAVEN'T WASHED MY HANDS
I FELT A MILLION POUNDS LIGHTER...
THE THERAPY WENT ON FOR WEEKS...
PUBLIC RESTROOM
GOOD JOB...

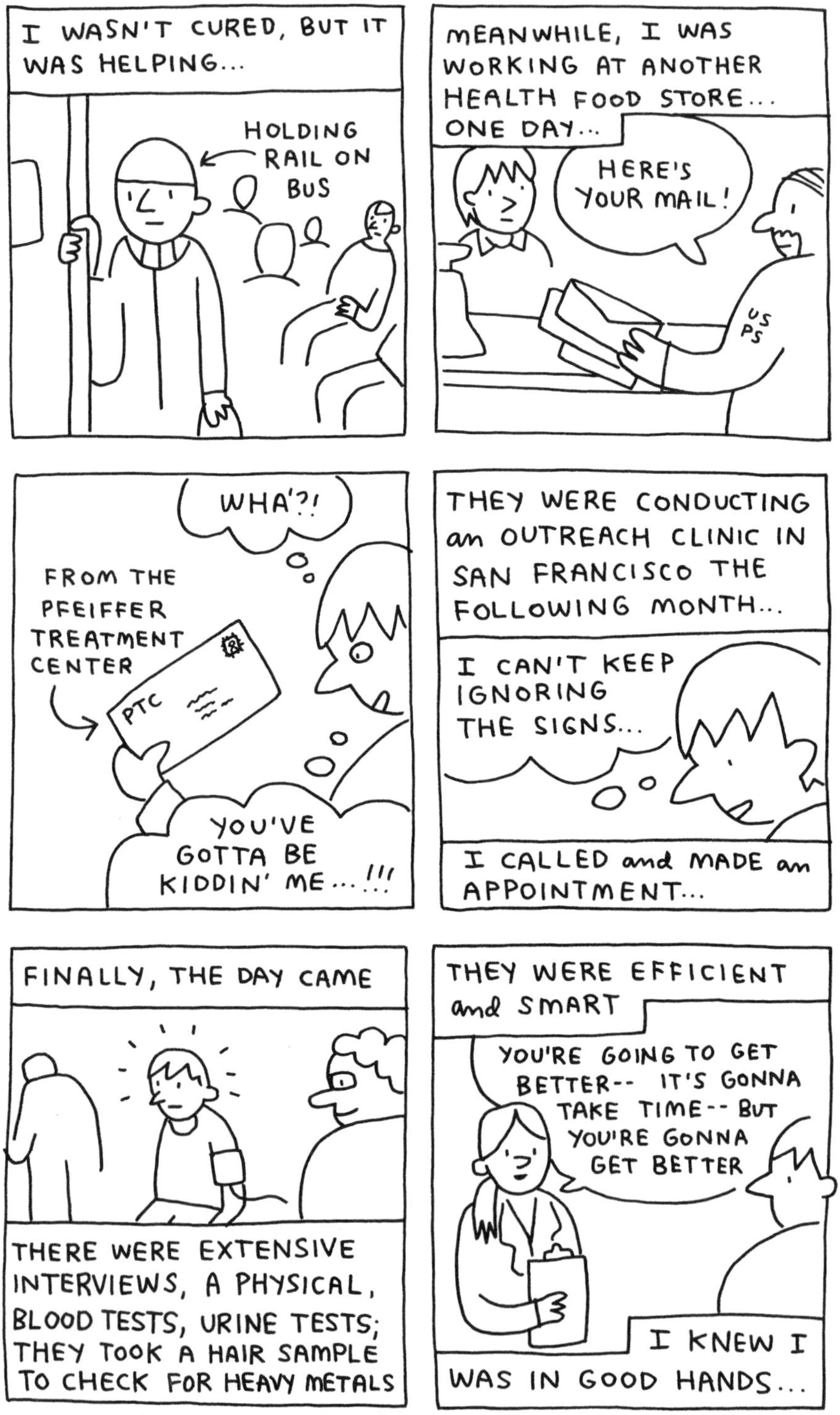
I WASN'T CURED, BUT IT WAS HELPING...
HOLDING RAIL ON BUS
MEANWHILE, I WAS WORKING AT ANOTHER HEALTH FOOD STORE... ONE DAY...
HERE'S YOUR MAIL!
USPS
WHA'?!
FROM THE PFEIFFER TREATMENT CENTER
PTC
YOU'VE GOTTA BE KIDDIN' ME...!!!
THEY WERE CONDUCTING an OUTREACH CLINIC IN SAN FRANCISCO THE FOLLOWING MONTH...
I CAN'T KEEP IGNORING THE SIGNS...
I CALLED and MADE an APPOINTMENT...
FINALLY, THE DAY CAME
THERE WERE EXTENSIVE INTERVIEWS, A PHYSICAL, BLOOD TESTS, URINE TESTS; THEY TOOK A HAIR SAMPLE TO CHECK FOR HEAVY METALS
THEY WERE EFFICIENT and SMART
YOU'RE GOING TO GET BETTER-- IT'S GONNA TAKE TIME-- BUT YOU'RE GONNA GET BETTER
I KNEW I WAS IN GOOD HANDS...

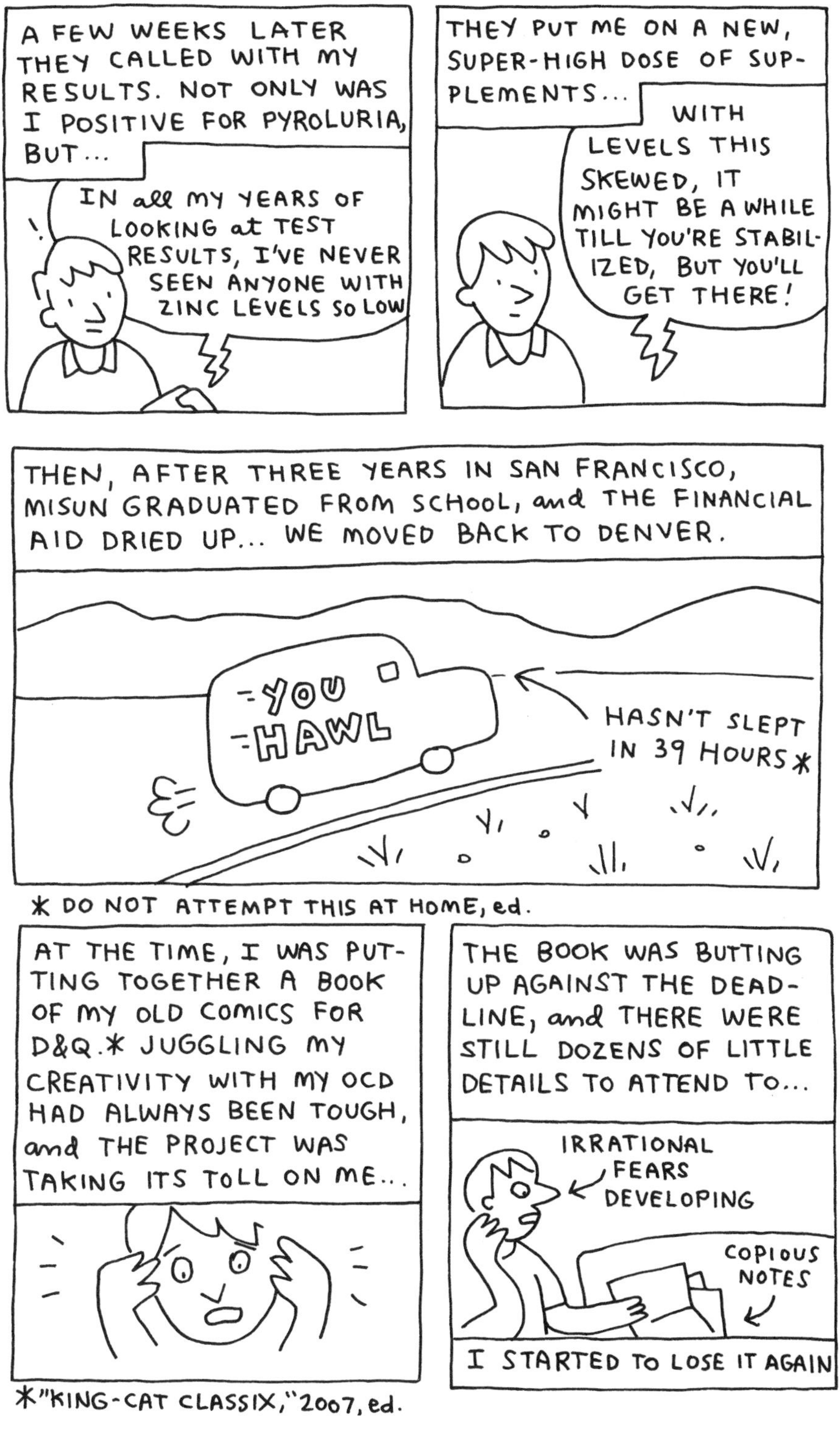
A FEW WEEKS LATER THEY CALLED WITH MY RESULTS. NOT ONLY WAS I POSITIVE FOR PYROLURIA, BUT...
IN all MY YEARS OF LOOKING at TEST RESULTS, I'VE NEVER SEEN ANYONE WITH ZINC LEVELS SO LOW
THEY PUT ME ON A NEW, SUPER-HIGH DOSE OF SUPPLEMENTS...
WITH LEVELS THIS SKEWED, IT MIGHT BE A WHILE TILL YOU'RE STABILIZED, BUT YOU'LL GET THERE!
THEN, AFTER THREE YEARS IN SAN FRANCISCO, MISUN GRADUATED FROM SCHOOL, and THE FINANCIAL AID DRIED UP... WE MOVED BACK TO DENVER.
YOU HAWL
HASN'T SLEPT IN 39 HOURS*
* DO NOT ATTEMPT THIS AT HOME, ed.
AT THE TIME, I WAS PUTTING TOGETHER A BOOK OF MY OLD COMICS FOR D&Q.* JUGGLING MY CREATIVITY WITH MY OCD HAD ALWAYS BEEN TOUGH, and THE PROJECT WAS TAKING ITS TOLL ON ME...
*"KING-CAT CLASSIX," 2007, ed.
THE BOOK WAS BUTTING UP AGAINST THE DEADLINE, and THERE WERE STILL DOZENS OF LITTLE DETAILS TO ATTEND TO...
IRRATIONAL FEARS DEVELOPING
COPIOUS NOTES
I STARTED TO LOSE IT AGAIN

WHAT IF ELVIS COMES AFTER ME? WHAT IF THE BOOK GETS PULPED? IS COLLAGE A CRIMINAL OFFENSE?

← OUT WALKING TO TRY TO CALM DOWN *

* IT'S NOT WORKING, ed.

THE PRINTER WAS WAITING FOR ME AS I OBSESSIVELY EDITED and RE-EDITED THE JACKET COPY...

Em dash OR semi-colon ?!?

FINALLY, THE BOOK WAS DONE, BUT AT The EX-PENSE OF ANOTHER NERVOUS BREAKDOWN...

DURING WHICH MY OCD HAD MADE A SWIFT and TOTAL RETURN.

WASH HANDS BEFORE LEAVING APT. ↘

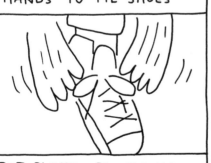

PUT PLASTIC GLOVES ON HANDS TO TIE SHOES

PUT PLASTIC GLOVES IN BOX BY FRONT DOOR

USE PAPER TOWEL TO OPEN APARTMENT DOOR

SAME PAPER TOWEL OPENS THE DOOR TO THE OUTSIDE

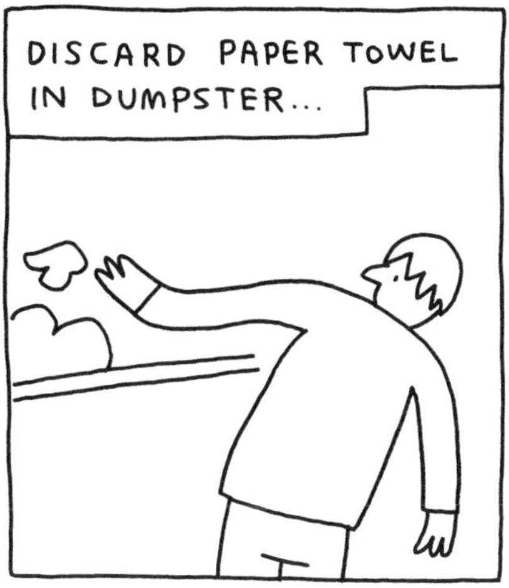
DISCARD PAPER TOWEL IN DUMPSTER...

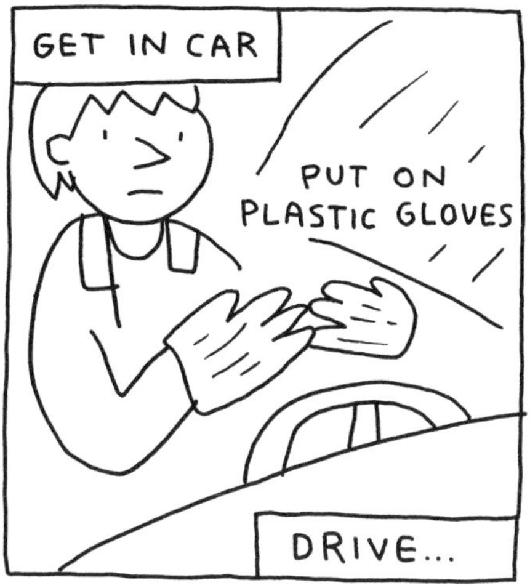
GET IN CAR
PUT ON PLASTIC GLOVES
DRIVE...

ALL MY EFFORTS TO HEAL MYSELF -- MEDITATION, YOGA, DIET, THERAPY, SUPPLEMENTS -- HAD EACH TRULY HELPED TO A DEGREE... BUT THEY NEVER REALLY TOOK ME OVER THE HUMP. I JUST BEGAN LIVING WITH IT...

FOR DAYS OR EVEN WEEKS NOW, I MIGHT GET BY WITHOUT A MAJOR CRISIS — BUT IN ORDER TO DO SO, ALMOST MY ENTIRE LIFE HAD BECOME an ELABORATE and INTRICATELY PERFORMED RITUAL...

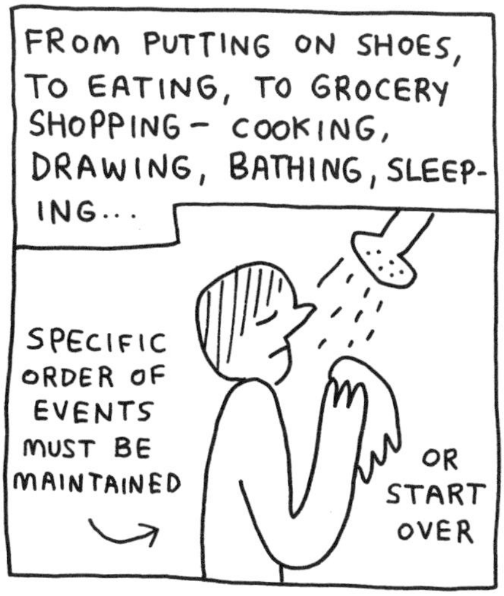
FROM PUTTING ON SHOES, TO EATING, TO GROCERY SHOPPING — COOKING, DRAWING, BATHING, SLEEPING...
SPECIFIC ORDER OF EVENTS MUST BE MAINTAINED
OR START OVER

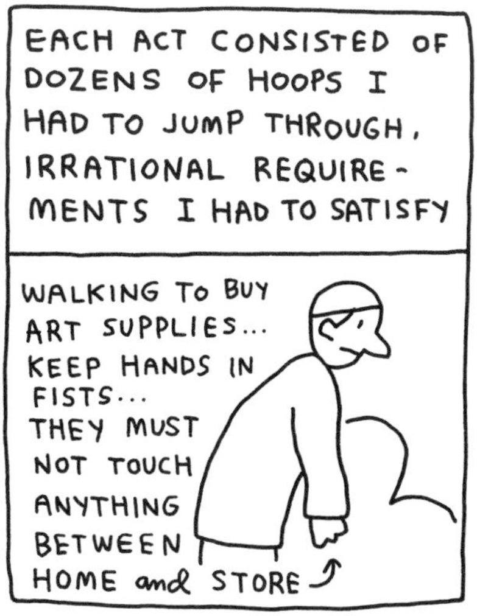
EACH ACT CONSISTED OF DOZENS OF HOOPS I HAD TO JUMP THROUGH, IRRATIONAL REQUIREMENTS I HAD TO SATISFY
WALKING TO BUY ART SUPPLIES... KEEP HANDS IN FISTS... THEY MUST NOT TOUCH ANYTHING BETWEEN HOME and STORE

I DIDN'T EVEN CARE WHO KNEW IT ANYMORE

I DRIVE WITH PLASTIC BAGS ON MY HANDS-- DEAL WITH IT!!

NOAH VAN SCIVER

STILL, THERE WERE MO- MENTS WHEN IT WAS SIMPLY IMPOSSIBLE TO COPE:

FUCKIN' KILL ME!!!

FOR THE COVER OF KING- CAT #69, I DREW THE VIEW FROM MY OFFICE, LOOKING OUT OVER THE ALLEY...

ONE OF THE BUILDINGS WAS an OLD GARAGE THAT HAD BEEN CON- VERTED TO AN APART- MENT

FROM ITS FLAT ROOF, AN ENORMOUS, MAKESHIFT ALU- MINUM CHIMNEY ROSE...

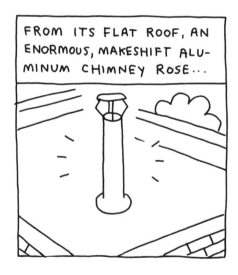

IT RUINED THE DRAW- ING...

IT THROWS THE WHOLE COMPOSITION OFF... AH, WELL, I'LL JUST RE- DRAW IT WITHOUT THE CHIMNEY...

* 100° IN ROOM CUZ I'M TOO AFRAID TO OPEN THE WINDOWS, ed.

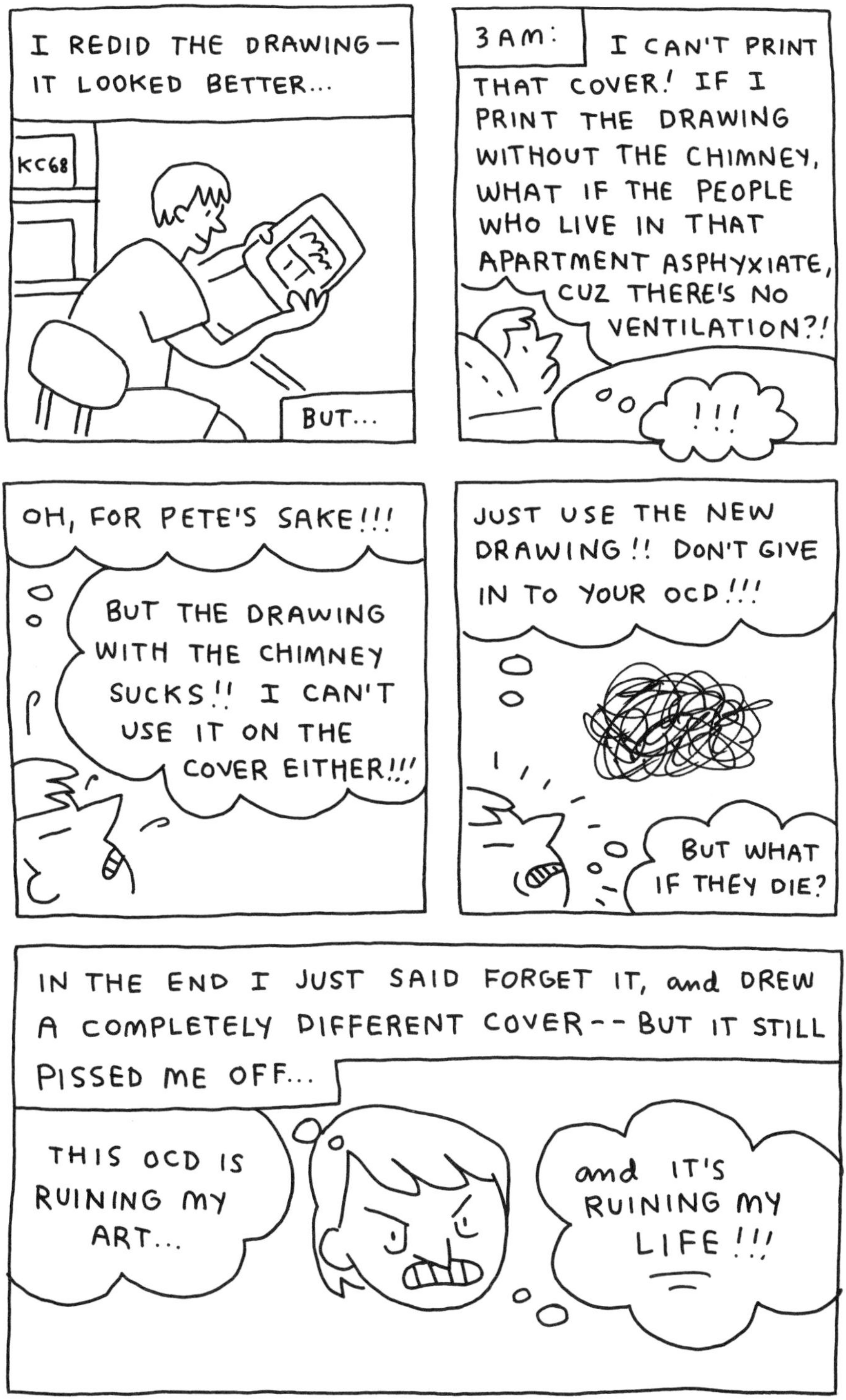
I REDID THE DRAWING—
IT LOOKED BETTER...
KC68
BUT...
3 AM:
I CAN'T PRINT THAT COVER! IF I PRINT THE DRAWING WITHOUT THE CHIMNEY, WHAT IF THE PEOPLE WHO LIVE IN THAT APARTMENT ASPHYXIATE,
CUZ THERE'S NO VENTILATION?!
!!!
OH, FOR PETE'S SAKE!!!
BUT THE DRAWING WITH THE CHIMNEY SUCKS!! I CAN'T USE IT ON THE COVER EITHER!!!
JUST USE THE NEW DRAWING!! DON'T GIVE IN TO YOUR OCD!!!
BUT WHAT IF THEY DIE?
IN THE END I JUST SAID FORGET IT, and DREW A COMPLETELY DIFFERENT COVER-- BUT IT STILL PISSED ME OFF...
THIS OCD IS RUINING MY ART...
and IT'S RUINING MY LIFE!!!

OR HOW ABOUT THE TIME THE LANDLORD WAS GOING TO SPRAY FOR BUGS IN THE HALLWAY... SO I STAYED UP *all* NIGHT, TAPING CLOSED EVERY POSSIBLE CRACK IN OUR APARTMENT??

I TAPED SHUT EVERY WINDOW, *all the* DOOR JAMBS...

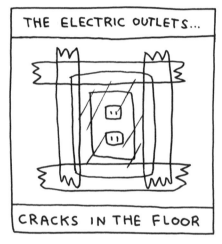

THE ELECTRIC OUTLETS...

CRACKS IN THE FLOOR

I TAPED PLASTIC GARBAGE BAGS OVER EVERY CEILING LIGHT...

4AM

I REALLY DID THAT.

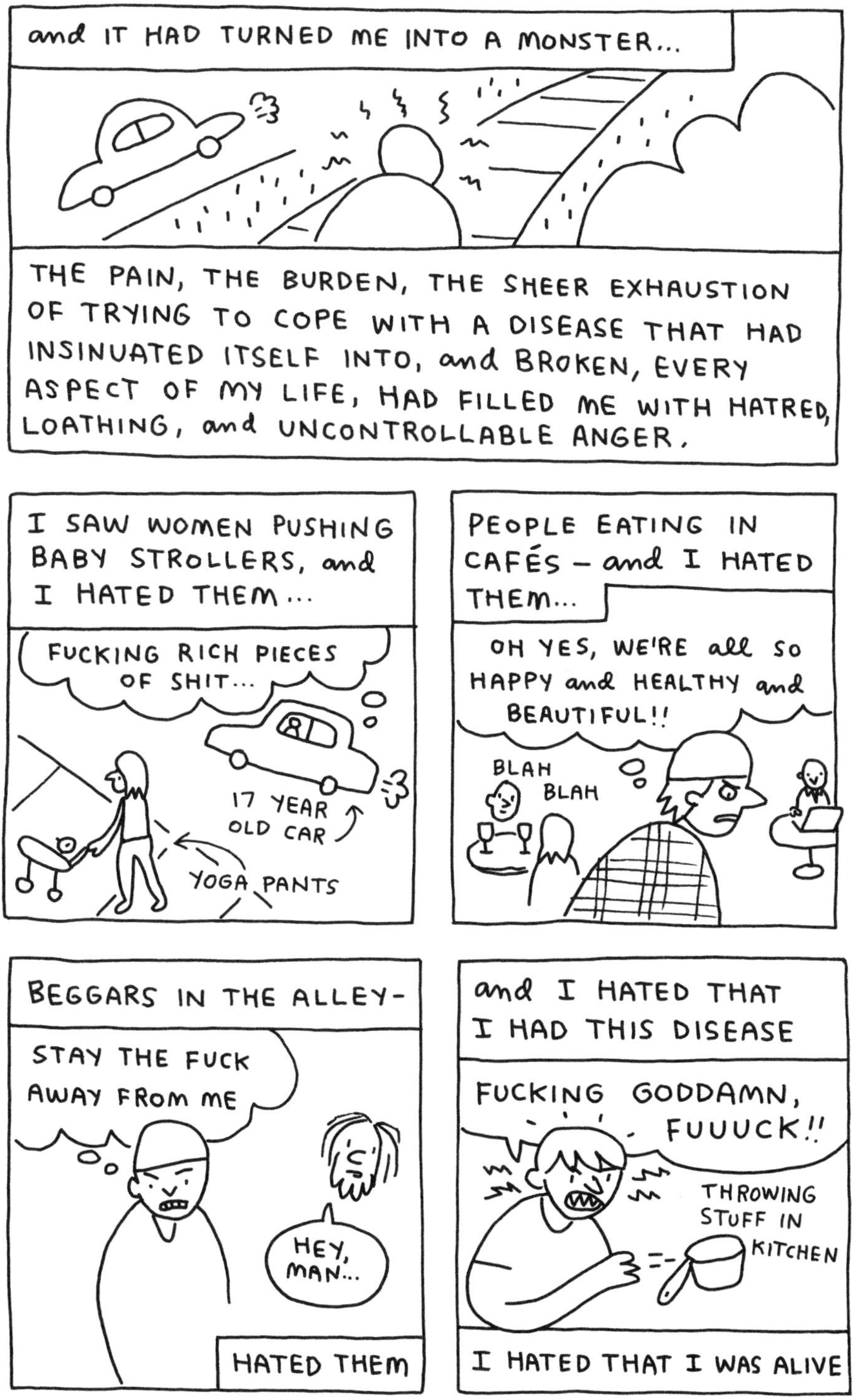
and IT HAD TURNED ME INTO A MONSTER...
THE PAIN, THE BURDEN, THE SHEER EXHAUSTION OF TRYING TO COPE WITH A DISEASE THAT HAD INSINUATED ITSELF INTO, and BROKEN, EVERY ASPECT OF MY LIFE, HAD FILLED ME WITH HATRED, LOATHING, and UNCONTROLLABLE ANGER.
I SAW WOMEN PUSHING BABY STROLLERS, and I HATED THEM...
FUCKING RICH PIECES OF SHIT...
17 YEAR OLD CAR
YOGA PANTS
PEOPLE EATING IN CAFÉS – and I HATED THEM...
OH YES, WE'RE all SO HAPPY and HEALTHY and BEAUTIFUL!!
BLAH BLAH
BEGGARS IN THE ALLEY-
STAY THE FUCK AWAY FROM ME
HEY, MAN...
HATED THEM
and I HATED THAT I HAD THIS DISEASE
FUCKING GODDAMN, FUUUCK!!
THROWING STUFF IN KITCHEN
I HATED THAT I WAS ALIVE

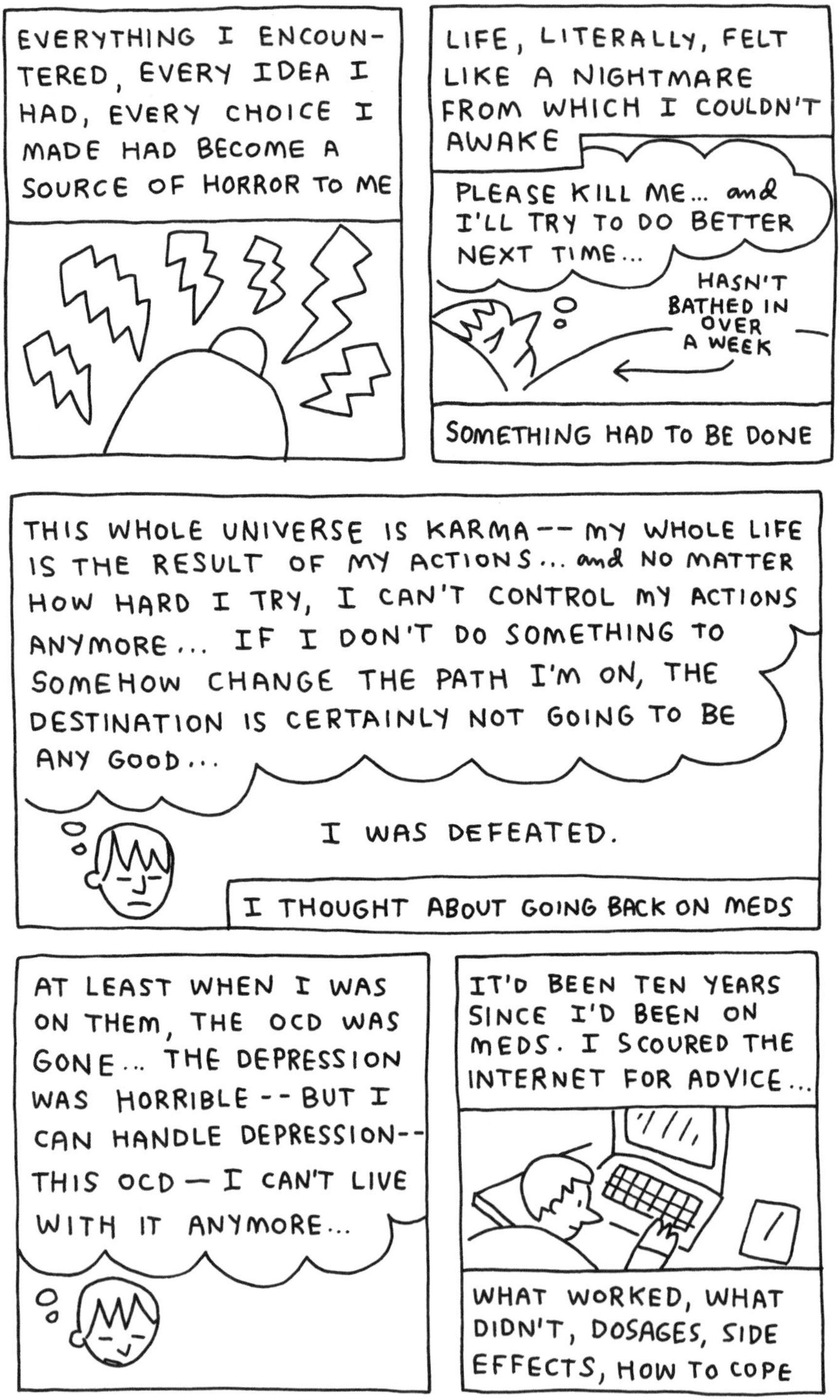
EVERYTHING I ENCOUNTERED, EVERY IDEA I HAD, EVERY CHOICE I MADE HAD BECOME A SOURCE OF HORROR TO ME
LIFE, LITERALLY, FELT LIKE A NIGHTMARE FROM WHICH I COULDN'T AWAKE
PLEASE KILL ME... and I'LL TRY TO DO BETTER NEXT TIME...
HASN'T BATHED IN OVER A WEEK
SOMETHING HAD TO BE DONE
THIS WHOLE UNIVERSE IS KARMA -- MY WHOLE LIFE IS THE RESULT OF MY ACTIONS... and NO MATTER HOW HARD I TRY, I CAN'T CONTROL MY ACTIONS ANYMORE... IF I DON'T DO SOMETHING TO SOMEHOW CHANGE THE PATH I'M ON, THE DESTINATION IS CERTAINLY NOT GOING TO BE ANY GOOD...
I WAS DEFEATED.
I THOUGHT ABOUT GOING BACK ON MEDS
AT LEAST WHEN I WAS ON THEM, THE OCD WAS GONE... THE DEPRESSION WAS HORRIBLE -- BUT I CAN HANDLE DEPRESSION -- THIS OCD — I CAN'T LIVE WITH IT ANYMORE...
IT'D BEEN TEN YEARS SINCE I'D BEEN ON MEDS. I SCOURED THE INTERNET FOR ADVICE...
WHAT WORKED, WHAT DIDN'T, DOSAGES, SIDE EFFECTS, HOW TO COPE

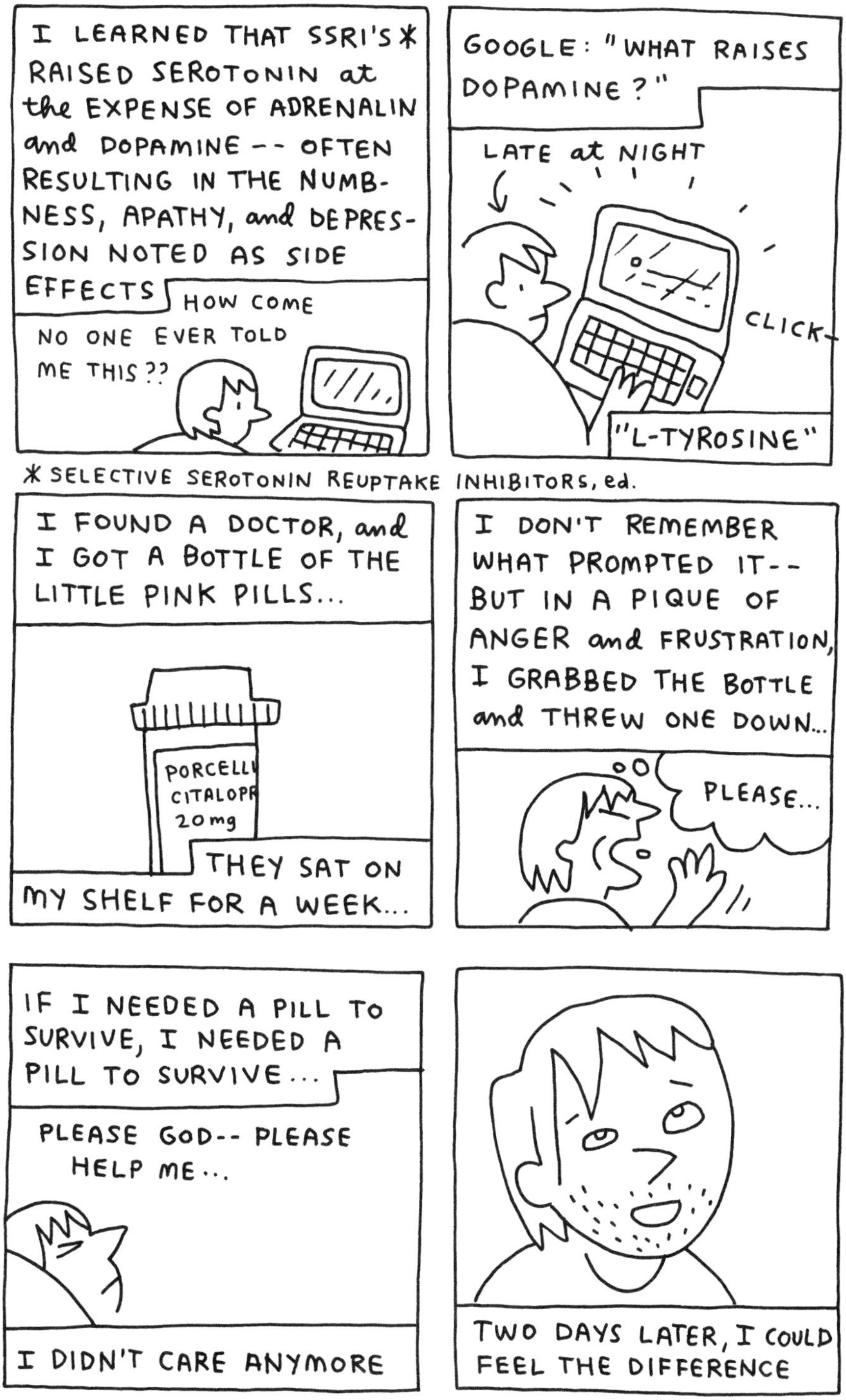
I LEARNED THAT SSRI'S* RAISED SEROTONIN at the EXPENSE OF ADRENALIN and DOPAMINE -- OFTEN RESULTING IN THE NUMBNESS, APATHY, and DEPRESSION NOTED AS SIDE EFFECTS
HOW COME NO ONE EVER TOLD ME THIS??
GOOGLE: "WHAT RAISES DOPAMINE?"
LATE at NIGHT
CLICK
"L-TYROSINE"
* SELECTIVE SEROTONIN REUPTAKE INHIBITORS, ed.
I FOUND A DOCTOR, and I GOT A BOTTLE OF THE LITTLE PINK PILLS...
PORCELL
CITALOPR
20mg
THEY SAT ON MY SHELF FOR A WEEK...
I DON'T REMEMBER WHAT PROMPTED IT-- BUT IN A PIQUE OF ANGER and FRUSTRATION, I GRABBED THE BOTTLE and THREW ONE DOWN...
PLEASE...
IF I NEEDED A PILL TO SURVIVE, I NEEDED A PILL TO SURVIVE...
PLEASE GOD-- PLEASE HELP ME...
I DIDN'T CARE ANYMORE
TWO DAYS LATER, I COULD FEEL THE DIFFERENCE

I FELT LIGHTER...

I FELT MY BRAIN BEGIN TO WORK BETTER--

IT STARTED TO STOP GOING TO BAD PLACES...

IT WAS A MIRACLE

A FEW WEEKS LATER, WHEN I REALIZED THAT I'D JUST SPENT an ENTIRE WEEKEND ON THE COUCH WATCHING TV PREACHERS, I BOUGHT A BOTTLE OF TYROSINE -- and IT WORKED!

I WASN'T CRAZY ANYMORE...

BUT I'M STILL NUTS

RESEARCHING EVERY BRIDGE IN SOUTH BELOIT, ILLINOIS

I'M STILL WEIRD.

STEPHANIE? IS THIS A PIG OR A WOMBAT?

SQUIRM SQUIRM MYOW!

I STILL HAVE GOOD DAYS and BAD DAYS...

...and I STILL HAVE A LOT OF OLD HABITS TO LEARN TO UNDO...

I CAN DRAW THOUGH... and I CAN THINK

THE SKY LOOKS BEAUTIFUL AGAIN

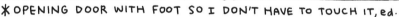

* OPENING DOOR WITH FOOT SO I DON'T HAVE TO TOUCH IT, ed.

WHEN I MEET YOU, LET'S SHAKE HANDS

John Porcellino 2013-2014

APPENDICES

THE ORIGINAL "TRUE ANXIETY" ZINES

When I started *King-Cat* in 1989, it quickly became the home for most of my comics output, but occasionally I'd draw little "one-shot" or oddball comics like 1992's *True Anxiety #1*, and publish them in very small editions.

The *True Anxiety* series became an outlet for my more OCD-focused strips, and ran for three issues, from 1992–1993, reproduced here.

true ANXIETY COMICS
At WORK I told my BOSS, JANE:
JANE, I think I might move to Denver in APRIL
SHE SAID SHE'D BE SAD to see me go. I could tell SHE WAS A Little mad.
Well then I'm gonna be a bitch to you for the next 3 months.
the IDEA OF MOVING WAS FREAKING ME OUT
I Got Home, fell asleep
KAthy CALLED
...I could tell she was mad
JIM CALLED
you gotta draw the fucking line, JOHN
NERVOUSNESS SET IN...
How can I leave all these people?
I COOKED DINNER, LISTENED to BOW WOW WOW
I'll call Jeff
Jeff is going with to Denver
DON SAID come in the middle of a month, not
BLA
BLA
OKAY JOHN-talk to ya later
It was official I was freaking
I LAID ON the Bed, looking at the WALL

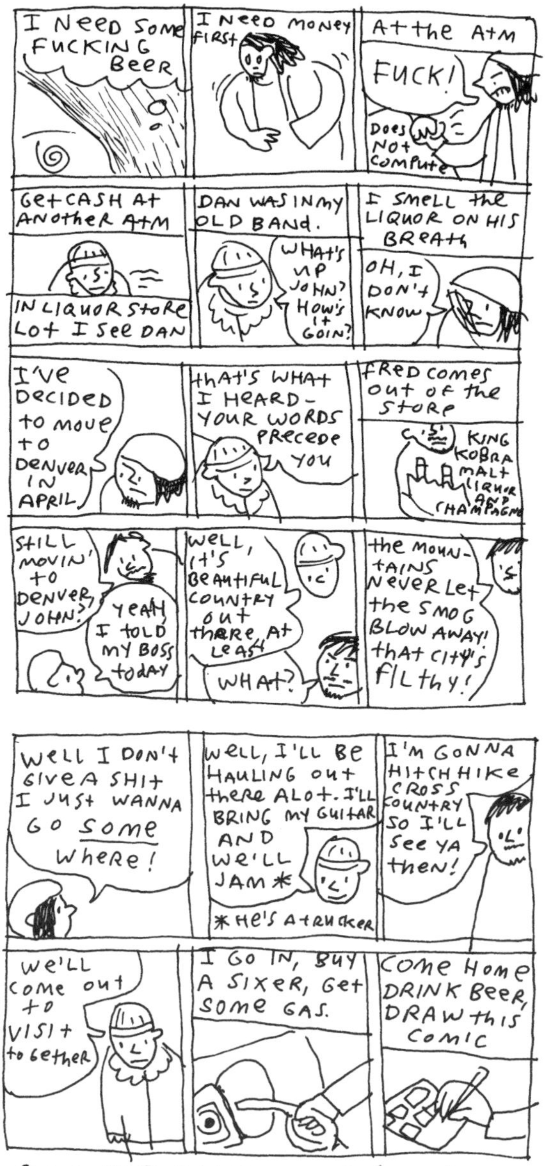
I Need Some FUCKING Beer
I Need money first
At the ATM
FUCK!
Does Not Compute
Get CASH At Another ATM
IN LIQUOR STORE Lot I See DAN
DAN WAS IN my OLD BAND.
WHAT's up JOHN? How's it GOIN?
I SMELL the LIQUOR ON HIS BREATH
OH, I DON'T KNOW
I've Decided to move to Denver in April
That's what I heard- your words precede you
Fred comes out of the store
KING KOBRA MALT LIQUOR AND CHAMPAGNE
Still movin' to Denver, John?
Yeah I told my boss today
Well, it's beautiful country out there, at least
WHAT?
The mountains never let the smog blow away! That city's filthy!
Well I don't give a shit I just wanna go some where!
Well, I'll be hauling out there alot. I'll bring my guitar and we'll jam *
* He's a trucker
I'm gonna hitchhike cross country so I'll see ya then!
We'll come out to visit together
I go in, buy a sixer, get some gas.
Come Home DRINK Beer, DRAW this comic

HAPPENED 12/30/91
DRAWN A.S.A.P. 8:45 to 10:15 P.M.
BY JOHN PORCELLINO
MAP OF DENVER: DONAL OGILVIE
WRITE TO ME BEFORE APRIL:
J.P./427 N. 11th St. DEKALB, IL 60115

TRUE ANXIETY #2

TODAY I WENT OUT I BOUGHT the BALDO REX C.D.

BALDO REX IS MY FAVORITE COLORADO BAND

I WAS IN MY ROOM LISTENING to It. and DRAWING COMIX

I WAS HAPPY BECAUSE SOMETIMES MY C.D. PLAYER WON'T WORK RIGHT, But the DISC PLAYED JUST FINE.

See, I REALLY WORRY ABOUT things. EVERY time I PUT A C.D. IN the PLAYER I GET NERVOUS that It WON'T WORK

But It WORKED and the C.D. WAS VERY GOOD

WHEN It WAS OVER I PUT It BACK IN the CASE, BUT It KIND OF SLID IN, A LITTLE, Not PERFECT

I GOT REALLY SCARED THAT I "SCRATCHED" It and THAT It WOULDN'T WORK ANYMORE

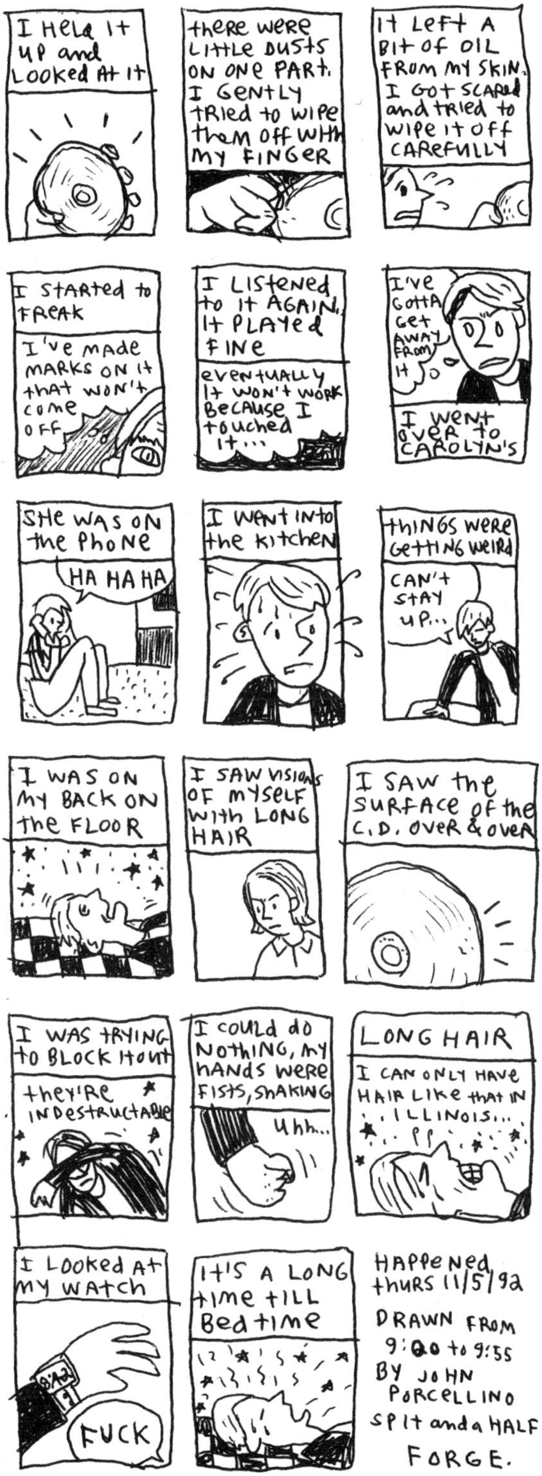
I Held it up and Looked At it
there were little dusts on one part. I gently tried to wipe them off with my finger
It left a bit of oil from my skin. I got scared and tried to wipe it off carefully
I started to freak
I've made marks on it that won't come off
I listened to it again, it played fine
eventually it won't work because I touched it...
I've gotta get away from it
I went over to Carolyn's
She was on the phone
HA HA HA
I went into the kitchen
things were getting weird
Can't stay up...
I was on my back on the floor
I saw visions of myself with long hair
I saw the surface of the C.D. over & over
I was trying to block it out
they're indestructable
I could do nothing, my hands were fists, shaking
Uhh...
LONG HAIR
I can only have hair like that in Illinois...
I looked at my watch
FUCK
It's a long time till bedtime
Happened thurs 11/5/92
Drawn from 9:20 to 9:55
By John Porcellino
Spit and a Half
Forge.

TRUE ANXIETY #3

that's the best I CAN DO...
KINKO'S
I WAS WORKING ON A BOOKLET to GO with A RECORD I had RECENTLY PUT OUT
PROFILES IN COURAGE
I WAS WORRIED BECAUSE I WAS GOING to HAVE to HAVE it PRINTED AT KINKO'S (their MACHINE HAS A PHOTO SCREEN that MAKES PHOTOGRAPHS COPY BETTER) and EVERYONE KNOWS KINKO'S SUCKS and IS OVER-PRICED to BOOT, BUT AFTER WEIGHING the OPTIONS I DECIDED I HAD to DEAL WITH KINKO'S...
I'LL JUST GO LATE AT NIGHT and FORCE them to DO A GOOD JOB NO MATTER HOW LONG IT TAKES!
SO I WORKED ON the BOOK FOR A WEEK, TRYING to LAY IT OUT WELL, WRITE IT JUST RIGHT, etc...
COMMA- OR SEMI-COLON?
?!
ANYHOW I FINALLY FINISHED it and that NIGHT DON and I WENT OVER to KINKO'S
500 copies of each please
O.K.
it TOOK ABOUT 45 MINUTES and COST $100 but LO and BEHOLD - the copies looked great!
those LOOK GOOD JOHN! Let's GO.
DON
When we got HOME it WAS ABOUT MID-NIGHT BUT I WAS excited so I PUT [redacted] A COPY OF the BOOKLET TOGETHER to SHOW CAROLYN
Fold
STAPLE
But she WAS AL-READY ASLEEP. I WANTED to LOOK AT the BOOK SO I RETREATED to the WELL LIT BATHROOM
ON TOP OF the WORLD

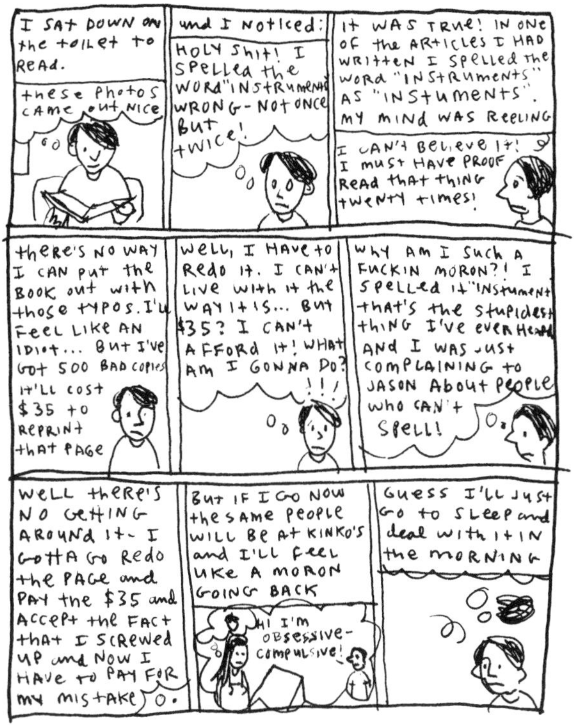
I SAT DOWN ON the toilet to READ.
these Photos CAME out NICE
and I Noticed:
HOLY Shit! I SPELLed the WORD "INSTRUMENTS" WRONG - NOT ONCE But twice!
It WAS TRUE! IN ONE of the ARTICLES I HAD WRITTEN I SPELLED the WORD "INSTRUMENTS" AS "INSTUMENTS". MY MIND WAS REELING
I CAN'T BELIEVE IT! I MUST HAVE PROOF READ that thing TWENTY times!
there's NO WAY I CAN put the BOOK out with those typos. I'll FEEL LIKE AN IDIOT... But I've Got 500 BAD copies It'll cost $35 to REPRINT that PAGE
WELL, I HAVE to Redo it. I CAN'T LIVE With it the WAY It IS... But $35? I CAN'T AFFORD it! WHAT AM I GONNA DO?
!!!
WHY AM I SUCH A FUCKIN MORON?! I SPELLED It "INSTUMENTS" that's the STUPIDEST thing I've ever Heard And I WAS JUST COMPLAINING to JASON About People who CAN'T SPELL!
WELL there's NO GETTING AROUND It- I GOTTA GO Redo the PAGE and PAY the $35 and ACCEPT the FACT that I SCREWED UP and NOW I HAVE to PAY FOR my mistake
But IF I GO NOW the SAME PEOPLE WILL BE At KINKO'S and I'LL FEEL LIKE A MORON GOING BACK
HI I'M OBSESSIVE-COMPULSIVE!
GUESS I'LL JUST GO to SLEEP and deal with it IN the MORNING

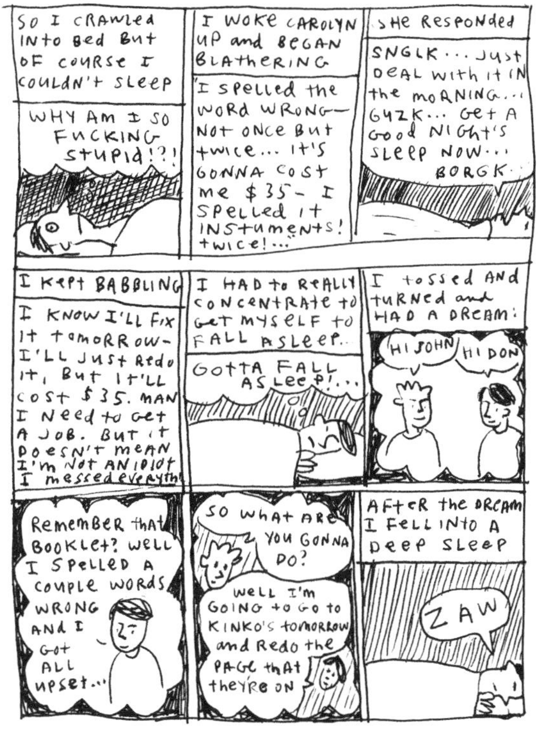
SO I CRAWLED INTO BED But OF COURSE I COULDN'T SLEEP
WHY AM I SO FUCKING STUPID!?!
I WOKE CAROLYN UP and BEGAN BLATHERING
I SPELLED the WORD WRONG— NOT ONCE But twice... It's GONNA COST me $35 - I SPELLED it INSTUMENTS! twice!...
SHE RESPONDED
SNGLK... JUST DEAL with it IN the MORNING... GUZK... Get A Good NIGHT'S SLEEP NOW... BORGK...
I KEPT BABBLING
I KNOW I'LL FIX It tomorrow- I'LL JUST Redo it, But It'LL cost $35. MAN I Need to Get A JOB. But it DOESN'T MEAN I'M NOT AN IDIOT I messed everyth
I HAD to REALLY CONCENTRATE to Get MYSELF to FALL ASLEEP...
GOTTA FALL ASLEEP!...
I tossed AND turned and HAD A DREAM:
HI JOHN
HI DON
Remember that BOOKLET? WELL I SPELLED A COUPLE WORDS WRONG AND I Got ALL upset...
SO WHAT ARE YOU GONNA DO?
WELL I'M GOING to Go to KINKO'S tomorrow and Redo the PAGE that they're ON
AFTER the DREAM I FELL INTO A DEEP SLEEP
ZAW

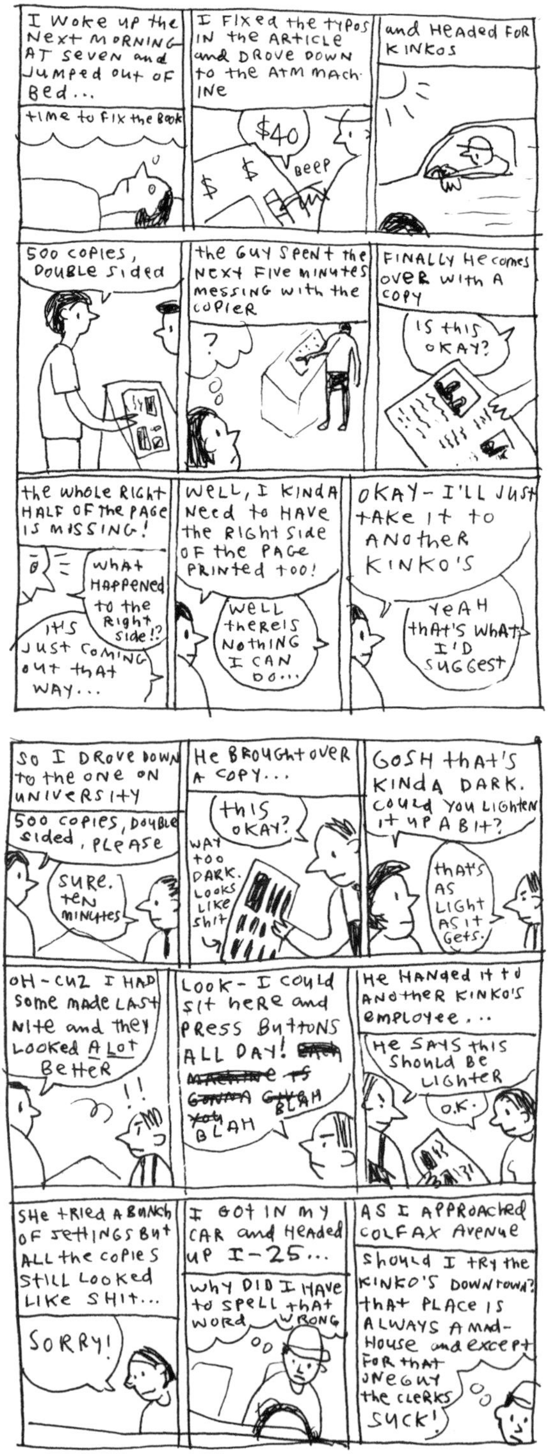
I woke up the next morning at seven and jumped out of bed...
time to fix the book
I fixed the typos in the article and drove down to the ATM machine
$40
$
$
BEEP
and headed for Kinkos
500 copies, double sided
the guy spent the next five minutes messing with the copier
?
finally he comes over with a copy
Is this okay?
the whole right half of the page is missing!
what happened to the right side!?
It's just coming out that way...
Well, I kinda need to have the right side of the page printed too!
Well there's nothing I can do...
Okay- I'll just take it to another Kinko's
Yeah that's what I'd suggest
So I drove down to the one on University
500 copies, double sided, please
Sure. ten minutes
He brought over a copy...
this okay?
way too dark. looks like shit
Gosh that's kinda dark. Could you lighten it up a bit?
that's as light as it gets.
Oh- cuz I had some made last nite and they looked a lot better
!!
Look- I could sit here and press buttons all day! each machine is gonna give you blah blah blah
He handed it to another Kinko's employee...
He says this should be lighter
O.K.
She tried a bunch of settings but all the copies still looked like shit...
Sorry!
I got in my car and headed up I-25...
why did I have to spell that word wrong
As I approached Colfax Avenue
Should I try the Kinko's downtown? that place is always a mad-house and except for that one guy the clerks suck!

HAPPENED: JUNE 26-27, 1993
DRAWN: BY JOHN PORCELLINO
FIRST HALF: 7/11/93 IN SAN FRANCISCO, CALIF.
SECOND HALF: 7/16/93 IN DENVER, COLO.

THANKS TO: CAROLYN and BRIAN at the LAKEWOOD KINKO'S

KINKO'S COSTS TOO MUCH! | FORGE

/ce Hammer was formed in the summer of 1983 by John |
off as a duo. In the Fall of 1984 John got a guitar for his |
| bass. Later in the year John Jakubowski, who owned a micr|
ability to play their instuments, the band began writing songs |
ur Night in August, 1985- the first release on their own Spit a|
Senior year of High School, they were soon joined by Jeff Jenl|
tarted on fire in Fred's basement during a band practice, he swi|
lized lineup, they began recording, and released their sophon|

WRite to JOHN P.: P.O. Box 18510 DeNVeR, CO 80218

MERCY

"Mercy" originally appeared in *The Comics Journal Special Edition Volume Two: Cartoonists on Music*, June 2002, Fantagraphics Books.

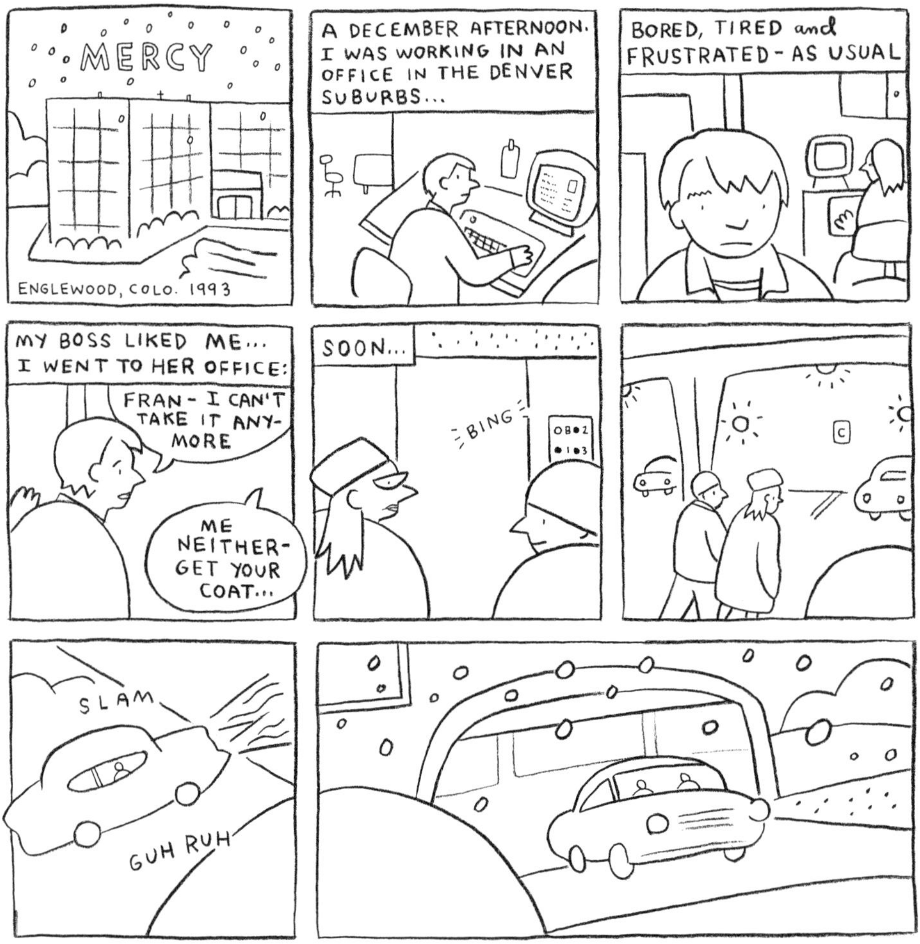
MERCY
ENGLEWOOD, COLO. 1993
A DECEMBER AFTERNOON. I WAS WORKING IN AN OFFICE IN THE DENVER SUBURBS...
BORED, TIRED and FRUSTRATED - AS USUAL
MY BOSS LIKED ME... I WENT TO HER OFFICE:
FRAN - I CAN'T TAKE IT ANY-MORE
ME NEITHER- GET YOUR COAT...
SOON...
BING
SLAM
GUH RUH

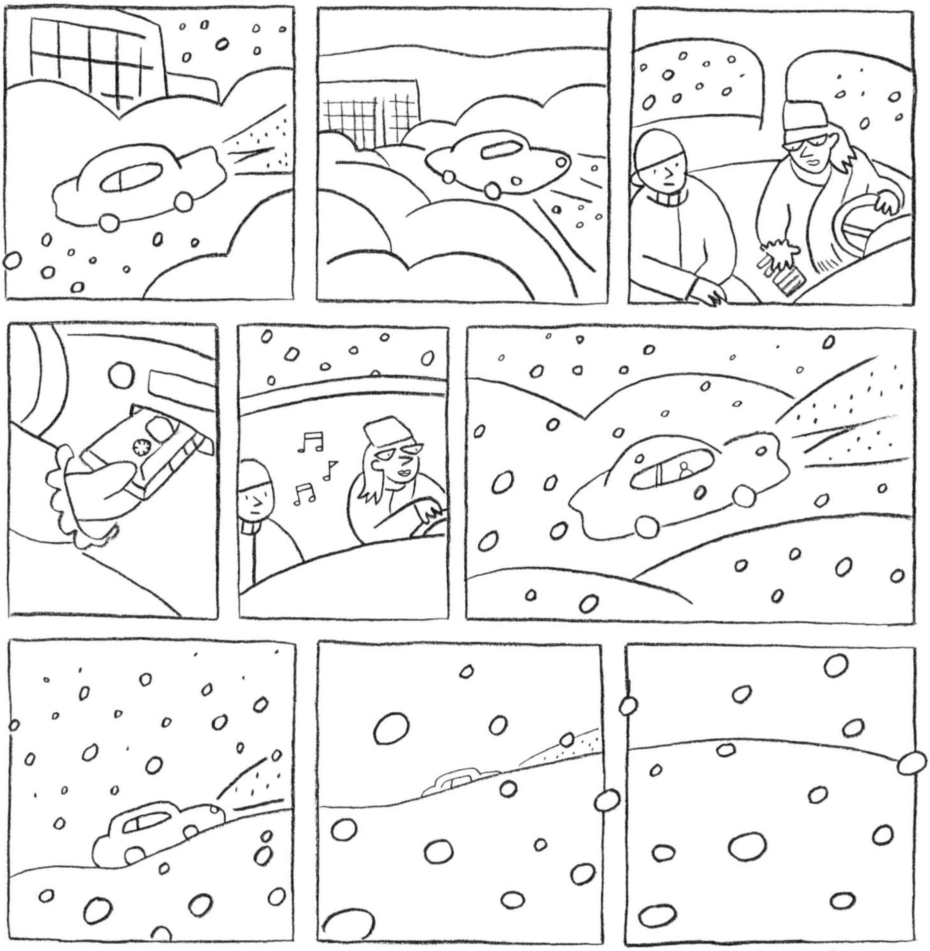

JOHN P. 3-10-02

ZEN STORIES

Known as kōans, these short but profound stories point directly at the heart of reality, and are used as aids to meditation practice. The word kōan means, literally, "public case," and they often-times record interactions between Zen teachers and their students.

YUN-MEN'S "DRIED SHITSTICK"

A monk asked Yun-Men, "What is Buddha?"

Yun-Men replied, "Dried shitstick."

SOYEN SHAKU'S "IF YOU DIE"

When Nyogen Senzaki was a young monk,
he was afflicted with tuberculosis.

So for one year, he lived in isolation in a small hut
on the edge of the monastery.

His teacher, Soyen Shaku, would visit him.

Once, when he was in the grip of despair, Nyogen
cried out to Soyen, "What if I should die?!?"

Soyen said. "If you die, just die."

THE HEART SUTRA
(PRAJÑĀ PĀRAMITĀ HRIDAYA)

The Bodhisattva of Compassion
from the depths of prajñā wisdom
saw the emptiness of all five skandhas
and sundered the bonds that cause all suffering.

Know then:
Form here is only emptiness;
emptiness only form.
Form is no other than emptiness;
emptiness no other than form.

Feeling, thought, and choice—
consciousness itself—
are the same as this.

Dharmas here are empty;
all are the primal void.
None are born or die,
nor are they stained or pure,
nor do they wax or wane.

So in emptiness no form,
no feeling, thought, or choice,
nor is there consciousness.
No eye, ear, nose, tongue, body, mind,
no color, sound, smell, taste, touch,
or what the mind takes hold of,
nor even act of sensing.
No ignorance or end of it,
nor all that comes of ignorance:
No withering, no death, no end of them.

Nor is there pain, or cause of pain,
or cease in pain,
or noble path to lead from pain;
not even wisdom to attain:
Attainment too is emptiness.

So know that the Bodhisattva,
holding to nothing whatever,
but dwelling in prajñā wisdom,
is freed of delusive hindrance,
rid of the fear bred by it,
and reaches clearest nirvana.

All buddhas of past and present,
buddhas of future time,
through faith in prajñā wisdom,
come to full enlightenment.
Know then the great dharani,
the radiant, peerless mantra,
the supreme, unfailing mantra,
the Prajñā Pāramitā,
whose words allay all pain.
This is highest wisdom,
true beyond all doubt;
know and proclaim its truth:

Gate, gate
pāragate
pārasamgate
bodhi, svāhā!

The Mahaprajñāpāramitā Hridaya Sutra, *or Heart Sutra, is a concise distillation of what are known as the Buddha's Perfection of Wisdom teachings. It was originally taught by the Bodhisattva of Compassion, Avalokiteshvara (Quan Yin, Ch.; Kannon, Jap.) to Shariputra, one of the Buddha's earliest disciples. It is chanted daily by millions of Buddhists worldwide.*

Prajñā *translates as* "Wisdom." (Prajñāpāramitā *means* "Perfection of Wisdom"). Skandhas *(form, feeling, thought, choice, consciousness) are the composite sensations that delimit our experience, and create the idea of separateness.* Dharmas *refer to all compound things experienced in the world.* "Form" *and* "Emptiness" *are the two sides of reality, the Relative and Absolute.*

The final line of the Sutra is in Sanskrit, and is pronounced, roughly: Guh-tay, guh-tay, pahruh guh-tay, pahruh sahm guh-tay, boh-dee, svah-hah. *It translates (again, roughly) as* "Beyond, beyond, further beyond, even further beyond, wisdom, hooray!"

For Further Reading

Dillard, Annie. *Three by Annie Dillard: The Writing Life, An American Childhood, Pilgrim at Tinker Creek*. New York: Harper Perennial, 1990.

Dōgen, Eihei. *Moon in a Dewdrop: Writings of Zen Master Dōgen*. Edited by Kazuaki Tanahashi. New York: North Point Press, 1985.

Freke, Timothy. *The Wisdom of the Christian Mystics*. New York: Journey Editions, 1998.

Mathews-Larsen, Joan. *Depression Free Naturally*. New York: Ballantine, 2001.

Pfeiffer, Carl C. *Nutrition and Mental Illness*. Boston: Healing Arts Press, 1988.

Uchiyama, Kōshō. *Opening the Hand of Thought/Approach to Zen*. Translated by Shohaku Okumura and Tom Wright. New York: Penguin Arkana, 1997.

John at home in Denver, after his hospital stay in 1997, with Maisie Kukoc.

John Porcellino was born in Chicago, Illinois, in 1968. He wrote and photocopied his first zine in 1982, at the age of fourteen. In 1989, Porcellino began writing his celebrated *King-Cat* mini-comic series, which has been ongoing for more than twenty-five years, winning acclaim from *Time*, *Entertainment Weekly*, *USA Today*, *Punk Planet*, and the *Globe & Mail*. His work in *King-Cat* has been translated into French, German, Italian, Spanish, and Swedish.

Porcellino is the author of *Diary of a Mosquito Abatement Man*, *King-Cat Classix*, *Map of My Heart*, *Perfect Example*, and *Thoreau at Walden*, and the illustrator of *The Next Day*. He lives in Beloit, Wisconsin, with his girlfriend and two cats and two dogs, and continues to produce new issues of *King-Cat* on a regular basis.